SECRET WARS

Princeton Studies in International History and Politics

G. John Ikenberry, Marc Trachtenberg, and
William C. Wohlforth, Series Editors

For a full list of books in this series see https://press.princeton.edu/catalogs/series /title/princeton-studies-in-international-history-and-politics.html

RECENT TITLES

Secret Wars: Covert Conflict in International Politics by Austin Carson

Who Fights for Reputation: The Psychology of Leaders in International Conflict by Keren Yarhi-Milo

Aftershocks: Great Powers and Domestic Reforms in the Twentieth Century by Seva Gunitsky

Why Wilson Matters: The Origin of American Liberal Internationalism and Its Crisis Today by Tony Smith

Powerplay: The Origins of the American Alliance System in Asia by Victor D. Cha

Economic Interdependence and War by Dale C. Copeland

Knowing the Adversary: Leaders, Intelligence, and Assessment of Intentions in International Relations by Keren Yarhi-Milo

Nuclear Strategy in the Modern Era: Regional Powers and International Conflict by Vipin Narang

The Cold War and After: History, Theory, and the Logic of International Politics by Marc Trachtenberg

America's Mission: The United States and the Worldwide Struggle for Democracy, Expanded Edition by Tony Smith

Liberal Leviathan: The Origins, Crisis, and Transformation of the American World Order by G. John Ikenberry

Secret Wars

Covert Conflict in International Politics

Austin Carson

PRINCETON UNIVERSITY PRESS

PRINCETON AND OXFORD

Published by Princeton University Press
41 William Street, Princeton, New Jersey 08540
6 Oxford Street, Woodstock, Oxfordshire OX20 1TR

press.princeton.edu

Editorial: Fred Appel and Thalia Leaf
Production Editorial: Brigitte Pelner
Cover Design: Amanda Weiss
Cover Credit: Men of the 3rd Ranger Company, 3rd Infantry Division, adjust their gear before
undertaking a dawn patrol across the Imjin River, Korea. 17 April 1951. Korea / US Army Center
of Military History
Production: Erin Suydam
Publicity: Tayler Lord
Copyeditor: Karen Verde

This book has been composed in Adobe Text Pro and Gotham

For Sarah, Kai, and Zoe. You are my world.

CONTENTS

1 Introduction   1

2 A Limited-War Theory of Secrecy   26

3 The Emergence of Covert Warfare   75

4 The Spanish Civil War (1936–1939)   99

5 The Korean War (1950–1953)   142

6 The Vietnam War (1964–1968)   187

7 The War in Afghanistan (1979–1986)   238

8 Conclusion   283

Index   317

ACKNOWLEDGMENTS

The idea for the book came when I was a graduate student in a superb creative environment in Columbus, Ohio. The Ohio State graduate program produced excellent International Relations (IR) scholars during the time I was there. Several of my fellow Ph.D. students were especially helpful as I shaped the idea into a dissertation, including Eric Grynaviski, Jason Keiber, Josh Kertzer, and Eleonora Mattiacci. The IR faculty at Ohio State created the perfect environment for me to flourish. Bear Braumoeller, Rick Herrmann, Ted Hopf, Jennifer Mitzen, Randy Schweller, Alex Thompson, Alex Wendt, and others encouraged us to creatively analyze the diverse theoretical and empirical world of IR. Rick, Jennifer, and Randy were critical in helping me mold the idea into a dissertation as committee members.

Developments in my wife's career brought me to Washington, D.C., and George Washington University, where I wrote every word of the dissertation that would become this book. Charlie Glaser generously provided visiting fellowships for two years at his Institute for Security and Conflict Studies, where I was integrated into a new and vibrant intellectual community. Several people were especially important to my development as a scholar and the substance of my project, including Alex Downes, Elizabeth Saunders, and Caitlin Talmdage. Graduate students there formed a new peer support group. Particularly important for comments and friendships were Julia MacDonald, Tristan Volpe, Lindsey O'Rourke, and Josh Shifrinson.

Princeton's Niehaus Center for Globalization and Governance under Helen Milner provided much-needed time for converting a messy dissertation into more polished work. As a postdoctoral fellow, the seeds of two articles that would later appear in *International Organization* ("Facing Off and Saving Face" and "The Spotlight's Harsh Glare") were planted. You could do a lot worse in ten months in central New Jersey. My friendship and collaboration with Keren Yarhi-Milo also started at Princeton, for which I remain extremely grateful. Most memorable, however, was the colorful cohort of postdocs. I spent many hours laughing with, and learning from, Allison Carnegie, Julia Gray, Jeff Kucik, Don Leonard, Nimah Maza-heri, Thomas Zeitzoff, and Bo Zhu.

My time at Georgia State was brief but significant. Carrie Manning and John Duffield were model senior colleagues, both welcoming and wise in their advice. Shawn Powers and Amelia Arsenault were colleagues but, more importantly, dear friends who made my time in Reynoldstown in-credibly enjoyable. Their only mistake was selfishly keeping Fidel the cat. Being a colleague of the incomparable Jelena Subotic was a highlight. Her advice, solicited and unsolicited, was equal parts useful and hilarious.

Two experiences before the academy also shaped the book I would go on to write. One was the decade I spent in competitive policy debate. While hundreds of coaches, teammates, friends, and rival debaters contributed along the way, especially important were my head coaches. Ellen Zwaren-steyn watched my first practice debate as a high school sophomore and coached me to a win in my last debate at the Michigan state championship. I can never repay her for what she invested in me. Later, the only thing I cared about while at Michigan State was success at debate. Will Repko saw talent in me that I couldn't see myself. His tactical and strategic acumen, his passion, and his humor were essential to my achieving success and deeply influenced my intellectual development.

My time at the Center for Strategic and International Studies was an-other formative experience that influenced the ideas in this book. Immer-sion in the Washington, D.C., policy environment shaped how I think about IR and gave me my first taste of archival research. Watching the run-up to the Iraq War inspired my enduring interest in how governments use se-crecy and intelligence to manage optics. The opportunity all started with Alex Lennon opening the door to CSIS with an internship in 2002, for which I remain eternally grateful. My writing and thinking were vastly im-proved by the mentorship of Bob Einhorn. More significantly, he gave me my first salaried job and, later, helped me get into a great Ph.D. program. I can only hope to emulate his generosity with the students I now mentor.

Turning to the present, the University of Chicago has been an ideal en-vironment to complete the book. My colleagues have played an essential role. I owe a particularly large debt of gratitude to John Mearsheimer, Bob Pape, Paul Poast, and Paul Staniland, whose countless points of advice on issues large and small have been invaluable. Cathy Cohen and Will Howell have, as department chairs, provided generous support and advice. Three cohorts of undergraduates in my Secret Side of International Politics class gave thoughtful, constructive reactions to book-related material. Faculty and graduate student participants in my book workshop were also extremely helpful in sharpening the manuscripts. A special thanks to Bob Jervis, Michael Barnett, and Marc Trachtenberg, who provided detailed comments and considerable wisdom during and after the workshop.

This book could not have been written without excellent research assistance at various stages. Essential to the final product was help from Andrea Bartoletti, Matt Conklin, Zarek Drozda, Adam Saxton, Laura Sipe, Madeleine Stevens, and Behnam Taleblu. Several others provided advice at various stages of the manuscript, including Jon Brown, Mike Poznansky, and Josh Rovner. The great support I received from Princeton University Press was also vital. It is hard to overstate the importance of Eric Crahan in making this book happen. He has been instrumental along every step of the way, leaving an imprint on both its form and substance. Most importantly, he had a vision for what the book might become back when it was still a dissertation. Three anonymous reviewers provided excellent comments. The manuscript's editors, Madeleine Adams and Karen Verde, were both extremely helpful. I was privileged to have the book interpreted visually by cover designer Amanda Weiss.

Two friends have been especially important in this book's substance and in my emotional well-being. Allison Carnegie is the perfect academic collaborator: brilliant, creative, enthusiastic, hard-working, and even-keeled in the face of criticism. Again and again, she has provided sage advice on everything from parenting to publishing. I am forever grateful she suggested we work on a paper together back in 2013. Bentley Allan has been a best friend and my single most important intellectual sounding board for a decade and counting. My career would not be half of what it is without him. Most important, perhaps, is the inspiration I draw from the ambition of his ideas and his work ethic. I am beyond lucky to continue to share this strange academic journey with him.

Finally, the most important people have been my family. My parents, Bruce and Nancy, provided a foundation of love and opportunity that I can only hope to repay to my own children. Their unwavering faith in my abilities always exceeded my own and helped me get through many rough patches. Jessica, Jon, and Carson are the trio I could always count on for joy and laughter, the essential antidote to book-writing blues. Kai arrived when I was first drafting the full book manuscript. For the past three years, he has been the gentle, thoughtful, and funny little boy I had always hoped I would get a chance to raise. His sister Zoe has just arrived, mere months before the book is in print. She has her life ahead of her and I feel deeply fortunate that I get to be an essential part of it. Lastly, my wife Sarah has been the perfect spouse and life partner. She is unflappable, loving, and fantastically smart; an expert traveler and food enthusiast; an unbelievably loving, thoughtful, and inspiring parent to our children. No one knows the emotional adventure of writing a book like a spouse. Without her steady support, wisdom, and love, this book would not exist.

SECRET WARS

1

Introduction

An irony of the end of the Cold War was confirmation that it was, in fact, never cold in the first place. In the early 1990s, interviews with Soviet veterans and newly opened archives verified that Soviet pilots covertly participated in air-to-air combat with American pilots during the Korean War for two years.[1] About a decade later, declassification of 1,300 American intelligence documents confirmed an even more striking fact: US intelligence agencies knew about the operation.[2] One intelligence review from July 1952, a full year before the end of the war, estimated that 25,000–30,000 Soviet military personnel were "physically involved in the Korean War" and concluded that "a de facto air war exists over North Korea between the

---

1 Early accounts appear in Robert F. Futrell, *The United States Air Force in Korea 1950–1953* (Washington, DC: Office of Air Force History, 1983), 401; post–Cold War works include Jon Halliday, "Air Operations in Korea: The Soviet Side of the Story," in *A Revolutionary War: Korea and the Transformation of The Postwar World*, ed. William J. Williams (Chicago: Imprint Publications, 1993); Kathryn Weathersby, "The Soviet Role in the Early Phase of the Korean War: New Documentary Evidence," *Journal of American-East Asian Relations* 2, no. 4 (Winter 1993): 425–58; Mark O'Neill, "The Other Side of the Yalu: Soviet Pilots in the Korean War" (Dissertation, Florida State University, 1996); William B. Breuer, *Shadow Warriors: The Covert War in Korea* (New York: Wiley, 1996); Mark O'Neill, "Soviet Involvement in the Korean War: A New View from the Soviet-Era Archives," *OAH Magazine of History* 14, no. 3 (April 1, 2000): 20–24; Kathryn Weathersby, "The Soviet Role in the Korean War: The State of Historical Knowledge," in *The Korean War in World History* (Lexington: University Press of Kentucky, 2004).

2 "Baptism by Fire: CIA Analysis of the Korean War." Collection available at Freedom of Information Act website for the Central Intelligence Agency. https://www.cia.gov/library/readingroom/collection/baptism-fire-cia-analysis-korean-war-overview.

UN and the USSR."[3] In short, the Cold War started hot.[4] Yet neither Moscow nor Washington gave any public indication that direct combat was taking place.

This episode is a dramatic example of the two related phenomena this book seeks to understand. The Soviet entry in the Korean War is a case of *covert military intervention*, in which an external power secretly provides military assistance during a war. The American decision to stay silent after detecting Russian pilots is a case of *collusion*, in which one government detects but does not publicize or confirm the secret intervention of another government. The episode raises two related but distinct questions. First, why use a covert form of intervention, especially if it will be detected by an adversary? Second, why would an adversary play along?

The conspiracy of silence that emerged in the Korean War is but one example of a broader phenomenon. In political campaigns, rival candidates may uncover evidence of secret legal or ethical violations by their opponents. While going public with such information is tempting, exposure could force the rival candidate to respond in kind and lead to a rash of attack ads and inflammatory accusations. Such mudslinging could depress turnout and open the door for other candidates, creating good reason for mutual restraint regarding secrets.[5] Childhood family dynamics also feature reciprocal secret keeping. Two siblings often know about one another's secrets, be it hidden Halloween candy, forged homework, or a clandestine romantic relationship. Exposing the other's secret to teachers or parents, while tempting, might prompt a reaction that neither sibling wants. If this scenario looms, then a sustainable conspiracy of silence could emerge. Finally, firms may find evidence that their competitor uses offshore bank accounts to evade taxes. The detecting firm may be tempted to expose and undermine its competitor's advantage. Yet doing so risks provoking regulators to more closely scrutinize the industry as a whole. One reasonable response would be mutual restraint in keeping secret such tax evasion.

---

3 National Intelligence Estimate, "Communist Capabilities and Probable Courses of Action in Korea," NIE-55/1, 30 July 1952, *Foreign Relations of the United States*, 1952–1954, Korea, volume 15, part 1.

4 Other well-known episodes in which casualties were inflicted despite the "Cold War" moniker include the shootdown of U-2 surveillance flights in 1960 and during the Cuban Missile Crisis. On shootdown incidents, see the account of twenty-nine such incidents in Alexander L. George, *Case Studies of Actual and Alleged Overflights, 1930–1953——Supplement*, RAND Research Memorandum, August 15, 1955, RM-1349 (S).

5 E.g., Wioletta Dziuda and William Howell, "Political Scandal," unpublished manuscript, University of Chicago, 2018.

In each example, a mutually unacceptable outcome influences both the initial act of secrecy and the response by one who finds the secret. The central insight is that mutual silence may result if individuals, firms, or governments can act secretly, observe one another doing so, and share fear of a mutually damaging outcome. Cooperative secrecy of this sort is not so surprising for siblings that live together or firms that might price fix or collude in other ways. However, such behavior is quite surprising in world politics, especially during war. That collusive secrecy would emerge *among rivals under anarchy* is especially unexpected.

This book analyzes the politics of secrecy in war and puzzling features like tacit collusion among adversaries. Secrecy has long been a hallmark of international politics where "incentives to misrepresent" can be powerful for governments that must fend for themselves.[6] Seeing states act covertly is not surprising per se. After all, secrecy can be essential for protecting military forces in the field and for operational surprise.[7] Hence the adages that "loose lips sink ships" and "tittle tattle lost the battle." Yet secrecy in the Korean War example appears to be serving different ends. Covert activity was *observable* to the rival. Rather than being in the dark, Moscow's adversary had a unique window into its covert behavior. Moreover, secrecy in this case seems to have been mutually beneficial. Both the American and the Soviet leaders appeared to derive value from keeping the public and other governments in the dark.

This book links such decisions to limited war dynamics and the desire for escalation control. Large-scale conflict escalation is a mutually damaging outcome that is influenced by exposure decisions. I develop a theory in which initial covertness and reactive secrecy are driven by the need to control escalation and avoid large-scale conflict. When escalation risks are significant, adversaries will tend to share an interest in prioritizing control. External military involvement in a local war raises the prospect of expansion in scope and scale. Intervening covertly, however, allows both the intervener and its rivals to better control what scenario unfolds following the intervention. Keeping an intervention covert—that is, acting on the "backstage" rather than the "frontstage"—has two limited-war benefits: easing constraints from a domestic audience and improving communication about

---

6 James D. Fearon, "Rationalist Explanations for War," *International Organization* 49, no. 3 (Summer 1995): 379–414.

7 Robert Axelrod, "The Rational Timing of Surprise," *World Politics* 31, no. 2 (January 1979): 228–46; Branislav L. Slantchev, "Feigning Weakness," *International Organization* 64, no. 3 (2010): 357–88.

interest in limited war. Covertness minimizes domestic hawkish pressures and expresses a mix of resolve and restraint that supports limited war. In the Korean War, covertness regarding the Soviet role allowed each side to operate with fewer constraints, to save face as it limited war, and to have confidence that its adversary valued limiting the conflict. This happened because of, rather than in spite of, detection by the other side. A central finding of the book is that this is not one-of-a-kind. Rather, covertness and collusion are an important part of wars ranging from the Spanish Civil War in the 1930s to the American occupation of Iraq in the 2000s.

Beyond developing a novel logic for secrecy in war, this book also offers new insights into the very nature of modern war. In the wake of two devastating world wars in the first half of the twentieth century, how did great powers avoid a third? Nuclear weapons, democracy, and bipolarity are typical answers.[8] This book provides a different take on this question. As O'Brien notes, wars still erupted after 1945 despite these larger changes but were "guided by the principle that the conflict should be geographically limited to the immediate overt belligerents."[9] I show that leaders learned over time to use covertness and collusion to avoid domestic constraints and miscommunication that might otherwise lead to large-scale escalation. This book underscores that *overtness* is an important qualification and identifies how it came to be. Conflicts like the Korean and Vietnam Wars featured direct casualties among the major powers on the backstage. Moreover, understanding these historical links between limited war and secrecy offers practical lessons for policymakers responding to tragic and potentially explosive civil wars in places like Syria, Ukraine, and Yemen.

Secret Wars also holds broader theoretical implications for scholars of International Relations (IR) beyond the study of secrecy itself. For example, the secret side of war I analyze yields new insights about domestic politics and statecraft. Subsequent chapters feature infamous personalist dictators like Adolf Hitler cautiously navigating the dangers of conflict escalation via

8 E.g., Kenneth N. Waltz, *Theory of International Politics*, 1st ed. (New York: McGraw-Hill Humanities/Social Sciences/Languages, 1979); John Mueller, "The Essential Irrelevance of Nuclear Weapons: Stability in the Postwar World," *International Security* 13, no. 2 (1988): 55–79; John Mueller, *Retreat from Doomsday: The Obsolescence of Major War* (New York: Basic Books, 1989); Steven Pinker, *The Better Angels of Our Nature: The Decline of Violence In History And Its Causes* (New York: Penguin Books Limited, 2011).

9 William V. O'Brien, *The Conduct of Just and Limited War* (New York: Praeger, 1981), 230; emphasis added.

covertness and collusion. These otherwise unobservable policy decisions showcase caution on the part of leaders and regime types better known for reckless aggression. Regarding democracies, the book shows that democratic leaders often detect but stay silent about covert activity by other governments. This is an under-recognized way in which presidents and prime ministers can deceive and manipulate domestic elites and public opinion which raises questions about accountability and transparency in democracy. The book also provides new insight into how states under anarchy communicate. Covert intervention takes place in a distinct communicative venue during war. This backstage is visible to other major powers and can allow governments to send and receive messages, including regarding escalation and limited war. This metaphor of a theater provides a heuristic use for the study of war more generally. Rather than conceptualizing war as simply a bargaining process dividing up finite spoils, the book suggests the promise of conceptualizing war as a kind of performance. Later chapters show how major powers move between visible and hard-to-observe spaces to manage the image and meaning of their clashes. Doing so protects the performance of limited war and produces collaborative patterns like collusion that are otherwise hard to explain.

The Topic

This book addresses two questions. First, why do states intervene covertly rather than overtly? Second, when covert interventions take place, why do detecting states collude rather than expose? Secrecy, defined as intentional concealment of information from one or more audiences, is simply one way of making decisions and behaving in the world. Secrecy can be used regarding state deliberations, government decisions, communications among heads of state, or externally oriented policy activity. Secrecy, moreover, requires effort. Especially for complex organizations like states, effectively concealing decisions and actions requires information control in the form of physical infrastructure, rules, penalties, and organizational habits. A term closely related to secrecy, which I use when discussing military intervention specifically, is "covert." Covertness is defined as government-managed activity conducted with the intention of concealing the sponsor's role and avoiding acknowledgment of it. It has a narrower scope than the term "secrecy" because it is specific to a state's externally oriented behavior rather than discrete decisions, refers to the sponsor's identity rather than operational details or outcomes, and explicitly incorporates the concept of non-acknowledgment.[10]

I specifically assess secrecy regarding external military interventions. An intervention is combat-related aid given by an outside state to a combatant in a local civil or interstate conflict that includes some role for personnel. An *overt intervention* involves weaponry and personnel sent to a war zone without restrictions on visibility and with behavioral and verbal expressions of official acknowledgment. A *covert intervention*, in contrast, features an external power providing such aid in a way that conceals its role and does not feature official acknowledgment. Covert intervention is a specific form of covert operation, distinct from covert surveillance, regime change, or other operation that does not aim to alter battlefield dynamics.[11] States can covertly intervene by providing weaponry that lacks military labeling or appears to originate from a different source; they may send military personnel in unmarked civilian uniforms, as "volunteers," or as "military advisors." Much existing research has focused on why states intervene and on intervention's effect on war duration and other outcomes. I focus on the *how* of intervention, specifically, covert compared to overt forms. Such a focus is both theoretically important and timely. Just in the last ten years, the list of countries that have reportedly featured covert external involvement by major powers includes Ukraine, Syria, Libya, Somalia, Pakistan, and Yemen. [12]

---

10 See chapter 2 for additional discussion of these terms. Note that clandestine is a related term which tends to connote concealment of both sponsor and the fact that there was an operation. See Alexandra H. Perina, "Black Holes and Open Secrets: The Impact of Covert Action on International Law," *Columbia Journal of Transnational Law* 53 (2014): 512.

11 Alexander B. Downes and Mary Lauren Lilley, "Overt Peace, Covert War?: Covert Intervention and the Democratic Peace," *Security Studies* 19, no. 2 (2010): 271–72.

12 Roy Allison, "Russian 'Deniable' Intervention in Ukraine: How and Why Russia Broke the Rules," *International Affairs* 90, no. 6 (2014): 1255–97. On Syria, see Greg Miller, "CIA Ramping up Covert Training Program for Moderate Syrian Rebels," *Washington Post*, October 2, 2013, http://www.washingtonpost.com/world/national-security/cia-ramping-up-covert-training-program-for-moderate-syrian-rebels/2013/10/02/a0bba084-2af6-11e3-8ade-a1f23cda135e_story.html; Mark Mazzetti, Adam Goldman, and Michael S. Schmidt, "Behind the Sudden Death of a $1 Billion Secret C.I.A. War in Syria," *New York Times*, August 2, 2017, sec. Middle East, https://www.nytimes.com/2017/08/02/world/middleeast/cia-syria-rebel-arm-train-trump.html. For Libya, Mark Hosenball, "Exclusive: Obama Authorizes Secret Help for Libya Rebels," *Reuters*, March 30, 2011, https://www.reuters.com/article/us-libya-usa-order/obama-authorizes-secret-support-for-libya-rebels-idUSTRE72T6H220110330; "France Gave Libyan Rebels Weapons," *BBC News*, June 29, 2011, sec. Africa, http://www.bbc.com/news/world-africa-13955751. For Somalia, Mark Mazzetti, "U.S. Is Said to Expand Secret Military Acts in Mideast Region," *New York Times*, May 24, 2010, http://www.nytimes.com/2010/05/25/world/25military.html?hp.

Covert interventions raise a second-order question regarding secrecy: If detected, will others keep the secret too? This question is especially germane for other major powers that are most likely to detect a given covert intervention. Providing military aid beyond one's borders for months or years is a significant undertaking, no matter the scope. Doing so without partial exposure is difficult enough. In addition, major powers tend to invest significant resources in intelligence bureaucracies. To be clear, detectors often remain in the dark about many details. However, the sponsor of a covert intervention is often discernible. Any detector has two basic options: collude or expose. Exposure involves publicly revealing evidence that a covert intervention is underway and/or publicly validating allegations by others. Collusion, in contrast, involves staying silent. There is an informational component of collusion; the detector must keep evidence of a covert intervention private rather than share it widely. There is also an acknowledgment component: a colluder must publicly deny or stay silent about allegations of a covert intervention made by others such as the media.

Two Puzzles

The study of secrecy, deception, and related aspects of informational misrepresentation are at last getting their due in IR. In the past ten years, new research has been published on secrecy in diplomacy and deal-making, prewar crisis bargaining, military operations, elite decision-making, alliances, and international institutions.[13] This has been joined by related work

---

For Pakistan, "Secret Memos Reveal Explicit Nature of U.S., Pakistan Agreement on Drones," *Washington Post*, October 23, 2013. For Yemen, Robert Booth and Ian Black, "WikiLeaks Cables: Yemen Offered US 'open Door' to Attack Al-Qaida on Its Soil," December 3, 2010, http://www .guardian.co.uk/world/2010/dec/03/wikileaks-yemen-us-attack-al-qaida; Karen McVeigh, "'Trump's Secret Yemen War': UK Role in US Counter-Terrorism Causes Unease," *Guardian*, September 25, 2017, https://www.theguardian.com/global-development/2017/sep/25/trump-secret-yemen -war-uk-role-us-counter-terrorism-causes-unease.

13 On diplomacy, David Stasavage, "Open-Door or Closed-Door? Transparency in Domestic and International Bargaining," *International Organization* 58, no. 04 (2004): 667–703; Keren Yarhi-Milo, "Tying Hands Behind Closed Doors: The Logic and Practice of Secret Reassurance," *Security Studies* 22, no. 3 (2013): 405–35; Jonathan N. Brown, "Immovable Positions: Public Acknowledgment and Bargaining in Military Basing Negotiations," *Security Studies* 23, no. 2 (April 3, 2014): 258–92; Jonathan N. Brown, "The Sound of Silence: Power, Secrecy, and International Audiences in US Military Basing Negotiations," *Conflict Management and Peace Science* 31, no. 4 (September 1, 2014): 406–31; Corneliu Bjola and Stuart Murray, *Secret Diplomacy: Concepts, Contexts and Cases* (New York: Routledge, 2016); Shawn L. Ramirez, "Mediation in the Shadow of an Audience: How Third Parties Use Secrecy and Agenda-Setting to Broker Settlements," *Journal of Theoretical Politics*, September 25, 2017, 0951629817729227. On crisis bargaining,

on covert operations, deception and lying, intelligence, and declassification.[14] Two predominant logics for the appeal of secrecy provide initial intuition about the book's two specific research questions. The most prevalent view is that information misrepresentation helps insecure states protect their security under anarchy. Here secrecy is directed at adversaries. Especially during war, effective concealment of new weapons, troop locations, or an operational naval vulnerability can be essential to avoiding losses and harnessing the power of surprise. A second strand of research emphasizes secrecy's link to domestic politics. For research on security and conflict, the dominant emphasis is on *democratic* leaders avoiding *dovish*, antiwar constraints. Leaders might circumvent public constraints to initiate war against a threatening foe or change the regime of a fellow democracy.

Shuhei Kurizaki, "Efficient Secrecy: Public Versus Private Threats in Crisis Diplomacy," *American Political Science Review* 101, no. 03 (2007): 543–58; Jonathan N. Brown and Anthony S. Marcum, "Avoiding Audience Costs: Domestic Political Accountability and Concessions in Crisis Diplomacy," *Security Studies* 20 (April 2011): 141–70. On operational benefits of surprise, Adam Meirowitz and Anne E. Sartori, "Strategic Uncertainty as a Cause of War," *Quarterly Journal of Political Science* 3, no. 4 (December 2008): 327–52; Slantchev, "Feigning Weakness"; David Lindsey, "Military Strategy, Private Information, and War," *International Studies Quarterly* 59, no. 4 (December 1, 2015): 629–40; Austin Carson, "Facing Off and Saving Face: Covert Intervention and Escalation Management in the Korean War," *International Organization* 70, no. 01 (2016): 103–31; Austin Carson and Keren Yarhi-Milo, "Covert Communication: The Intelligibility and Credibility of Signaling in Secret," *Security Studies* 26, no. 1 (January 2, 2017): 124–56. On elite decision-making, Elizabeth N. Saunders, "War and the Inner Circle: Democratic Elites and the Politics of Using Force," *Security Studies* 24, no. 3 (July 3, 2015): 466–501. On alliances, Jeffrey Ritter, *"Silent Partners" and Other Essays on Alliance Politics* (Cambridge, MA: Harvard University Press, 2004); Muhammet Bas and Robert Schub, "Mutual Optimism as a Cause of Conflict: Secret Alliances and Conflict Onset," *International Studies Quarterly* 60, no. 3 (September 1, 2016): 552–64. On international organizations, Emilie M. Hafner-Burton, Zachary C. Steinert-Threlkeld, and David G. Victor, "Predictability versus Flexibility: Secrecy in International Investment Arbitration," *World Politics* 68, no. 3 (June 23, 2016): 413–53.

14 Downes and Lilley, "Overt Peace, Covert War?"; Lindsey A. O'Rourke, *Covert Regime Change: America's Secret Cold War* (Ithaca, NY: Cornell University Press, 2018); Michael Poznansky, "Stasis or Decay? Reconciling Covert War and the Democratic Peace," *International Studies Quarterly*, March 1, 2015; Michael F. Joseph and Michael Poznansky, "Media Technology, Covert Action, and the Politics of Exposure," *Journal of Peace Research*, November 16, 2017, 0022343317731508. On deception and lying, John M. Schuessler, "The Deception Dividend: FDR's Undeclared War," *International Security* 34, no. 4 (2010): 133–65; John J. Mearsheimer, *Why Leaders Lie: The Truth about Lying in International Politics* (New York: Oxford University Press, 2011); Dan Reiter, "Democracy, Deception, and Entry into War," *Security Studies* 21, no. 4 (2012): 594–623; John M. Schuessler, *Deceit on the Road to War: Presidents, Politics, and American Democracy* (Ithaca, NY: Cornell University Press, 2015); Erik Gartzke and Jon R. Lindsay, "Weaving Tangled Webs: Offense, Defense, and Deception in Cyberspace," *Security Studies* 24,

To be clear, each of these perspectives sheds light on covert aspects of war. Yet some shortcomings suggest there is more to the story, presenting two empirical puzzles. First, existing research provides little reason to expect adversaries to collude. The operational security logic sees information manipulation as part of the broader pursuit of security at the expense of rivals, whereas the domestic dove logic focuses on domestic concerns that are not directly related to an adversary's interests. If anything, these logics would expect a rival that detects a covert intervention to expose it, either to neutralize any operational advantage or to trigger domestic dovish constraints in the intervener. And yet we have historical documentation of cases in which rival powers did allow detection of covert operations and did collude in this way. Examples include Chinese and Soviet border clashes before 1969, aerial clashes from covert American surveillance flights over Soviet territory, and the covert dimension of Iran-Israel rivalry today.[15]

A second puzzle also underscores the need for a fresh approach. Whether or not major powers collude, covert intervention can be widely exposed by non-state actors like media organizations. This can be due to enterprising journalism on the ground or simple bureaucratic leaks. Recent examples include the Russian covert role in eastern Ukraine and the

---

no. 2 (April 3, 2015): 316–48. On intelligence, Joshua Rovner, *Fixing the Facts: National Security and the Politics of Intelligence* (Ithaca, NY: Cornell University Press, 2011); Robert Jervis, *Why Intelligence Fails: Lessons from the Iranian Revolution and the Iraq War* (Ithaca, NY: Cornell University Press, 2011); James Igoe Walsh, *The International Politics of Intelligence Sharing* (New York: Columbia University Press, 2013); Keren Yarhi-Milo, "In the Eye of the Beholder: How Leaders and Intelligence Communities Assess the Intentions of Adversaries," *International Security* 38, no. 1 (2013): 7–51; Keren Yarhi-Milo, *Knowing the Adversary: Leaders, Intelligence, and Assessment of Intentions in International Relations* (Princeton, NJ: Princeton University Press, 2014); Jonathan N. Brown and Alex Farrington, "Democracy and the Depth of Intelligence Sharing: Why Regime Type Hardly Matters," *Intelligence and National Security* 32, no. 1 (January 2, 2017): 68–84. On declassification, Michael P. Colaresi, *Democracy Declassified: The Secrecy Dilemma in National Security* (New York: Oxford University Press, 2014).

15 Thomas W. Robinson, "The Sino-Soviet Border Dispute: Background, Development, and the March 1969 Clashes," *American Political Science Review* 66, no. 04 (1972): 1175–1202. On surveillance flights, George notes that "in fourteen cases of Soviet action against a Western plane, neither side disclosed the incident either diplomatically or publicly ... the Russians prefer to make no disclosure at all of action they take against an intruding foreign plane. In only three of the thirty-one cases did the Soviets themselves initiate disclosure." Alexander L. George, *Soviet Reaction to Border Flights and Overflights in Peacetime*, RAND Research Memorandum, 15 October 1954, RM-1346 (TS-1106), p. 2. On Iran-Israel, Karl Vick, "Spy Fail: Why Iran Is Losing Its Covert War with Israel," *Time*, February 13, 2013, http://world.time.com/2013/02/13/spy-fail-why-iran-is-losing-its-covert-war-with-israel/.

American covert aid program in the Syrian Civil War. Widely exposed covert interventions become a kind of *open secret*. Such a scenario would obviate secrecy's value as a device to address dovish critiques (domestic dove logic) or deceive an adversary (operational security logic). A puzzle therefore arises when covert interveners maintain a covert posture despite open secrecy. This is possible because covert activity can remain *officially unacknowledged* even if is widely visible. Examples of exposed-but-unacknowledged state behavior include Israel's nuclear weapons arsenal, the American drone strike program in Pakistan, and Russia's "little green men" in Eastern Ukraine.[16] If the pretense of covertness is valuable even after wide exposure, then we must look beyond existing work for insights into a more complex story.

The Argument

I argue that escalation control and a shared desire to limit war can motivate covert intervention up front, collusion by major powers that detect it, and official non-acknowledgment if it is widely exposed. Since World War I, large-scale escalation of war has become unacceptably costly, yet leader control of the escalation process has been simultaneously weakened. While a range of factors influence the escalation potential for war, my theory focuses on two specific escalation-control problems: constraints created by domestic hawks and misunderstandings among adversaries about the value of limited war. My theory claims that backstaging military intervention allows rival leaders to insulate themselves and one another from domestic hawkish constraints. In addition, embracing the backstage communicates shared interest in keeping war limited. This basic relationship provides a unifying logic for the initial decision to intervene covertly, a detector's decision to collude after detection, and an intervener's continuing non-acknowledgment of a widely exposed intervention.

THE CHALLENGE OF ESCALATION CONTROL

In general, war escalation is the expansion in scale or scope of violence. What I refer to as "large-scale escalation" is when a local conflict expands to a regional or global level with at least one major power's participation.

---

16 One analyst concluded the drone strike program was the "worst kept covert secret in the history of U.S. foreign policy." Interview with Micah Zenko, "Raising the Curtain on U.S. Drone Strikes," Council on Foreign Relations, June 2, 2010. On Russian involvement in Ukraine, see Andrew Higgins, Michael Gordon, and Andrew Kramer, "Photos Link Masked Men in East Ukraine to Russia," *New York Times*, April 20, 2014.

Industrialized warfare is ruinous to cautious and reckless states alike. As I develop in chapter 3, World War I made clear that mechanized warfare using industrial-era innovations produced astounding levels of violence. The advent of nuclear weaponry only exacerbated this. As a result, leaders and governments seek to control the pathways to large-scale escalation. Cautious governments hoping to preserve the status quo will tend to see entanglement in a regional or global conflict as gravely damaging. Yet even risk-acceptant states with revisionist goals will find escalation dangerous. The current debate about China and the United States demonstrates this dynamic. Even if China is risk acceptant and revisionist in East Asia, a regional war involving Japan, Korea, and/or the United States could inflict fatal damage on the Communist Party's hold on power, dislocate the Chinese economy, and risk a military humiliation harmful to long-term security. Even if more modest forms of "escalation" are tolerable or even useful, large-scale escalation is strategically counterproductive for major powers in the modern era.

Techniques for building and maintaining control over the escalation process are therefore appealing. In Clausewitzian terms, war tends toward escalation but can be limited if leaders can impose political purpose.[17] Two threats to control are especially relevant. First, domestic politics can undermine escalation control. When one or both sides of a rivalry face strong nationalist pressure, leaders can have little choice but to push forward a tit-for-tat escalation process. While dovish and hawkish sentiment varies, managing hawkish pressure is an especially pressing problem during crises in which a major power has interests. Literatures on domestic rally-round-the-flag effects, nationalism and hypernationalism, audience costs, and the nature of limited war all point to the way mobilization of elites and masses can make restraint during a crisis or war very costly.[18] Moreover, this holds across regime type. Elite or mass criticism in a single-party authoritarian regime can constrain a head of state's options, especially during an ongoing crisis.[19]

17 Peter Paret, "Clausewitz," in *Makers of Modern Strategy from Machiavelli to the Nuclear Age,* ed. Peter Paret, Gordon A. Craig, and Felix Gilbert (Princeton, NJ: Princeton University Press, 1986), 199–200.

18 Stephen Van Evera, "Hypotheses on Nationalism and War," *International Security* 18, no. 4 (April 1, 1994): 5–39; Jack Snyder and Karen Ballentine, "Nationalism and the Marketplace of Ideas," *International Security* 21, no. 2 (October 1, 1996): 5–40; John Mueller, *War, Presidents and Public Opinion* (New York: Wiley, 1973).

19 Jessica L. Weeks, "Autocratic Audience Costs: Regime Type and Signaling Resolve," *International Organization* 62, no. 01 (2008): 35–64; Jessica Chen Weiss, "Authoritarian Signaling,

The second escalation-control problem is between heads of state. It is a product of the complexity of communicating under anarchy, specifically regarding interest in limited war. As Schelling first developed, adversaries seeking to compete while bounding conflict face numerous challenges in accurately and intelligibly expressing their goals.[20] This applies to both resolve and restraint. Most important is the temptation to see an adversary in pessimistic terms, especially when they transgress limits during a war. Accurately understanding one another, however, is essential to controlling escalation because limited war takes two to tango.[21] Escalation control requires identifying "salient thresholds," such as political borders, which allow both sides to show that they are able and willing to localize war.[22] Either side failing to indicate a degree of resolve *and* restraint can lead to misunderstanding that fuels tit-for-tat escalation.

COVERTNESS AND COLLUSION AS ESCALATION CONTROL

This book posits that *how* states intervene and *how* detectors react affect these two escalation problems. In general, each intervention by an outside power raises questions about the continued viability of limits. Nonintervention by outside powers is itself one of the "salient thresholds" that can bound war. Not all interventions are alike, however. An intervention that is a public spectacle (i.e., overt) tends to exacerbate these two escalation-control problems; hawkish domestic constraints become sharper and an adversary tends to see a provocation and infer the absence of restraint. Placing an intervention on the backstage, however, does the opposite, preserving escalation control. On the one hand, covertly crossing the salient threshold of foreign entry reduces the inflammation of domestic hawkish constraints in responding states. Such hawks may not be aware of the entry

Mass Audiences, and Nationalist Protest in China," *International Organization* 67, no. 01 (January 2013): 1–35.

20 Thomas Schelling, *The Strategy of Conflict* (Cambridge, MA: Harvard University Press, 1960); Thomas C. Schelling, *Arms and Influence* (New Haven, CT: Yale University Press, 1966).

21 "Limited war requires limits; so do strategic maneuvers if they are to be stabilized short of war. But limits require agreement or at least some kind of mutual recognition and acquiescence. And agreement on limits is difficult to reach, not only because of the uncertainties and the acute divergence of interests but because negotiation is severely inhibited both during war and before it begins and because communication becomes difficult between adversaries in time of war." Schelling, *The Strategy of Conflict*, 53; see also Jeffrey Legro, *Cooperation Under Fire: Anglo-German Restraint During World War II* (Ithaca, NY: Cornell University Press, 1995).

22 Schelling, *Arms and Influence*, 135.

and will be less able to mobilize pressure to escalate. The absence of official acknowledgment, moreover, can reduce the degree to which an intervention is seen as a provocation. On the other hand, covertness communicates a balanced message. Using a low profile provides a legible and credible indicator of both resolve and restraint. Yet a covert intervention is still an intervention. It also shows an adversary that the intervener is serious about its interests and will give observable (to the adversary) assistance to a local client. This blend of moderate resolve and moderate restraint can be ideally suited to producing the shared understanding that is key to controlling escalation and limiting war.[23]

The mechanisms in my argument differ significantly from the operational security and domestic dove logics. Covert intervention is valuable in part *because* it is observable to the adversary. Moreover, to the extent that domestic politics matter, punishment by elites or masses with hawkish, nationalist preferences is the problem, both for the intervener and those reacting. Finally, escalation control is a goal that is often shared by adversaries and that, I argue, benefits from both information manipulation and non-acknowledgment. These two insights make sense of the two puzzles in the opening: collusion and open secrecy.

THEATER ANALOGY

Herein I use an analogy of the theater to refer to how major powers navigate publicity and secrecy in intervention scenarios. Doing so highlights the shared interests adversaries have in managing impressions during war and the role of limited war and outside audiences in shaping decisions about secrecy. In important respects, major powers are "actors" moving between a space in which their behavior is known and acknowledged to all (frontstage) and a place where actions are visible only to other performers (backstage). Navigation happens in light of the observation of an "audience," which in my theory is domestic observers with hawkish views. One advantage of the theater metaphor is highlighting the shared interest adversaries have in limited war, which is akin to the shared interest actors have in protecting the performance. Limited war is also a co-produced outcome that relies on mutual restraint, just as a performance on stage is a co-production of actors. Finally, just as actors can step out of character on the

---

23 On covert communication and the resolve side of the signal, see Carson and Yarhi-Milo, "Covert Communication."

backstage, major powers during war can direct their behavior to the covert sphere out of the view of domestic hawks. Yet this backstage behavior is not fully concealed; other performers, i.e., other major powers with access to the backstage, can witness that behavior.

The theater analogy captures the key structural features of the strategic setting I theorize. The backstage insulates actors from the humiliation and damage to the performance that would result if mistakes or costume changes were on the frontstage. Backstaging an intervention similarly protects the public-facing image of a limited war and helps major powers save face. Moreover, actors that see one another using the backstage to protect a performance can learn. Stage maneuvers are an indication of commitment to the performance. This is akin to the way observing covert intervention rather than an overt form can communicate a mix of resolve and restraint that supports limited war. Chapter 2 develops the analogy in more detail and links it to the mechanisms and puzzles the book addresses.

BALANCING PUBLICITY AND SECRECY

Any theory of the *choice* for secrecy must specify the temptation to reject it. Put differently, why should we observe *variation* in overt and covert intervention if escalation is easier to control with the latter? Why not always conceal and collude?

This book suggests that major powers have some basic temptations to use the frontstage. For interveners, there are logistical advantages to overtly providing weapons and personnel. It implies simpler logistics and a broader range of scope and scale. Moreover, public interventions are, by definition, more likely to be highly visible vehicles for signaling. Overtness therefore sends the broadest and strongest indication of resolve. For detectors of covert intervention, there are also powerful reasons to consider public exposure. Exposure is tempting primarily due to its impact on the covert intervener's prospects of success. Exposure will heighten awareness among third-party states and tend to better trigger diplomatic, economic, and other forms of punishment. Doing so can raise the costs to the intervener and undermine its goals.

When do interveners and detectors prioritize escalation control or, alternatively, embrace the operational and symbolic advantages of overt intervention and exposure? I argue that the *severity* of escalation risks determines how this balance is struck. When escalation risks are severe and control of escalation via the backstage is feasible, major powers will prioritize escalation control by embracing covertness and collusion. This was the case in the Korean War: both Soviet and American leaders saw escalation risks as severe and believed control via the backstage was feasible. In contrast, the initial American intervention in Korea was overt despite the same structural features. Why? The answer is that a *first-mover intervention* that was *geographically localized* to the Korean peninsula presented a much milder escalation problem. With more manageable risks, the United States prioritized logistics and symbolism, best achieved through an overt intervention. The historical cases that this book assesses follow this basic approach, analyzing the way escalation dynamics often give rise to covertness and collusion but also shed light on why rivals sometimes seize the spotlight.

Empirical Analysis

I use a comparative case study design to analyze five wars: the Spanish Civil War, Korean War, Vietnam War, the Soviet occupation of Afghanistan, and the US occupation of Iraq. I decompose them into a number of cases of intervention and exposure/collusion within each war. This empirical strategy is especially important for three reasons. First, a qualitative approach allows me to analyze within and across wars that each feature multiple interventions. My empirical chapters therefore assess up to three different interventions, often varying in overtness and covertness. This allows me to assess differences among different interveners and detectors. Such controlled comparisons also help identify the causal importance of escalation and the theory's specific mechanisms.[24] Second, central to my theory is a contextually specific phenomenon: behavior vis-à-vis a set of "salient thresholds" that are limiting a war. Identifying how major powers understand the limits bounding a war, and how publicity and secrecy influence them, requires drawing on qualitative evidence that documents conflict-specific, shared beliefs. Third, the practical challenges of studying covert intervention and intelligence-based detection are significant. After all, states are selecting themselves out of traditional data sources. Archival resources are often essential to documenting the very fact of a covert intervention, the fact of detection, as well as the internal debates about what to do and why. American

24 On the promise of multiplying observations with "subcases" within a single case, see John Gerring, "What Is a Case Study and What Is It Good For?," *American Political Science Review* 98, no. 2 (May 2004): 342; Peter Hall, "Aligning Ontology and Methodology in Comparative Politics," in *Comparative Historical Analysis in the Social Sciences*, ed. James Mahoney and Dietrich Rueschemeyer (Cambridge, UK: Cambridge University Press, 2003), 395.

covert operations in Laos during the Vietnam War demonstrate this. Only by relying on now-declassified records from the ambassador and White House managers of this program can we see why leaders perceived political utility in refusing to acknowledge a widely exposed covert program. For each war, I draw on existing archival collections, newly accessed archival materials, and work by historians specializing in states whose records are not publicly available. Only these data can provide the raw material for drawing the descriptive and theoretical inferences this book proposes.

Each empirical chapter addresses two questions. First, I explain *how* and *why* intervening states adopt a particular form of military intervention (the dependent variable) based on the perceived escalation features of a given conflict (the independent variable). Second, I explain *whether* and *why* detector states choose to collude or expose (the dependent variable) based on the same escalation features as well as the level of exposure by other actors. Two clarifications are important in this regard. One is that other logics for secrecy can and do coexist with my own. Secrecy in war serves multiple purposes and they are not mutually exclusive within the same conflict. My empirical analysis therefore focuses on assessing relative importance rather than refuting other logics. A second clarification is that escalation is part of the causal story and not the outcome of interest. As I argue in chapter 2, the magnitude of escalation is ultimately the product of a number of factors. Covertness and collusion handle two escalation-control problems (domestic hawks and miscommunication) but these are not the only problems. A war may widen despite these efforts if a commander in the field goes rogue, for example. The test for my theory is why we see covertness and collusion, not whether they provide perfect escalation control when we see them.

The book focuses on conflicts that balance inferential leverage with a broad and historically informed chronological scope. The theory applies to ongoing local conflicts with some major power involvement that have not escalated to a large scale, as I define it. The theory does not make sense of secrecy's role in a war like World War II; conflicts that quickly reach a regional or global scope will not have escalation control as an important constraint. Moreover, I purposefully and explicitly bound my empirical analysis to post–World War I conflicts because, as chapter 3 describes, that conflict consolidated systemwide changes that sharpened escalation costliness and the problem of escalation control. Within these bounds, I analyze a set of conflicts that feature multiple, nested interventions across seven decades. This results in chapters on five wars and their related interventions (see table 1.1). Each covert intervention also gives rise to separate cases

TABLE 1.1. Conflicts and Cases of Intervention

	Case	Date	Form	Details
Spanish Civil War (1936–1939)	Germany	1936–1939	Covert	Aircraft with pilots in Spain
	Italy	1936–1939	Mixed	"Volunteer" ground troops, aircraft with pilots in Spain; submarines with crews in Mediterranean
	Soviet Union	1936–1938	Covert	Tanks with tank crews, aircraft with pilots in Spain
Korean War (1950–1953)	United States	1950–1953	Overt	Ground, air units in Korea
		1951–1953	Covert	Weapons, training for insurgency and raids into mainland China
	Soviet Union	1950–1953	Covert	Aircraft with pilots in China and North Korea
	China	1950–1953	Mixed	"Volunteer" ground troops in Korea; aircraft with pilots in Korea
Vietnam War (1964–1968)	United States	1964–1973	Overt	Air, ground operations in North and South Vietnam
		1964–1973	Covert	Air, ground operations in Laos
	China	1965–1969	Covert	Air defense weapons and crews in North Vietnam
	Soviet Union	1965	Covert	Air defense weapons and crews in North Vietnam
Afghanistan (1979–1986)	Soviet Union	1979	Covert	Ground, air personnel in Afghanistan
		1979–1988	Overt	Ground, air units in Afghanistan
		1982–1987	Covert	Air, ground raids into Pakistan
	United States	1979–1986	Covert	Weapons supply to rebels in Afghanistan
		1986	Overt	US-only weaponry (Stinger) to rebels
U.S.-occupied Iraq (2003–2011)	Iran	2003–2011	Covert	Iranian-suppled weaponry, advisors for insurgents

of detector exposure or collusion. Each chapter therefore assesses these reactions as well.

Regarding generalizability, I include cases from outside the Cold War, such as the Spanish Civil War (chapter 4), and a shorter case study of US-occupied Iraq in the 2000s (chapter 8). I also include conflicts that feature democracies and non-democracies in both intervener and detector roles. These choices ensure the book can weave a coherent historical narrative that holds across a broad range of contexts. It is important to note that I explicitly reject the treatment of each conflict as an independent event. I follow others in conceptualizing limited war as a learned state practice akin to other learned practices like nuclear deterrence. Moreover, key mechanisms such as backstage communication benefit from experience. Thus, escalation control becomes easier with more interactions. My selection of conflicts allows me to specifically identify cross-conflict influence. For example, a leader in one war (say, the Korean War) may observe and understand its rival's covert intervention in terms of similar events during a prior war (say, the Spanish Civil War). This, in turn, may improve the leader's confidence that limited war is the rival's goal. I present primary documentation of exactly these intertemporal comparisons in later chapters. Moreover, this evidence of cumulative learning is a distinct form of evidence that limited-war issues are important.

Contributions

The theory and findings presented here make contributions to scholarship on international relations, histories of war, and policy.

For scholars of International Relations, the theory and empirical findings most directly contribute to the growing research on secrecy-related themes. I develop a distinct escalation-focused understanding of why states value covertness during war and why collusion often follows. Moreover, while anchored in the dynamics of limited war and intervention, the basic structure of the argument is broadly applicable to situations with a mutually damaging outcome. More broadly, the book develops several conceptual tools—e.g., how secret behavior is detected, the phenomenon of collusive secrecy, and the distinct effects of acknowledgment—that can inform future research on secrecy in other domains.

My findings also have implications for broader themes in the study of war. The book makes clear that information plays a more complex role in war than often assumed. Scholars of IR have long viewed information primarily as a strategic resource wielded against rival states to secure tactical or strategic advantage.[25] Deception along these lines has been seen as one

---

25 Fearon, "Rationalist Explanations for War"; Stephen Van Evera, *Causes of War: Power and the Roots of Conflict* (Ithaca, NY: Cornell University Press, 1999); As one recent entry notes, "states planning aggression may seek to hide this or appear peaceful to lull potential adversaries

key reason two sides can believe war will pay; such mutual optimism makes war more likely.[26] While information revelation is often useful, this book shows how restricting some specific kinds of information can be important to preserving leaders' ability to control escalation. The implication is that more transparency and more information, especially when it fuels hawkish domestic constraints, can worsen the prospect for containing war.[27]

The book also makes a case for reviving the study of escalation and sheds new light on its dynamics. Studies of limited war and escalation largely fell out of fashion with the end of the Cold War. Yet developments in the last ten years—the rise of China; the emergence of cyberwarfare; Russia's revisionism in Eastern Europe—have generated renewed interest in escalation dynamics.[28] My theory draws attention to a largely overlooked aspect of limited war: transgressions that are covert and unacknowledged. Earlier work on limited war has simplified the choice regarding limits to "obey" or "violate."[29] This book shows that governments often have a third

---

into a false sense of security. Similarly, states with peaceful intentions may hide their designs or appear aggressive to deter aspiring predators." Sebastian Rosato, "The Inscrutable Intentions of Great Powers," *International Security* 39, no. 3 (January 1, 2015): 87.

26 Geoffrey Blainey, *The Causes of War*, 3rd ed. (New York: Free Press, 1988); Fearon, "Rationalist Explanations for War"; Meirowitz and Sartori, "Strategic Uncertainty as a Cause of War"; Bas and Schub, "Mutual Optimism as a Cause of Conflict."

27 My claims therefore build on a smaller literature on the dangers of more information in crises and wars, such as Bernard I. Finel and Kristin M. Lord, "The Surprising Logic of Transparency," *International Studies Quarterly* 43, no. 2 (June 1999): 315–39; Bernard I. Finel and Kristin M. Lord, *Power and Conflict in the Age of Transparency*, 1st ed. (New York: Palgrave Macmillan, 2002); Dan Lindley, *Promoting Peace with Information: Transparency as a Tool of Security Regimes* (Princeton, NJ: Princeton University Press, 2007); Kristin M. Lord, *The Perils and Promise of Global Transparency: Why the Information Revolution May Not Lead to Security, Democracy, or Peace* (Albany: SUNY Press, 2006).

28 Avery Goldstein, "First Things First: The Pressing Danger of Crisis Instability in U.S.-China Relations," *International Security* 37, no. 4 (April 1, 2013): 49–89; Caitlin Talmadge, "Would China Go Nuclear? Assessing the Risk of Chinese Nuclear Escalation in a Conventional War with the United States," *International Security* 41, no. 4 (April 1, 2017): 50–92; Martin C. Libicki, *Cyberdeterrence and Cyberwar* (Santa Monica, CA: RAND Corporation, 2009); Martin C. Libicki, *Crisis and Escalation in Cyberspace*, MG-1215-AF (Santa Monica, CA: RAND Corporation, 2012), http://www.rand.org/pubs/monographs/MG1215.html; Jon R. Lindsay, "Stuxnet and the Limits of Cyber Warfare," *Security Studies* 22, no. 3 (July 1, 2013): 365–404; Alexander Lanoszka, "Russian Hybrid Warfare and Extended Deterrence in Eastern Europe," *International Affairs* 92, no. 1 (January 1, 2016): 175–95.

29 The literature on limited war and forms of escalation is vast and addressed in more detail in chapter 2. Classics are Robert E. Osgood, *Limited War: The Challenge to American Strategy* (Chicago: University of Chicago Press, 1957); Schelling, *The Strategy of Conflict*; Schelling, *Arms and Influence*; Robert E. Osgood, *Limited War Revisited* (Boulder, CO: Westview Press, 1979); a more recent treatment is Legro, *Cooperation Under Fire*.

option: covertly violate them. I argue this third option has unique and important consequences for escalation.[30] These mechanisms can provide insight into whether, say, a clash in the South China Sea escalates. The book suggests concealment, ambiguity, and non-acknowledgment can be important tools for managing the domestic pressures and miscommunication risks in the aftermath of such a clash. Moreover, analyzing the backstage can reveal unique and meaningful forms of adversary collaboration that might otherwise be overlooked. This is dramatized by the mutually concealed Soviet-American casualties that helped keep the Korean War limited.

Taking the covert side of conflict seriously also yields new insights about domestic politics. A consistent finding across conflicts is that autocratic regimes exhibit caution and insight about democratic domestic constraints that is often not observable when only analyzing overt behavior. The covert sphere also appears to host instances of democratic leaders suppressing intelligence findings that might endanger limited war which is a novel purpose for deception. The book also has important implications for new forms of covert warfare, such as non-attributable cyberattacks. One important rationale for using a cyber offensive attack instead of a kinetic use of force is escalation control. Moreover, the theory provides important insight into the diplomatic and domestic implications of publicizing forensic analysis of a cyberattack, as in the American intelligence findings about Russian interference in the 2016 election. Similarly, collusive secrecy could emerge among adversaries in civil wars or between governments and terror groups if one conceptualizes escalation more broadly. I discuss many of these extensions in more depth in chapter 8.

The broadest implications of the book reach beyond issues of conflict and communication. The intuition of the theory has implications for states struggling to avoid any worst-case outcome, not just large-scale escalation. Leaders that hope to avoid an all-out trade war or a diplomatic crisis over blame for past war crimes, for example, might find tools like covertness and collusion to be useful in similar ways as limited-war scenarios. The book builds this logic, in part, by drawing on insights from comparisons to performance and the stage. Previous scholars drawing on dramaturgical concepts and the work of sociologist Erving Goffman have focused on widely

---

30 The book therefore builds on a finding mentioned by Legro. He finds evidence of concealed and unacknowledged chemical weapons use during World War II and finds evidence that a desire to keep mutual restraint led the British and German governments to avoid drawing attention to these limit violations. He does not theorize the unique mechanisms of secrecy and non-acknowledgment. Legro, *Cooperation Under Fire*, chap. 4.

visible impressions, roles, and performances.[31] This book adds consideration of the backstage. Theorizing what states conceal as part of performing is useful in its own right; it also helps shed light on the production of cohesive frontstage performances. Moreover, conceptualizing limited war as a kind of performance recognizes that states often must work together, explicitly or tacitly, to define the nature of their encounters. Secrecy and nonacknowledgement are therefore part of a process of instantiating limited war. This basic insight—that states, even adversaries, can use secrecy to cultivate a definition of specific encounters as a way to maintain political control—has wide applicability.

The book also highlights events and episodes in the covert sphere that change how we understand specific wars and modern war more broadly. A dedicated analysis of the backstage and escalation dynamics sheds new light on conflicts ranging from Vietnam to the Spanish Civil War. Archival records I review show that, for example, Nazi Germany tracked Soviet covert involvement during the war in Spain and carefully calibrated covert German combat participation in light of hawkish domestic sentiment in London and Paris. I review unusually candid declassified American records that show that US leaders anticipated the covert involvement of Chinese and Soviet personnel in the Korean War and detected their presence after entry. Newly reviewed archival material from the US covert intervention in Laos during the Vietnam War shows that leaders foresaw media leaks and carefully calibrated their response in order to limit the war. Subsequent empirical chapters note the episodes that add new details to the histories of these wars.

The covert sphere is more than a venue for rivals to deceive and outmaneuver one another during war. The backstage is also a segregated space that can help major powers, even adversaries, manipulate perceptions and control the escalation risks of war. The book also shows that the domestic politics that shape secrecy decisions are complex. Rather than the evasion of antiwar mass mobilization to initiate and maintain intervention, I demonstrate that secrecy is alluring to democratic leaders seeking to insulate

---

31 E.g., Michael N. Barnett, *Dialogues in Arab Politics* (New York: Columbia University Press, 1998); Frank Schimmelfennig, "Goffman Meets IR: Dramaturgical Action in International Community," *International Review of Sociology: Revue Internationale de Sociologie* 12, no. 3 (2002): 417; Rebecca Adler-Nissen, "Stigma Management in International Relations: Transgressive Identities, Norms, and Order in International Society," *International Organization* 68, no. 1 (2014): 143–76; Todd H. Hall, *Emotional Diplomacy: Official Emotion on the International Stage* (Ithaca, NY: Cornell University Press, 2015).

themselves from hawkish reactions that would make *limiting* war more difficult. This results in two very different stories about secrecy in a case like the Vietnam War. Nixon and Kissinger used secrecy to minimize antiwar constraints late in the war, but this book tells the story of the early and middle years, in which the Johnson White House saw secrecy and non-acknowledgment as critical to keeping the war localized to Vietnam.[32] This book therefore joins with well-known observations of war theorists like Clausewitz and Schelling that controlling escalation during war is challenging. It differs, however, in linking that process to secrecy-related tactics and outcomes.

Finally, the book has implications for policy analysts and decision-makers who use and react to the covert side of war. First, I find a recurring pattern of communication and collusion in covert interventions. While it is tempting to focus on operational considerations when assessing or using covert methods, this book highlights a specific set of *political* considerations relevant to exposure and acknowledgment. For example, my theory suggests leaders may need to bridge traditional analytic divides by combining analysis of domestic political constraints abroad with expertise on covert operations and military considerations. Failure to do so may lead to an inaccurate understanding of the value of covertness for rivals. Second, the book suggests that policymakers need to be attentive to differences among covert interventions. Policy design should account for the timing and location of different interventions as well as the severity of the specific escalation problems I develop in chapter 2. Users of covert military tools should specifically assess different exposure scenarios and whether effective secrecy or mere non-acknowledgment can achieve key goals.

Third, the book's findings provide policymakers with a rare set of cross-case historical comparisons that can guide efforts to decipher the meaning of rivals' activity in the covert sphere. This is especially important and timely in an era when leaders in countries like Russia and China increasingly seem to favor tactics that draw on covertness and non-acknowledgement in "hybrid warfare" or "gray zone conflicts." Fourth, the book provides important lessons about when to expect collusion from other governments. I find that adversaries often share an interest in avoiding competitive embarrassment by exposing one another. Yet I also I find that collusion is most reliable when other major powers also seek to control escalation *and* have unique

---

32 See chapter 6.

knowledge of covert activity. These incentives and constraints can be assessed if leaders seek to anticipate when a rival will participate or abandon secrecy-related restraint in a limited war.

Plan of the Book

In chapter 2, I develop my core concepts and theoretical claims. I define and take stock of the challenge of war escalation and the practice of limited war. I argue that secrecy generally addresses two common pathways for unwanted escalation: political constraints and miscommunication. The heart of the chapter argues that covert forms of military intervention can simultaneously insulate leaders from outside audience reactions and communicate to adversaries one's interest in maintaining a limited-war framework. I then connect these themes to the two puzzles by showing that limited-war dynamics make sense of collusion by an adversary and the continued value of widely exposed interventions. The chapter ends by explaining how the severity of escalation dangers influences the choice between frontstage and backstage and identifies process-related observable implications.

Chapter 3 describes the confluence of political, technological, and social changes that prompted the emergence of covert military intervention as an escalation-control technique. The chapter therefore places my case studies in historical context and lays the foundation for assessing how more recent political and technological changes, such as cyberwarfare and drones, influence the covert sphere. It highlights the special role of World War I. I conceptualize the Great War as a critical juncture that dramatized the dangers of large-scale war escalation and accelerated political, social, and technological developments that influenced escalation control. These changes sharpened the problem of escalation control by making leaders more vulnerable to hawkish domestic constraints and making intentions about limited war harder to discern. Yet it also made possible new ways of using military force anonymously through, for example, the development of airpower.

Chapters 4 through 7 move chronologically and assess secrecy in four wars. In chapter 4, I analyze foreign combat participation in the Spanish Civil War. Fought from 1936 to 1939, the war hosted covert interventions by Germany, Italy, and the Soviet Union. The chapter leverages variation in intervention form among those three states, as well as variation over time in the Italian intervention, to assess the role of escalation concerns and limited war in the use of secrecy. Hitler's German intervention provides especially interesting support for the theory. An unusually candid view of Berlin's thinking suggests that Germany managed the visibility of its covert "Condor Legion" with an eye toward the relative power of domestic hawkish voices in France and Great Britain. The chapter also shows the unique role of direct communication and international organizations. The Non-Intervention Committee, an ad hoc organization that allowed private discussions of foreign involvement in Spain, helped the three interveners and Britain and France keep the war limited in ways that echo key claims of the theory.

Chapter 5 shifts the focus to the early Cold War. I review primary materials on a poorly understood aspect of the Korean War: Soviet-American air-to-air combat over North Korea. Records released since the end of the Cold War document how Washington and Moscow engaged in a deadly multiyear struggle for air supremacy and used secrecy to contain its effects. The chapter includes new archival material on American intelligence showing anticipation, detection, and concealment of the Soviet covert entry. The chapter also assesses the United States' initial decision to intervene overtly, its turn to covert action against mainland China, and China's complex role in the war. I argue that China's initial ground intervention used secrecy to achieve surprise, following an operational security logic, but used an unacknowledged "volunteer" intervention to limit the war.

Chapter 6 focuses on the covert side of the Vietnam War. Secrecy famously helped Richard Nixon cope with dovish domestic opposition toward the end of the war. In contrast, I highlight the role of covert intervention in helping both sides compete in Vietnam while keeping the war limited during the earlier Johnson years (i.e., 1964–1968). Even as he greatly expanded US military activity in Vietnam, President Lyndon Johnson acted to avoid provoking a larger war with China or the Soviet Union. Covert US military operations in places like Laos, though an open secret, were a way to prosecute a counterinsurgency while keeping a lid on hostilities. China and the Soviet Union similarly sought to control escalation dangers through covertness. Both communist patrons provided military personnel covertly to improve air defense in North Vietnam. The chapter suggests that all three outside powers worked hard to avoid public and acknowledged clashes up through 1968.

In chapter 7, I analyze the end of the Cold War and external involvement in Afghanistan. On the Soviet side, the December 1979 invasion was preceded by six months of covert involvement in counterinsurgency military operations. I review evidence on the motives for covertness and the detection of it by American leaders. The chapter then assesses covertness in the American weapons supply program after the overt Soviet invasion. Escalation fears—in particular, fear of provoking Soviet retaliation against Pakistan and a larger regional war—led to consistent efforts to keep the expanding US aid program covert from 1979 to 1985. By the mid-1980s, however, American leaders embraced a more aggressive strategy and identified key changes that largely eliminated the risk of escalation, leading them to approve an overt form of weaponry (the Stinger missile system). The chapter also reviews covert Soviet cross-border operations into Pakistan and US inferences from its detection of these activities.

The book concludes in chapter 8. I summarize the key empirical findings and address extension of the basic argument to cyberconflict and violence within states (i.e., civil wars, terrorism). I then present a brief case study of a post–Cold War conflict: the Iranian covert weapons supply program during the US occupation of Iraq (2003–2011). The chapter also addresses questions about the initial choice to intervene, mistakes and exploitation, and the possible implications of social media and leaks in the contemporary era. I conclude by discussing the implications of secrecy's role in escalation control for policy and scholarship.

2

A Limited-War Theory of Secrecy

This chapter develops a logic for secrecy based on shared fears of large-scale conflict escalation. The theory is anchored in the nature of escalation dynamics in modern war and the difficulty of bounding conflict. Industrialization, nationalism, and the advent of nuclear weapons have made large-scale escalation astoundingly destructive and costly. I argue that interveners use covert means and detectors react with collusion to cope with two threats to escalation control: hawkish domestic pressure and poor communication among adversaries. While overt intervention and exposure are tempting, acute escalation risks cause leaders to prioritize escalation control and embrace the backstage. This logic makes sense of the initial choice to intervene covertly, collusion reactions by those detecting covert interventions, and unusual cases of "open secrecy."

The first section defines the structure of intervention scenarios, identifying the relevant actors and research questions. Next, I briefly review the answers offered in extant scholarship, describe three analytical moves my theory makes that distinguish it from existing work, and introduce the theater analogy. The third section develops two escalation-control problems and the mechanisms through which covertness and collusion improve control. I also connect these limited-war dynamics to the two puzzles—collusion and open secrecy—introduced in chapter 1. The fourth section situates limited-war dynamics among other considerations relevant to choices about secrecy and how competing considerations are balanced against escalation control. I conclude by discussing process-related observable implications, which will be the focus of my empirical analysis in subsequent chapters.

Intervention Scenarios and Two Questions

Secrecy, defined as intentional concealment of information from one or more audiences, is simply one way of making decisions and behaving in the world.[1] Secrecy can play many roles in war and peace. This book focuses on the role of secrecy in foreign military interventions. Figure 2.1 identifies the core features of the conflicts I analyze. Two major powers (A and B) are sympathetic to opposed local actors (X and Y) who are engaged in ongoing violent conflict within some bounded geographic space (L). I define major powers as states capable of waging sustained military campaigns beyond immediate neighboring territory.[2] Moreover, X and Y may either be sovereign states (e.g., North and South Korea) or a government and rebel group (e.g., Afghanistan's central government and rebel groups). Figure 2.1 makes one important distinction about where war is taking place. The existing conflict is surrounded by other territory and waters, designated as peripheral areas (P). These peripheral areas may be territory across a political border, territory above a certain latitude or longitude, or distinct geographic zones like a nearby sea. The key point is that combat activities may or may not move to these peripheral areas.

Major Powers A and B may express their support for local actors through a variety of means, including military intervention. I define military intervention as combat-related aid to a state or non-state participant that includes some role for personnel.[3] This is represented by the arrows in

---

1 Sissela Bok, *Secrets: On the Ethics of Concealment and Revelation* (New York: Vintage Books, 1989), 5–6.

2 Note that I do not define this in terms of global power projection. Interwar Italy (chapter 4) was capable of sustained ground and naval operations in Europe and North/East Africa but not beyond. I count it as a major power because its operations were in non-contiguous territory. On extraregional power projection and great power status, see Nuno P. Monteiro, *Theory of Unipolar Politics* (New York: Cambridge University Press, 2014), 43–44. See also Joshua Shifrinson, *Rising Titans, Falling Giants: How Great Powers Exploit Power Shifts* (Ithaca, NY: Cornell University Press, 2018).

3 This definition occupies a middle ground vis-à-vis existing definitions in the literature, including both aid and some minimal personnel role. Regan defines third-party intervention as "the supply or transfer of troops, hardware, or intelligence and logistical support to the parties in conflict." Patrick M. Regan, "Conditions of Successful Third-Party Intervention in Intrastate

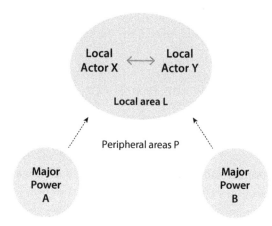

FIGURE 2.1. Local conflict and foreign intervention.

figure 2.1. Moreover, A and B can observe one another. As I discuss below, major powers observe interventions either because they are publicly announced, covert but detected via intelligence resources, or covert but widely exposed by third parties like the media. To simplify, I refer to any intervening state as an "intervener" and a state detecting a covert intervention as a "detector." Note that although these two roles are treated separately for analytical clarity, the same major power often both intervenes and detects others.

The central problem framing intervention scenarios and at the heart of my theory is conflict escalation. Escalation, or the expansion in the scale or scope of violence during war, increases the magnitude of destruction during war.[4] Escalation occurs in two basic ways: by expanding the kinds of weaponry and intensity of battle (vertical escalation) or by expanding

Conflicts," *Journal of Conflict Resolution* 40, no. 2 (1996): 342, 339fn1; Corbetta and Dixon include in intervention combat participation, military assistance, military sanctions, and threats to use force. Renato Corbetta and William Dixon, "Danger Beyond Dyads: Third-Party Participants in Militarized Interstate Disputes," *Conflict Management and Peace Science* 22, no. 1 (2005): 44; Saunders defines intervention as the deployment of one thousand combat-ready troops. Elizabeth N. Saunders, *Leaders at War: How Presidents Shape Military Interventions* (Ithaca, NY: Cornell University Press, 2011), 20.

4 Richard Smoke, *War: Controlling Escalation* (Cambridge, MA: Harvard University Press, 1977), 17, 32, 35; this definition excludes intensification of prewar disputes, which coercive bargaining studies often refer to as "escalation," i.e., James D. Fearon, "Domestic Political Audiences and the Escalation of International Disputes," *American Political Science Review* 88, no. 3 (September 1994): 577–92. It also excludes expansion in state goals, though see Jeffrey Larsen and Kerry Kartchner, *On Limited Nuclear War in the 21st Century* (Stanford, CA: Stanford University Press, 2014), 5–6.

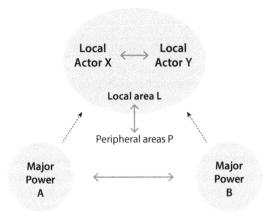

FIGURE 2.2. Large-scale escalation amid foreign intervention.

the physical space in which active combat takes place (horizontal escalation).[5] Escalation is an inherently relational and context-dependent phenomenon.[6] The same act—for example, bombing a city—is an "escalation" in one war (e.g., cities had been off-limits) and not in another (e.g., cities were already being bombed). Escalation can therefore be redefined as both sides settle on, transgress, and even restore limits.

In reality, escalation is not dichotomous. Wars can vary along a nearly infinite spectrum; Herman Kahn famously identified dozens of stepwise escalations in the context of the Cold War.[7] To build a theory, however, this infinite variety must be simplified to theoretically important forms of escalation. I focus on what I call *large-scale escalation*, or a war that has spread to a regional or larger scope and/or features direct, large-scale, and publicly acknowledged combat among major powers.[8] Large-scale escalation is distinguished from lesser forms of escalation like newly targeting civilians or cities or the act of military intervention itself. Figure 2.2 adds detail to figure 2.1, illustrating large-scale escalation. One new arrow, linking L to P, represents combat widening beyond geographic boundaries and

5 Herman Kahn, *On Escalation: Metaphors and Scenarios* (New York: Praeger, 1965); Smoke, *War: Controlling Escalation.*

6 Thomas Schelling, *The Strategy of Conflict* (Cambridge, MA: Harvard University Press, 1960), 162–66.

7 Kahn, *On Escalation: Metaphors and Scenarios.*

8 This definition excludes diplomatic crises or ruptures short of war. As I discuss in chapter 4 (Spanish Civil War) and chapter 7 (Afghanistan), these outcomes can also influence covertness and collusion. While in the spirit of the theory, such a finding is technically outside its bounds.

assuming a regional or larger scope. A second new arrow, linking Major Powers A and B, represents the emergence of direct, large-scale, and publicly acknowledged combat among opposed major powers. Both constitute large-scale escalation.

Limited war is an ongoing intra- or interstate conflict in which violence is used within a relatively fixed scale and scope. Like escalation, limited war can be defined in different ways, is context-dependent, and can be redefined over time. Yet all limits must serve as what Schelling calls "salient thresholds."[9] Salient thresholds are implicit or explicit rules about *who* uses violence, *where* it is used, and/or *how* it is used. They can be tacit or explicit; literal lines or figurative distinctions; moreover, they can be codified in trans-historical normative rules like the prohibition on targeting civilians in the laws of war.[10] In some eras, limited war has a specific connotation, such as "conventional not nuclear war" during the Cold War. In this book, limited war refers to any conflict in which intervention takes place but which lacks large-scale escalation.

Because limits in war are vulnerable, leaders often value control of the escalation process. In intervention scenarios like figure 2.1, violations of some salient thresholds "may carry the possibility of sparking an open-ended action-reaction cycle."[11] Yet one state's transgression of a threshold (e.g., say, bombing of a hospital) may not necessarily be followed by counter-escalation (i.e., retaliatory bombing of hospitals). The reaction is therefore a question of *further* escalation which may result in large-scale escalation. Leaders respond to this risk by seeking to maintain political control of the escalation process. I refer to this as "escalation control," or the capacity of heads of state to manipulate and calibrate the level of hostilities in a given conflict.[12]

9 Thomas C. Schelling, *Arms and Influence* (New Haven, CT: Yale University Press, 1966), 135; as Smoke notes, a war's limits are transgressed when a state's wartime conduct "crosses a saliency which defines the current limits of a war." Smoke, *War: Controlling Escalation*, 35.

10 Schelling, *The Strategy of Conflict*, 258–59.

11 Smoke, *War: Controlling Escalation*, 32; on a hard-to-control, step-by-step process, Smoke (24) notes, "escalation can feed on itself: earlier escalations threaten wider and deeper interests, which heighten the motivation on both sides to win"; on cycles of counter-escalation in the spiral model, see Robert Jervis, *Perception and Misperception in International Politics* (Princeton, NJ: Princeton University Press, 1976); Charles L. Glaser, "Political Consequences of Military Strategy: Expanding and Refining the Spiral and Deterrence Models," *World Politics* 44, no. 4 (July 1992): 497–538; Andrew Kydd, "Game Theory and the Spiral Model," *World Politics* 49, no. 3 (April 1997): 371–400.

12 This definition is similar to definitions of "escalation management" in Alexander L. George, ed., *Managing U.S.-Soviet Rivalry: Problems of Crisis Prevention* (Boulder, CO: West-

TWO QUESTIONS

Regarding secrecy and intervention scenarios, the first question this book addresses is *how* a major power intervenes, specifically whether Major Power A intervenes covertly or overtly. While secrecy is intentional concealment of information from one or more audiences, covertness refers to government-managed activity that is conducted with the intention of concealing and avoiding acknowledgment of the sponsor's role.[13] In practice, military aid can be provided visibly and with official acknowledgment (overtly) or in a concealed way and without official acknowledgment (covertly). Note an important feature of the definition of "covert intervention": it does not stipulate that secrecy is universal or effective and includes the distinct issue of non-acknowledgment. "Covertness and secrecy are distinct characteristics," Perina observes, "but … secrecy facilitates the masking of unacknowledged programs."[14] Put differently, a covert intervention may remain "covert" even if partially visible (i.e., exposed to those with intelligence capabilities) or even widely exposed.[15]

Major powers can use several techniques to obfuscate their role and avoid official acknowledgment. Some states alter the distinctive markings of their weaponry and personnel to make them resemble the local ally recipient's own forces. This is, in essence, impersonation. Foreign personnel may literally don the uniform of the local ally or personnel may be limited to those that share ethnic and linguistic commonalities with the local client. A second approach is to overtly send non-combat equipment or civilian

---

view Press, 1983); Forrest E. Morgan et al., *Dangerous Thresholds: Managing Escalation in the 21st Century* (Santa Monica, CA: RAND Publishing, 2008).

13 In American law, covert action is defined as "an activity or activities of the U.S. Government to influence political, economic, or military conditions abroad, where it is intended that the role of the U.S. Government will not be apparent or acknowledged publicly." Alexandra H. Perina, "Black Holes and Open Secrets: The Impact of Covert Action on International Law," *Columbia Journal of Transnational Law* 53 (2014): 512; also see Elizabeth E. Anderson, "The Security Dilemma and Covert Action: The Truman Years," *International Journal of Intelligence and CounterIntelligence* 11, no. 4 (1998): 403–27.

14 She further notes that "accretions of information or allegations may incrementally diminish a secret's depth, until in some cases it may be considered an 'open secret' even if it continues to be unacknowledged." Perina, "Black Holes and Open Secrets," 539–40.

15 Widely exposed operations are sometimes called "overt-covert" operations, as in Reagan-era operations in Nicaragua. See Gregory F. Treverton, "Covert Action: From 'Covert' to Overt," *Daedalus* 116, no. 2 (1987): 95–123; for a more recent treatment using the "open secret" language I prefer, see Perina, "Black Holes and Open Secrets."

personnel but secretly adopt combat roles.[16] A third method is to imitate private or unofficial alternatives. Outside powers may provide personnel in the guise of "private" or "volunteer" actors; weaponry can be limited to that which is available on the black market or seized from other states.[17] Finally, some technologies create space for anonymity and allow an outside power to influence a war covertly without special adaptations.[18] Limiting an intervention to non-surfacing submarines or high-altitude drones, for example, may avoid indication of whose forces are being used without physical changes. Later chapters showcase each of these techniques, including Soviet "military advisors" operating missile systems in North Vietnam (chapter 6), Italy disguising ships to resemble the Spanish Nationalist fleet (chapter 4), and American "civilian advisors" in Laos (chapter 6).[19]

The second question I address in the book is about *reactions* to covert intervention. As I document in chapters 3 through 7, effectively concealing distant military aid over months or years is logistically difficult. This is especially the case regarding other major powers with sophisticated intelligence capabilities and strong incentive to direct those intelligence assets to monitoring ongoing conflicts with potential for foreign participation. This second question asks: How does any detector react? There are two basic options. Collusion is defined as the detector (say, Major Power B) reinforcing the covert intervener's position of non-involvement. It can involve B

---

16 During the 1970 War of Attrition, for example, Soviet military advisors already stationed within Egypt were quietly tasked with serving active air defense roles against Israeli-flown air missions. David A. Korn, *Stalemate: The War of Attrition and Great Power Diplomacy in the Middle East, 1967–1970* (Boulder, CO: Westview Press, 1992).

17 Examples of putative "volunteers" that were not acknowledged as organized military personnel include the Spanish Blue Division in World War II and, more recently, Russian combat-related personnel in Eastern Ukraine. See Denis Smyth, "The Dispatch of the Spanish Blue Division to the Russian Front: Reasons and Repercussions," *European History Quarterly* 24, no. 4 (October 1, 1994): 537–53; David M. Herszenhorn, "Fears Rise as Russian Military Units Pour into Ukraine," *New York Times,* November 12, 2014, http://www.nytimes.com/2014/11/13/world /europe/ukraine-russia-military-border-nato.html. On private or mercenary forces, the CIA relied on two putatively private airlines (Civil Air Transport and Air America) for many covert air missions in Asia. See the now-declassified four-volume collection, "CIA's Clandestine Services: Histories of Civil Air Transport," at https://www.cia.gov/library/readingroom/collection/cias -clandestine-services-histories-civil-air-transport.

18 See additional discussion of technology and anonymity around World War I in chapter 3.

19 Note that each of these tactics can be combined and that they may evolve over time within a given covert intervention. For example, South Africa steadily progressed from arms-length weaponry to active combat operations in its covert intervention in Angola in 1975–1976. Jamie Miller, "Yes, Minister: Reassessing South Africa's Intervention in the Angolan Civil War, 1975–1976," *Journal of Cold War Studies* 15, no. 3 (July 1, 2013): 4–33.

withholding private information about A's concealed military role and refusing to officially confirm allegations about A's activity. The detector can instead publicly refute A's public-facing narrative, which I refer to as exposure. Exposure can include B publicly revealing unique intelligence-derived information that shows A's concealed involvement and/or B publicly confirming allegations made by others about A.

Existing Literature and a Different Approach

My theory aims to provide a unified logic for decisions about covertness and collusion. What does existing scholarship in IR suggest about these two questions?

Intervention in general has received extensive scholarly attention in the last twenty years. Research on civil wars has analyzed intervention in the form of peacekeeping and its impact on war duration, recurrence, or democratization.[20] Other work has focused on intervention as military or economic aid to combatants and its impact on the ability and willingness to reach peace, including interventions specifically motivated by humanitarian goals.[21] Still others address intervention in civil wars in the form of diplomatic mediation.[22] Despite acknowledging several different forms of

20 E.g., Paul F. Diehl, Jennifer Reifschneider, and Paul R. Hensel, "United Nations Intervention and Recurring Conflict," *International Organization* 50, no. 4 (October 1996): 683–700; Virginia Page Fortna, "Does Peacekeeping Keep Peace? International Intervention and the Duration of Peace After Civil War," *International Studies Quarterly* 48, no. 2 (June 1, 2004): 269–92; Virginia Page Fortna, *Does Peacekeeping Work?: Shaping Belligerents' Choices After Civil War* (Princeton, NJ: Princeton University Press, 2008).

21 E.g., Patrick M. Regan, "Third-Party Interventions and the Duration of Intrastate Conflicts," *Journal of Conflict Resolution* 46, no. 1 (February 1, 2002): 55–73; Patrick M. Regan, *Civil Wars and Foreign Powers: Outside Intervention in Intrastate Conflict* (Ann Arbor: University of Michigan Press, 2002). On humanitarian goals, see Martha Finnemore, *The Purpose of Intervention: Changing Beliefs about the Use of Force* (Ithaca, NY: Cornell University Press, 2004); Jon Western, "Sources of Humanitarian Intervention: Beliefs, Information, and Advocacy in the U.S. Decisions on Somalia and Bosnia," *International Security* 26, no. 4 (April 1, 2002): 112–42; Ian Hurd, "Is Humanitarian Intervention Legal? The Rule of Law in an Incoherent World," *Ethics & International Affairs* 25, no. 03 (2011): 293–313; Robert A. Pape, "When Duty Calls: A Pragmatic Standard of Humanitarian Intervention," *International Security* 37, no. 1 (July 1, 2012): 41–80.

22 E.g., Andrew H. Kydd, "When Can Mediators Build Trust?," *American Political Science Review* null, no. 03 (August 2006): 449–462; Kyle Beardsley, "Agreement without Peace? International Mediation and Time Inconsistency Problems," *American Journal of Political Science* 52, no. 4 (October 1, 2008): 723–40; Patrick M. Regan, Richard W. Frank, and Aysegul Aydin, "Diplomatic Interventions and Civil War: A New Dataset," *Journal of Peace Research* 46, no. 1 (January 1, 2009): 135–46; Kyle Beardsley, *The Mediation Dilemma* (Ithaca, NY: Cornell University Press, 2011).

intervention, few civil war studies have addressed covert military intervention. Kristian Gleditsch's observation a decade ago remains true today: "covert support to one of the parties ... seems at least as important as direct intervention in ongoing civil wars but has received little attention."[23] At the interstate level, military intervention during a war has been analyzed under the headings of war diffusion, war widening, and alliance politics.[24] These studies, many of which draw on the Militarized Interstate Dispute dataset, tend to neglect covert options by limiting their scope to "explicit, overt, nonaccidental, and government sanctioned."[25] Qualitative studies do this as well. Saunders, for example, draws on archival evidence to assess leader beliefs about transformative or non-transformative interventions but explicitly defines intervention as "an overt, short-term deployment" with an "explicit, visible decision to commit forces."[26] Because covert involvement is less visible, she argues, "the decision to intervene covertly may be gov-

23 On varieties of intervention, see Patrick M. Regan and Aysegul Aydin, "Diplomacy and Other Forms of Intervention in Civil Wars," *Journal of Conflict Resolution* 50, no. 5 (October 1, 2006): 736–56. On covert being under-analyzed, Kristian Skrede Gleditsch, "Transnational Dimensions of Civil War," *Journal of Peace Research* 44, no. 3 (May 1, 2007): 296; note that some studies do identify "alleged" vs. "explicit" external aid to insurgencies, as in Idean Salehyan, Kristian Skrede Gleditsch, and David E. Cunningham, "Explaining External Support for Insurgent Groups," *International Organization* 65, no. 04 (2011): 709–44.

24 E.g., Randolph Martin Siverson and Harvey Starr, *The Diffusion of War: A Study of Opportunity and Willingness* (Ann Arbor: University of Michigan Press, 1991); Alastair Smith, "To Intervene or Not to Intervene: A Biased Decision," *Journal of Conflict Resolution* 40, no. 1 (March 1, 1996): 16–40; Stacy Bergstrom Haldi, *Why Wars Widen: A Theory of Predation and Balancing* (New York: Routledge, 2004); Renato Corbetta, "Determinants of Third Parties' Intervention and Alignment Choices in Ongoing Conflicts, 1946–2001," *Foreign Policy Analysis* 6, no. 1 (2010): 61–85; Kyle A. Joyce, Faten Ghosn, and Reşat Bayer, "When and Whom to Join: The Expansion of Ongoing Violent Interstate Conflicts," *British Journal of Political Science* 44, no. 1 (January 2014): 205–38.

25 Much work on intervention in interstate war draws on the Militarized Interstate Dispute dataset, which defines MIDs as "a set of interactions between or among states involving threats to use military force, displays of military force, or actual uses of military force. To be included, these acts must be explicit, overt, nonaccidental, and government sanctioned." Charles S. Gochman and Zeev Maoz, "Militarized Interstate Disputes, 1816–1976: Procedures, Patterns, and Insights," *Journal of Conflict Resolution* 28, no. 4 (December 1, 1984): 587; later iterations refer to "overt action taken by the official military forces or government representatives" and clarify that "when regular forces are disguised as non-regular forces, operate with or command non-regular forces, or engage in covert operations, their actions are excluded unless and until further militarized incidents involving official forces take place, or when the targeted state responds—militarily or diplomatically—to the act in question." Daniel M. Jones, Stuart A. Bremer, and J. David Singer, "Militarized Interstate Disputes, 1816–1992: Rationale, Coding Rules, and Empirical Patterns," *Conflict Management and Peace Science* 15, no. 2 (1996): 169–70.

26 Saunders, *Leaders at War*, 21–22.

erned by a different causal process than decisions to intervene overtly."[27] As I argue below, my theory focuses on the unique escalation issues that arise in decisions about covertness and collusion.

More helpful for my questions are studies that focus on the appeal of secrecy and publicity.[28] Two clusters are most prominent in extant work. First, secrecy is often part of misrepresentation among adversaries. Information manipulation about capabilities and military operations can provide strategic and tactical advantages over a rival. An adversary-centric logic can also inform peacetime choices, as when leaders conceal research into new surveillance technology or quietly forge a new alliance. The distinguishing characteristic in all of these applications is that secrecy can be used to create an information asymmetry vis-à-vis a rival to achieve operational gains. I refer to this as the operational security logic for secrecy. It provides one important foil. Exactly this claim has been made about China's use of secrecy when entering the Korean War.[29] A second cluster focuses on domestic politics. Secrecy helps leaders avoid domestic political punishment. But what is the domestic problem? In the security context, the typical domestic problem is antiwar or war-reluctant publics that constrain democratic leaders. This provides a second foil for my theory in which covertness is useful for democratic leaders seeking to influence an overseas conflict without triggering dovish criticism. This logic has been used to make sense of secrecy's role initiating and maintaining American military forces in Vietnam.[30]

What about the appeal of publicity for interveners? A key trend in IR literature since the 1990s has been theorizing the hands-tying and other communicative benefits of publicity for both words and actions, often drawing on Fearon's influential audience cost mechanism.[31] These ideas offer

27 Saunders, *Leaders at War*, 54.

28 For a list of recent work on secrecy and diplomacy, crisis bargaining, military operations, and alliances, see sources in footnote 13 in chapter 1.

29 E.g., Robert Axelrod, "The Rational Timing of Surprise," *World Politics* 31, no. 2 (January 1979): 228–46; Branislav L. Slantchev, "Feigning Weakness," *International Organization* 64, no. 3 (2010): 357–88.

30 E.g., David N. Gibbs, "Secrecy and International Relations," *Journal of Peace Research* 32, no. 2 (1995): 213–228; John M. Schuessler, *Deceit on the Road to War: Presidents, Politics, and American Democracy* (Ithaca, NY: Cornell University Press, 2015), chap. 3.

31 E.g., Fearon, "Domestic Political Audiences and the Escalation of International Disputes"; James D. Fearon, "Signaling Foreign Policy Interests: Tying Hands versus Sinking Costs," *Journal of Conflict Resolution* 41, no. 1 (February 1997): 68–90; Kenneth A. Schultz, "Domestic Opposition and Signaling in International Crises," *American Political Science Review* 92, no. 4

one set of insights about why overt intervention might be attractive; it should be more effective in demonstrating resolve and a credible commitment to adversaries and allies. A distinct reason public or overt state behavior can be useful involves operational considerations.[32] Secrecy is effortful and, while potentially cheap, is inherently constraining. Working to avoid broad exposure and acknowledgment of an intervention can lead to constraints on what is provided (i.e., pilots, tank operators, small groups of antiaircraft artillery, generic weaponry) and its sophistication (i.e., not foreign-born infantry or highly advanced weaponry).[33] Covert options also tend to lack wide policy discussion and vetting which can increase the risk of poor planning.[34] By contrast, overt operations can involve robust amounts of aid, more advanced technologies, and optimally trained personnel; may feature lively debate that better vets policy ideas; and can use more efficient transport networks.

My second question focuses on detectors and the reaction. Why would detectors choose to expose or collude? On the one hand, extant research and intuition provide good reason to expose. Major Power B revealing A's covert intervention can have large potential diplomatic effects. Exposing a rival's covert intervention can serve as a form of "naming-and-shaming" that refutes the claims of legitimacy of an intervener.[35] It can also raise hypocrisy costs by highlighting the gap between the intervener's words and

---

(December 1998): 829–44; Kenneth A. Schultz, *Democracy and Coercive Diplomacy* (New York: Cambridge University Press, 2001).

32 See discussion in Lindsey A. O'Rourke, *Covert Regime Change: America's Secret Cold War* (Ithaca, NY: Cornell University Press, 2018), chap. 3.

33 This is akin to the operational benefits of acting unilaterally rather than multilaterally noted in Alexander Thompson, "Coercion Through IOs: The Security Council and the Logic of Information Transmission," *International Organization* 60, no. 01 (2006): 1–34; Sarah E. Kreps, *Coalitions of Convenience: United States Military Interventions After the Cold War* (New York: Oxford University Press, 2011); on the value of policy vetting and the danger of distortions, see Chaim Kaufmann, "Threat Inflation and the Failure of the Marketplace of Ideas: The Selling of the Iraq War," *International Security* 29, no. 1 (July 1, 2004): 5–48.

34 Dan Reiter and Allan C. Stam, *Democracies at War* (Princeton, NJ: Princeton University Press, 2010), 159–61.

35 On naming and shaming benefits in other contexts, see Martha Finnemore and Kathryn Sikkink, "International Norm Dynamics and Political Change," *International Organization* 52, no. 04 (1998): 887–917; Emilie M. Hafner-Burton, "Sticks and Stones: Naming and Shaming the Human Rights Enforcement Problem," *International Organization* 62, no. 4 (October 1, 2008): 689–716; exposure can counter the legitimating strategies of rising powers that draw on interventions; see Stacie E. Goddard, "When Right Makes Might: How Prussia Overturned the European Balance of Power," *International Security* 33, no. 3 (2011): 110–42. On downsides of expos-

deeds.[36] This can build support from the international community for moral, diplomatic, economic, and other forms of punishment, raising the costs and potentially undermining the intervener's ability to achieve its goals. The logic for collusion, in contrast, is less clear. Collusion does not provide an operational advantage to the detector; if anything, it does the covert intervener a favor by keeping others in the dark that might otherwise adapt. If covertness is helping the intervener avoid their own dovish domestic audiences, then there is little incentive for a detector to collude. In fact, both extant logics for secrecy provide powerful reasons for exposure. A detector exposing a covert intervention can eliminate any residual operational advantages and invoke dovish constraints for the intervener; both can do real damage to the intervention and even prompt withdrawal.

To summarize, existing work points to intuitive reasons overt intervention and exposure can be appealing. Publicity has diplomatic and operational benefits. At the same time, existing work identifies two important rationales for secrecy with clear applications to covertness in intervention. Yet the potential value of a different approach is dramatized by the continued puzzle of collusion. If anything, existing logics sharpen the puzzle.

A DIFFERENT APPROACH TO SECRECY

One key limit in existing work is its assumptions. The operational security logic assumes that information manipulation, like other policy tools available to insecure states, serves as a vehicle for security competition. While surely part of the story of secrecy, this assumption obscures the possibility of *mutually advantageous* secrecy. The domestic dove logic, meanwhile, tends to conceptualize domestic politics narrowly. It focuses on one specific regime type (democratic leaders) and one specific domestic preference (dovish or antiwar). This leaves us ill equipped to understand what domestic problems adversaries might share and how covertness might address them. In contrast, I make three broad theoretical moves that lay the foundation

---

ing violations, see Allison Carnegie and Austin Carson, "The Spotlight's Harsh Glare: Rethinking Publicity and International Order," *International Organization*, forthcoming.

36 Martha Finnemore, "Legitimacy, Hypocrisy, and the Social Structure of Unipolarity: Why Being a Unipole Isn't All It's Cracked Up to Be," *World Politics* 61, no. 1 (2009): 58–85; Henry Farrell and Martha Finnemore, "The End of Hypocrisy," *Foreign Affairs*, October 15, 2013; Michael Poznansky, "Intervention and Secrecy in International Politics" (Dissertation, University of Virginia, 2016).

for a different understanding of the dynamics surrounding covert conflict. I introduce these three theoretical moves here and develop them in more detail in subsequent sections.

1. Secrecy and exposure. Exposure is the revelation of concealed information. In IR scholarship, secrecy has typically been assumed to "work" when chosen by states; exposure is not intended and is, in fact, fatal to secrecy's function.[37] The practical reality is that secrets are hard to keep, especially for complex organizations like states where inadvertent exposure is common.[38] Effective information security requires a complex constellation of formal and informal rules, penalties, and physical infrastructure that regulate the hundreds or thousands of individuals in an organization.[39] Secrecy in policy behavior that unfolds over time is especially vulnerable to exposure, as in a military intervention. Secrets are also vulnerable to exposure when other actors, such as a major power rival, detect them.[40] Rather than assume effective concealment, my theory explicitly assumes that the secrecy used in covert intervention is effortful, difficult, and imperfect. I further assume that exposure varies in terms of who witnesses what, and with what level of detail.

37 This is most obvious for the operational security logic in which exposure undermines security and surprise (i.e., "loose lips sink ships"). An exception is work that incorporates potential exposure seriously, i.e., Keren Yarhi-Milo, "Tying Hands Behind Closed Doors: The Logic and Practice of Secret Reassurance," *Security Studies* 22, no. 3 (2013): 405–35; Austin Carson and Keren Yarhi-Milo, "Covert Communication: The Intelligibility and Credibility of Signaling in Secret," *Security Studies* 26, no. 1 (January 2, 2017): 124–56; Michael F. Joseph and Michael Poznansky, "Media Technology, Covert Action, and the Politics of Exposure," *Journal of Peace Research*, November 16, 2017, 0022343317731508.

38 David E. Pozen, "The Leaky Leviathan: Why the Government Condemns and Condones Unlawful Disclosures of Information," *Harvard Law Review* 127, no. 2 (December 2013): 512–635; Rahul Sagar, *Secrets and Leaks: The Dilemma of State Secrecy* (Princeton, NJ: Princeton University Press, 2013).

39 On partial and other forms of exposure, see Kim Lane Scheppele, *Legal Secrets: Equality and Efficiency in the Common Law*, 1st ed. (Chicago: University of Chicago Press, 1988), 14–22; on effortful secrecy in social contexts, see Thomas Gregor, "Exposure and Seclusion: A Study of Institutionalized Isolation among the Mehinaku Indians of Brazil," in *Secrecy, a Cross-Cultural Perspective*, ed. Stanton K. Tefft (New York: Human Sciences Press, 1980); on the uniquely effortful nature of secrecy in organizations, see Hans Geser, "Towards an Interaction Theory of Organizational Actors," *Organization Studies* 13, no. 3 (January 1, 1992): 429–51; David R. Gibson, "Enduring Illusions: The Social Organization of Secrecy and Deception," *Sociological Theory* 32, no. 4 (December 1, 2014): 283–306.

40 Yarhi-Milo, "Tying Hands Behind Closed Doors."

My theory specifically draws out the different implications of two exposure scenarios: covert-but-visible *to other major powers only*, and covert-but-visible to *all publics and states*.[41]

2. Knowledge vs. acknowledgment. Secrecy's most obvious effect is on the distribution of knowledge. Given that exposure threatens knowledge manipulation, taking exposure seriously invites consideration of other, additional effects of acting secretly. One distinct effect identified in sociological studies of secrecy and denial is *acknowledgment*. Knowledge is simply one actor's possession of information, in this case awareness of the fact of a major power's military intervention. Acknowledgment, in contrast, involves the additional step of a government or other social actor positively, explicitly, and officially admitting the truth of a proposition.[42] Hints of its significance can be found in the effort social actors put forth to avoid acknowledgment of the dying process, family secrets, and sexual orientation.[43] In the context of intervention, official acknowledgment puts an exposed covert intervention on the record; non-acknowledgment allows a widely exposed covert intervention to still remain an "open secret." My theory explicitly incorporates a role for secrecy in enabling official non-acknowledgment and, as a result, the value of an open secret intervention.

3. Secrecy and social stability. Extant IR scholarship tends to see information manipulation as useful for selfish ends, such as bargaining advantages or operational success. One theme in much of the literature on secrecy in sociology and anthropology is that structures and uses of secrecy help groups collectively *define*

41 On Soviet and American leaders accepting the inevitability of mutual detection of their covert operations in the earliest years of the Cold War, see Gregory Mitrovich, *Undermining the Kremlin: America's Strategy to Subvert the Soviet Bloc, 1947–1956* (Ithaca, NY: Cornell University Press, 2000), 45.

42 For discussions of acknowledgment's distinct relevance, see Stanley Cavell, *Must We Mean What We Say? A Book of Essays*, 2nd ed. (Cambridge, UK: Cambridge University Press, 2002); Eviatar Zerubavel, *The Elephant in the Room: Silence and Denial in Everyday Life* (New York: Oxford University Press, 2006); Barry O'Neill, *Honor, Symbols, and War* (Ann Arbor: University of Michigan Press, 1999), 183–87.

43 Barney G. Glaser and Anselm L. Strauss, *Awareness of Dying* (New Brunswick, NJ: Aldine Publishing, 1965); Barbara Ponse, "Secrecy in the Lesbian World," *Urban Life* 5, no. 3 (October 1976); Zerubavel, *The Elephant in the Room*; Stanley Cohen, *States of Denial: Knowing about Atrocities and Suffering* (Cambridge, UK: Polity, 2001).

situations and *maintain social stability.*[44] The sociologist Erving Goffman, for example, noted that specific social encounters in everyday life are ambiguous until defined by participants through their gestures, words, and behavior.[45] Individually and collectively hiding discordant events is a central part of "impression management" and the creation and maintenance of a well-defined social encounter.[46] Even competitors share an interest in maintaining a stable definition of a competitive encounter; this can produce a "general conspiracy to save face so that social situations can also be saved."[47] My theory connects this broad insight to limited war. I develop how secrecy by interveners and detectors helps maintain the appearance of a well-structured, limited conflict and often leads to tacit or explicit collusion. States do this not out of generosity but out of their own strategic interest in avoiding a worst-case scenario of large-scale war.

Although I depart from typical assumptions regarding secrecy, it is important to bear in mind that different logics for secrecy can, and do, coexist. Secrecy in war clearly serves multiple purposes, both for the intervener and detector. There is no single logic or "master cause" of secrecy; this book does not purport to provide one. The logics of secrecy in existing work and my own theory can coexist in the same war. Vietnam (chapter 6) demonstrates: secrecy about US military activity was used to deal with antiwar domestic problems after 1968 even as escalation control prompted collusive secrecy and open secrets in the earlier 1964–1968 period. Because they are not mutually exclusive, empirical analysis needs to assess relative importance.

---

44 Goffman describes individuals' taking precautions "to prevent disruption of projected definitions" as "defensive practices." See Erving Goffman, *The Presentation of Self in Everyday Life* (Garden City, NY: Doubleday, 1959), 14.

45 See description of combined performances and "the definition of the situation that its performance fosters" in Goffman, *The Presentation of Self in Everyday Life*, 141.

46 See discussions of secrecy in Goffman, *The Presentation of Self in Everyday Life*; secrecy is critical to managing impressions of stigma; see Erving Goffman, *Stigma: Notes on the Management of Spoiled Identity* (Englewood Cliffs, NJ: Prentice-Hall, 1963).

47 Philip Manning. *Erving Goffman and Modern Sociology* (Palo Alto, CA: Stanford University Press, 1992), 39.

WAR AND THE BACKSTAGE

The metaphor of the theater serves as a useful heuristic in the book.[48] In drawing on this analogy, I build on and extend previous work that has used theater analogies in IR,[49] as well as Goffman's original development of it.[50] Importantly, the theater captures the intuition in each of the three theoretical moves I describe above, i.e., the varieties of exposure in using secrets; the distinct act of acknowledging exposed secrets; and the shared incentive in using secrecy to define and stabilize social encounters.

The notion of a theater invokes a particular structure. There is a frontstage, actors that perform, and an audience that observes. The frontstage is where a performance comes together; it is where actors collaborate using rules, roles, and characters to create a particular performance's genre (e.g., drama or comedy) and content (e.g., *Death of a Salesman*). Because words and behavior are visible to the audience, role-breaking moments are in full view; they can humiliate and endanger the larger performance. There is also a backstage. This is a separate space where actors talk and behave beyond the view of the audience. On the backstage, actors can step out of character without suffering humiliation or undermining the performance in the eyes of the audience.[51] The backstage and frontstage are therefore linked: a

48 On war in general as a spectacle, see Anastasia Bakogianni and Valerie M. Hope, *War as Spectacle: Ancient and Modern Perspectives on the Display of Armed Conflict* (New York: Bloomsbury, 2015); Ulrich Keller, *The Ultimate Spectacle: A Visual History of the Crimean War* (New York: Routledge, 2013).

49 Other adaptations of Goffman's dramaturgical metaphor in IR tend to focus on the frontstage and other performances besides limited war. See, for example, Michael N. Barnett, *Dialogues in Arab Politics* (New York: Columbia University Press, 1998); Nina Eliasoph, *Avoiding Politics: How Americans Produce Apathy in Everyday Life* (New York: Cambridge University Press, 1998); Frank Schimmelfennig, "Goffman Meets IR: Dramaturgical Action in International Community," *International Review of Sociology: Revue Internationale de Sociologie* 12, no. 3 (2002): 417; Ayse Zarakol, *After Defeat: How the East Learned to Live with the West* (Cambridge, UK: Cambridge University Press, 2010); Rebecca Adler-Nissen, *Opting Out of the European Union: Diplomacy, Sovereignty and European Integration* (Cambridge, UK: Cambridge University Press, 2014); Todd H. Hall, *Emotional Diplomacy: Official Emotion on the International Stage* (Ithaca, NY: Cornell University Press, 2015).

50 Goffman defines a staged interaction as any social interaction "set before an audience. What is presented in this way may be a talk, a contest, a 'formal' meeting, a play, a movie, a musical offering, a display of dexterity or trickery, a round of oratory, a ceremony, a combination thereof. The presenters will either be on a raised platform or encircled by watchers." Erving Goffman, "The Interaction Order: American Sociological Association, 1982 Presidential Address," *American Sociological Review* 48, no. 1 (1983): 7.

51 Goffman defines the backstage or back region as "a place, relative to a given performance, where the impression fostered by the performance is knowingly contradicted as a matter of

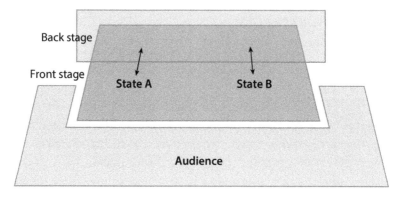

FIGURE 2.3. War as theater.

secluded refuge enables actors to bring to life a performance for the audience. Figure 2.3 summarizes this basic structure.

I conceptualize limited war as featuring similar stage dynamics. Limited war is co-produced by adversaries and requires specific roles and rules to distinguish it from alternative "performances" (e.g., peace; total war). Only if adversaries follow such roles and rules will a militarized encounter appear to be a well-structured limited war to the audience. The actors are major powers capable of intervention, not smaller states or non-state entities like NGOs. The audience from whom backstage activity is obscured consists of domestic publics, specifically domestic elites and mass publics that favor hawkish, escalatory policy during a crisis. This analogy usefully highlights the way violations of limits in war can happen in two places. Violations on the frontstage are visible to the audience; they provoke, humiliate, and can endanger the integrity of the performance of "limited war." Violations on the backstage, in contrast, are typically unseen by the audience. They will not provoke, humiliate, or affect the perceived performance of a well-bounded war. Yet the actors—for my theory, major powers—share access to the backstage. This is equivalent to the reality that other major powers, using intelligence, observe the backstage activity (i.e., covert involvement) of their counterparts. Figure 2.4 adds these details to the spare version of the theater in figure 2.3.

---

course. There are, of course, many characteristic functions of such places. It is here that the capacity of a performance to express something beyond itself may be painstakingly fabricated; it is here that illusions and impressions are openly constructed." Goffman, *The Presentation of Self in Everyday Life*, 112–13.

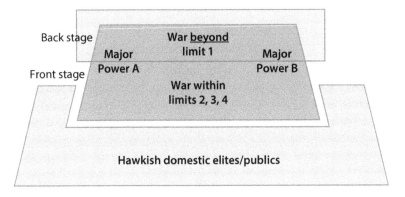

FIGURE 2.4. Limited war and the theater metaphor.

The backstage therefore features two key dynamics: (1) actors protecting a performance by concealing role and rule violations from the audience; and (2) actors having a space where they can see one another at all times and even explicitly coordinate.[52] Two clarifications about the theater are important. First, nothing about the theater analogy is meant to imply war is not real. Combat inflicts real human suffering and death; it is not simply a theatrical exercise. Second, international politics and limited war are riven with rivalry and competition. A theater troupe might connote cooperative, friendly relationships. This difference is important to keep in mind as major powers balance competitive advantage with the preservation of the larger structure of limited war. The theater metaphor can accommodate competitive elements quite easily. Actors in the same play often have profound, sometimes petty, personal and professional rivalries. These rivalries can even impede the successful performance of roles on the frontstage. Yet the "performers" share a basic interest in protecting the integrity of the overall performance lest they lose the very vehicle that allows them to showcase their talents.

One advantage of the theater metaphor is highlighting aspects of war that are often neglected in alternative metaphors, such as the bargaining model of war.[53] Conceptualizing war as a bargaining process highlights the

---

52 On actors' mutual visibility on the backstage, see Goffman, *The Presentation of Self in Everyday Life*, 112–13.

53 See reviews in Dan Reiter, "Exploring the Bargaining Model of War," *Perspectives on Politics* 1, no. 01 (2003): 27–43; Kristopher W. Ramsay, "Information, Uncertainty, and War," *Annual Review of Political Science* 20, no. 1 (2017): 505–27.

division of stakes or goods and the role of deception and commitment devices in altering the size of the pie for each side.[54] The theater metaphor highlights how leaders simultaneously manage the public image of a conflict and compete for spoils within that conflict. The theater metaphor's distinctiveness is in highlighting leaders' desire to explicitly or implicitly *collaborate* in grooming the basic *definition* of their conflict encounter.[55] This is not to suggest bargaining and theater metaphors are "right" or "wrong"; instead, they are useful in different ways and highlight different aspects of war.

Escalation and the Challenge of Limiting War

I argue that escalation dynamics provide a unifying logic for both decisions to intervene covertly and the collusion that may follow. My theory builds on the basic insight that modern international politics features a dangerous combination of destructive military technology and imperfect escalation control. As a result, large-scale escalation has simultaneously become universally counterproductive *and* difficult to control. This section reviews the widely shared view that major powers of all stripes seek to avoid large-scale escalation in the modern system.[56] I then identify two recurring escalation-control problems to which covertness and collusion respond.

War on a regional or global scale has become counterproductive and potentially ruinous. Scholars of limited war have, since Clausewitz, cited the uniformly negative impact of total war. For Clausewitz, this was in reaction to the French Revolution and Napoleon, which married mass political and war participation with nationalism.[57] Yet technological limitations and the restoration of absolutism in Europe delayed the onset of the modern esca-

---

54 James D. Fearon, "Rationalist Explanations for War," *International Organization* 49, no. 3 (Summer 1995): 379–414.

55 Note that bargaining model techniques can incorporate some domestic political dynamics and concern for imagery, as in Fearon, "Domestic Political Audiences and the Escalation of International Disputes."

56 For the unique importance of World War I in creating this modern predicament, see chapter 3.

57 Bernard Brodie, "On Clausewitz: A Passion for War," ed. Roger Parkinson, *World Politics* 25, no. 2 (1973): 288–308; Peter R. Moody, "Clausewitz and the Fading Dialectic of War," *World Politics* 31, no. 3 (April 1979): 417–33; Stephen J. Cimbala, *Clausewitz and Escalation: Classical Perspective on Nuclear Strategy* (New York: Frank Cass, 1991).

lation predicament.[58] Twentieth-century thinkers like Liddell Hart and Quincy Wright focused on the special devastation of industrialized "total war."[59] Hans Morgenthau wrote that mechanization had "enormously increased destructiveness of twentieth-century warfare" and "the ability to eliminate an unprecedented number of enemies through one single operation."[60] The central lesson from both world wars was that total war would be incapacitating. Note that this was not solely a product of atomic weaponry.[61] The nuclear era certainly sharpened the view that major powers could now "destroy each other, neither being able to conquer; or the least weakened may conquer, presiding over universal devastation."[62] Yet, as I develop further in chapter 3, the costliness and control problems central to my theory were the result of a confluence of changes—democratization, nationalism, industrialization, transoceanic power projection—consolidated by World War I.[63]

Fear of large-scale escalation is most sensible for leaders of major powers that have cautious, conservative goals. A state that seeks to preserve the territorial status quo and prioritizes economic stability, for example, will view entanglement in a regional or global conflict as gravely threatening.[64] Yet even major powers with less cautious strategic priorities will likely view

58 As Moody notes, "total war requires both a technology of mass destruction and a high level of mass mobilization. Mobilization is achieved when the stake in war is ideological or religious, as in the near-total conflicts of the Thirty Years' War and the French Revolutionary Wars. These wars, however, were restricted by the relatively limited technology. Today the technology of mass destruction must be taken as given." Moody, "Clausewitz and the Fading Dialectic of War," 432.

59 Liddell Hart, *Paris: Or, The Future of War* (New York: E.P. Dutton, 1925); Quincy Wright, "The Causation and Control of War," *American Sociological Review* 3, no. 4 (1938): 461–74.

60 Hans Morgenthau, Kenneth Thompson, and David Clinton, *Politics Among Nations*, 7th ed. (New York: McGraw-Hill Humanities/Social Sciences/Languages, 2005), 384.

61 John Mueller, "The Essential Irrelevance of Nuclear Weapons: Stability in the Postwar World," *International Security* 13, no. 2 (1988): 55–79; John Mueller, *Retreat from Doomsday: The Obsolescence of Major War* (New York: Basic Books, 1989).

62 Morgenthau, Thompson, and Clinton, *Politics Among Nations*, 396.

63 Osgood's classic Cold War–era treatment of limited war acknowledges that, with the Great War, "all the latent conditions underlying the decline of limited war—democratization, messianic nationalism, dissolution of moral consensus, deterioration of the balance-of-power system—became the actual sources of unlimited war." Robert E. Osgood, *Limited War: The Challenge to American Strategy* (Chicago: University of Chicago Press, 1957), 92.

64 On different state "types" and the difference between security seeking and greedy states, see Charles L. Glaser, *Rational Theory of International Politics: The Logic of Competition and Cooperation* (Princeton, NJ: Princeton University Press, 2010), 38–39.

large-scale escalation as deeply problematic. A rising power like China may well seek to change the territorial status quo in its neighborhood (e.g., resource rights in the South China Sea) and address any military inferiority vis-à-vis others (e.g., military buildup to balance the United States). Yet China will still find regional or global war extremely dangerous. A regional war involving the United States or its allies might endanger the Communist Party's hold on power, dislocate the Chinese economy, and risk a military humiliation.[65]

The China example underscores how large-scale escalation poses economic, domestic political, and more obvious military dangers. A regional or global war may undermine the economic basis of a state's power, destroy and divert vital military assets, and risk a humiliating defeat that invites future military challenges. Domestically, large-scale escalation can also create a governing crisis, risking revolution and even removal from office by election, death, or other means. This is not to deny that regional wars happen. They do. The point is simply that modern technology and political conditions make a *preference* for such an outcome extremely rare. The forms and pathways for *inadvertent* escalation are therefore critical to understand.[66]

My theory posits that, whether state goals are conservative or assertive, status quo or revisionist, major powers have powerful and overlapping reasons to view large-scale escalation (as I define it) as counterproductive for geostrategic, economic, or domestic political reasons. Put differently, I assume that all major powers prefer to avoid what I call "large-scale" escalation. When conflicts create a plausible risk of large-scale escalation, this assumption means major powers will value—but not necessarily prioritize— escalation control. To be clear, I do not argue that all forms of escalation have this quality. Rather, the claim is specifically regarding *large-scale escalation* for *major powers* in the *modern era*. Thus, leaders do not always avoid

---

65 See, for example, damage that local rivals and the United States could inflict in Michael Beckley, "The Emerging Military Balance in East Asia: How China's Neighbors Can Check Chinese Naval Expansion," *International Security* 42, no. 2 (November 1, 2017): 78–119; on the risks of inadvertent escalation, see Avery Goldstein, "First Things First: The Pressing Danger of Crisis Instability in U.S.-China Relations," *International Security* 37, no. 4 (April 1, 2013): 49–89; Caitlin Talmadge, "Would China Go Nuclear? Assessing the Risk of Chinese Nuclear Escalation in a Conventional War with the United States," *International Security* 41, no. 4 (April 1, 2017): 50–92.

66 Barry R. Posen, *Inadvertent Escalation: Conventional War and Nuclear Risks* (Ithaca, NY: Cornell University Press, 1991); Talmadge, "Would China Go Nuclear?"

escalation risks in my story.[67] Embracing lesser forms of incremental escalation can be consistent with seeking control of the escalation process in light of the dangers of large-scale escalation.

CULTIVATING ESCALATION CONTROL

This specter of large-scale escalation raises a key question: How do states control escalation more or less effectively? If the limits of a given war are challenged or transgressed, what influences whether leaders will be able to manipulate a subsequent action-reaction process to avoid large-scale escalation?

Escalation control allows leaders to strike a Clausewitzian balance between the drive for military effectiveness and the need for strategic purpose.[68] While many conditions and variables affect whether wars *can* escalate, escalation-control problems affect whether that potential is realized.[69] Experience and learning can be important in this regard. Controlling escalation requires adversaries to identify forms of wartime restraint and communicate their willingness to abide by them. Given the high stakes in war and poor channels of communication, converging on mutual restraint benefits from experience.[70] Adversaries with a track record of such encounters will tend to find salient thresholds easier to identify and communicate. The modern form of limited war is therefore a kind of learned state practice that has evolved over time.[71] Subsequent empirical chapters show that covert

---

67 See, for example, risk-raising strategies in Schelling, *Arms and Influence*, chap. 3.

68 Cimbala, *Clausewitz and Escalation*.

69 Scholars have identified alliances, territorial contiguity, large shifts in relative military power, military organizational norms, deterrence, military strategy, and accidents as important as well. See, respectively, John A. Vasquez, *The War Puzzle Revisited* (New York: Cambridge University Press, 2009); Thomas J. Christensen and Jack Snyder, "Chain Gangs and Passed Bucks: Predicting Alliance Patterns in Multipolarity," *International Organization* 44, no. 02 (1990): 137–68; D. Scott Bennett and Allan C. Stam III, *The Behavioral Origins of War* (Ann Arbor: University of Michigan Press, 2003); Alex Weisiger, *Logics of War: Explanations for Limited and Unlimited Conflicts* (Ithaca, NY: Cornell University Press, 2013); Haldi, *Why Wars Widen*; Jeffrey Legro, "Military Culture and Inadvertent Escalation in World War II," *International Security* 18, no. 4 (April 1, 1994): 108–42; Richard Smoke, *War: Controlling Escalation* (Cambridge, MA: Harvard University Press, 1977); Posen, *Inadvertent Escalation*; Bruce G. Blair, *The Logic of Accidental Nuclear War* (Washington, DC: Brookings Institution, 1993); a classic treatment is Clausewitz, as analyzed in Cimbala, *Clausewitz and Escalation*; another classic analysis is Herman Kahn, *On Escalation: Metaphors and Scenarios* (New York: Praeger, 1965).

70 Schelling, *The Strategy of Conflict*, 260–62.

71 Emanuel Adler and Vincent Pouliot, "International Practices," *International Theory* 3, no. 01 (February 2011): 1–36.

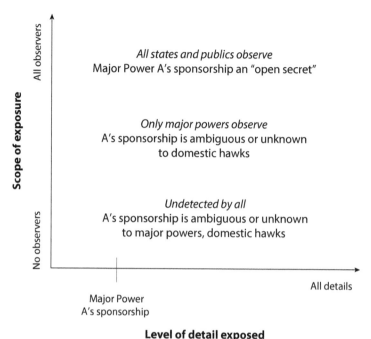

FIGURE 2.5. Variation in exposure.

intervention and collusion were refined as a result of cumulative experience, a topic I develop in more detail in chapter 3.

My theory highlights two specific escalation-control problems: domestic hawkish constraints and miscommunication among adversaries. One important ingredient for what follows is a conceptualization of how exposure works. As noted earlier in this chapter, I explicitly integrate the practical reality that secrets by complex organizations regarding overseas activities during war are hard to keep. Yet exposure's forms can vary. I simplify the range of possible exposure scenarios to two, captured in figure 2.5. The figure suggests the identity of the sponsor of a covert intervention may be only partially exposed where only other major powers with intelligence systems detect it. This was the case when the United States detected Soviet pilots flying planes in North Korea via communications intercepts (chapter 5). Alternatively, the sponsor of a covert intervention may be widely exposed to all publics and states. This results in an "open secret," or a situation in which "the entire community knows a tremendous amount" about a previously hidden fact but there is "no official confirmation."[72] Examples

72 Pozen, "The Leaky Leviathan," 560.

of open secret covert interventions that regularly appeared in news stories include the American covert intervention in Afghanistan (chapter 7) and Italy's ground role in the Spanish Civil War (chapter 4).

Several observations are worth noting regarding figure 2.5. First, I assume that covert intervention is *always* visible to other major powers. This gives it the communicative potential I link to limited war. It also means the bottom scenario in figure 2.5—a covert intervention "undetected by all"—is functionally off the table in my theoretical logic.[73] Second, covert intervention is *sometimes* visible to domestic publics as well. When it is unseen by domestic audiences, covertness has an insulating effect which I link to hawkish audiences. When it is widely exposed (i.e., open secret), the emphasis shifts to communicative effects of non-acknowledgment. Moreover, the two scenarios in figure 2.5 correspond to two different scenarios in the theater analogy. Backstage behavior by major powers is always visible to other major powers who share access to the backstage due to their intelligence capabilities. Moreover, just as backstage activity is occasionally exposed to the audience, covert intervention can be an open secret and widely exposed to domestic hawkish elites and mass publics.

PROBLEM #1: DOMESTIC HAWKS AND ESCALATION CONTROL

First consider domestic politics and escalation dynamics. Decisions by leaders to escalate or act restrained are not made in a vacuum. Reactions of others, such as domestic elite rivals or mass public opinion, can shape the costliness of acting restrained and the rewards for retaliating and escalating. Clausewitz identified domestic politics as a problem, arguing that large-scale escalation was harder to avoid when nationalism, mass participation in politics, and mass conscription were invoked.[74] Hobbes, too,

---

73 As I note elsewhere, the practicalities of effectively concealing an intervention are especially difficult, making total concealment exceedingly rare. My theory therefore makes the simplifying assumption that all covert interventions are detected by motivated adversaries with good intelligence capabilities.

74 Vennesson summarizes Clausewitz's views about the erosion of leaders' political control, noting that "depending on the relative involvement of the people—and on policymakers' perceptions of these social and political conditions—political and social structures can impose or remove constraints on the conduct of war. These socio-political conditions can favour the trend towards absolute war, or they can contribute to the limitation of warfare." Pascal Vennesson, "War Without the People," in *The Changing Character of War*, ed. Hew Strachan and Sibylle Scheipers (Oxford: Oxford University Press, 2011), 244–45; see also Fuller's description, drawn

feared the dangers created by "the Seditious roaring of a troubled Nation" in his defense of an all-powerful sovereign.[75] Alexis de Tocqueville famously analyzed early American democracy; one of his concerns was that if war "roused the whole community from their peaceful occupations and ruined their minor undertakings, the same passions that made them attach so much importance to the maintenance of peace will be turned to arms."[76]

The common thread is that the move away from absolutist domestic political authority, specifically in Western Europe, had implications for the scope and scale of war. Contemporary IR scholarship has substantiated the myriad ways that domestic politics in the twentieth century exacerbate this. Studies of limited war, for example, built on this theme. Writing in the shadow of an escalating Vietnam War, Morton Halperin lamented that "once the American government commits combat forces, or major aid short of that, as it did in Vietnam in 1962, to a local war, there will be pressure to see the war through to decisive victory.... Any hobbling of power which prevents the decisive local victory will generate intense domestic political pressures."[77]

Consider several discrete research areas. Scholarship on nationalism and war, for example, shows that states' restraint can become politically infeasible if calls for belligerence are severe, both in democratic and non-democratic settings.[78] Weiss's study of nationalist mobilization argues that hawkish protests strengthen China's hand in coercive diplomacy precisely because such protests risk the Communist Party's hold on domestic power.[79] Bargaining models of coercive diplomacy also suggest that domestic polit-

---

heavily from Clausewitz, about Napoleon's shift from "wars of Kings" to "wars of peoples." J.F.C. Fuller, *The Conduct of War, 1789–1961: A Study of the Impact of the French, Industrial, and Russian Revolutions on War and Its Conduct* (New York: Da Capo Press, 1992), 28–58; Moody, "Clausewitz and the Fading Dialectic of War," 424.

75 Thomas Hobbes, *Leviathan* (London: Penguin, 2003), 141.

76 Alexis de Tocqueville, *Democracy in America* (New York: Colonial Press, 1900), 290.

77 Morton H. Halperin, *Limited War in the Nuclear Age* (New York: Wiley, 1963), 24–25.

78 Stephen Van Evera, "Hypotheses on Nationalism and War," *International Security* 18, no. 4 (April 1, 1994): 5–39; Jack Snyder and Karen Ballentine, "Nationalism and the Marketplace of Ideas," *International Security* 21, no. 2 (October 1, 1996): 5–40; Jessica Chen Weiss, "Authoritarian Signaling, Mass Audiences, and Nationalist Protest in China," *International Organization* 67, no. 01 (January 2013): 1–35; John D. Ciorciari and Jessica Chen Weiss, "Nationalist Protests, Government Responses, and the Risk of Escalation in Interstate Disputes," *Security Studies* 25, no. 3 (July 2, 2016): 546–83.

79 Weiss, "Authoritarian Signaling, Mass Audiences, and Nationalist Protest in China"; Ciorciari and Weiss, "Nationalist Protests, Government Responses, and the Risk of Escalation in Interstate Disputes."

ical constraints on leaders can influence the likelihood that one side capitulates during a prewar crisis. Audience cost theory, for example, posits that leaders can be punished by hawkish domestic constituents if caught visibly and clearly bluffing.[80] Indeed, one line of criticism of the theory is that hawkish domestic constraints are so threatening that leaders avoid clear and public threats in the first place.[81] Studies of the domestic rally-round-the-flag effects prompted by crises and war make clear that context matters.[82] While domestic moods shift and sway, rally dynamics suggest an ongoing conflict specifically boosts belligerence and support for strong leadership. Each of these strands of research suggest frontstage events in modern wars can trigger domestic political dynamics that make escalatory behavior more rewarding.

Moreover, leaders need to worry about more than just their own backyard. The interactive nature of escalation and limited war means that others' domestic constraints are potentially problematic. Even a leader free of *their own* constraints should attend to the possibility that nationalism, rally effects, and audience costs *constrain their adversary* and fuel a tit-for-tat cycle of escalation. To return to the Korean War example from the opening of chapter 1, even a leader like Stalin can be indirectly endangered by domestic hawkish constraints if his counterpart (the American president Harry Truman) succumbs to nationalist, anti-communist demands for direct retaliation against the Soviet Union. This dynamic is similar to the problems that arise from others' domestic constraints noted in Putnam's two-level games and in work on private diplomacy and compromise.[83] Moreover, these hawkish domestic dynamics can interact to create feedback loops.

80 Fearon, "Domestic Political Audiences and the Escalation of International Disputes."

81 On domestic hawkish views locking leaders into escalation in the context of audience cost theory, see Jack Snyder and Erica D. Borghard, "The Cost of Empty Threats: A Penny, Not a Pound," *American Political Science Review* 105, no. 3 (August 2011): 437–56. As Trachtenberg (20) concludes, "these sorts of pressures could not be turned on and off like a faucet; they might get out of hand and limit the government's freedom of action in very unpalatable ways." Marc Trachtenberg, "Audience Costs: An Historical Analysis," *Security Studies* 21, no. 1 (2012): 3–42.

82 John Mueller, *War, Presidents and Public Opinion* (New York: Wiley, 1973); Matthew A. Baum and Philip B. K. Potter, "The Relationships Between Mass Media, Public Opinion, and Foreign Policy: Toward a Theoretical Synthesis," *Annual Review of Political Science* 11, no. 1 (2008): 39–65.

83 E.g., Robert D. Putnam, "Diplomacy and Domestic Politics: The Logic of Two-Level Games," *International Organization* 42, no. 3 (Summer 1988): 427–60; David Stasavage, "Open-Door or Closed-Door? Transparency in Domestic and International Bargaining," *International Organization* 58, no. 04 (2004): 667–703; Shuhei Kurizaki, "Efficient Secrecy: Public Versus Private Threats in Crisis Diplomacy," *American Political Science Review* 101, no. 03 (2007): 543–58.

One side's constraint can lead to policy choices that inflame hawkish constraints in its adversary, and so on.

To be clear, domestic politics can be a force for peace and de-escalation.[84] Domestic publics or elites can turn inward, oppose a war, or demand that a leader limit their country's involvement. War weariness, for example, can set in leading to disaffection, distrust, and demands for peace.[85] So why assume that hawks are the relevant domestic challenge for decisions about covert conflict? The reason is *context*. Recall that I am analyzing intervention scenarios. As defined in the first section of this chapter, this involves an ongoing war with at least one major power intervening with military aid and personnel. Four features elevate the role of hawks. First, a war is already under way, meaning that military considerations will be salient. This also empowers military imagery, rhetoric, and decision-making power that can sharpen hawkish perceptions.[86] Second, the presence of at least one major power intervention means that the conflict already has stakes beyond the local dispute. This sharpens questions of national interest and honor in ways that distant wars with no foreign involvement do not. Third, the relevant decisions about how to intervene and what to expose are in the early or middle periods of a war. Intervention at the end is rare. Dovish sentiment is most prevalent after casualties and disillusionment set in late in a war. Fourth, any overt intervention will tend to constitute an intuitive and provocative act. As I argue below, this stimulates rallying effects and nationalism that might not otherwise lay dormant. To emphasize the point: my theory does *not* assume that hawks always dominate domestic decisions about war. My theory allows for fluctuations of dovish and hawkish views

---

84 Bear F. Braumoeller, "Deadly Doves: Liberal Nationalism and the Democratic Peace in the Soviet Successor States," *International Studies Quarterly* 41, no. 3 (1997): 375–402; Ole R. Holsti, *Public Opinion and American Foreign Policy*, Rev. ed., Analytical Perspectives on Politics (Ann Arbor: University of Michigan Press, 2004); Jonathan D. Caverley and Yanna Krupnikov, "Aiming at Doves: Experimental Evidence of Military Images' Political Effects," *Journal of Conflict Resolution*, 61, no. 7 (2017): 1482–1509.

85 Christopher Gelpi, Peter D. Feaver, and Jason Reifler, "Success Matters: Casualty Sensitivity and the War in Iraq," *International Security* 30, no. 3 (Winter 2005): 7–46.

86 On imagery, see Caverley and Krupnikov, "Aiming at Doves: Experimental Evidence of Military Images' Political Effects"; on militarized rhetoric, see Joachim Krause, "Assessing the Danger of War: Parallels and Differences Between Europe in 1914 and East Asia in 2014," *International Affairs* 90, no. 6 (November 1, 2014): 1421–51; on military leaders and decision-making, see Samuel P. Huntington, *The Soldier and the State: The Theory and Politics of Civil-Military Relations* (Cambridge, MA: Harvard University Press, 1957).

at other times and at the end of a war. I only assume that, in the specific kinds of conflicts I analyze, domestic views tilt toward support for firmness, retaliation, and even outright war.

Addressing the Domestic Hawks Problem

How might leaders address domestic constraints during intervention scenarios? The key insight is that the provocation of a major power intervention depends on it being visible to domestic audiences. Sending military aid and personnel into a local conflict awakens hawkish domestic constraints when it is known and acknowledged as a provocation. Intervening covertly, in contrast, can reduce this liability.

These claims build on several strands of existing work. Although it does not address escalation dynamics during war or covert intervention, existing research suggests that secrecy can be useful for maneuvering around belligerent domestic audiences and useful to more than one state. For example, others have found that leaders can use secrecy during crisis bargaining to reduce their own domestic audience costs for concessions.[87] Shuhei Kurizaki specifically argues that secrecy can help blunt the audience costs for *other states* should they make dramatic concessions.[88] Other studies have analyzed instances of leaders using secret-but-detectable military maneuvers, such as mobilizing bombers capable of delivering atomic bombs, to signal to an adversary without inflaming domestic hawks at home.[89] This comports with my theory's claim that leaders use secrecy with awareness of the implications of their actions for the hawkish domestic constraints on their rivals. To be clear, these studies seek to understand concession during prewar crises and reactions to explicit threats.[90] Yet they highlight information manipulation of aggressive rather than dovish domestic voices.

87 Jonathan N. Brown and Anthony S. Marcum, "Avoiding Audience Costs: Domestic Political Accountability and Concessions in Crisis Diplomacy," *Security Studies* 20 (April 2011): 141–70.

88 Kurizaki, "Efficient Secrecy."

89 Roger Dingman, "Atomic Diplomacy during the Korean War," *International Security* 13, no. 3 (1988): 50; Scott D. Sagan and Jeremi Suri, "The Madman Nuclear Alert: Secrecy, Signaling, and Safety in October 1969," *International Security* 27, no. 4 (2003): 150–83.

90 For related work on private threat effectiveness, see Anne E. Sartori, "The Might of the Pen: A Reputational Theory of Communication in International Disputes," *International Organization* 56, no. 01 (2002): 121–49; Robert F. Trager, "Diplomatic Calculus in Anarchy: How Communication Matters," *American Political Science Review* 104, no. 02 (May 2010): 347–68.

These, too, show that leaders may be drawn to backstage activity with an eye toward constraints from domestic hawks.

More broadly, covertness can be conceptualized as a tool to manipulate the provocation of intervention. As Todd Hall argues, provocations prompt "outraged reactions" at both individual and mass levels by symbolically challenging status and honor.[91] Covertness blunts the provocation an intervention would otherwise represent. Covertness reduces the symbolic intensity of a challenge and can meaningfully limit knowledge of it. Regarding challenges, Barry O'Neill observes that "there is no important sense in which a challenge is real apart from the expectations of the audience and the challenge."[92] But what influences what the audience—in this case, domestic hawks—understands and expects? The answer depends on the form of intervention.[93] An overt intervention ensures wide public knowledge about a major power's involvement and carries with it official acknowledgment of that role. In contrast, covert intervention may be unseen by domestic hawkish groups and will lack official acknowledgment. The overt scenario improves the chances that an intervention will be seen by mass and elite groups already predisposed to seeing it as a threatening challenge to their interests. As William O'Brien notes, observably violating limits in war communicates to domestics at home and abroad, not just adversaries.[94] Thus, hawkish mobilization is more likely and its constraints on leaders more powerful if an intervention is overt.

An absence of acknowledgment can further loosen constraints from domestic hawks. In everyday social life, confining affronts to the backstage can blunt the need to respond. As Erving Goffman argues, a visible and acknowledged provocation "can have the effect of plunging his opponent into the business of exerting immediate negative sanctions" where the ad-

---

91 Todd H. Hall, "On Provocation: Outrage, International Relations, and the Franco-Prussian War," *Security Studies* 26, no. 1 (January 2, 2017): 10.

92 Barry O'Neill, *Honor, Symbols, and War* (Ann Arbor: University of Michigan Press, 1999), 115.

93 George's review of a case study of Angola notes that highly visible interventions by Cuba and South Africa magnified the reputational stakes of the civil war and the domestic political complications. In contrast, less visible interventions in places like Rhodesia did not attract such attention and kept stakes low. The space for diplomatic resolution was greater in the latter. See Alexander L. George, "Crisis Prevention Reexamined," in *Managing U.S.-Soviet Rivalry: Problems of Crisis Prevention*, ed. Alexander L. George (Boulder, CO: Westview Press, 1983), 365–66.

94 Violations of geographic limits are "important in respect to at least three different audiences: the enemy, the world at large, and the home front." William V. O'Brien, *The Conduct of Just and Limited War* (New York: Praeger, 1981), 231.

versary "may not be primarily concerned with strategy or self-interest, or even with successful enforcement; his first need may be to stand up and be counted."[95] In contrast, unacknowledged behavior "need not be faced up to," which allows one to "be warned that this current line or the current situation is leading to loss of face, without this warning itself becoming an incident."[96] Even an implausibly denied intervention may conserve ways for states to respond in a restrained manner without domestic hawkish punishment. O'Neill's study of threats and provocation notes that communicating publicly or "on the record" sharpens an insult and makes a forceful response more important.[97] Avoiding acknowledgment, even if unconvincing, can reduce the perception of provocation.

To be clear, the mechanism through which covertness affects domestic hawks depends on the scope of exposure. If an intervention is effectively kept secret from the "audience" (but visible to the other major powers on the "backstage"), then domestic hawkish actors on both sides are less of a concern because they lack the knowledge and details necessary to sense provocation and mobilize to constrain leaders. If the covert intervention becomes widely exposed, the lack of acknowledgment can still minimize the perceived provocation. However, hawks will have the raw informational material to mobilize and constrain.

These domestic-escalation links also provide a rationale for collusion. Mobilized domestic hawks can make it more likely that the detector itself or other states will react with an escalatory counter-intervention. This creates an incentive for collusion to keep a known covert intervention on the backstage. Domestic hawkish constraints can be activated by exposure. If a detector publicizes a covert intervention, this will tend to empower its own domestic hawkish voices and those in other states. Greater knowledge alone will then reduce room for maneuver and opportunities to save face. Those reacting can "act as if they have not officially received the message contained in the hint."[98] Moreover, acknowledgment by the detector can sharpen the expectation that it will respond. In contrast, collusion by the detector allows it to retain escalation control. Collusion can preserve uncertainty about whether Major Power A has intervened. This can expand

---

95 Erving Goffman, *Strategic Interaction* (Philadelphia, PA: University of Pennsylvania Press, 1969), 134.

96 Erving Goffman, *Interaction Ritual; Essays on Face-to-Face Behaviour*, 1st ed. (Garden City, NY: Anchor Books, 1967), 30.

97 O'Neill, *Honor, Symbols, and War*, 153; see also 112–13, 125–26.

98 Goffman, *Interaction Ritual; Essays on Face-to-Face Behaviour*, 30.

the capacity for Major Power B (or C, D, etc.) to react with restraint. Refusing to acknowledge allegations of Major Power A's covert intervention also reduces the domestic expectations for a belligerent response. If large-scale escalation is a concern for a detector, then retaining escalation control through collusion can make political and strategic sense.

The rationale for collusion is supported by the fundamentally interdependent nature of limited war. Just as it only takes one side to end a limit in war, it only takes one major power—the intervener or a detector—to activate domestic hawks. Collusion thus provides a stopgap measure that can reduce elite alarm and minimize any public outcry that would otherwise likely follow exposure of the intervention. Collusion is akin to keeping another actor's transgressions backstage in an effort to preserve the integrity and success of the frontstage performance. Collusion also has a mutually reinforcing effect. As Hall notes, "displaying outrage can serve to communicate that an actor is unafraid to confront those perceived as having committed offense."[99] Collusion is the opposite of displaying outrage, which may communicate a "live-and-let-live" message.[100]

PROBLEM #2: COMMUNICATION AND ESCALATION CONTROL

Autonomy from domestic actors does not guarantee leaders will be able to manipulate and calibrate the level of hostilities in a war. Even an absolutist monarch with perfect domestic control can lose the capacity to manipulate and modulate escalation. Avoiding large-scale escalation also requires effective inter-adversary communication. Misunderstandings among heads of state can encourage rivals to bid each other further up the escalation ladder, out of either fear or predation. Adversaries must understand the nature of such thresholds (i.e., intelligibility) and tacitly cooperate in observing them.[101]

---

99 Hall, "On Provocation," 10.

100 On adversary cooperation in behavior rather than information and secrecy, see Robert Axelrod, *The Evolution of Cooperation* (New York: Basic Books, 1984); Jeffrey Legro, *Cooperation Under Fire: Anglo-German Restraint During World War II* (Ithaca, NY: Cornell University Press, 1995); a small literature on oligopolies in economics is also relevant, i.e., Helder Vasconcelos, "Tacit Collusion, Cost Asymmetries, and Mergers," *RAND Journal of Economics* 36, no. 1 (2005): 39–62.

101 "Traditions or conventions are not simply an analogy for limits in war, or a curious aspect of them; tradition or precedent or convention is the essence of the limits … The limits may correspond to legal and physical differences or to moral distinctions; indeed, they usually have

The central problem is that communication during war is difficult, especially among adversaries with little experience and direct diplomatic contact. Adversaries during a limited war often lack channels for direct communication, have ideological and other reasons for distrust, and find credibility hard to come by.[102] What messages are important for avoiding unwanted large-scale escalation? Escalation control and limited war rest on mutual understanding about two things. First, adversaries need to understand each side has some measure of resolve to defend its interest. If Major Power A believes Major Power B has very low willingness to defend its interests, escalation to a wider war may take place via deterrence failure.[103] Avoiding this scenario thus requires that both sides provide credible and intelligible proof that they care enough about a local conflict to defend it. Second, adversaries must believe the other side seeks to limit the conflict. This is a message of restraint rather than resolve. Loss of escalation control can result if Major Power A believes Major Power B has unlimited goals in the local theater and a large appetite for risk.[104] The problem in this

---

to correspond to something that gives them a unique and qualitative character and that provides some focus for expectations to converge on. But the authority is in the expectations themselves, and not in the thing that expectations have attached themselves to." Schelling, *The Strategy of Conflict*, 260–61; on intelligibility, see Austin Carson and Keren Yarhi-Milo, "Covert Communication: The Intelligibility and Credibility of Signaling in Secret," *Security Studies* 26, no. 1 (January 2, 2017): 124–56. On tacitly cooperating, "the maintenance of limits in a war requires some cooperation from both sides." States pursue their own goals during war while jointly seeking to establish "ground rules" that can define the "nature of the conflict." Smoke, *War: Controlling Escalation*, 14–15; on tacit cooperation in restraint, see Legro, *Cooperation Under Fire*.

102 Schelling, *The Strategy of Conflict*, chap. 1; Fearon, "Rationalist Explanations for War."

103 The literature on rational deterrence games is vast; see, for example, Robert Powell, "Nuclear Brinkmanship with Two-Sided Incomplete Information," *American Political Science Review* 82, no. 1 (March 1988): 155–78; on conventional deterrence, see John J. Mearsheimer, *Conventional Deterrence* (Ithaca, NY: Cornell University Press, 1983); on airpower and coercion, see Robert Pape, *Bombing to Win: Airpower and Coercion in War* (Ithaca, NY: Cornell University Press, 1996).

104 Robert Jervis, "Review: Deterrence Theory Revisited," *World Politics* 31, no. 2 (January 1979): 289–324; Alexander L. George and Richard Smoke, "Deterrence and Foreign Policy," *World Politics* 41, no. 2 (January 1989): 170–82; Robert Jervis, "Rational Deterrence: Theory and Evidence," *World Politics* 41, no. 2 (January 1989): 183–207; the comparative lack of attention to conditions that produce inadvertent or spiral-based escalation is noted in Smoke, *War: Controlling Escalation*, 10–11; Jervis cites fears of losing control in the writings of both Kennedy and Khrushchev during the Cuban Missile Crisis. He notes that "when an army is put in motion, the other side has to be concerned not only with the evidence that this provides about the state's willingness to stand firm, but with the risk that, as Kennedy put it to Khrushchev immediately after the climax of the Cuban Missile Crisis, 'developments [are] approaching a point where events could ... become unmanageable.'" Robert Jervis, *The Meaning of the Nuclear Revolution: Statecraft and the Prospect of Armageddon* (Ithaca, NY: Cornell University Press, 1989), 83–84.

scenario is an escalation sequence driven by fear of predation, akin to spirals of conflict.[105] Avoiding this scenario requires states to credibly and intelligibly give indication of their willingness to restrain themselves and keep war contained. Thus, these two communication challenges correspond with two different paths to large-scale escalation—which are by no means mutually exclusive in a given war—that are associated with the deterrence model and spiral model, respectively.[106]

The central point is that avoiding large-scale escalation involves communicating both resolve *and* restraint. A vast literature on costly signaling addresses the conditions and tactics that can credibly communicate resolve.[107] The central theme in this work is that military actions and diplomatic proclamations that feature either ex ante or ex post costs are credible indications of resolve. A smaller literature on limited war addresses how restraint can be conveyed and inferred.[108] Here the focus is on "conspicuous constraint," or actions and commitments that are detectable, legible sacrifices. These can convince an adversary that limited aims and limited means are acceptable.[109]

To be clear, this communication challenge is similar to, but distinct from, the challenge of diagnosing grand strategic aims. Inferences about limited war are not inferences about grand strategic plans. As chapter 4 illustrates, assessing the grand strategic appetite of a leader like Adolf Hitler was related to, but distinct from, leaders in Paris and London assessing whether Germany sought to keep the conflict in Spain bounded. In short, diagnosing intentions about limited war and escalation demand less heroic insights than the traditional debate about grand strategic intentions.[110]

---

105 "Unlike deterrence, they root the source of overt, aggressive behavior in the acute vulnerability of adversaries." Richard Ned Lebow, "Deterrence and Reassurance: Lessons from the Cold War," *Global Dialogue* 3, no. 4 (Autumn 2001): 128; on the spiral model / security dilemma, see Robert Jervis, *Perception and Misperception in International Politics* (Princeton, NJ: Princeton University Press, 1976); Robert Jervis, "Cooperation Under the Security Dilemma," *World Politics* 30, no. 2 (January 1, 1978): 167–214; Charles L. (Charles Louis) Glaser, "The Security Dilemma Revisited," *World Politics* 50, no. 1 (1997): 171–201.

106 Jervis, *Perception and Misperception in International Politics*, chap. 3.

107 James D. Fearon, "Signaling Foreign Policy Interests: Tying Hands versus Sinking Costs," *Journal of Conflict Resolution* 41, no. 1 (February 1997): 68–90.

108 Andrew Kydd, "Trust, Reassurance, and Cooperation," *International Organization* 54, no. 2 (Spring 2000): 325–57.

109 The term "conspicuous constraint" is from Smoke, *War: Controlling Escalation*.

110 E.g., Sebastian Rosato, "The Inscrutable Intentions of Great Powers," *International Security* 39, no. 3 (January 1, 2015): 48–88.

Addressing the Communication Problem

Once one incorporates covert activity as an option, the aforementioned "salient thresholds" provide sites for both kinds of messages. First, imagine a world in which Major Power A only has a choice between violating or abiding by a salient threshold. On the one hand, violating a limit will be seen as clearly expressing resolve which might force an adversary to concede (compellence) or can dissuade it from new aggression (deterrence).[111] On the other hand, obeying the limit will clearly show mindful and costly restraint.[112] As O'Brien argues, geographic limits are especially useful in this regard. "Geographic confinement is one of the most explicit signals of the intention to wage limited war," he writes, noting that "it can become a kind of symbol ... of an overall desire to keep a conflict limited."[113]

This two-choice situation creates a dilemma between communicating resolve and restraint. Signaling one message seems to undermine communicating the other. This dilemma is acute in the case of external military intervention. Such interventions violate a widely understood and intuitive "salient threshold"; moreover, interventions involve the costly deployment of materiel and personnel. Thus, an intervention can be interpreted as a strong indicator of resolve and exacerbate risks of miscommunicating about interest in limited war. While choosing no intervention minimizes the risk of a conflict spiral, it also can create a deterrence problem by expressing an absence of resolve.

This dilemma changes when adding a third option: covert transgression. Covertness allows a quiet transgression, which indicates both Major Power A's resolution to help a local ally *and* its commitment to competing within limits. In terms of the theater analogy, states do not simply choose to follow roles or break them. They can choose to seclude a break in character within the backstage. Backstaging the violation of a limit communicates a distinct message to the major powers that share access and can observe covert intervention. On the one hand, the intervener is seen to have *rejected* an overt intervention, or a publicly visible and acknowledged violation of a limit. The logistical alterations used in covert interventions, along with the absence of an effort to capture public relations gains from the intervention, will be understandable forms of "conspicuous restraint." Note that this does

---

111 Schelling, *Arms and Influence*, chap. 3.

112 Schelling, *The Strategy of Conflict*; Schelling, *Arms and Influence*, 135; Smoke, *War: Controlling Escalation*, 15–16.

113 O'Brien, *The Conduct of Just and Limited War*, 230.

not require effective concealment: an intervener's non-acknowledgment is an intelligible gesture that indicates continued desire to maintain limits in war. These communicative properties help address spiral problems by communicating continued interest in limiting war.[114] On the other hand, covertly intervening is still intervening. Choosing it over "no intervention" can be seen as a willingness to exceed the costs and risks of non-involvement. It can be a significant and consequential investment of resources by the intervener and raises the possibility of additional escalation beyond those that would exist with no intervention.[115] This allows an intervener to express resolve, though to a lesser degree than overtness would. In short, disaggregating *how* intervention takes place reveals that an intervention may simultaneously be an expression of *both* resolve and restraint.

It is worth noting that the communicative properties of acting secretly have typically been ignored or discounted in IR studies. In part, this is because secrecy is often conceptualized as an alternative to messaging or signaling: If Major Power A cares more about operational issues than signaling, it will use secret rather than public methods.[116] The communicative function of covertness has been under-analyzed partly because it is hard to observe and considered "cheap talk."[117] My claims therefore build on newer studies that identify the communicative potential of secrecy by adapting them to the particular dynamics of limited war and integrating acknowledgment dynamics.[118]

One payoff of the unique communication properties of covertness is insight regarding the puzzle of open secrecy. Acknowledging a covert-but-widely-exposed intervention can independently communicate an absence of restraint. In contrast, an intervener's commitment to limited war is reinforced by refusing to acknowledge its role even after exposure. Outside the intervention context, O'Neill notes that, in the case of Israel, "keeping its nuclear status off the record may lessen the pressure on surrounding coun-

---

114 My usage of "restraint" and "reassurance" in this context is specific to the issue of war's scope. A broader treatment of reassurance in cooperation is in Kydd, "Trust, Reassurance, and Cooperation."

115 Carson and Yarhi-Milo, "Covert Communication."

116 See, for example, Branislav L. Slantchev, "Feigning Weakness," *International Organization* 64, no. 3 (2010): 357–88.

117 Sagan and Suri, "The Madman Nuclear Alert."

118 Kurizaki, "Efficient Secrecy"; Carson and Yarhi-Milo, "Covert Communication"; some intuition is also drawn from studies of communication methods akin to covert action, as in John H. Fleming and John M. Darley, "Mixed Messages: The Multiple Audience Problem and Strategic Communication," *Social Cognition* 9, no. 1 (March 1, 1991): 25–46.

tries to respond in kind. The adversaries are not fooled, of course—they know the objective facts—but whether a certain situation constitutes a forceful challenge is about something other than objective facts."[119] Conspicuous non-acknowledgment of an exposed secret can take on symbolic significance, as when Israeli non-acknowledgment is seen as less provocative and admission dangerous.[120] This also finds expression in the theater metaphor: actors are reassured of one another's commitment to the performance when they see one another ignoring exposed backstage behavior even if it is visible to the audience. The alternative—pointing out the mistake on stage (i.e., publicly confirming the intervention)—can be seen as an indication that other actors (i.e., major powers) are prepared to accept a breakdown in the performance (i.e., unlimited war).

SUMMARY

To summarize, political and technological change has rendered large-scale escalation universally counterproductive for states. Control of escalation is endangered by two threats: domestic hawkish constraints and miscommunication. Covertness and collusion address both. Concealing and not acknowledging an intervention reduces the relevance of domestic hawkish reactions. Moreover, because covert interventions are observable to other major powers, covertness provides an indication of both resolve and restraint. In the theater metaphor, backstaging the crossing of a limit in war both reduces the relevance of the "audience" reaction and informs other "actors" that share access to the backstage that one is committed to the "performance." Table 2.1 reprises these points. I have also argued that one

---

119 O'Neill, *Honor, Symbols, and War*, 126; on informing while avoiding imposing on others the need to respond, see Stanley Cohen, *States of Denial: Knowing about Atrocities and Suffering* (Cambridge, UK: Polity, 2001), 81.

120 As Cohen notes, "Israel's nuclear bargain has many praiseworthy aspects ... Israel has committed to both resolve and caution, thereby avoiding the either-or structure of the nuclear dilemma." Avner Cohen, *The Worst-Kept Secret: Israel's Bargain with the Bomb* (New York: Columbia University Press, 2010), xxxii; non-acknowledgment was originally designed to avoid a cascade of proliferation in the region ("A declared nuclear stance would undermine the American nonproliferation policy and Israel's interest in not introducing nuclear weapons into the Arab-Israeli conflict"); Avner Cohen, *Israel and the Bomb* (New York: Columbia University Press, 1998); on the provocation of official disclosure, see Avner Cohen and Marvin Miller, "Facing the Unavoidable: Israel's Nuclear Monopoly Revisited," *Journal of Strategic Studies* 13, no. 3 (1990): 71–73.

TABLE 2.1. Covertness and Collusion: Solutions to Two Escalation Problems

Escalation Problem	Relevant Audience(s)	Mechanism	General Solution	How Backstaging Helps
Loss of domestic political autonomy	Domestic "hawks"	Negative reactions to restraint makes it prohibitively costly (for either side)	Minimize the role of domestic reactions in escalation decisions	Minimizes perception of provocation in eyes of domestic hawks via knowledge manipulation and avoiding acknowledgment
Poor adversary communication	Adversary leaders	Adversaries doubt one another's interest in limited war, both resolve and restraint	Find ways to simultaneously communicate moderate resolve and restraint	Covert line-crossing behavior sends a message to adversary of willingness to resist *and* interest in limiting war

payoff of my limited war theory is insight into the puzzles of collusion and open secrecy.[121]

Several clarifications are worth noting before proceeding further. My theory assumes that domestic politics matters for escalation for all regime types.[122] I specifically assume that hawkish views of domestic publics and elites not only are non-trivial but tend to dominate during crises and conflicts, and that they can effectively constrain leaders by making retaliation less costly and restraint more costly. Note also that "hawkish" is broader than explicit calls for war; hawkish views may be articulated simply as a desire to defend national honor or to enact eye-for-an-eye retaliation. Yet domestic politics is not all-powerful in my story. I also assume that escalation depends on how well adversaries understand one another. Moreover, my theory assumes that adversaries are capable of understanding one another's intentions about limited war under the right circumstances and

121 Goffman notes that "collusion involves falseness knowingly used as a basis for action. Something of a conspiracy is therefore entailed … Collusion serves to maintain for the excolluded a definition of the situation that is unstable, one that would be disrupted and discredited were the colluders to divulge what they know, and were they to relax in their management of evidence available to the excolluded." Erving Goffman, *Relations in Public: Microstudies of the Public Order* (New York: Penguin Books, 1971), 339; Goffman, *Strategic Interaction*, 16–17; on tacit vs. explicit collusion, see Rom Harre, *Key Thinkers in Psychology* (London: Sage, 2006).

122 I follow others in assuming autocracies are vulnerable, e.g., Jessica L. P. Weeks, *Dictators at War and Peace* (Ithaca, NY: Cornell University Press, 2014); Weiss, "Authoritarian Signaling, Mass Audiences, and Nationalist Protest in China."

with use of the right tools. As I develop further below, a history of inter-action or other means of reinforcing messages can enable covert activity to serve as a useful indication of resolve and restraint. Although mistakes in communication are possible in my theory, I assume that governments are capable of Bayesian updating in reaction to new information and do not suffer from persistent perceptual biases. Finally, it bears repeating that my limited-war theory does not claim to be a "master cause" of all secrecy in war. Alternative logics are compatible with my own logic even within the same conflict. Thus, while I argue covert interventions are detected by ad-versaries, secrecy could allow deception of an adversary in the short term with accompanying operational advantages. While I posit that leaders are most concerned about hawkish domestic critiques, long wars can give rise to war weariness and antiwar sentiment. Covertness could then shift to serving a domestic dove purpose later in a war. Even though I focus on limited-war dynamics, later chapters discuss episodes in the wars I analyze where other logics appear to be important.

Balancing Frontstage and Backstage

Even if this limited-war logic is a valid description of some of the appeal of covertness and collusion, two questions remain. First, how do major pow-ers balance the escalation control benefits of secrecy with other consider-ations? How are other issues, such as operational effectiveness, weighed against improved ability to limit war? Under what conditions do major powers (de)prioritize escalation concerns? Second, what conditions im-prove the viability of specific ways secrecy can limit war? What factors help or hinder management of domestic hawkish pressures and communication about limited war?

BALANCING PRIORITIES: INTERVENER

Thus far, my theory has focused on identifying threats to escalation con-trol and the role of covertness and collusion in retaining that control. This depiction of how major powers analyze intervention scenarios is incom-plete. Addressing escalation issues is but one of many possible goals major powers might prioritize in intervention scenarios. Moreover, publicity can advance such goals. Major powers intervene to address a range of in-terests including preservation or revision of a territorial or geopolitical status quo, improved economic opportunities, to protect the intervener's reputation, or to address humanitarian crises.[123] Because the *form* of intervention is immaterial to many of these goals, my theory makes minimal assumptions about what positively motivates intervention.[124] My only assumption is that an intervener cares enough about some goal (economic, geostrategic, or otherwise) to give overseas military aid during an ongoing war.

Some issues in intervention are influenced by the form of involvement. As noted earlier, overtness can have symbolic and operational benefits. I argue that, along with escalation control considerations, major powers also consider operational effectiveness of their intervention and the symbolic benefits of involvement. An overt form of intervention can be larger and less logistically complex than a covert alternative. In general, avoiding broad exposure requires covert interveners to send particular kinds of military aid (i.e., pilots, tank operators, small groups of antiaircraft artillery, generic weaponry) that are less easily detectable (i.e., not foreign-born infantry or highly advanced weaponry). Moreover, overt intervention will tend to be more effective in demonstrating maximum resolve and symbolic commitment to principles like assistance to allies. These two factors constitute the appeal of the frontstage.

In situations in which escalation control and other priorities are relevant, how are these priorities reconciled?[125] In the language of the theater analogy, how do states balance the appeal of the front and backstages? On the one hand, overt interventions are more operationally effective and symbolically laden. Exposure, moreover, can tighten the screws on a rival that has covertly intervened. On the other hand, covertness and collusion allow

123 On the range of positive goals in interventions, see Alexander L. George and Richard Smoke, *Deterrence in American Foreign Policy: Theory and Practice* (New York: Columbia University Press, 1974), 50; Martha Finnemore, *The Purpose of Intervention: Changing Beliefs about the Use of Force* (Ithaca, NY: Cornell University Press, 2004); Haldi, *Why Wars Widen*.

124 For example, stopping a genocide or securing mining rights can be done through either covert or overt aid to a local ally with little difference in outcome.

125 To be clear, wars with no plausible path to escalation allow interveners to prioritize the operational and symbolic benefits of overtness. One example is the 1990–1991 Persian Gulf War in which Saddam Hussein had no major power support allowing a one-sided, United Nations-blessed intervention to protect Kuwait. Similarly, a local conflict that fails to attract any external involvement lacks escalation potential. Yet, by definition, this kind of war will attract no intervention in the first place, so the relative priority of operational effectiveness or other considerations is irrelevant. Note also that wars that have *already* reached regional or global proportions (i.e., large-scale escalation) would obviate the priority of escalation control. Both scenarios reflect scope conditions of the theory: when no potential for large-scale escalation exists or it has already taken place, covertness and collusion to control escalation are irrelevant.

superior escalation-control opportunities by minimizing domestic hawkish pressure and communicating interest in limiting war. This tension begs the question: How do major powers prioritize these different considerations?

I argue that the *severity* of escalation risks is the factor that determines how major powers balance competing priorities. To do so, I draw on a central insight from theories of limited war: the risk of large-scale escalation is a function of whether clear thresholds that localize the war remain secure. As Smoke's study of escalation notes, violating a limit during war "does not prompt all the limits of a war to disappear." Instead, he argues, it is possible that "certain limits become discredited and irrelevant and new limits appear."[126] This reflects the reality that each war features a variety of limits that may or may not be interdependent. The Bosnian War, for example, was effectively limited with regard to external participants (European vs. non-European uses of force, ground troops vs. airpower) even as other limits were ultimately transgressed (mass civilian killings).

Within a given conflict, then, the severity of escalation varies. The logic of salient thresholds suggests that escalation danger is highest when an intervener's entry would endanger the most important thresholds that localize war: geographic confinement and the absence of direct major power combat encounters. As O'Brien notes, "placing geographic limits on conflicts ranks second only to avoidance of direct superpower confrontation and of nuclear war as a guideline for modern limited war."[127] Restoration of limits to avoid large-scale escalation is especially difficult in such scenarios. External intervention can specifically endanger the geographic bounds of combat (i.e., L vs. P in figure 2.2) and raise the risk of direct major power clashes. Such transgressions risk triggering dynamics that can result in large-scale escalation as I define it.

This insight provides a logic for one core empirical expectation of the theory: the timing and location of intervention influences the relative priority of escalation control and therefore the form (i.e. covert vs. overt) of intervention. Figure 2.6 shows two kinds of intervention (represented here as actions by Major Power A) that endanger these thresholds and therefore engender severe escalation risks. If A's intervention follows the entry of Major Power B (left panel of figure 2.6), then A's intervention creates a new and serious possibility of direct combat clashes of their nationals. Even if those remain within the local area (L), the possibility of a larger direct

126 Smoke, *War: Controlling Escalation*, 16.
127 O'Brien, *The Conduct of Just and Limited War*, 230.

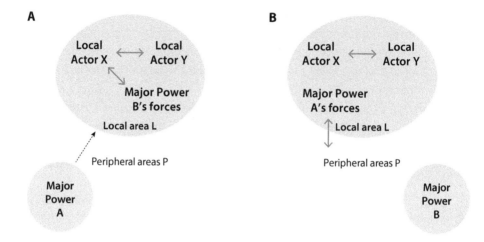

FIGURE 2.6. Interventions that trigger severe escalation risks.

confrontation is hard to avoid. Alternatively, if A's intervention expands the geographic area of combat into peripheral areas (P) (right panel), then it creates a new and significant spatial expansion of that war. Both are pathways to large-scale escalation, sharply increasing domestic constraints and the risks of misunderstanding for leaders. My theory suggests either situation will prompt the prioritization of escalation control via covertness.

Now consider the alternative: an intervention by A that is narrowly tailored to the local area (L) *and* that precedes any other major power's entry. By respecting spatial bounds and being a first mover, A avoids threatening the war's limiting thresholds. This allows considerations other than escalation control to take priority and the attraction of the frontstage to prevail. The implications are straightforward and intuitive. For interveners, my escalation-centric theory expects a choice for overtness only in the third scenario (local intervention, first mover) and a choice for covert intervention otherwise (see figure 2.7). Measuring this requires a straightforward assessment of the sequence and scope of each intervention.

BALANCING PRIORITIES: DETECTOR

Now consider the detector's choice. My second research question focuses on whether detected covert interventions are publicized (i.e., expose) or kept secret (i.e., collude). Similar considerations affect a detector's choice.

Intervention timing
(risk of direct major power clashes)

		First in (low)	Nth in (high)
Intervention location (risk of geographic expansion)	Local (low)	Overt intervention	Covert intervention
	Periphery (high)	Covert intervention	Covert intervention

FIGURE 2.7. Theoretical expectations for intervention form.

As noted earlier, there is considerable appeal in exposing an adversary's covert involvement. Doing so can prompt naming-and-shaming, dramatize hypocrisy, and generally damage the prospects of success for the intervener. At the same time, the prior section on domestic pressures described considerable escalation problems from exposure. Doing so can alert domestic hawks in multiple states, for example, which can make a tit-for-tat escalation process harder to avoid.

A key conclusion in the previous subsection on intervener choices, however, is that interventions that are covert will be in reaction to severe escalation risks. Thus, the logic of my claims puts detectors in a situation where escalation risks are significant. What, then, explains variation in exposure and collusion? Governments in the detector role have an additional issue to consider: the uniqueness of their information. As noted above, my theory assumes that other major powers and non-state actors might publicize interventions. For any given detector, this is an exogenous possibility largely outside of their control.[128] Wide exposure would convert a covert intervention into "open secret." The critical implication is that any given detector's decision to collude is then diluted. There is a reduction in the independent impact of collusion when wide exposure has already taken place. Limited war dynamics therefore suggest that an open secret renders

128 This is similar to the exogenous risk of exposure in Yarhi-Milo, "Tying Hands Behind Closed Doors," 405–35.

B's collusion decision less important because, regardless of its choice, domestic politics will be altered for A and B. Collusion does still influence what is *acknowledged* by B, but this is less potent. In contrast, B's collusion decision can influence *both* acknowledgment and knowledge if no other sources have exposed it.

This is the foundation for a second core expectation of the theory: detectors should vary in how they react to detection of a covert intervention based on *the extent of third-party exposure*. When third-party exposure follows a covert intervention, the theory expects detecting major powers to further expose a covert intervention in light of its diplomacy benefits. When third-party exposure is low, in contrast, the theory expects the detector to keep its intelligence information private and avoid confirming accusations by others. This will tend to preserve face-saving space for restraint on all sides. Measuring this condition requires a straightforward survey of the date and frequency of stories regarding a particular intervention and its sponsor's identity in high-circulation, English-language newspapers.[129]

CONDITIONS INFLUENCING FEASIBILITY

I argue that covertness and collusion can preserve escalation control by affecting both domestic hawkish constraints and miscommunication problems. This section discusses several factors that influence the effectiveness of these two control mechanisms.[130]

First consider the potential communicative function of covertness and collusion. One important factor influencing whether adversaries can make effective inferences to limit war based on observed covert activity is the clarity of messages. The distinguishability of any message from a covert intervention can vary. At times the legibility and meaning of covert behavior is difficult to establish. One clear lesson from the learned nature of limited war is that experience matters. Inexperience among adversaries in

---

129 See discussion of news coverage in chapters 4–7 regarding the extent of third-party exposure for details on how this is coded. I assume that regular reporting on a covert intervention in other languages will be picked up by English-language papers, and that regular appearance in high-circulation news sources represents a form of elite and literate public "common knowledge."

130 For this discussion, I assume that major powers have the institutional capacity to intervene covertly, should it be valuable for escalation-control purposes. I also assume that the costliness of large-scale escalation is high and the control problems I analyze are active. Major powers here face realistic domestic hawkish constraints and risks of miscommunication that both could drive escalation.

intervention-related scenarios or limiting war in general can degrade the quality of communication.[131] Similarly, ambiguity about the rationale for covertness—for example, due to overlapping potential reasons for observing another major power using secrecy—can also degrade the quality of communication.[132] In contrast, past experience and the absence of overdetermined reasons for resorting to covertness can foster high distinguishability and improved communication.

Now consider domestic politics and the ability to use covertness and collusion to insulate leaders from hawkish, pro-escalation pressure. The feasibility of this tactic is mainly a function of the likelihood of wider exposure by actors other than the relevant major powers. This, in turn, is influenced by a range of issues. For example, the accessibility of the battlefield and the specific nature of a foreign power's physical presence there can influence the likelihood others can expose. As I argue in chapter 3, technological changes like the development of airpower make hard-to-observe conflict participation more feasible. Similarly, media exposure is more or less likely depending on the proximity of the local conflict to international media sources and the nature of media technology.[133]

These considerations suggest that the ideal conditions for limiting war draw on both mechanisms. Covert activity and collusion are most viable when adversaries are likely to be able to effectively insulate themselves from domestic constraints and can clearly infer a mix of resolve and restraint that supports limited war. An example is the Soviet-American covert air war in Korea, in which sound inferences reinforced effective domestic insulation. In other situations, one control mechanism will prove more feasible than the other. Open secret scenarios are a special case when effective concealment from domestic audiences is infeasible but non-acknowledgment of a widely visible covert action still helps communicate interest in limited war.[134] Finally, a worst-case scenario for both mechanisms exists when adversaries'

131 As I argue in chapter 4, inexperience can be addressed through direct diplomatic communication, as when the ad hoc multilateral institution (i.e., the Non-Intervention Committee) allowed major powers without much experience to privately communicate regarding interventions.

132 Overlapping motivations is akin to the difficulty in identifying offensive and defensive operational maneuvers, as in Posen, *Inadvertent Escalation*.

133 Joseph and Poznansky, "Media Technology, Covert Action, and the Politics of Exposure."

134 An example of this is US covert involvement in Laos (chapter 6) during Vietnam after 1965. Media reporting rendered this activity an "open secret" and energized hawkish domestic voices. Yet Soviet and Chinese leaders understood Washington's careful refusal to acknowledge as symbolically meaningful support for Laotian neutrality and the limits these provided for the Vietnam War.

covert behavior is likely to be widely exposed and when inexperience or overlapping logics for secrecy lead to poor messaging effects. Because they have very little prospect for success, adversaries will tend to resort to escalation control through other means or simply accept the risks of escalation.

Additional Observable Implications

The previous section derived two core expectations of the theory about the conditions under which interveners should adopt a covert or overt form and when detectors should expose or collude. Each of the subsequent empirical chapters assesses each war to see whether this basic expectation holds. My research design conceptualizes each war as a set of nested cases and focuses on how different major powers resolve the tension differently within a single conflict. As noted in chapter 1, qualitative analysis and a comparative case study research design provide unique advantages for my particular research questions. The conflicts I analyze all meet the most important scope condition of the theory: the potential for large-scale escalation. As noted above, this excludes three kinds of local wars: those that lack any potential major power involvement, those in which major powers all back just one side, and those that have already escalated to large-scale global war (i.e., World War I or II). Among those wars with potential for large-scale escalation, I analyze variation in the severity of escalation risk to understand variation in the use of covertness and collusion. Table 1.1 in chapter 1 features a complete list of conflicts and cases.

This section derives additional observable implications that focus on *process* rather than *outcome* that are especially useful for assessment with qualitative archival evidence. My research design often allows me to observe the private decision-making process for interveners and detectors, comparing different states within a conflict and across time. What does an escalation-based theory expect decision-makers to observe and articulate in these settings? What would alternative theories of the choice for secrecy expect? I divide the discussion into three groups of implications: (1) for intervening states; (2) for detector states; and (3) for alternative logics.

INTERVENERS

In broad terms, my theory suggests that deliberations by intervening states should include careful analysis of escalation dynamics and risks. Leaders should generally acknowledge that large-scale escalation can be inadvertent, unwanted, or otherwise a function of "forced" choices and miscommunication. Leaders might specifically cite risks from hawkish domestic reactions or misunderstandings among adversaries. For intervening states choosing a covert form, the theory expects leaders to anticipate and accept the reality of exposure to their adversary, though they may still expect effective secrecy regarding domestic actors. It expects reason-giving in internal debates to focus on the risks of conflict escalation when comparing to overt alternatives.

The theory's claims about escalation-control problems and mechanisms provide additional expectations. Leaders should see a link between their use of covertness and the flexibility their adversary has vis-à-vis domestic hawkish actors. They might also link their use of covertness to the severity of the perceived challenge created by an intervention. Regarding the danger of escalation by miscommunication, my theory would expect leaders to be aware that *how* they intervene will influence how their rival(s) interprets their intentions. Leaders should see a messaging opportunity in adopting a covert intervention, allowing them to express a combination of resolve and restraint that supports limited war. The theory also has specific expectations about the two puzzles. Covert interveners should anticipate detection but also monitor and assess the likelihood of exposure by their adversary. They should anticipate that collusion is a plausible response if the detector also seeks escalation control. Regarding the second puzzle, the theory expects covert interveners whose role is widely exposed to find utility in maintaining a covert posture. Leaders should specifically discuss the unique risks of acknowledging what has been exposed, expressing a practical sense of the distinction between knowledge and acknowledgment.

For interveners that choose an overt form, the theory expects leaders to discuss and identify the lower escalation risk in bounding their overt intervention to the local area and in arriving first. They may specifically address a kind of "first-mover advantage" given that their own overt intervention will make subsequent overt interventions much more fraught. Moreover, the theory specifies the kinds of advantages leaders should see in choosing an overt form. They might cite the greater operational flexibility that an overt posture allows and balance that against the escalation-control advantages of covert involvement. Leaders should also be aware of the broader signal sent by an overt intervention. To be clear, all the conflicts I analyze have some base level of escalation risks. The theory does *not* expect overt interveners to dismiss the costs of escalation or see escalation as impossible. Rather, when escalation risks are not severe, the theory expects interveners to cite escalation issues but deprioritize them in favor of the advantages of public, acknowledged involvement.

An escalation-centric theory also has implications for change over time, especially interventions that evolve over time from covert to overt. My theory has a straightforward explanation: this should be in response to changes in escalation features of the war and the relative importance of logistics. Suppose, for example, that the behavior of other major powers changes from potential interveners to uninterested. A major power may react to this change in escalation risks by shifting from a covert to overt role. Similarly, my theory would expect a change if escalation risks were constant but a change in the need for logistical flexibility was introduced. A major power might prioritize escalation control early in a conflict but, as the need for a larger and more complex role developed, opt for an overt role. My theory would not expect this transition, however, if doing so would create severe escalation risks (i.e., "nth" mover, intervening in peripheral areas).

DETECTORS

Like interveners, my theory expects detectors to carefully assess escalation dynamics, view large-scale escalation as potentially inadvertent or unwanted, and specifically identify the dangers of hawkish domestic reactions or misunderstanding among adversaries. Moreover, my theory expects them to identify benefits in exposing covert interventions, specifically in damaging its prospects for success. When selecting collusion, I expect detectors to cite concern about escalation, and the mechanisms I identify in particular, rather than other motives. Detectors should cite the specific risks of relaxing geographic or nationality-based limits on a war. They should assess that collusion can make a meaningful difference in what is known about the covert intervention and in the domestic constraints on themselves and others to react. The theory also has implications for exposure. Detecting states deciding to expose should cite the wide dissemination of knowledge about the covert intervention by others. Finally, the theory has implications for change over time. Detectors should be most likely to collude early in a detected covert intervention, when uncertainty about escalation is highest and exposure by other sources least likely. Exposure should be more common later in the war, as limits of a conflict settle and others identify the covert intervention.

ALTERNATIVE LOGICS

Alternative logics, such as building operational advantages over rivals (operational security logic) or insulating from domestic dovish punishment (domestic dove logic), have distinct observable implications. Each has implications for when covertness should be preferred (outcome) and what kind of reason-giving and beliefs should be articulated by policymakers (process). An operational security logic for covertness would expect its adoption when an intervener is helping a losing local ally and is capable of effectively concealing its intervention from an adversary. In terms of process, an operational security logic expects leaders to focus on the importance of adversary ignorance for protecting forces in the field or exercising surprise maneuvers. They should cite battlefield disadvantages which can be overcome through misinformation and seek covertness to enable their intervention to turn the tide. More broadly, an operational security logic for covertness is most likely when the intervener is weaker than the likely opponent, which elevates the value of surprise. It is also particularly suited to small, one-off covert operations where effective deception of an adversary is most plausible. A domestic dove logic would expect covertness for democratic leaders facing a strongly antiwar public mood. Leaders should cite the infeasibility of a proposed intervention should antiwar elite statements or mass protests follow an intervention. Covertness would then be most likely when elite and public attention in the intervening state are focused on the conflict and strongly disfavor intervention.

Regarding reactions to detected covert interventions, neither the operational security nor the domestic dove logic provides a rationale for collusion. As noted in chapter 1, each provides some important reasons for a detecting power to expose regardless of escalation conditions. Exposure can ensure operational advantages are neutralized (operational security logic) and improve the chances that constraints result in a circumscribed intervention or withdrawal altogether (domestic dove).

Conclusion

This chapter has developed a logic for secrecy's role in attempts to control the dangers of large-scale conflict escalation. I argue that interveners and those detecting covert interventions can use secrecy to cope with two escalation-control problems: hawkish domestic pressure and poor communication among adversaries. When escalation risks are severe, leaders will prioritize escalation control and embrace a tacitly collusive use of the backstage. The theory provides a single logic to address the appeal of secrecy both to an intervener and to a rival that detects it. Doing so also sheds light on the appeal of overtness and exposure as well as the puzzles of collusion and open secrecy that were introduced in chapter 1. Next, I turn to anchoring the theory in history. Chapter 3 identifies political and technological changes that prompted the emergence of covert conflict as a means to deal with escalation, focusing on the critical importance of World War I. This gives a sense of when and why escalation control became a key concern in the modern era and how secret, unacknowledged military interventions have evolved into an important tool for doing so.

3

The Emergence of Covert Warfare

What historical changes prompted states to experiment with new ways of limiting war? What innovations made the concealed, unacknowledged use of force possible? This chapter describes the confluence of political, technological, and social changes that led to the emergence of covert military intervention as an escalation-control technique. In doing so, I primarily focus on developments during and in the wake of World War I. One purpose of the chapter is to place subsequent empirical chapters in historical context. By the end, we are left with an image of the technological and political landscape that would shape decisions by European leaders as civil war broke out in Spain in 1936 (chapter 4). Second, by identifying when widespread concern about large-scale escalation and the problem of control emerged, the chapter identifies temporal scope conditions for the theoretical assumptions I make about escalation. In particular, World War I crystallized the link between the magnitude of modern war, domestic hawkish constraints, and the dangers of miscommunication. Last, identifying conditions that prompted the emergence of covertness as a limited war-technique also lays the foundation for assessing the impact of more recent political and technological developments, such as democratization and cyber-technology, which I return to in chapter 8.[1]

I conceptualize World War I as a kind of "critical juncture" that dramatized the dangers of large-scale war escalation in the modern era. Beyond

1 See chapter 8 for discussion.

its symbolic importance, the war also accelerated political, social, and technological developments that simultaneously sharpened the problem of escalation control and made possible new ways of using military force covertly.[2] The chapter is divided into three sections. I first review how World War I led to a widely shared perception of the costliness of war in the industrial age via the raw numbers of mobilized, injured, and killed and the searing imagery of gas masks and trench warfare. The section then describes how World War I also bore important lessons about how war escalates, making salient the twin challenges of hawkish domestic pressures and communicating interest in limited war. The first section ends by reviewing the long-run historical changes, consolidated by the fighting of World War I itself, that sharpened these escalation problems. The second section then turns to technological changes which allowed foreign powers to more easily use military force anonymously. Focusing on airpower and submarines as examples, I argue that World War I–era innovations allowed major powers to provide useful military aid without disclosing the national identity of their personnel. Most of the covert interventions in later chapters drew on these developments. A third section provides early examples of post–World War I experimentation in ways to limit war. The lessons of World War I translated into undeclared wars, use of "volunteers," and early efforts to conceal involvement. This provided the context for the covert interventions in Spain in the late 1930s, covered in the next chapter.

One theme that emerges from this analysis is the importance of learning. World War I prompted major powers to experiment with ways of limiting war; this included manipulation of the form of external military intervention. Although early precursors to covert intervention preceded the Great War, its emergence as a recurring and coherent state practice required the emergence of new ideational and material realities.[3] This chapter's themes echo Martha Finnemore's analysis of the earlier emergence of intervention

---

2 Paul Pierson, *Politics in Time: History, Institutions, and Social Analysis* (Princeton, NJ: Princeton University Press, 2011).

3 To be clear, some isolated episodes of covert activity and related practices like privateers preceded World War I. I am arguing that the Great War accelerated and consolidated conditions that led to the emergence of covert intervention as a distinct and coherent practice. An early precursor was state-sponsored privateers which in effect allowed low-level undeclared naval warfare between England and Spain in the New World. See Janice E. Thomson, *Mercenaries, Pirates, and Sovereigns: State-Building and Extraterritorial Violence in Early Modern Europe* (Princeton, NJ: Princeton University Press, 1996), 22–23.

itself.[4] Subsequent empirical chapters show that covert intervention and collusion were refined as a result of cumulative experience. Learning is an admittedly fraught concept in IR, and assessing its causal weight in specific foreign policy decisions is difficult.[5] I draw a parallel with the experimentation and learning identified by scholars of nuclear deterrence.[6] Soviet and American leaders or, more recently Indian and Pakistani leaders, have drawn on experience and precedent to develop systems of command and control, nuclear doctrine, relatively stable deterrence, and arms control.[7] Limited war is a distinct kind of state practice constituted by a set of rules about how force is used (i.e., the "salient thresholds" described in chapter 2), which serve to distinguish a limited war from "peace" and "total war."[8] It is therefore a blend of cooperation and competition.

World War I and the Problem of Escalation

No event showcased modern warfare's destructiveness more vividly than World War I. As one recent review of research on the centennial of the war noted, the Great War marked "a rupture in modern European, indeed global, history" which "transformed people's understanding of international relations."[9] The destruction and arc of escalation in World War I therefore

---

4 Martha Finnemore, *The Purpose of Intervention: Changing Beliefs about the Use of Force* (Ithaca, NY: Cornell University Press, 2004).

5 Jack S. Levy, "Learning and Foreign Policy: Sweeping a Conceptual Minefield," *International Organization* 48, no. 2 (Spring 1994): 279–312.

6 Joseph S. Nye, "Nuclear Learning and U.S.–Soviet Security Regimes," *International Organization* 41, no. 03 (June 1987): 371–402; Emanuel Adler and Vincent Pouliot, "International Practices," *International Theory* 3, no. 01 (February 2011): 1–36.

7 On precedents, Elizabeth Kier and Jonathan Mercer, "Setting Precedents in Anarchy: Military Intervention and Weapons of Mass Destruction," *International Security* 20, no. 4 (1996): 77–106; see also discussion of precedents and conventions in limited war in Thomas Schelling, *The Strategy of Conflict* (Cambridge, MA: Harvard University Press, 1960); Thomas C. Schelling, *Arms and Influence* (New Haven, CT: Yale University Press, 1966); on learning generally, see Jeffrey W. Knopf, "The Importance of International Learning," *Review of International Studies* 29, no. 2 (April 2003): 185–207; on India and Pakistan and nuclear learning, see sections in Peter R. Lavoy, *Asymmetric Warfare in South Asia: The Causes and Consequences of the Kargil Conflict* (New York: Cambridge University Press, 2009).

8 See discussion of focal points and limited war as a distinct state practice ("focal points stem from the patterned nature of social practices. It is the regularity of players' moves that makes the convergence of expectations and coordination possible") in Adler and Pouliot, "International Practices," 11.

9 William Mulligan, "The Trial Continues: New Directions in the Study of the Origins of the First World War," *English Historical Review* 129, no. 538 (June 1, 2014): 642, 666. See also Barry

left a searing legacy on the international system. "All were haunted by the 1914 experience," John Mueller observes in his analysis of societal attitudes about war. The dominant view afterward was that "war was no longer supreme theater, redemptive turmoil, a chess game for high stakes, a riveting diversion, a natural progression, or an uplifting affirmation of manhood." Rather, war had become "repulsive, immoral, uncivilized, and futile."[10] Beyond pure destructiveness, the Great War was also a turning point in a range of broader political trends, including the trajectory of global governance, democratization, ideology, and empire.[11] Put differently, the symbolic, ideational, and material changes wrought by World War I created a new purpose, escalation control, for which covert intervention was well suited.[12]

DEMONSTRATING THE COSTS OF ESCALATION

World War I became synonymous with the threat of total war. As the military historian Hew Strachan notes, during the decade following World War I, "total war became part of the language of warning, an attempt to scare states from undertaking major war again and to create an architecture of self-deterrence."[13] Bernard Brodie's influential analysis of the novelty of nuclear weapons traces the horror of war to World War I. In his book *Strategy in the Missile Age*, for example, Brodie argues that "the most ominous lesson of World War I" was a feature many would later attribute to nuclear weaponry: "The vast advance in the technology of war which distinguishes the twentieth century from the nineteenth has been attended by suppression of rational coercion.... [A] war that was clearly not being fought for total objectives, such as the political extirpation of the enemy state, was allowed to become total in its methods and intensity."[14] The scale of de-

---

Buzan and George Lawson, *The Global Transformation: History, Modernity and the Making of International Relations* (New York: Cambridge University Press), 2015.

10 John Mueller, *Retreat from Doomsday: The Obsolescence of Major War* (New York: Basic Books, 1989), 54–55, 60.

11 For an overview, see David Reynolds, *The Long Shadow: The Legacies of the Great War in the Twentieth Century* (New York: W. W. Norton, 2014).

12 Finnemore, *The Purpose of Intervention*.

13 Strachan concludes that with the advent of nuclear weapons, "the idea of 'total war' now underpinned the stability of the international order. And so the shadow of Verdun fell across the Cold War world." Hew Strachan, "The Strategic Consequences of the World War," *American Interest* 9, no. 6 (June 2, 2014), http://www.the-american-interest.com/2014/06/02/the-strategic-consequences-of-the-world-war/.

14 Bernard Brodie, *Strategy in the Missile Age* (Princeton, NJ: Princeton University Press, 1959), 67.

struction in World War I also had an impact on how analysts of international politics understood war. Influential realists like Hans Morgenthau, for example, described the Great War in language akin to a critical juncture when noting that there was "a type of limited war that prevailed, with the sole significant exceptions of the Wars of Religion and the Napoleonic Wars, throughout modern history up to the First World War."[15]

The sheer numerical scale of World War I was a key reason it altered perceptions of the costliness of war. The conflict lasted 1,564 days and included thirty-three belligerents. Recent estimates conclude that, across all participants, 70 million people were mobilized as part of the war effort. The war resulted in the deaths of 10 million military personnel and an additional 10 million civilians from hunger and disease.[16] This included more than 1.3 million French and more than 2 million German military personnel.[17] More than 15 percent of Serbia's total population before the war would be killed; 630,000 war widows were estimated to live in France by 1918.[18] These totals reflected a staggering accumulation of daily, weekly, and monthly destruction. In the first four months of the war, 300,000 Frenchman were killed and 600,000 wounded. One estimate is that 7,000 British were killed in the trenches of the Western front each day.[19]

Geographic scale and the impact on basic government function further underscore the impact of the war. The burden on governments and social services was profound. The war was truly global in scale and fought in an estimated fourteen theaters of action.[20] The Western front featured an estimated 6,250 miles of French trenches and 25,000 miles of trenches overall on both sides, enough to encircle the earth.[21] As a percentage of total economic size, war-related expenses grew from 10 percent in 1914 to more than 50 percent in 1918 for France and Germany.[22] The destruction of nonhuman assets was also enormous. One recent estimate places the percentage of prewar domestic physical assets destroyed in France at 60 percent.

---

15 Hans Morgenthau, Kenneth Thompson, and David Clinton, *Politics Among Nations*, 7th ed. (New York: McGraw-Hill Humanities/Social Sciences/Languages, 2005), 378.

16 Stephen Broadberry and Mark Harrison, *The Economics of World War I* (Cambridge, UK: Cambridge University Press, 2005), 35.

17 Broadberry and Harrison, *The Economics of World War I*, 15.

18 John Keegan, *The First World War* (New York: Knopf Doubleday, 2012), 6–7.

19 Paul Fussell, *The Great War and Modern Memory* (New York: Oxford University Press, 1975), 41.

20 Broadberry and Harrison, *The Economics of World War I*, 35.

21 Fussell, *The Great War and Modern Memory*, 37.

22 Broadberry and Harrison, *The Economics of World War I*, 15.

The cost of German war reparations was estimated to be 52 percent of its prewar capital assets.[23]

Yet these data do not capture the widespread sense of a qualitative change in the character of war. For many, the war was a harbinger of a shift toward conflict on a far larger scale and for a purpose that was more difficult to bound or limit. Morgenthau quotes the French marshal Ferdinand Foch, who argued in 1917 that "a new era had begun, that of national wars which were to absorb into the struggle all the resources of the nation." This kind of conflict featured disputes over "philosophic ideas" and "were destined to bring out the interest and faculties of each soldier, to take advantage of sentiments and passions never before recognized as elements of strength."[24] Paul Fussell documents ways in which the war experience infiltrated English-language literature and culture. The haunting imagery of trench warfare left a legacy in idioms ("in the trenches," "over the top," "entrenched in power") and new references ("trenchcoat").[25] The meaning of the most basic elements of daily life, including the rising and setting of the sun, were altered by the war. A recurring theme in British literature was "new, modern associations of dawn: cold, the death of multitudes, insensate marching in files, battle, and corpses too shallowly interred."[26] Disillusionment with the war was so profound that it cast doubt on the very virtues and purpose of society in Western Europe. Especially in the decades immediately following the war, a deep cynicism appeared in literature and elsewhere in popular culture, supplanting and often directly questioning the culture of honor and glory before 1914. A common interpretation of the Great War was that it shattered a climate of romantic innocence that had previously suffused daily life and soldiering in war.[27]

DEMONSTRATING THE CHALLENGE OF CONTROLLING ESCALATION

Beyond the numerical scale of death and the senselessness of trench warfare, the process of escalation in 1914 raised other concerns. Leaders drew lessons about the seeming loss of control over the conflict escalation process. Popular and elite perceptions in the interwar period emphasized that

---

23 Broadberry and Harrison, *The Economics of World War I*, 28.
24 Morgenthau, Thompson, and Clinton, *Politics Among Nations*, 378.
25 Fussell, *The Great War and Modern Memory*, 36, 189.
26 Fussell, *The Great War and Modern Memory*, 63.
27 Fussell, *The Great War and Modern Memory*, 21, 24.

the Great War "might have been prevented ... through calm negotiation." If leaders had been allowed "some breathing space," Mueller argues, "the protagonists might have eventually abated or diverted the momentum toward war."[28] Leaders' shared desire to avoid blame for the war only encouraged narratives of inadvertence and loss of control.[29] As Michael Howard notes, "those who were so accused disclaimed responsibility for the events of 1914, throwing it on others or saying the whole thing was a terrible mistake for which no one was to blame."[30] Lessons from this war about the dangers of fixed military mobilization plans and tight alliances influenced how states subsequently handled crisis diplomacy and war escalation.[31] Most important for this book's arguments, however, is the way the conflict dramatized the role of hawkish domestic pressures and misunderstanding about interest in limited war, showing both could fuel a tit-for-tat process to large-scale escalation.

One particular anxiety in the wake of World War I was the problem of domestic, nationalist constraints in fueling escalation, a concern that first appeared in the latter half of the nineteenth century. A common interpretation of the process leading to the Crimean War, for example, was that domestic hawkish constraints on British and French leaders exacerbated misunderstandings among those states and Russia. Dramatized news coverage of Russia's attack on Sinope harbor, for example, triggered "frenzied emotions," which helped incentivize escalatory interventions.[32] Historians also cite the role of "yellow journalism" in sensationalizing events during the Spanish-American War in 1898. The realist George Kennan's disdain for mass popular opinion was influenced by the way the crisis with Spain was

---

28 Mueller, *Retreat from Doomsday*, 60.

29 On the politics of blame shifting in storytelling about war guilt, see Keir A. Lieber, "The New History of World War I and What It Means for International Relations Theory," *International Security* 32, no. 2 (Fall 2007): 155–91; Jack Snyder and Keir A. Lieber, "Defensive Realism and the 'New' History of World War I," *International Security* 33, no. 1 (June 26, 2008): 174–94. Note that the truth of German strategic goals is not germane to the question of what lessons interwar leaders derived at the time.

30 Michael Howard, "The Causes of Wars," *Wilson Quarterly (1976–)* 8, no. 3 (1984): 94.

31 Stephen Van Evera, "The Cult of the Offensive and the Origins of the First World War," *International Security* 9, no. 1 (Summer 1984): 58–107; Jack L. Snyder, *The Ideology of the Offensive: Military Decision Making and the Disasters of 1914* (Ithaca, NY: Cornell University Press, 1984); Thomas J. Christensen and Jack Snyder, "Chain Gangs and Passed Bucks: Predicting Alliance Patterns in Multipolarity," *International Organization* 44, no. 02 (1990): 137–68; Barbara W. Tuchman, *The Guns of August* (New York: Random House Digital, 2009).

32 Richard Smoke, *War: Controlling Escalation* (Cambridge, MA: Harvard University Press, 1977), 184, 190, 193.

influenced by swings in public opinion that produced dangerous constraints on leaders.[33] The Agadir Crisis of 1911 foreshadowed these themes on the eve of World War I. Germany's lead diplomat in the crisis, Alfred von Kiderlen-Waechter, cultivated ultra-nationalist press coverage in Germany to strengthen Germany's hand vis-à-vis French claims in Morocco. This fueled hawkish press and elite opinion in France. The result was uncertainty on both sides about each other's interest in controlling the crisis and limiting any war.[34]

Yet World War I showed that a resolution short of war, as in the Agadir Crisis, was no guarantee. The Great War was largely interpreted as an object lesson in the difficulty of reaching a shared understanding of interest in limited war. This is a key reason the conflict is a standard reference point for security dilemma and spiral model theories.[35] Schelling's theorization of limited-war dynamics and the difficulty of tacit communication among adversaries looks to the Great War. He describes "mutual alarm" in Europe during July and August 1914 and argues that a key reason for escalation beyond Serbia and Austria was the difficulty of inferring intentions. Military mobilization for a country like Russia was inherently ambiguous with respect to limited war. The tsar's precautionary mobilization in case Germany backed Austria would "confront Germany with an Eastern enemy mobilization as though for total war."[36] The central problem was leaders' lack of military preparations that expressed an intuitive difference in defensive, limited versus offensive, aggressive aims: "The mobilization systems of continental countries in 1914 did not discriminate."[37] Mixed signals and misunderstanding even influenced allies: as Jack Levy observes, Austria had difficulty reading Germany's intentions due to confusion over which center of power in Germany held sway. This made restraint in Vienna more difficult to accept.[38]

More recent historiographical interpretations have kept alive the debate about the reason for escalation and the specific question of German inten-

---

33 George F. Kennan, *American Diplomacy*, expanded edition (Chicago: University of Chicago Press, 1985), 9–10.

34 Christopher Clark, *The Sleepwalkers: How Europe Went to War in 1914* (New York: Harper Collins, 2013), 207.

35 Robert Jervis, *Perception and Misperception in International Politics* (Princeton, NJ: Princeton University Press, 1976).

36 Schelling, *Arms and Influence*, 223.

37 Schelling, *Arms and Influence*, 225.

38 Jack S. Levy, "Preferences, Constraints, and Choices in July 1914," *International Security* 15, no. 3 (1990): 177.

tions. Yet even advocates of a harsher view of Germany note that the dominant perception in the two decades following World War I emphasized misperception and a "slide to war." As Lieber describes, early revisions to the assignment of German war guilt simply spread blame and elevated the theme of a tragic misunderstanding. The result was that, by the 1930s, "the consensus view in much of Europe held that no country wanted war in 1914 and that all the major powers deserved blame for allowing the diplomatic crisis that summer to escalate out of control."[39] The escalation-by-misunderstanding view was so prominent and so enduring precisely because the war "had been so horrific." As a result, "many people were more comfortable with the notion that it must have been started inadvertently. Surely nobody could have desired such a catastrophe."[40]

A specific strand of this inadvertence interpretation emphasized a toxic combination of domestic politics and nationalism. As Ja Chong and Todd Hall recently summarized, a key lesson from 1914 is that "pressure groups increased the stakes and payoffs of prestige politics ... tilting the scales of domestic political incentives in the direction of confrontation."[41] Vasquez's review of new work on World War I in the past two decades identifies the theme of domestic politics. He notes that this research suggests that each of the major European powers struggled to cope with domestic constraints on the way to large-scale escalation.[42] These findings build on earlier work on the role of hawkish domestic actors in Germany specifically.[43] Thus, World War I was more than an object lesson in "war by timetable."[44]

The problems of domestic elite and mass political constraints are best described in Christopher Clark's recent analysis of World War I, referred to in one review as "the most significant single contribution to the debate on

---

39 Lieber, "The New History of World War I and What It Means for International Relations Theory," 158.

40 Lieber, "The New History of World War I and What It Means for International Relations Theory," 158.

41 Ja Ian Chong and Todd H. Hall, "The Lessons of 1914 for East Asia Today: Missing the Trees for the Forest," *International Security* 39, no. 1 (July 1, 2014): 29.

42 John A. Vasquez, "The First World War and International Relations Theory: A Review of Books on the 100th Anniversary," *International Studies Review* 16, no. 4 (December 1, 2014): 624–27.

43 Konrad H. Jarausch, "The Illusion of Limited War: Chancellor Bethmann Hollweg's Calculated Risk, July 1914," *Central European History* 2, no. 1 (March 1969): 48–76.

44 A.J.P. Taylor, *War by Time-Table: How the First World War Began* (London: Macdonald & Co., 1969); see the refutation of this thesis in Marc Trachtenberg, "The Meaning of Mobilization in 1914," *International Security* 15, no. 3 (1990): 120–50.

the origins of the war since Fischer's 1961 book."[45] As Clark summarizes, "the last decades before the outbreak of the war saw a dramatic expansion of the political public sphere and broader public discussion of issues linked to international relations."[46] This proved fertile ground for the articulation of nationalist political agendas and, specifically, criticism of restraint during crises. The result was a widely shared concern for domestic reactions in European capitals:

> Monarchs, ministers and senior officials thus had good reason to take the press seriously. In parliamentary systems, positive publicity might be expected to translate into votes, while negative coverage supplied grist for the mills of the opposition. In more authoritarian systems, public support was an indispensable ersatz for democratic legitimacy. Some monarchs and statesmen were positively obsessive about the press and spent hours each day poring through cuttings. Wilhelm II was an extreme case, but his sensitivity to public criticism was not in itself unusual. "If we lose the confidence of public opinion in our foreign policy," Tsar Alexander III had told Foreign Minister Lamzdorf, "then all is lost." It is hard to find anyone in the executives of early twentieth-century Europe who did not acknowledge the importance of the press for the making of foreign policy.[47]

There were implications for strategic interaction as well. Domestic vulnerability and hawkish press reactions could affect the capacity for *other* capitals to act with restraint, echoing one theme in chapter 2. Each of the major protagonists in 1914 was justified in worrying that its counterpart might find itself unable to resist pressure for mobilization or escalation. This domestic uncertainty, in turn, fueled broader uncertainty about intentions. While systemic shifts in relative military power (i.e., between Russia and Germany) set the stage for the July Crisis, hawkish press coverage seemed to feed fears about such shifts. German internal deliberations quoted hawkish Russian press coverage verbatim as evidence of the tsar's aggressive intentions and the dominance of a "war party."[48] Combining the two

45 Mulligan, "The Trial Continues," 664. Mulligan (658) also notes that "[m]astering literature in six languages and drawing on archival and documentary sources for each belligerent, Christopher Clark's book represents the most complete international analysis of the origins of the war since Luigi Albertini's three-volume study published in the 1940s."

46 Clark, *The Sleepwalkers*, 226.

47 Clark, *The Sleepwalkers*, 226–27.

48 Clark, *The Sleepwalkers*, 362–63.

escalation-control problems developed in chapter 2, Clark observes that in World War I,

> a striking feature of the interactions between the European executives was the persistent uncertainty in all quarters about the intentions of friends and potential foes alike. The flux of power across factions and office-holders remained a problem, as did worries about the possible impact of popular opinion.... Beneath all the paranoia and aggression was a fundamental uncertainty about how to read the mood and intentions of the other chancelleries, let alone how to anticipate their reactions to as yet unrealized eventualities.[49]

To be clear, a descriptive claim about how leaders in the 1920s and 1930s understood the lessons of the Great War is distinct from weighing in on the analytical claims about the "true" causes of World War I. I am not commenting on anything but perceptual issues here. In short, both kinds of claims could be true: interwar leaders may have *perceived* the conflict as a case study in the difficulty of limited war even if *in reality* German or Russian leaders sought a larger continental war. Whatever the "true" intentions of the combatants, limited war was elusive. As one historian notes about Germany, limited war was an "illusion." Many in Berlin believed a localized crisis was preferable but difficult to pull off; as a result, "the concept of limited war proved elusive and drew Germany deeper and deeper into the vortex."[50]

CONSOLIDATING LONG-RUN CHANGES

Beyond serving as an exemplar, World War I also changed the world in which interwar leaders operated. Many of these changes intensified the problems of escalation costliness and escalation control. The end of the war consolidated trends that made war more destructive and leaders more vulnerable to miscommunication and domestic hawkish pressure. World War I launched a boom in the spread of democracy, such that "by 1923 almost a quarter of the independent political systems in the world had achieved that status."[51] This included a "dramatic expansion of the electorate" as the

49 Clark, *The Sleepwalkers*, 362–63.

50 Jarausch, "The Illusion of Limited War," 75.

51 Renske Doorenspleet, "Reassessing the Three Waves of Democratization," *World Politics* 52, no. 3 (April 2000): 393.

franchise was expanded to larger sectors of the population.[52] Many worried in the interwar period about the consequences of this democratization, as it coincided with the rise of ideologies like fascism which could be rewarded at the ballot box. David Reynolds's review of the legacies of World War I notes that "the introduction of a democratic franchise, coupled often with parliamentary government, amounted to a political explosion.... [T]he real problem was making democracy safe for the world."[53]

World War I also dramatically increased the number of independent states in the international system, sharpening and spreading the appeal of nationalism. The collapse of the Ottoman, Austro-Hungarian, and Russian empires expanded the places where local conflicts could tempt foreign powers to intervene. While some territory was simply transferred to British and French control, other territory (i.e., Eastern and Central Europe) hosted newly independent states where nationalist sentiment flourished.[54] The war also "sharpen[ed] national consciousness," due to the fighting itself and the postwar Wilsonian emphasis on self-determination.[55] This resulted in an "explosive fusion of national particularism and moral universalism," which, in future conflicts, could drive war "toward its utmost material limits."[56]

World War I also accelerated military technological innovations that deepened the costliness and reach of large-scale escalation. Perhaps most consequential was the shift to what McNeill calls "command invention," in which deliberate innovation was fostered through public-private partnerships that harnessed corporate rationality and industrial-scale production for mass production of military armaments.[57] Specific weapons were developed or refined that enabled far more efficient killing, symbolized by the machine gun and gas warfare.[58] In addition to specific technological devel-

---

52 Reynolds, *The Long Shadow*, 45.

53 Reynolds, *The Long Shadow*, 82.

54 As Reynolds notes, the war "spawned a tribe of fractious nation-states whose instability and enmities were at the root of." Reynolds, *The Long Shadow*, 83.

55 Reynolds, *The Long Shadow*, 8–9.

56 Robert E. Osgood, *Limited War: The Challenge to American Strategy* (Chicago: University of Chicago Press, 1957), 92.

57 William H. McNeill, *The Pursuit of Power: Technology, Armed Force, and Society Since A.D. 1000* (Chicago: University of Chicago Press, 1982), 358.

58 Martin Van Creveld, *The Transformation of War: The Most Radical Reinterpretation of Armed Conflict Since Clausewitz* (New York: Free Press, 1991), 85.

opments, military doctrine and strategy were "shaped by Great War precedents" as the likelihood of war in Europe became greater in the 1930s.[59]

Together, these changes confronted leaders in the 1920s and 1930s with
an even more acute challenge than in 1914.

Anonymizing Military Force

Beyond lethality, changes brought about by World War I also created new
ways for governments to use military force anonymously. This, in turn,
expanded the ways in which major powers could engage in unpublicized,
unacknowledged military intervention. By anonymity I specifically mean
the *ease of identifying the national origin of military personnel on the battlefield.* To be clear, anonymity was not the primary purpose of such innovations. Rather, obfuscating who was participating in war was typically the
unintended by-product of the development of technologies serving other
military purposes. However, changes in how states could use military force
on land, at sea, and in the air created new ways in the interwar period for
sending military aid and personnel without disclosing it.

Historians and theorists of technology have long noted how technology
can alter legibility and provide new methods for both social concealment
and discovery. James C. Scott, for example, argues that innovations in car-
tography and information management allowed sovereign authorities to
"see" in ways previously unavailable.[60] New technology can also enable new
forms of anonymity. In some cases, this purpose is an intentional part of its
development. For example, the spread of commercial satellite technology
is prompting civilian and military organizations to adopt new techniques
to conceal sensitive facilities.[61] Other technological changes produce anonymity as an unintended by-product. Studies of driving behavior have
shown that aggressiveness and road rage are influenced by the anonymity
of operating an automobile.[62] Studies of physical violence suggest that the

---

59 Reynolds, *The Long Shadow*, 246.

60 Professor James C. Scott, *Seeing Like a State: How Certain Schemes to Improve the Human
Condition Have Failed* (New Haven, CT: Yale University Press, 1999).

61 Chris Perkins and Martin Dodge, "Satellite Imagery and the Spectacle of Secret Spaces,"
Geoforum 40, no. 4 (July 2009): 557.

62 P. A. Ellison et al., "Anonymity and Aggressive Driving Behavior: A Field Study," *Journal
of Social Behavior and Personality; Corte Madera, CA* 10, no. 1 (January 1, 1995): 265–72; David
Shinar, "Aggressive Driving: The Contribution of the Drivers and the Situation," *Transportation
Research Part F: Traffic Psychology and Behaviour* 1, no. 2 (December 1, 1998): 137–60.

simple "technology" of a disguise or mask can lead to "deindividuation" and more aggressive behavior.[63] The constellation of technologies that allow modern urban living has been critiqued for fostering social anonymity and a resulting absence of social bonds that tend to exist in small, non-urban communities.[64]

Military innovations can influence anonymity as well. Piracy's economic viability was a function of the inability to detect and monitor pirates while operating on a ship at sea. Thus, naval innovations created "elusiveness and anonymity," which combined with the "ease of disposal of incriminating evidence" to make punishment extremely difficult.[65] A consistent theme in contemporary reactions to the introduction of iron-hulled, submerged naval vessels during the American Civil War was increased anonymity. A Union officer reflecting on the USS *Monitor* differentiated it from traditional combat, suggesting that the new vessels gave rise to "a mode of warfare strangely differing from the dashing cavalry service on the outposts."[66] The American writer Nathaniel Hawthorne noted visibility issues, predicting that heroism "will become a quality of very minor importance, when its possessor cannot break through the iron crust of his own armament and give the world a glimpse of it."[67] Similar concerns greeted the development of camouflage at the end of the nineteenth century. Martin Van Creveld argues that the introduction of more deadly armaments, symbolized by Maxim's rapid-fire machine gun invented in 1884, altered the traditional emphasis on highly visible and distinguishable uniforms during battle. Shifting from traditional battlefield dress to muted colors that blended with the landscape ("Drabness quite suddenly became the order of the day") enabled greater anonymity for individuals and groups.[68] Even more subtle uses of technology can be used to produce anonymity. At sea, "changing the con-

---

63 Andrew Silke, "Deindividuation, Anonymity, and Violence: Findings from Northern Ireland," *Journal of Social Psychology* 143, no. 4 (August 1, 2003): 493–99.

64 "Urban society, in contrast, encourages anonymity and independence; it offers material abundance and individual privacy, but at the price of unraveling knots in the total social fabric." George Klaus Levinger and Harold L. Raush, *Close Relationships: Perspectives on the Meaning of Intimacy* (Amherst, MA: University of Massachusetts Press, 1977), 11.

65 J. L. Anderson, "Piracy and World History: An Economic Perspective on Maritime Predation," *Journal of World History* 6, no. 2 (1995): 178–79.

66 David A. Mindell, *Iron Coffin: War, Technology, and Experience Aboard the USS Monitor* (Baltimore, MD: Johns Hopkins University Press, 2012), 5.

67 Mindell, *Iron Coffin*, 8.

68 Martin Van Creveld, *Technology and War: From 2000 B.C. to the Present* (New York: Simon & Schuster, 2010), 171–72.

figuration of lights aboard a warship" in specific ways can result in a ship that "appears to be something other than it really is."[69]

More than a century later, the development of stealth aircraft technology illustrates the link to anonymity and the back-and-forth evolution of technology. Stealth was a conscious military innovation in reaction to a previous technological change (radar) that had reduced the anonymity of pilots and their aircraft. Stealth restored anonymity by rendering aircraft invisible to even state-of-the-art technologies of detection.[70] Most recently, unmanned aerial vehicles, or drones, have raised both issues. On the one hand, drones allow an unprecedented capacity to see targets of surveillance, revealing landscapes and behavior that would otherwise be undetected.[71] On the other hand, using drones for military strikes allows anonymized killing. Much of the debate about the legality and ethics of drone-based military strikes is a result of the physical separation of the operator from the battlefield and a sense that drone strikes appear to come from "nowhere."[72]

As drones and stealth demonstrate, innovations are often part of a complex interplay over time. In the case of unmanned platforms, a single innovation can simultaneously render targets of surveillance more visible and operators more anonymous. Yet an aggregate effect of this process can be a steady disjuncture between what is visible to powerful governments compared to non-state actors. Even innovations that restore visibility are only possessed by powerful governments and so create a privileged view. Stealth demonstrates this: the innovation that reduced anonymity (radar) was initially available only to states, and the innovation that restored anonymity (stealth) was exclusively available to states. This is one reason I distinguish in chapter 2 between two kinds of exposure. Rather than a dichotomy of "exposed" or "concealed," I assume that secret external military involvement is often *partially visible* due to the privileged insights that technology provides major powers. Unique decryption and signals interception technologies, for example, allowed American leaders to detect Soviet involvement in the Korean War that was otherwise not visible.

---

69 Matthew G. Morris, "Hiding amongst a Crowd and the Illegality of Deceptive Lighting," *Naval Law Review* 54 (2007): 236.

70 Benjamin S. Lambeth, "The Technology Revolution in Air Warfare," *Survival* 39, no. 1 (March 1, 1997): 65–83.

71 Nasser Hussain, "The Sound of Terror: Phenomenology of a Drone Strike," text, *Boston Review*, October 16, 2013, http://bostonreview.net/world/hussain-drone-phenomenology.

72 Hugh Gusterson, *Drone: Remote Control Warfare* (Cambridge, MA: MIT Press, 2016); Alaa Hijazi et al., "Psychological Dimensions of Drone Warfare," *Current Psychology*, September 14, 2017, 1–12.

Several technological innovations were especially significant in opening up new ways for major powers to intervene covertly after World War I. I focus on two: airpower and submarines. Both innovations made it more difficult to identify the national origin of military personnel participating in war-related activities.

AIRPOWER

The earliest attempts to apply aviation technology to military purposes were military ballooning and the German Zeppelin.[73] Italian bombing in Libya in 1911 and 1912 marked the first use of airplanes for combat missions and, specifically, bombing of ground targets.[74] At the start of World War I, the major European powers "had not yet embraced aviation as an essential part of their armed forces," but each possessed rudimentary air armies.[75] During World War I, aircraft primarily served a surveillance role. The addition of cameras to surveillance aircraft allowed the British, for example, to photograph German trenches and enable more effective artillery and ground attack methods.[76] As the war progressed, bombing and fighter roles were added. As one historian of airpower notes, the contrast between 1914 and the end of the war was striking because "by 1918, almost every element of modern airpower would be demonstrated or experimented with."[77] Even this broad experimentation did not change the fact that "the fighter aeroplane was only a subsidiary element to what was anyway a subsidiary facet of the war."[78]

Experimentation in the Great War did give rise to significant debate about how to use airpower in the interwar period. Analysts like Giulio Douhet developed doctrines that often focused on using aircraft for bombing and "causing general social collapse through the precision bombing of key industrial nodes."[79] It also prompted further technological innovation

---

73 Walter J. Boyne, *The Influence of Air Power Upon History* (Philadelphia, PA: Casemate Publishers, 2005), 22–23.

74 Robin D. S. Higham, *One Hundred Years of Air Power and Aviation* (College Station, TX: Texas A&M University Press, 2003).

75 Boyne, *The Influence of Air Power Upon History*, 45.

76 Boyne, *The Influence of Air Power Upon History*, 67–68.

77 Boyne, *The Influence of Air Power Upon History*, 62.

78 Trevor Wilson and Robin Prior, "Conflict, Technology, and the Impact of Industrialization: The Great War 1914–18," *Journal of Strategic Studies* 24, no. 3 (September 1, 2001): 144.

79 Robert Pape, *Bombing to Win: Air Power and Coercion in War* (Ithaca, NY: Cornell University Press, 1996), 62.

that would restore anonymity to the targets of surveillance and bombing. Camouflage and decoys used during World War II, for example, allowed ground units to mislead or avoid detection by bombing and surveillance aircraft. As Isla Forsyth notes, "the aeroplane offered new aerial visualizations and targeting of the battlespace" but, at the same time, "camouflage offered a means from the earth through which to undermine and subvert the aerial view."[80]

Doctrinal debates aside, a fundamental feature of aerial missions in war was anonymity. A pilot of aircraft engaging in surveillance, bombing, or fighter missions "was a shrouded, hidden entity whose only features were those you could see in the control of the airplane."[81] One theme in contemporary reactions to the advent of airpower was this concern: as Sherry notes, "the chief danger of the dreadnought or the machine gun or the airplane was that they might make men superfluous or anonymous in war."[82] The result was that, from the point of view of an external observer, "the pilot was so merged with machinery that his human/nonhuman status was blurred."[83] The central point for covert intervention is less about the merging of machine and man. Instead, airpower allowed influence on the battlefield from a distance. The nationality of the crew in a bomber's cockpit was inherently difficult to observe, as Nazi Germany and others would show in the Spanish Civil War (chapter 4). This technological innovation therefore created new opportunities for outside powers to influence combat.

SUBMARINES

The submarine was another technological innovation that matured during World War I and influenced the feasibility of covert military intervention in the years after. Undersea naval vessels equipped with torpedoes capable of sinking other ships were in development as early as the 1850s.[84] In the decade preceding World War I, "the development of the submarine was being

80 Isla Forsyth, "Designs on the Desert: Camouflage, Deception and the Militarization of Space," *Cultural Geographies* 21, no. 2 (April 1, 2014): 261.

81 Sina Najafi and Peter Galison, "The Ontology of the Enemy: An Interview with Peter Galison," *Cabinet Magazine*, 12 (Fall/Winter 2003): 63.

82 Michael S. Sherry, *The Rise of American Air Power: The Creation of Armageddon* (New Haven, CT: Yale University Press, 1987), 6.

83 Najafi and Galison, "The Ontology of the Enemy: An Interview with Peter Galison," 64.

84 Michael Gunton, *Submarines at War: A History of Undersea Warfare from the American Revolution to the Cold War* (New York: Basic Books, 2005), 12.

carried out with enthusiasm by all the major naval powers."[85] Thus, in contrast with airpower's experimentation during World War I, "by the outbreak of World War I, the submarine had already assumed a form which was to change little over the next thirty years."[86]

Germany's U-boat, first developed in 1905, would play a central role in the war. By 1915, the British had armed merchant ships to defend against U-boat attacks, while the German government adopted an expansive view of the war zone at sea in a warning to British allies.[87] The maturation of submarine technology during the early years of the war led to increasing temptations to adopt unrestricted usage of submarines, a view that became "more solid and acceptable, despite international agreements that were signed to the contrary."[88] By 1916, Germany embraced unrestricted warfare, and its sinking of the *Lusitania* would play a role in the entry of the United States into the war. As with other technological innovations, adaptations by other governments could reduce or eliminate the anonymity of the submarine. The hydrophone, invented in the early 1900s, offered the potential for sophisticated navies to detect submarines. During World War I, early versions of sonar—the ASDIC system used by American and British convoys to cross the Atlantic—improved the detection capacity of navies targeted by submarines. The interwar period featured continued refinement of underwater acoustical detection in Germany, the United Kingdom, and the United States.[89]

The anonymous nature of submarine attacks, along with their deployment against "defenseless" civilian ships like the *Lusitania*, fed a widely shared view that something about submarine warfare was different. A common association was that the submarine attack was cowardly, or somehow at odds with traditional notions of proper and honorable battle. As one author notes, a "typical opinion was that the submarine was at best a nuisance and a cowardly weapon employed only by weak naval powers."[90] Popular culture texts in Britain tended to describe German submarines as staying out of sight ("skulked about and hid beneath the waves in cowardly fash-

---

85 Gunton, *Submarines at War*, 15.

86 Van Creveld, *Technology and War*, 208.

87 Nachman Ben-Yehuda, *Atrocity, Deviance, and Submarine Warfare: Norms and Practices During the World Wars* (Ann Arbor: University of Michigan Press, 2013), 109, 165.

88 Ben-Yehuda, *Atrocity, Deviance, and Submarine Warfare*, 55.

89 Willem D. Hackmann, "German Navy Sonar Development During the Two World Wars and Interwar Years," *Journal of the Acoustical Society of America* 141, no. 5 (2017): 3706.

90 Robert P. Haffa and James H. Patton, "Analogues of Stealth: Submarines and Aircraft," *Comparative Strategy* 10, no. 3 (July 1, 1991): 257–71.

ion") and viewed the "half-submerged … peculiar shape" as reminiscent of an "antediluvian animal."[91] Though noting the self-serving nature of this view for British victims of German attacks, a summary of contemporary perceptions written in 1937 noted that "the submarine has been subjected to all kinds of abuse. It has been denounced on numberless occasions as a cruel, cowardly, inhumane weapon."[92] To be clear, anonymity was not the only reason for this view, but it played an important part.

Even as the visibility of submarine activity among the most powerful navies changed, the sponsor of undersea naval attacks continued to be almost impossible to establish definitively for outside observers. This produced a yawning gap between the visibility of submarine activity to major naval powers and to other states and non-state actors. By the mid-1930s, a European power like Italy could conduct covert submarine operations during the Spanish Civil War (chapter 4) confident that, at worst, its culpability for submarine attacks could be established only by major naval powers with sufficient submarine detection and intelligence capabilities. As I argue, this had a profound impact on Italy's involvement in the civil war at sea.

Experimentation: The Emergence of Covert Intervention

So far, this chapter has argued that, in the interwar years, World War I served as a powerful demonstration of the costliness of large-scale escalation and the difficulty leaders could have in avoiding it. The Great War also unleashed deep political and technological changes that simultaneously exacerbated the costliness of war and the difficulty of controlling it, as well as providing new weapons systems that could allow concealed, unacknowledged war participation. This final section reviews events during the interwar period that suggest that leaders understood the need for new tools to limit war and experimented with new ways of using force. Part of that experimentation included covert involvement in local conflicts.

The destruction in the Great War, as Mueller notes, produced "a revulsion against wars" and long-term "desire to prevent similar wars from taking

91 Michael L. Hadley, *Count Not the Dead: The Popular Image of the German Submarine* (Buffalo, NY: McGill-Queen's Press, 1995), 42; the author quotes a novel from 1917 about a German submarine by Charles Gibson.
92 Walton L. Robinson, "The Submarine in the Next War," *Scientific American* 157, no. 1 (1937): 22.

place."[93] That desire was channeled in different ways. Some sought to re-form the very system itself. As symbolized by the Kellogg-Briand pact to ban aggressive war, a strand of pacifism during the 1920s and 1930s led to attempts to overthrow the system of power politics itself.[94] Another re-sponse was to assess how war could be limited. World War I challenged leaders and non-governmental reformers to consider "whether [war] could be contained in order to avoid another great war across the Continent."[95] Influential voices like Liddell Hart criticized pacifism and theorized limited war as a method of maintaining strategic purpose and political control in the face of mass mobilization and possible total war.[96]

Experimentation in how military force was used—in particular, reject-ing declared war in favor of synonyms for using force—was one result of this impulse to avoid another large-scale war. "Hardly was the ink dry on the League [of Nations] Covenant," one historian of international law notes, "when states began to circumvent its restrictions by characterizing their armed actions otherwise than as wars."[97] The very effort to regulate war prompted innovations to circumvent those regulations, which "increase[d] the significance of the distinction between wars and the various measures short of war."[98] Wars in the 1930s, such as the undeclared Sino-Japanese War, showcased how leaders were pursuing their geopolitical goals with force while avoiding declared, overt military clashes. This experimentation weakened multilateral institutions like the League of Nations; it also served as the seedbed for later covert, "volunteer," and undeclared wars in the Cold War era. As David Foglesong insightfully summarizes, "the era of total war and unprecedented public involvement in foreign relations brought not only the withering of the old aristocratic statecraft but also the seed-time for modern methods of covert action."[99] To be clear, experimentation

93 John Mueller, "The Essential Irrelevance of Nuclear Weapons: Stability in the Postwar World," *International Security* 13, no. 2 (1988): 75.

94 Oona A. Hathaway and Scott J. Shapiro, *The Internationalists: How a Radical Plan to Outlaw War Remade the World* (New York: Simon & Schuster, 2017).

95 Reynolds, *The Long Shadow*, 204.

96 Robert H. Larson, "B. H. Liddell Hart: Apostle of Limited War," *Military Affairs* 44, no. 2 (1980): 70–74.

97 Stephen C. Neff, *War and the Law of Nations: A General History* (Cambridge, UK: Cambridge University Press, 2005), 279.

98 Neff, *War and the Law of Nations*, 279.

99 David S. Foglesong, *America's Secret War Against Bolshevism: U.S. Intervention in the Russian Civil War, 1917–1920* (Chapel Hill: University of North Carolina Press, 2001), 3.

along these lines was not solely driven by escalation fears and lessons from the Great War, but they played an important role.[100]

The contrast between World War I and these new forms of warfare was striking. In the Great War, "the conventional provisions in regard to the declaration of war were observed" so faithfully that states' formal consecration of war could be traced to a specific minute on a specific day.[101] This reflected a norm of overt, declared war formed in the crucible of monarchical rule and debates about just war.[102] However, "new concepts, such as aggression, insurrection, defense, support, sanctions" were blurring the old distinctions between peace and war, and between neutrality and belligerence. In 1931, Japan invaded and occupied Chinese Manchuria. The conflict was referred to with a variety of increasingly creative synonyms—an "attack," "severe hostilities," an act of "aggression," a "police action" to restore order—but Japan carefully avoided invoking "war against the state of China itself."[103] A similar tactic was used by Mussolini's Italy in its invasion of Ethiopia in 1935. Italy justified the war on grounds of self-defense and the conflict featured "no declaration of war by either side" and thus "lacked the traditional trappings of a war."[104] Writing presciently in 1940, Quincy Wright accurately predicted that "it seems probable that these new concepts are here to stay."[105] "The result," Stephen Neff summarizes, "was a sharp decrease in wars during this period—but in the perverse, and extremely restricted, sense that armed conflicts largely ceased to be classified as wars."[106]

100 Avoiding harsh treatment at the League of Nations or circumventing neutrality laws also provided reasons to experiment with undeclared wars and covert involvement. While escalation concerns and avoiding abrogation of international law appear to be separate considerations, in practice they were reinforcing. Declaring wars triggered domestic and international legal rules about neutrality which both damaged an aggressor's military prospects and could generate wider participation in a war, as the British entry into World War I in reaction to German violations of Belgian neutrality illustrated.

101 George Grafton Wilson, "War Declared and the Use of Force," *Proceedings of the American Society of International Law at Its Annual Meeting* 32 (1938): 113–14.

102 Eric Grynaviski, "The Bloodstained Spear: Public Reason and Declarations of War," *International Theory* 5, no. 02 (2013): 238–72. See examples before World War I when states occasionally engaged in undeclared hostilities (239–41).

103 Neff, *War and the Law of Nations*, 305.

104 Neff, *War and the Law of Nations*, 306. Note that the League of Nations ultimately found Italy had created a state of war without a declaration and issued sanctions.

105 Quincy Wright, "The Present Status of Neutrality," *American Journal of International Law* 34, no. 3 (1940): 407.

106 Neff, *War and the Law of Nations*, 286; though Fazal's study of the decline in declarations of war dates the transition as the post–World War II period, her data show a sharp decline

One early example of experimentation using covertness was the quasi-covert American intervention in the Russian Civil War. In the two years after the end of World War I, President Woodrow Wilson authorized covert support to anti-Bolshevik factions inside the Soviet Union. This aid included financial assistance, war supplies, and sabotage operations.[107] Moreover, a publicly acknowledged military expedition to Siberia, which was putatively unrelated to the civil war, covertly supported anti-Bolshevik forces.[108] Foglesong describes how the Soviet government, foreshadowing the mutual visibility of covert activity in later decades, tracked American activities through sources like "captured agents of U.S. intelligence services" and was therefore aware that, although it did not acknowledge official participation, the United States provided "arms and other military supplies" to anti-Bolshevik factions.[109] Because of his highly visible advocacy of self-determination, Wilson therefore "pursued methods of assisting anti-Bolshevik forces that evaded public scrutiny and avoided the need for congressional appropriations.... [P]reserving public faith in the essential idealism of Wilsonian foreign policy required a high level of secrecy."[110]

Japan's occupation of China in the late 1930s featured unpublicized military clashes. Japan engaged in periodic military clashes with Soviet forces. Border incidents between Soviet and Japanese forces in places like Mongolia and Manchuria were visible but served as additional examples of the new trend in undeclared "quasi-war."[111] Yet Stalin also secretly provided China with aircraft and pilots, labeled the Soviet Air Force Volunteers, under the auspices of "Operation Zet." Moscow provided five air wings of planes and pilots in mid-1938 to help avoid Japanese expansion but was also "reluctant ... to risk becoming involved in hostilities with Japan."[112] Interestingly, a similar American group of "volunteer" airmen was sent to assist China against Japan in early 1941, before US entry into the war. The "American Volunteer Group" was a clandestinely deployed expeditionary unit

---

following World War I that is only punctuated by the declarations issued during World War II. See Tanisha M. Fazal, "Why States No Longer Declare War," *Security Studies* 21, no. 4 (2012): 564.

107 Foglesong, *America's Secret War Against Bolshevism*.

108 Foglesong, *America's Secret War Against Bolshevism*, chap. 7.

109 Foglesong, *America's Secret War Against Bolshevism*, 6.

110 Foglesong, *America's Secret War Against Bolshevism*, 2, 5.

111 Clark W. Tinch, "Quasi-War between Japan and the USSR, 1937–1939," *World Politics* 3, no. 02 (1951): 174–99. This article, written during the Korean War, is explicitly framed as an exercise in comparing behavior in Korea to the Japanese-Soviet experience in the late 1930s.

112 Bradford A. Lee, *Britain and the Sino-Japanese War, 1937–1939: A Study in the Dilemmas of British Decline* (Stanford, CA: Stanford University Press, 1973), 137–38.

under the command of Claire Chennault and was approved by President Franklin Roosevelt as a method for countering Japan's imperial expansion in East Asia without a declaration of war.[113] As one historian of the US air strategy wrote, the "origins of clandestine air warfare" are traceable, not just to the Cold War, but to the earlier "clandestine military attacks on Japan" prior to the US joining World War II.[114]

Such experimentation—shifting away from declared war; adopting the fig leaf of unorganized "volunteer" involvement; using secrecy to hide clashes and operations—illustrates the fusion of interest in new ways of using military force and escalation control in the interwar period. It is evidence that covertness as a technique of external military intervention was, in many ways, an evolutionary response to a new purpose (escalation control) relevant to intervention.[115] This setting framed the decisions of major European powers when civil war broke out in Spain in 1936. As I describe in the next chapter, fear that this civil war could spiral into a large-scale European or world war was widely shared. In response to the most acute escalation problems, Soviet, German, and Italian governments covertly provided military aid to different sides in the civil conflict. When nuclear weapons and the Cold War rivalry challenged escalation control again, these early interwar experiments would prove useful reference points for new attempts at limited war.

Conclusion

This chapter describes the historical context of the emergence of covertness as an escalation-control technique. Although secrecy in war is as old as war itself, I argue that the specific use of secrecy to produce ignorance and ambiguity about a sponsor's participation in war, and its application to the problem of limiting war, is a distinctly modern phenomenon. Moreover, while this chapter focuses on World War I as the critical juncture, other conflicts also shaped views of the nature of escalation and limited war. For example, the process of escalation in World War II supplied its own lessons about the threat of expansive and aggressive bids for hegemony and the

---

113 Michael Schaller, "American Air Strategy in China, 1939–1941: The Origins of Clandestine Air Warfare," *American Quarterly* 28, no. 1 (1976): 3–19; Guangqiu Xu, "The Issue of US Air Support for China during the Second World War, 1942–45," *Journal of Contemporary History* 36, no. 3 (July 1, 2001): 459–84.

114 Schaller, "American Air Strategy in China, 1939–1941," 4.

115 Finnemore, *The Purpose of Intervention.*

risks of buck-passing and appeasement in confronting such bids.[116] This combined with the advent of atomic weaponry to focus significant attention on deterrence dynamics in postwar scholarship.[117] The combined lessons of both world wars was that large-scale escalation could result from multiple pathways and that it was likely to be ruinous. Controlling escalation and fostering limited war was therefore a consistent theme in research and government deliberations in the wake of both world wars.[118]

One theme of this chapter is the iterated, evolutionary nature of limited war and techniques to achieve it. This lays the foundation for evidence presented in the next four chapters about how lessons from previous conflicts affected efforts to limit war through covertness and collusion. In each war, I provide evidence that previous conflicts helped shape the approach to escalation control and, specifically, the adoption and interpretation of covert meddling by outside powers. This evolutionary theme is extended in chapter 8, when I describe connections between Cold War covert conflict and the Iranian covert aid to militias in US-occupied Iraq. Thus, the book provides connective tissue that stretches from World War I to the modern day and suggests the consistent role of escalation considerations in shaping the choices major powers make when deciding whether to operate on the backstage or frontstage.

116 See the discussion of the contrasting legacies of World War I (i.e., spiral model) and World War II (i.e., deterrence model) in Lieber, "The New History of World War I and What It Means for International Relations Theory."

117 See, for example, the influence of Munich on deterrence and credibility in the Vietnam War. Yuen Foong Khong, *Analogies at War: Korea, Munich, Dien Bien Phu, and the Vietnam Decisions of 1965* (Princeton, NJ: Princeton University Press, 1992).

118 Michael W. Cannon, "The Development of the American Theory of Limited War, 1945–63," *Armed Forces & Society* 19, no. 1 (October 1, 1992): 71–104; Christopher M. Gacek, *The Logic of Force: The Dilemma of Limited War in American Foreign Policy* (New York: Columbia University Press, 1994).

4

The Spanish Civil War
(1936-1939)

The peace in Europe following World War I ended in Spain. The Spanish Civil War, fought from 1936 to 1939, featured a clash of ideologies in fascism and communism that gave it global relevance. The war for control of the Spanish state was waged by the incumbent Popular Front government (referred to as the Republicans) and a coalition of rebelling groups led by Spanish military officers (referred to as the Nationalists). Within two months of a coup led by Francisco Franco, three major powers—Italy, Germany, and the Soviet Union—had begun covertly sending military hardware and personnel to one of the two sides. This chapter analyzes these external interventions and how the desire to control escalation drove leaders to conceal and avoid acknowledging foreign involvement.

The Spanish Civil War was historically significant. On the military plane, it hosted the first sustained, symmetric combat since World War I and became a venue for experimentation and innovation in modern warfare. The war also hosted an unprecedented level of combat participation by genuine foreign volunteers, most famously in the International Brigades, setting the stage for future conflicts and the bedeviling problem of foreign volunteer participation.[1] Finally, the Spanish Civil War represented the most serious

---

1 On critical innovations in military technology and tactics in the Spanish Civil War, see Raymond L. Proctor, *Hitler's Luftwaffe in the Spanish Civil War* (Westport, CT: Greenwood

challenge to European peace since World War I. It was a microcosm of the ideological clash between communism, fascism, and liberal democracy, and its outcome shaped the diplomatic alignments and ambitions of the states that would start World War II a few years later.[2]

Analyzing this conflict is valuable for theoretical and historical purposes. The presence of multiple major power interventions, along with variation within one of those interventions (i.e., Italy), provide opportunities to evaluate a broad set of observable implications. Moreover, the conflict features particular interveners, such as Hitler's Germany, that are unlikely cases for escalation caution and attentiveness to domestic political constraints. Evidence of a limited-war logic in how states like Germany used covertness and collusion would be especially valuable. Table 4.1 lists the intervention cases I focus on in the chapter. Each of the covert interventions also raised the possibility of detection and the question of exposure or collusion. Table 4.2 provides an overview of the instances of detection and the related outcomes.

Beyond my core findings, the chapter describes several additional features of the conflict that are worth noting. First, an ad hoc international institution enabled adversaries to successfully collude and control escalation despite being inexperienced in limited war and covert activity. The intervening states and two bystanders (the UK and France) formed an ad hoc international organization to monitor intervention. The Non-Intervention Committee (NIC), founded in August 1936 in response to the fighting in Spain, was explicitly designed to avoid public diplomatic crises and smooth out disputes about foreign intervention. It allowed the airing of intelligence-based claims about intervention behind closed doors and, more fundamentally, continuous diplomatic contact among the key powers that could drive escalation. This showcases a unique role for such institutions and illustrates

---

Press, 1983), 95; Robert H. Whealey, *Hitler and Spain* (Lexington: University Press of Kentucky, 1989), 105–8; Stanley G. Payne, *Franco and Hitler: Spain, Germany, and World War II* (New Haven, CT: Yale University Press, 2008), 35; Hugh Thomas, *The Spanish Civil War*, revised updated edition (New York: Modern Library, 2001), 910–11; recent analysis of volunteers in war and their ambiguities include Thomas Hegghammer, "The Rise of Muslim Foreign Fighters: Islam and the Globalization of Jihad," *International Security* 35, no. 3 (December 1, 2010): 53–94; Nir Arielli and Bruce Collins, *Transnational Soldiers: Foreign Military Enlistment in the Modern Era* (New York: Palgrave Macmillan, 2012).

2 On the importance of the Spanish Civil War to World War II alignments and the timing of the war, see Payne, *Franco and Hitler*, 25, 42, and chap. 3 generally; John F. Coverdale, *Italian Intervention in the Spanish Civil War* (Princeton, NJ: Princeton University Press, 1975), 405; Whealey, *Hitler and Spain*.

TABLE 4.1. Intervention Cases in the Spanish Civil War

	Dates	Location	Timing	Form	Details	Theory support
Germany	1936–1939	Local (Spain)	Subsequent intervener	Covert	Concealed, unacknowledged aircraft with pilots	Strong
Soviet Union	1936–1938	Local (Spain)	Subsequent intervener	Covert	Concealed, unacknowledged artillery and operators, tanks and tank crews, aircraft with pilots	Strong but over-determined
Italy	1936–1939	Local (Spain)	First mover	Covert (open secret)	"Volunteer" ground, air combat role	Mixed
		Peripheral (Mediter-ranean Sea)	First mover	Covert	Concealed, unacknowledged submarines and crews	Strong

TABLE 4.2. Detector Behavior in the Spanish Civil War

	Detection	Third-party exposure	Expectation	Outcome	Theory support
Covert Germany (Spain)	Yes: UK, France	Low	Collusion	Collusion	Strong
Covert Italy (Spain)	Yes: UK, France	High	Exposure	Collusion	Weak
Covert Italy (naval)	Yes: UK, France	Low	Collusion	Collusion	Strong
Covert Soviet (Spain)	Yes: Germany, Italy	Low	Collusion	Collusion	Strong

one way inexperienced adversaries can limit war through covertness and collusion. Second, the conflict features an early and interesting example of an "open secret" intervention in Italy's ground role in Spain. This was facilitated by a diplomatic device that avoided acknowledgment: the language of "volunteers." The denied but observable presence that volunteers allowed was useful in limiting the war. As Smoke concludes, "The fact that policy-makers could observe others calculating their measures to control escalation encouraged them to do so as well, and reduced pressure for preemption."[3] As later chapters demonstrate, this set an important precedent for later conflicts.

The chapter is structured as follows. The first section provides an overview of the conflict and describes escalation-related features that influenced the three external interventions. I then analyze the German, Soviet, and Italian interventions in turn. Note that the fourth section on Italy's involvement compares and contrasts Rome's role at sea with its more visible ground intervention. A final section focuses on collusion, describing how an international forum (the NIC) and the diplomatic device of "volunteerism" allowed Britain, France, and the interveners to limit knowledge and avoid acknowledgment of covert involvement.[4]

Overview and Escalation Context

The war began with a military coup in July 1936 and concluded with Nationalist and Italian forces marching into Barcelona in March 1939. The coup cleaved Spanish territory and military in two. Officers participating in the coup secured the support of troops below them, as with General Franco's Army of Africa in Spanish Morocco.[5] Others did not defect, leaving the Republican government with nearly half the men under arms. It also retained the loyalty of much of the navy and air force. The loyalty of Spanish cities broke in different directions as well, with Nationalists controlling traditionally conservative cities and those garrisoned by coup-supportive generals while the Republican government controlled other areas including Madrid and Barcelona. Even after Nationalist victories in the north, "the

---

3 Richard Smoke, *War: Controlling Escalation* (Cambridge, MA: Harvard University Press, 1977), 70.

4 To assess covertness and collusion in the Spanish Civil War, I draw on a variety of sources. In addition to secondary sources, I draw most on primary document collections from Germany and the United Kingdom. The German records were seized during World War II and provide a rare opportunity to scrutinize the covert war involvement of a closed autocracy with considerable detail. The British records do double duty: they speak to British debates and perceptions as well as to the proceedings of the Non-Intervention Committee which was administered in London. I also take advantage of recent research drawing on materials available since the end of the Cold War on the Soviet side. The quality of evidence is weakest for the case of Italy. The best material available is from secondary histories of Italy's foreign policy during the interwar period, especially one book-length study (Coverdale) of Italy's intervention in Spain.

5 Well over half of Spain's officers joined the Nationalist cause, including all those with experience in the combat-tested Army of Africa. Thomas, *The Spanish Civil War*, 2001, 315–16.

stability of both Spains seemed such as would preserve a stalemate."[6] The war gradually tipped in favor of the Nationalists. Early victories allowed the Nationalists to capture southern cities like Badajoz and cut off military supplies to the Republicans from Portugal. After failing to take Madrid by 1936, the Nationalists shifted attention and led a successful offensive in the far north in 1937. After winning control of cities like Bilbao, the Nationalists renewed their offensive in the center of the country in 1938 and won control of Barcelona and the rest of Catalonia in February 1939.

Outsider military supplies and personnel played an important role in the war as "neither side in this unfolding conflict felt equipped to fight it successfully."[7] The rebelling Nationalist forces were supported via military supplies and combat participation from the Italian and German governments. The Republicans received aid primarily from multinational brigades of genuine foreign volunteers as well as weapons and combat participation from the Soviet Union. One unique feature of the Spanish Civil War was the creation of an ad hoc international organization, the Non-Intervention Committee, specifically designed to limit the war by prohibiting foreign involvement. This created opportunities for direct and repeated diplomatic interaction. As I argue below, a kind of explicit collusion about the fiction of non-intervention was facilitated by this institutional setting. The NIC was thus a symbolic center of diplomatic activity. Based in London and staffed by the British Foreign Office, twenty-seven states including all the relevant powers of Europe participated in regular, high-level diplomatic meetings.[8] The NIC was a center of public attention as well; fully one-third of BBC stories about the war between 1936 and 1939 include some discussion of the committee's activities.[9]

Escalation was a central concern during the war. In part this was because of the infusion of transnational ideological stakes which led to "passionate

---

6 Thomas, *The Spanish Civil War*, 2001, 728.

7 On the balance of forces on both sides immediately after the coup, see Thomas, *The Spanish Civil War*, 2001, 315–19. As Frank notes, "in the critical year from October 1936 until October 1937, it was a close match in the fighting ashore and in the battle for logistics" at sea. Willard C. Frank, Jr., "Naval Operations in the Spanish Civil War, 1936–1939," *Naval War College Review* 37, no. 1 (1984): 47.

8 The members were Albania, Austria, Belgium, Bulgaria, Czechoslovakia, Denmark, Estonia, Finland, France, Germany, Greece, Hungary, Irish Free State, Italy, Latvia, Lithuania, Luxemburg, Netherlands, Norway, Poland, Portugal, Romania, the Soviet Union, Sweden, Turkey, the United Kingdom, and Yugoslavia.

9 David Deacon, "A Quietening Effect? The BBC and the Spanish Civil War (1936–1939)," *Media History* 18, no. 2 (2012): 151.

interest" from those who "saw the Spanish war as a microcosm of European discontents."[10] Two specific forms of large-scale conflict escalation were particularly salient to leaders at the time. On land, leaders on all sides worried that clashes among major powers within Spain would give rise to broader hostilities among them. The tense relationship between France and Germany and the centrality of their conflict in World War I gave special significance to any scenarios that would produce French-German militarized encounters. A second kind of large-scale escalation could take place at sea. Military incidents in the Mediterranean were particularly dangerous because of the presence of vessels of other states, specifically the maritime hegemon Great Britain.[11] Naval interdiction or other clashes could produce destruction and death that might unleash hard-to-control political forces. The Royal Navy's extensive presence in the Mediterranean and Atlantic carried with it significant strategic interests. Figure 4.1 identifies the local combatants and conflict zone as well as the most salient peripheral area (i.e., Mediterranean Sea). It also identifies the three external interveners and one non-intervening, but important, major power (i.e., Great Britain).[12] Figure 4.2 highlights the two most salient scenarios for large-scale escalation: expansion into a broader naval war in the Mediterranean or wider direct combat between the outside interveners.

Finally, the specific threats to escalation control I identify in chapter 2—constraints from domestic hawks and miscommunication regarding intentions—were salient and significant in Spain. On the one hand, Germany's Hitler and Moscow's Stalin were personalist dictatorships with little to fear from domestic repercussions.[13] On the other hand, the two states whose involvement would create large-scale escalation, the United Kingdom and France, were parliamentary democracies in which foreign policy, ideology, and the danger of another European war were central topics during the interwar period. As noted in chapter 2 regarding World War I,

10 Thomas, *The Spanish Civil War*, 2001, 593.

11 On the unique dangers of Mediterranean naval incidents, see Coverdale, *Italian Intervention in the Spanish Civil War*, 304.

12 I also discuss France. However, as the final section argues, the British were the key "domino" determining whether France or the United Kingdom would enter. I therefore simplify discussion by largely focusing on London's decision-making.

13 Notably, one recent study cited these regime features to help explain revisionism by leaders like Stalin. I find the reverse: focusing on the covert sphere shows leaders like Hitler and Stalin exercising considerable caution. Jessica L. P. Weeks, *Dictators at War and Peace* (Ithaca, NY: Cornell University Press, 2014).

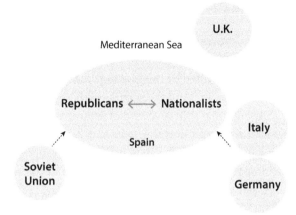

FIGURE 4.1. Structure of Spanish Civil War.

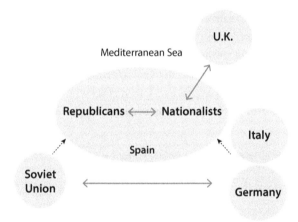

FIGURE 4.2. Key escalation scenarios, Spanish Civil War.

mass media coverage and nationalism were important possible constraints in any scenario in which militarized clashes produced casualties and outrage. Moreover, the Spanish Civil War had many of the same ingredients as the Great War: it was a civil war in Europe, amid social revolution and "extreme exacerbation of nationalism," featuring World War I–era military technology, and rife with potential for unintentional escalation.[14]

14 Stanley G. Payne, *The Spanish Civil War, the Soviet Union, and Communism* (New Haven, CT: Yale University Press, 2004), 313–14.

German Intervention

The centerpiece of Germany's covert combat participation was an expeditionary force of German pilots called the Condor Legion.[15] Air superiority and tactical bombing provided by this Condor Legion had a significant impact on the course of the war and the success of the Nationalists.[16] Overall, Germany's air expeditionary force, together with a similar Italian unit, allowed Nationalists to gain air superiority in mid-1937.[17] Moreover, Condor Legion bombing played a critical role in each of the Nationalist offensives after 1936, including the Basque/Asturias campaign in the north in 1937, the drive east to the Mediterranean ("Aragon Offensive") in 1938, and the final offensive in Catalonia in 1938/1939.[18]

In terms of sequence, Germany's entry into the Spanish war followed Italy's early aid and was in reaction to intelligence that the Soviet Union had initiated an aid program for the Republicans around October 1936. The location of Germany's involvement was carefully restricted to the Spanish mainland. As I describe below, the only exception was a short-lived, highly secret deployment of submarines which was quickly terminated in light of provoking a clash with Britain. Because Germany's involvement followed Italy, the theory suggests severe escalation risks would lead Berlin to prioritize escalation control by confining its role to the backstage.

COVERT AIR SUPPORT: THE CONDOR LEGION

Germany approved creation of a legion of German airmen for secret deployment to Spain at the request of Nationalist rebellion leader General Francisco Franco. Franco's need to outsource an air force was acute: the majority of the Spanish Air Force had stayed loyal to the incumbent gov-

---

15 Proctor describes a unit of separately organized German tank operators ("Drohne group"), but I omit discussion due to the small size of the contingent and the absence of discussion in other works. Proctor, *Hitler's Luftwaffe in the Spanish Civil War*, 60.

16 The German Condor Legion was "one of the decisive elements in the Spanish victory." James S. Corum, "The Luftwaffe and the Coalition Air War in Spain, 1936–1939," *Journal of Strategic Studies* 18, no. 1 (1995): 80.

17 On the turning point in air superiority in favor of the Nationalists, see Thomas, *The Spanish Civil War*, 2001, 694.

18 On the dominance of Condor Legion bombing during the campaigns in the north and northeast ("air power had proved repeatedly to be the deciding factor," on 142), see Proctor, *Hitler's Luftwaffe in the Spanish Civil War*, 119–43.

ernment and evidence of substantial Soviet military aid to the Republican side was mounting. The Condor Legion, managed out of the German Air Ministry by a new and secret Special Staff section ("W"), was to be a full-service, 5,000-person unit including bombing, fighter, reconnaissance, anti-aircraft artillery, and maintenance capabilities.[19] The unit remained under German command but was used in close coordination with Spanish Nationalist military planners.[20] The initial shipment of aircraft, related equipment, and personnel began in early November 1936, and the first combat missions were flown in the battles near Madrid later that month. The Condor Legion remained in Spain until the war concluded in spring of 1939. By the time it was withdrawn, 17,000 German soldiers and pilots had been deployed and participated in most major battles of the war.

German leaders went to great lengths to minimize the visibility of the unit and strongly refuted all public allegations of German personnel in Spain. A range of measures to ensure "strict secrecy on German military activities in Spain" were adopted and created logistical challenges both trivial and serious.[21] Condor Legion personnel were assembled in Germany under false pretenses, transported in civilian clothing, and stowed below deck; upon arrival, they were issued alternative uniforms with Spanish-style insignias.[22] Once in theater, Condor Legion personnel were housed in special trains which moved from battlefront to battlefront, minimizing on-the-ground interaction with Spanish nationals and journalists.[23] German personnel were not permitted to appear within Spain in German uniforms for fear of being recognized.[24] Hitler reduced the standard rotation cycle in and out of theater to reduce the number of personnel involved in the program and thus the risk of security leaks.[25] The German government gave no publicity to the successes or failures of the Legion as such during the war.[26] Avoiding exposure also required concealing bilateral consultations with Germany's partner, Italy. Regular private meetings helped the two Nationalist patrons coordinate on aid, its visibility, and diplomatic strategy at

---

19 Proctor, *Hitler's Luftwaffe in the Spanish Civil War*, 3–4; Thomas, *The Spanish Civil War*, 2001, 344.

20 Whealey, *Hitler and Spain*, 49.

21 Whealey, *Hitler and Spain*, 56.

22 Proctor, *Hitler's Luftwaffe in the Spanish Civil War*, 61, 97–98.

23 Thomas, *The Spanish Civil War*, 2001, 744.

24 Thomas, *The Spanish Civil War*, 2001, 377.

25 Whealey, *Hitler and Spain*, 56.

26 Whealey, *Hitler and Spain*, 56.

the NIC. A key theme was to avoid "open involvement" and steadfastly deny accusations of meddling.[27]

The strategic goals of Germany's intervention remain a point of debate among historians.[28] Most agree that Hitler's goals were some combination of a desire to (1) prevent the rise of an ideological and geostrategic adversary which would likely result if a radicalized Republican government won the war; (2) reap the geostrategic and economic benefits of a new ally should the Nationalists win, especially regarding mining rights; and, (3) accelerate the unraveling of the interwar order without a premature general European war.[29] Thus, in the language of positive goals discussed in chapter 2, Germany likely had a blend of defensive and offensive goals. Regardless of the precise blend of priorities, the next section demonstrates that escalation control and avoidance of a premature continental war was an important source of caution for Berlin.

COVERTNESS AND LIMITING WAR

Hitler and his advisors believed that a geographically bounded war in Spain was important for German interests. Regarding the general benefits of keeping the conflict in Spain bounded, even if simmering, the leading historian of the Spanish Civil War concludes, "Germany and Russia shared a disinclination to risk a general war breaking out over Spain."[30] Regarding German intervention, James Corum's review of primary materials concludes that military brass in Berlin sought a limited war and specifically feared "provoking French intervention on the side of the Spanish Loyalists (Republicans) and thereby starting a general European war—a war the Wehrmacht was not ready to fight in 1937 and 1938."[31] Hitler did plan for a larger European war; yet the mid-1930s was a time of rearmament and grand strategic

---

27 Regarding their combat participation, Thomas notes that Italy and Germany described their personnel "as if they were genuine volunteers—even to each other," in Thomas, *The Spanish Civil War*, 2001, 562; on Italy-Germany secret coordination, see also Frank, Jr., "Naval Operations in the Spanish Civil War, 1936–1939," 34; Proctor, *Hitler's Luftwaffe in the Spanish Civil War*, 36.

28 Alongside geostrategic and ideological rationales for siding with the fascist-supported Nationalist military generals, historians have debated whether the eventual military training and economic benefits accrued by Germany constituted part of the rationale for its original entry into the war. For a critique of this argument, see Payne, *Franco and Hitler*, 35.

29 Payne, *Franco and Hitler*, 23–29.

30 Thomas, *The Spanish Civil War*, 2001, 915.

31 Corum, "The Luftwaffe and the Coalition Air War in Spain, 1936–1939," 70.

preparation. In August and September 1936, Hitler had yet to occupy much-coveted land in Central Europe. None of the alliances with those who would end up as his critical wartime allies—Italy, Japan, and the Soviet Union—existed. He faced substantial gaps in military capabilities especially vis-à-vis Britain's Royal Navy.[32] As a result, "During the first year and a half of the civil war, Hitler subordinated his ambitions for German military action to his prime diplomatic aim of manipulating the other Great Powers because he was not yet ready for a showdown with France."[33]

The importance of escalation control was on display in several specific debates and exchanges. Internal German debates about an Italian proposal to send German infantry units rather than merely pilots, for example, demonstrates as much. In December 1936 and January 1937, the Italians pressed Germany in secret meetings to expand their combat role to improve Nationalist capabilities. Germany declined. Hitler's advisors warned that a more robust use of German troops would "unnecessarily provoke Great Britain and France" and "create needless international tension."[34] The international complications were feared "too severe." Citing the danger of a French response in particular, a German Foreign Ministry memo in January 1937 summarized why additional troops were rejected: "we were not prepared to do this, because we considered that such a step would seriously endanger the larger European situation. Unless we wanted to accept the risk of war, we would have to realize that the time was drawing near when we would have to abandon any further support of Franco."[35] Here the danger of the French response was motivated by concern over domestic hawks within France, supporting one key mechanism in chapter 2.

German leaders perceived important distinctions in whether troops were sent and who sent them. These reflect an early but emergent sense of how salient thresholds regarding the form of intervention shape limited war. Germany's ambassador in London, Joachim von Ribbentrop, assessed the danger of French/British entry and the risk of a European war in July 1937 ("the intensity of the Spanish war would probably increase considerably—a condition which in the long run would involve the possibility of complications of greater magnitude"). Ribbentrop argued the *form* of intervention

---

32 Compared to the British, the German navy believed they "just did not have enough firepower"; see Whealey, *Hitler and Spain*, 111.

33 Whealey, *Hitler and Spain*, 109.

34 Coverdale, *Italian Intervention in the Spanish Civil War*, 163, 173.

35 Memorandum by the Foreign Minister, January 13, 1937, *Documents on German Foreign Policy, 1918–1945*, Series D, Volume III (hereafter DGFP), Document 200.

was critical. France would likely intervene in reaction to organized ground units from Italy and Germany ("large, wholly German and Italian military units" which would "involve the danger of serious complications") but would not respond to more restrained assistance ("arms and air aid to Franco from Italy and from us without the dispatch of larger contingents of volunteers would in my opinion not cause any serious complications").[36] Note the assumption that France could distinguish among these gradations of involvement; this echoes the theme of backstage mutual awareness in chapter 2 and in the Cold War cases I analyze later. It also reflects the difficulty of concealing many of the details of German involvement from major powers with human and other intelligence sources, reducing the utility of covertness for tactical advantages.

Escalation considerations therefore make sense of the Fascist division of labor. German leaders believed the national identity of its external ground forces mattered. As John Coverdale summarizes, key voices in Berlin argued that "France would react far more violently to the presence of Germans than to the presence of Italians in Spain ... Germany could not justify the risks involved in provoking the French to such a degree."[37] This explains why Germany was comfortable with providing covert air support but not ground units. Allowing Italy to send "volunteers" could address the Nationalists' need for supplemental ground forces while avoiding a tit-for-tat process of escalation.

The role of limited war in determining the form of German covert intervention is also illustrated in debates about Germany's possible naval role. As I develop at length in the Italy section below, escalation risks were particularly acute at sea because being at sea rather than on land loosened the geographic bounds of combat. In addition to explaining greater Italian caution in its naval role, these same concerns led Hitler to limit German naval activity to a short-term, highly deniable form. The goal was simple: avoid "provoking Britain into a forceful reaction."[38] Two clandestine submarines were sent to patrol Spanish waters in November 1936 with false flags, painted over markings, and crews were required to surface exclusively at

36 Ambassador in Great Britain to Fuhrer and Chancellor, July 4, 1937, DGFP, Doc. 376.

37 Coverdale, *Italian Intervention in the Spanish Civil War*, 173; Goering advised Hitler that troops "might precipitate difficult international problems." Proctor, *Hitler's Luftwaffe in the Spanish Civil War*, 18.

38 Willard C. Frank, Jr., "Politico-Military Deception at Sea in the Spanish Civil War, 1936–1939," *Intelligence and National Security* 5, no. 3 (1990): 96; Frank also notes (91) the comparative caution by Germany in their use of force at sea vs. on land.

night and sworn to secrecy.[39] Even with these measures, Hitler and his advisors ended their interdiction role a month later. Importantly, the risk of a hard-to-control war escalation sequence that drew in the British was a critical consideration. Naval advisors invoked the problem of a perceived challenge and commitment, preferring "to remove the German Navy from clandestine naval war and its risks" given that revelation of Germany's role would prompt "unwanted complications or commitments." Hitler resisted Mussolini's pleas for continued naval aid, citing the problem of "uncontrolled complications" and a German desire to "avoid the risks of an escalation in intervention."[40] German naval planners saw a key pathway to premature escalation and a European war in a "provoked incident" in Spanish waters.[41]

Germany's restrictions on the use of the Condor Legion also reflected escalation-control concerns. The German High Command issued instructions that no Condor Legion aircraft fly within 50 kilometers of the French border and they were to avoid bombing ships in harbor that might be British.[42] Consistent with the theory, Germany saw a link between the strength of domestic advocates for war in France and the conduct of the air war. Cables from the German ambassador in Paris in March 1938, for example, noted the hawkish, pro-intervention French Left were using bombing behavior attributed to Italy and Germany to justify their position. Such behavior, the ambassador noted, was radicalizing the larger French population and creating conditions favorable to entry; discipline in how German airpower was used was therefore critical.[43]

The problem of hawkish domestic reactions in Britain and France was repeatedly invoked in Berlin's deliberations. The possibility that German intervention would undermine the NIC and unleash nationalist pressure for London or Paris to enter and widen the war was often how this was formulated. A dispatch to Berlin from the London embassy in September 1936 noted the author's "impression that with France and England, the two powers principally interested in the committee, it is not so much a question of taking actual steps immediately as of pacifying the aroused feelings of the Leftist parties in both countries ... I had the feeling that the British

39 Frank, Jr., "Politico-Military Deception at Sea in the Spanish Civil War, 1936–1939," 98.

40 Frank, Jr., "Naval Operations in the Spanish Civil War, 1936–1939," 36.

41 Whealey, *Hitler and Spain*, 111.

42 Thomas, *The Spanish Civil War*, 2001, 781; Proctor, *Hitler's Luftwaffe in the Spanish Civil War*, 207.

43 Ambassador in Spain to the Foreign Ministry, March 23, 1938, DGFP, Doc. 550.

Government hoped to ease the domestic political situation for the French Premier."[44] Two months later, another report on non-intervention diplomacy noted that "the British Government sees in the embargo committee a useful means of avoiding possibilities of conflict and that it is therefore encouraging as dilatory action as possible on the part of the committee. At the same time, the existence of the committee offers the Government a comfortable shield against Parliamentary pressure."[45]

German analysis regarding domestic politics in liberal democracies was strikingly precise and explicitly linked to escalation control. A cable analyzing British domestic politics and Spanish developments in July 1938, for example, notes a fissure between then Prime Minister Neville Chamberlain and the Opposition, led by Anthony Eden and Winston Churchill. Citing a specific speech by Eden, it notes the Opposition sees Spain as "an especially suitable platform from which they not only can cause difficulty for the Government as such, but, in addition, can attack Germany and Italy." Although non-intervention diplomacy was "easing the position of the Government in the House of Commons," this would be possible only if "no further opportunities for attack are offered the Opposition by any new bombing of British ships in Red Spanish harbors and waters."[46]

German analysis specifically worried that domestic political constraints in London and Paris could force the hands of leaders and create unwanted escalation. A November 1936 cable admitted that a French declaration of war was unlikely but replied that "It is another question whether and to what extent the Blum Government, under the pressure of the Second and Third Internationals, recently has been considering the idea of relaxing its non-intervention obligation to a great extent."[47] A December 1936 cable reports on a French ministerial meeting regarding "the landings of German troops—landings which had already taken place and additional landings which were still being planned." The landings at Cadiz were considered "extremely serious and dangerous."[48] The German ambassador in Paris warned his colleagues in late December 1936 that "nervousness prevails in political

---

44 Charge d'Affaires in Great Britain to the Foreign Ministry, September 9, 1936, DGFP, Doc. 79.

45 Charge d'Affaires in Great Britain to the Foreign Ministry, November 27, 1936, DGFP, Doc. 131.

46 Ambassador in Great Britain to the Foreign Ministry, July 14, 1938, DGFP, Doc. 637.

47 Ambassador in France to the Foreign Ministry, November 10, 1936, DGFP, Doc. 116.

48 Ambassador in France to the Foreign Ministry, December 22, 1936, DGFP, Doc. 160.

circles [in Paris] such as probably not existed since the end of the war" and that "the French Government will not be able to resist much longer the pressure that is being exerted on it by all parties."[49] A September 1937 memo similarly describes how, despite the French government's desire to renew a law banning their citizens from volunteering in Spain, the "rejection of such a law [is] probable in view of the sentiment in the country."[50]

Internal documents also show the presence of direct, private messaging between France and Germany about "backstage" behavior. This seems to have helped the two sides clarify their intentions despite having little prior experience in such scenarios. The previously cited cable concludes its analysis of French domestic reactions to the Cadiz landings by noting a back-channel French warning to Germany that "if the landing of troops continued, a general war would be unavoidable."[51] A note several days later updates the situation, relaying a quiet visit to the German embassy by French Foreign Minister Yvon Delbos. Delbos stated the "massing of German troops" in a country with an open border with France makes "many French patriots uneasy" and gives rise to talk of imminent war. France "could not permit the fate of this neighbor country to be decisively influenced, even determined, by another power." The memo writer also notes the domestic political mood in ways that echo the exact terminology used to describe World War I–era mobilization. Although Delbos appeared "calm and decisive" in his tone, there was "downright hysterical nervousness that has been evident among the public here for several days and has started crack-brained rumors circulating regarding the inevitability of a war."[52]

To the extent that historical comparisons played a role, one reference to Napoleonic France provides special insight into German thinking. A memo from a German foreign ministry advisor cited the risks of external involvement in Spain and the risk of a wider, and strategically counterproductive, conflict. Napoleon's involvement in war in Spain during a nineteenth-century Spanish uprising closely paralleled the 1930s scenario. French involvement in that war provoked the British to send troops to the continent, which ultimately helped defeat Napoleon. A German Foreign Ministry advisor,

49 Ambassador in France to the Head of the Extra-European Section of the Political Department, December 28, 1936, DGFP, Doc. 169.

50 Charge d'Affaires in Great Britain to the Foreign Ministry, September 2, 1937, DGFP, Doc. 412.

51 Ambassador in France to the Foreign Ministry, December 22, 1936, DGFP, Doc. 160.

52 Ambassador in France to the Foreign Ministry, December 24, 1936, DGFP, Doc. 164.

noting that a visible German division in Spain "would incur the same odium as the French had gathered in Spain in 1808," cited Napoleon to suggest the dangers of a visible German role and a wider European war with British participation.[53]

Soviet Intervention

The Soviet intervention resembled Germany's in many ways. In terms of sequence, the Soviet actions followed early Italian assistance to the Nationalists and so was subsequent to another major power's entry. The location of Soviet intervention was consciously limited to the main battlefronts within Spain. Because Moscow's entry followed Italy's and clearly created the conditions for a clash with another major power's forces, the theory suggests significant escalation risks should elevate the need to control the escalation process via secrecy and non-acknowledgment. Even before Stalin committed Soviet personnel and equipment to Spain, the Soviet Union was involved through a number of channels.[54] The Moscow-directed Communist International (Comintern) provided one avenue for non-lethal aid to the Republican side. It also allowed recruitment of left-leaning foreign volunteers to serve in "International Brigades." Thus, prior to any organized Soviet role, there were Russian and East European communists present in Spain. However, signs of Italian aid and the Nationalists' accumulating victories in summer 1936 led Stalin and the Soviet Politburo to consider deeper involvement. Stalin ultimately embraced an active military role with a first wave of Soviet tanks, aircraft, and operating crews secretly arriving in October. By the end of the war, more than 3,000 military personnel would serve in the war transported to and from the Soviet Union in sixty elaborately concealed long-haul shipments.[55]

COVERT INVOLVEMENT: OPERATION X

The program to provide modern Soviet military equipment and personnel to the Spanish Republicans was debated and approved in mid-September 1936. After two weeks of consideration, Stalin and the Politburo approved "Operation X," a plan to clandestinely provide military armaments, most importantly the newest models of Soviet aircraft, tanks, and the crews to

---

53 Thomas, *The Spanish Civil War*, 2001, 552.

54 Payne, *The Spanish Civil War, the Soviet Union, and Communism*, 146.

55 Payne, *The Spanish Civil War, the Soviet Union, and Communism*, 153.

handle them.[56] The program was run out of "Section X," a special secret subgroup within the NKVD, the Soviet Union's intelligence service.[57] Like Germany, Soviet personnel largely participated in air missions. Though its impact was temporary, Soviet pilots in fighter and bomber groups flying in Spain, along with other Soviet equipment, changed the course of the war in the fall of 1936 through early 1937.[58] Soviet forces specifically helped blunt a Nationalist offensive targeting Madrid and similarly helped win the battle for Guadalajara (March 1937) for the Republicans.[59] One difference with Germany was tanks. Soviet tanks and tank crews provided a boost in combat effectiveness for both of these campaigns. After the Nationalists and their patrons adapted to Soviet help, Stalin began scaling back Moscow's role. This decision was influenced by long supply lines from Russian ports and the problem of covert Italian naval interdiction and the depletion of the Republic's finances.[60] Soviet aid was also phased out as Spanish pilots trained in the Soviet Union came on line in May 1937.[61] Although not decisively winning the war, Soviet covert aid influenced some important early victories and postponed the defeat of the Republicans.[62]

The equipment and personnel provided under Operation X were "carried out under the highest level of secrecy."[63] Stalin insisted the transport and in-country visibility of Soviet military officers, airmen, and tank crews be kept extremely limited. Transport involved a number of logistically challenging concealment measures: within the Soviet Union, shipments of military equipment to port was done under false cover; loading equipment at ports was done under the supervision of intelligence officials inside heavily guarded harbors; elaborate disinformation plans for each shipment were developed to help provide false cover while at sea; the ships themselves had altered names, repainted hulls, foreign flags, and forged manifests; and

56 Daniel Kowalsky, *Stalin and the Spanish Civil War*, ACLS Humanities E-Book edition (2008) (New York: Columbia University Press, 2001), 496; Payne, *The Spanish Civil War, the Soviet Union, and Communism*, 141.

57 Kowalsky, *Stalin and the Spanish Civil War*, 459.

58 "Throughout the late fall of 1936 and into early 1937, the balance of air power weighed heavily in the Republic's favor." See Kowalsky, *Stalin and the Spanish Civil War*, 661.

59 Kowalsky, *Stalin and the Spanish Civil War*, 660–61; Payne, *The Spanish Civil War, the Soviet Union, and Communism*, 155.

60 The invasion of China by Japan, closer to the Soviet border, also played an important role in Stalin's thinking. See Kowalsky, *Stalin and the Spanish Civil War*, 521–22, 783–84; Payne, *The Spanish Civil War, the Soviet Union, and Communism*, 240–41, 266.

61 Thomas, *The Spanish Civil War*, 2001, 658.

62 Payne, *The Spanish Civil War, the Soviet Union, and Communism*, 172.

63 Kowalsky, *Stalin and the Spanish Civil War*, 463.

the shipping crews were given false pretenses and clothing. Concealment of the personnel included a number of important measures: recruiting and selection of personnel was carefully conducted under strict confidentiality by the Soviet Defense Commissariat; personnel were transported under civilian or other false pretenses; and, each person was given a pseudonym and corresponding papers. Once in the theater, Soviet personnel were carefully managed to avoid capture. Those not directly involved in combat were required to stay out of artillery range to avoid capture.[64] Any Soviet personnel captured were to be declared volunteers and their official status disavowed.[65] Within the Soviet Union, officially sanctioned press reports did not describe any Soviet combat role despite devoting ample space to extolling the virtues of communist solidarity in the Spanish Civil War. For example, the first successful bombing by Soviet pilots in late October 1936 was described by *Pravda* as victories by "Republican" air force squadrons of the Spanish government.[66] This secrecy was maintained for decades.

Historians disagree about Stalin's goals in approving his intervention. The predominant contemporary view is that Soviet goals were more geostrategic than ideological, a shift from early Cold War accounts which more commonly took claims of communist ideological sympathy at face value. In particular, the Soviet Union likely used military intervention to prevent the defeat of a friendly, incumbent government facing a rebellion by hostile fascist leaders.[67] Stalin also likely saw intervention as a way to place a victorious Republican government in his strategic debt. He may well have seen the conflict through the prism of competition within leftist ideology, where Soviet intervention could help ensure loyal communists were in power and deny rival leftists a victory.[68]

COVERTNESS AND LIMITING WAR

The Soviet intervention in Spain provides important, though qualified, support for the theory. In short, Soviet reasons for covertness are somewhat overdetermined, motivated by a desire to preserve limited war in Spain as

---

64 Thomas, *The Spanish Civil War*, 2001, 430.

65 Payne, *The Spanish Civil War, the Soviet Union, and Communism*, 160.

66 Kowalsky, *Stalin and the Spanish Civil War*, 658.

67 Payne, *The Spanish Civil War, the Soviet Union, and Communism*, 144–45, 295; Thomas, *The Spanish Civil War*, 2001, 326.

68 Payne, *The Spanish Civil War, the Soviet Union, and Communism*, 145, 295.

well as to avoid a diplomatic pivot away from Moscow by leaders in London and Paris. On one hand, Stalin's caution in Spain reflected a desire to avoid a wider war in Europe and awareness that knowledge and acknowledgment of Soviet intervention had significant diplomatic and domestic political implications. Preserving non-intervention diplomacy was an important constraint. On the other hand, the immediate Soviet concern was for geopolitical relationships rather than outright war. Stalin's specific concern was that a visible Soviet role would alienate British and French leaders and isolate Moscow. Because my theory focuses on the fear of large-scale escalation (see chapter 2), avoiding a diplomatic crisis or rupture is not directly supportive of the theory's logic. However, in another sense, Soviet geopolitical thinking was driven by fears of the consequences of a second war in Europe. Before a war in Spain could become a European war that endangered Soviet interests and even survival, it would first involve a breakdown in relations among the great powers.

In general, Stalin was cautious about the war in Spain and Soviet help to the Republicans. As Hugh Thomas notes, the Soviet leader approached the question of whether and how to intervene with "crablike caution." In 1936, he "would not permit the republic to lose" and sought to ensure that, if the war did escalate, it would be a "world war in which France, Britain, Germany, and Italy would destroy themselves, with Russia, the arbiter, staying outside."[69] The role of escalation was cited by communist supporters in Spain who observed initial Soviet hesitation to intervene. One specifically cited the risk of a delimited war for territories dear to Moscow, noting that "Russia regards her security as the apple of her eye. A false move on her part could upset the balance of power and unleash a war in East Europe."[70] The reactions of Britain and France were paramount in this regard. In 1936 and 1937, Stalin's strategy for coping with the growing risk of a war was, despite his later joining forces with Germany, via courting the liberal Western European powers against a rising Nazi Germany. Stalin's concept of "collective security" directed toward containing Germany necessitated good relations with the United Kingdom and France.[71] Given the great weight Paris and London placed on non-intervention diplomacy, Soviet intervention risked alienating both prospective allies.

69 Thomas, *The Spanish Civil War*, 2001, 326–27.

70 Thomas, *The Spanish Civil War*, 2001, 348, quoting Italian mathematician and communist leader Palmiro Tagliatti in late July 1936.

71 Thomas, *The Spanish Civil War*, 2001, 379.

The solution to this dilemma was for the Soviet Union to publicly abide by non-intervention while secretly providing military aid and personnel to the Spanish Republicans. Secrecy appears to have served a geopolitical rather than domestic or adversary-directed role. One historian of Soviet strategy and intervention in Spain concludes, "the emphasis on utmost secrecy in Operation X was designed to disguise or hide it as much as possible from the Western countries."[72] Stalin appeared to hope that "public denial and extreme secrecy might avoid alienating Britain and France."[73] Although the Soviet presence could be discovered, Stalin likely believed that "France and Britain would not be inhibited from embracing collective security with Moscow" if he kept a low profile and participated in the Non-Intervention Committee.[74] Daniel Kowalsky's review of Soviet primary documents made available after the Cold War similarly concludes "Stalin took precautions to ensure that the entire aid operation would be carried out in strict secrecy" so it "would not have adverse economic or diplomatic effects on the USSR."[75]

Other decisions besides approval of covert support corroborate the role of geopolitics and limited-war concerns. Like Hitler, Stalin considered but rejected proposals to send a division of Red Army troops to fight on behalf of the Republic, agreeing with top military commanders that it would be "too difficult and too risky."[76] In addition, Stalin issued instructions to deployed Soviet military personnel that were meant to specifically avoid generating evidence of Soviet involvement, such as staying out of artillery range where possible and withdrawing early when Republican forces were falling back. There are even allegations of quiet, high-level prisoner swaps of Soviet, German, and Italian personnel that had been captured by rival sides.[77]

Finally, German and Soviet reactions to the most potentially explosive combat encounter during the war show a shared concern for escalation and

72 Payne, *The Spanish Civil War, the Soviet Union, and Communism*, 145.
73 Payne, *The Spanish Civil War, the Soviet Union, and Communism*, 129.
74 Payne, *Franco and Hitler*, 7.
75 Kowalsky, *Stalin and the Spanish Civil War*, 778.
76 Payne, *The Spanish Civil War, the Soviet Union, and Communism*, 142.
77 On avoiding artillery range, see Thomas, *The Spanish Civil War*, 2001, 430; on prisoner exchanges, see Payne, *The Spanish Civil War, the Soviet Union, and Communism*, 160; in general, "Moscow took meticulous care to evacuate its entire contingent before the end of the war and ensure that very few Soviet participants fell into Nationalist hands," and word that two pilots had been captured was treated with "the most serious attention." Kowalsky, *Stalin and the Spanish Civil War*, 549.

the role of secrecy and denial in facilitating it. In May 1937, "untrained Soviet relief pilots" mistakenly bombed a German battleship, the *Deutschland*, while participating in non-intervention patrols.[78] This triggered a major international incident yet was handled by both sides in a way that contained the larger war. The incident itself was highly publicized and involved the deaths of almost two dozen German sailors, prompting urgent diplomatic requests that Germany not escalate the war.[79] Importantly, the nationality of the pilots was not apparent to outsiders. Germany directed its response to the Spanish Republicans rather than Soviet assets or leaders, shelling the Republican-held coastline. In turn, Spanish Republicans and Soviet representatives steered away from retaliation against Germany. The line from Moscow was that it had "no desire for world war" and cautioned the Spanish to ignore Germany's shelling.[80] The Republicans ultimately agreed, with one advocate of restraint cautioning that they "must ensure that *Deutschland* is not our *Maine*."

The reference to the USS *Maine* is significant. The explosion of the American warship in 1898 was a significant domestic political event that helped launch Spain and the United States to war. It suggests the role of historical parallels in helping shape the perception that publicity about naval incidents during war can constitute key drivers of wider escalation.[81] Moreover, this historical analogy and the reference to Napoleonic France (see previous section) represent attempts to understand escalation dynamics through history. They underscore that leaders during the Spanish Civil War could grasp for analogies and precedents to help inform their strategic decisions and the risks of escalation, though not to the same extent as in later Cold War–era conflicts.

Italian Intervention

Italy's combat participation was the largest of any foreign power. Rome provided equipment and personnel for artillery, tank, aircraft, naval interdiction, and infantry missions to the Nationalists. Italian-only infantry units with thousands fought on the front lines in critical battles for Malaga, Guadalajara, Santander, Valencia, Barcelona, and Madrid. Italian-piloted aircraft in the Aviazione Legionaria (Legionary Air Force) played major roles

---

78 Frank, Jr., "Naval Operations in the Spanish Civil War, 1936–1939," 40.

79 Whealey, *Hitler and Spain*, 110–11.

80 Thomas, *The Spanish Civil War*, 2001, 666.

81 Quoted in Thomas, *The Spanish Civil War*, 2001, 666.

throughout the war as well.[82] In fact, following the Nationalists' seizure of Madrid in 1939, more than 18,000 members of the Italian Corpo Truppe Volontarie (Corps of Volunteer Troops—CTV) led a victory parade through the streets of the capital. Italian naval crews operated submarines patrolling the Spanish coast and wider Mediterranean for shipments of military supplies headed toward Republican ports throughout the war. Official statistics now available state that more than 72,000 officers and troops participated in ground campaigns, more than 5,000 fought in the air, and at its height thirty-six submarines participated in interdiction missions.[83]

The objectives for intervening remain opaque. Historians of the Italian role suggest a mix of geopolitical considerations with a healthy dose of idiosyncratic domestic factors. Because of Franco's ideology and the role of Spanish fascist militia (i.e., the Falange, formed in the early 1930s) on the side of the Nationalists, Mussolini had an interest in the success of the rebellion. A fascist Spain would influence the balance of power in Europe with geopolitical benefits for Italy. Mussolini also sought Italian influence if not hegemony in the Mediterranean Sea (i.e., "mare nostrum"). A radicalized and victorious communist Spain could pose serious problems for Italian freedom of action in the western Mediterranean.[84] Italy may have specifically hoped to lay claim to naval facilities on Spanish islands like Majorca, an outcome to which the British were particularly sensitive, given their presence at Gibraltar.[85] Framing Italy's intervention as the product of genuine ideological solidarity and enthusiasm (i.e., "volunteers") was especially helpful. Moreover, battlefield victories for which fascist volunteers could claim credit boosted Mussolini's claims to martial prowess at home and abroad.[86]

In terms of theoretical expectations, my theory expects covertness in Italy's naval role and overtness in its ground intervention. Regarding se-

82 Italy participated in air combat missions as well in support of Italian ground units. With limited airpower of its own, the Nationalists relied heavily on Italian air forces (along with the German Condor Legion) which flew some 2,800 hours and dropped over 100,000 kilograms of bombs. Yet Mussolini did not view airpower as symbolically useful in the same way victorious infantry units could be. For reasons of space, I focus on the theoretically important contrast between naval and ground roles.

83 For overviews, see Coverdale, *Italian Intervention in the Spanish Civil War*, 396; Brian R. Sullivan, "Fascist Italy's Military Involvement in the Spanish Civil War," *Journal of Military History* 59, no. 4 (October 1995): 697–727.

84 Coverdale, *Italian Intervention in the Spanish Civil War*, 79–81.

85 Coverdale, *Italian Intervention in the Spanish Civil War*, 8–10 and chap. 5; Thomas, *The Spanish Civil War*, 2001, 340, 384.

86 Thomas, *The Spanish Civil War*, 2001, 340.

quence, Italy was the first outside power to join the conflict in Spain on land and at sea. Its role began conspicuously and early. General Franco's Army of Africa, stationed in Morocco, asked Italy to assist with an airlift of troops over the Mediterranean and into Spain in July 1936. Mussolini sent converted Italian bombers flown by Italian pilots in Spanish Foreign Legion uniforms and carrying false papers.[87] Despite these precautions, Italy's airlift was partially exposed when two of the twelve Italian planes were forced to land in French Morocco. Although Italy refused to acknowledge government authorization of the airlift, media reporting put publics and governments on notice of Italy's potential active military involvement.[88] Regarding location, the story is more complex. Italy's ground role was confined to the Spanish mainland; Italy did not engage in ground operations that would endanger the geographic limits of the war. Italy's naval role, however, was in the peripheral waters of the Mediterranean. Italian submarine interdiction patrols were conducted hundreds of miles from the Spanish coastline and prompted incidents involving military and civilian vessels from a range of other governments. Escalation risks for the latter were substantially higher than the former. I therefore expect Italy to have used overtness for its ground units (first-mover and localized) and covertness for its naval role (first-mover but peripheral).

ON THE GROUND

Following its airlift operations, Italy, in consultation with Germany, provided bombers, fighters, machine guns, hand grenades, and bombs to the Nationalists in September 1936. Rome authorized combat participation when Mussolini approved a shipment of equipment deemed too sophisticated for untrained Spanish Nationalists, such as tanks.[89] The decision to deploy large numbers of Italian infantry under the command of Italian generals, however, was reached in December 1936. In reaction to the successful Republican defense of Madrid, Mussolini and his advisors opted to send volunteers from Italian Fascist militia ("Black Shirts") and divisions of Italian regular infantry. By mid-December, three thousand Black Shirts arrived in Spain to be integrated into Nationalist forces.[90] By late December 1936,

87 Coverdale, *Italian Intervention in the Spanish Civil War*, 3–4, 69–74.

88 Coverdale, *Italian Intervention in the Spanish Civil War*, 4; Thomas, *The Spanish Civil War*, 2001, 350.

89 Coverdale, *Italian Intervention in the Spanish Civil War*, 106–10.

90 Coverdale, *Italian Intervention in the Spanish Civil War*, 168.

three shipments of autonomously commanded soldiers were on their way. All told, Italian military personnel in Spain swelled to 49,000 by February 1937.[91]

Italy's ground role was a classic case of a covert open secret. This provides mixed support for my claims. The timing and location of Italy's role would suggest an overt rather than putatively "volunteer" role; however, the use of non-acknowledgment to control escalation supports one key mechanism of the theory. Rome's official position was that all Italian nationals were volunteers. However, those "volunteers" were nakedly visible to anyone reading a newspaper. In part this was because Rome took few measures to effectively conceal its ground forces after December 1936 and, in fact, regularly praised their exploits. The lack of precautions led to regular and specific international news reports of the arrival of thousands of Black Shirts, an all-volunteer Italian militia, as early as January 5, 1937.[92] Later shipments included troops wearing distinctive Corpo Truppe Volontarie uniforms.[93] The unofficial-but-visible ground role for Italian forces was useful in part because official Italian propaganda could praise battlefield victories by Italian volunteers while diplomatically insisting it had not intervened.[94] In fact, Mussolini lobbied Franco hard to place autonomously organized Italian units in lead positions for offensives on Malaga (January) in the south and Guadalajara (March).[95] As a result, the government-controlled Italian media could be seen "trumpeting every minor victory" and "claiming Italian victories."[96]

Despite the publicity, both public and private official diplomatic statements stuck to a script of Italian "volunteers."[97] As Coverdale summarizes, although "no effort was made to hide the fact that Italian troops were pouring into Spain," there was an attempt by Italian Foreign Minister Galeazzo Ciano to "try to maintain the fiction that they were volunteers for whom

91 These were organized into three Black Shirt divisions and one royal army division. Details in Coverdale, *Italian Intervention in the Spanish Civil War*, 175–76, 182–83, 212.

92 Coverdale, *Italian Intervention in the Spanish Civil War*, 170.

93 Thomas, *The Spanish Civil War*, 2001, 566.

94 On the publicity surrounding perceived Italian failure in Guadalajara and success in Santander, see Coverdale, *Italian Intervention in the Spanish Civil War*, 250, 263, 282–83; Thomas, *The Spanish Civil War*, 2001, 696, 700.

95 Thomas, *The Spanish Civil War*, 2001, 576; Coverdale, *Italian Intervention in the Spanish Civil War*, 207–10, 212–50.

96 Corum, "The Luftwaffe and the Coalition Air War in Spain, 1936–1939," 77; Thomas, *The Spanish Civil War*, 2001, 700.

97 Italian Black Shirt personnel were legally volunteers but had few alternatives to deploying; see Thomas, *The Spanish Civil War*, 2001, 566; the non-militia military units were unquestionably not volunteer. Coverdale, *Italian Intervention in the Spanish Civil War*, 182–83.

the government was not responsible ... official intervention in Spain was systematically denied."[98] For example, Italian media reports on the "great victory" at Santander in August 1937 described Italy's role as "two divisions of Italian volunteers ... in fraternal and comradely collaboration with Franco's National forces."[99] Even during the attack on Barcelona at the war's end, Italy's representative to the United States privately maintained the bombing was done by Italian "volunteers" out of the government's control.[100] Such descriptions were not plausible, though they had important diplomatic consequences, which I review below. Confronted with news reports of Italians in Spain, Italy's representative to the NIC replied defensively that they hoped "no Italian volunteers would leave Spanish soil until Franco's victory was assured."[101]

Historians of Italy's decision-making in this period specifically emphasize the role of martial glory for Mussolini.[102] A glory motive required Italian nationals to win on the battlefield and do so with clear visibility and credit. This explains why Italy actually found effective concealment counterproductive. It is also consistent with my claim in chapter 2 that interveners tend to prefer overtness for operational and reputational reasons. Putting Italians in the front lines of battlefield victories—which Mussolini repeatedly insisted to Franco—ensured that "the glory of [autonomous Italian units] exploits would be reflected directly on Italy, on Fascism" and Mussolini himself.[103] Mussolini similarly insisted that "all Italians would act together" in the March 1937 Nationalist attack on Guadalajara "so that the victory to be gained would redound to the Italian credit."[104] Similar requests were made in 1938 as well.[105] Mussolini even sought to have Italians take the lead role in entering the final major city to fall despite Germans' insistence that the Spanish Nationalists themselves take credit.[106]

98 Coverdale, *Italian Intervention in the Spanish Civil War*, 200–201, 204.

99 Coverdale, *Italian Intervention in the Spanish Civil War*, 283.

100 Thomas, *The Spanish Civil War*, 2001, 785.

101 Coverdale, *Italian Intervention in the Spanish Civil War*, 301.

102 Thomas, *The Spanish Civil War*, 2001, 576–79; although the discussion here focuses on Mussolini, the second most important Italian decision-maker, Ciano, shared a similar interest in using the war in Spain as a source of his own personal prestige. This did not prevent the occasional disagreement about Italy's intervention (Ciano being more cautious in one important naval decision, noted below) but both tended to share a similar outlook. Sullivan, "Fascist Italy's Military Involvement in the Spanish Civil War," 704.

103 Coverdale, *Italian Intervention in the Spanish Civil War*, 169.

104 Thomas, *The Spanish Civil War*, 2001, 579.

105 Thomas, *The Spanish Civil War*, 2001, 746.

106 Corum, "The Luftwaffe and the Coalition Air War in Spain, 1936–1939," 78–79; Coverdale, *Italian Intervention in the Spanish Civil War*, 283.

Non-intervention diplomacy and escalation concerns appear to have driven Italy's preference for visible-but-unofficial intervention. Volunteerism avoided explicitly violating the legal and diplomatic non-intervention position of Italy's government. Maintaining the fiction of compliance with NIC rules helped manage the scope of the war. Coverdale recounts how Italy's Foreign Minister Ciano tried to "maintain the fiction that they were volunteers for whom the government was not responsible ... sending troops to Spain could not be said to be a violation of the terms of the agreement."[107] As more autonomous and identifiable Italian infantry units appeared in places like Guadalajara, Italy could observe how it was "more difficult for leaders in London and Paris to ignore the seriousness and extent of Italian violations of the Non-Intervention Agreement."[108] Italy's partners also saw the value of Italy maintaining the "volunteer" fiction. Franco, for example, cautioned Mussolini about the provocative nature of sending visible, Italian-led infantry units, saying they "might cause fruitless international tension and could create difficulties and even provoke other interventions."[109] German primary documents note the difference between genuine volunteers and the military units sent by Berlin and Rome. As negotiations about a coordinated withdrawal of "volunteers" intensified, a German memo from February 1938 showcases the risks of acknowledgment this posed. As the author notes, "it is out of the question either for the Italians or for us to permit the volunteers ... to be combed out by the methods of the Non-Intervention Committee"; doing so "would have to show our colors ... [and] would amount to an admission that they were contingents sent by the Government, that is, a proof of our intervention."[110]

AT SEA

Consistent with the theory's expectation, Italy was more cautious about the visibility of its activities at sea. It carefully avoided wider exposure of its naval operations. Even at the peak of Italian naval activity, its efforts maintained meaningful ambiguity about the sponsor of submarine operations. Only major powers with sophisticated naval intelligence could confirm and document Italy's hand. Moreover, as I show in the next section, this intelli-

107 Coverdale, *Italian Intervention in the Spanish Civil War*, 200–201.
108 Coverdale, *Italian Intervention in the Spanish Civil War*, 301.
109 Coverdale, *Italian Intervention in the Spanish Civil War*, 217.
110 Memorandum by Head of Political Division IIIa, February 28, 1938, DGFP, Doc. 538.

gence was kept private. Italy's covert naval operations had significant strategic importance. For most of the two-year period between October 1936 and October 1938, dozens of Italian submarines with Italian crews patrolled the Mediterranean, identifying and sinking Spanish Republican naval vessels. These patrols gave the Nationalists near-uncontested hegemony at sea and strangled off foreign aid to the Republicans.[111]

Although consistently covert and well-concealed, Italy's naval intervention varied in intensity. It began with carefully concealed operations and cautious rules of engagement. Mussolini agreed to clandestinely provide six Italian submarines to the Nationalists in fall 1936.[112] Mussolini had the Italian submarines physically altered by painting over distinguishing lettering before dispatch. Each submarine was required to raise the Spanish Nationalist flag if forced to surface in view of the coast or other ships. A Spanish liaison officer on board was instructed to pose as the commanding officer during any encounter. The rules of engagement required Italian submarines to abstain from firing on suspicion or at any convoy. Moreover, ships could only be attacked in Spanish territorial waters and not on high seas.[113] At the same time, Mussolini steadfastly denied Nationalist requests for surface ships, either under Italian or Spanish control, out of a desire to avoid making Italy's role at sea due to "the obvious impossibility of providing large surface ships without being detected."[114] He preferred submarines with their unique capability to evade identification.[115] Between October 1936 and February 1937, a total of twenty-four Italian submarines patrolled Spanish territorial waters, sinking several merchant vessels as well as severely damaging a Republican destroyer.[116]

Italy adopted a more aggressive posture during a four-week initiative in late summer 1937. Based on intelligence that new shipments of Soviet military aid were set to leave port, Franco requested that Italy scale up interdiction operations. Although still refusing large surface ships, Mussolini agreed to deploy fifteen submarines throughout the Mediterranean.[117] He

---

111 One historian's review of Italian primary documents concludes, "the navy's limited and often secret and illegal actions were crucial to Franco's victory." Sullivan, "Fascist Italy's Military Involvement in the Spanish Civil War," 713.

112 Frank, Jr., "Naval Operations in the Spanish Civil War, 1936–1939," 33–34.

113 On the variety of concealment measures, see Frank, Jr., "Naval Operations in the Spanish Civil War, 1936–1939," 34; Coverdale, *Italian Intervention in the Spanish Civil War*, 180.

114 Coverdale, *Italian Intervention in the Spanish Civil War*, 117.

115 Smoke, *War: Controlling Escalation*, appendix C.

116 Frank, Jr., "Naval Operations in the Spanish Civil War, 1936–1939," 37.

117 Coverdale, *Italian Intervention in the Spanish Civil War*, 307–8.

also relaxed rules of engagement to permit Italian vessels to fire on a wider range of ships.[118] The campaign began on August 10 and lasted until September 4, 1937. However, the sinking of vessels prompted an outcry in the rest of Europe. Merchant ships from Spain, Russia, the United Kingdom, Greece, France, and Denmark, among others, were sunk.[119] Such anger reached a dangerous climax when the British destroyer HMS *Havock* was hit with a torpedo. British and French leaders immediately convened a multilateral gathering in Nyon, Switzerland to discuss the "piracy" in the Mediterranean. The result was an agreement in which British and French warships would patrol the Mediterranean with the right to attack any suspicious submarine.[120] Italy's Italian Foreign Minister suspended the naval campaign days later. For the rest of the war, it reverted to more cautious interdiction. Mussolini agreed to deploy four Italian submarines under genuine Spanish control but with Italian crews to patrol the Spanish coast. He further stipulated strict rules of engagement leading to only three attacks in five months. In February 1938, the mission ended.[121]

Even when Italy engaged in more aggressive submarine activity, it maintained a posture which avoided more widespread public visibility at sea. Its naval vessels included significant concealment measures ("submarines bore no distinguishing marks; destroyers attacked only at night, and the auxiliary cruisers flew the Nationalist flag"). However, to the naval intelligence of other states, the Italian submarine behavior "was transparent" because "submarines brazenly surfaced in broad daylight near suspected merchant ships, their Italian profiles clearly outlined. Destroyers made no attempt to disguise their Italian identity as they trailed their targets by day."[122]

Escalation control is a consistent theme in Italy's naval activities and the fluctuations in rules of engagement within it. As Frank observes, Mussolini insisted on "an approach to clandestine submarine warfare less dangerous and extensive." After the Nationalists took Santander in August 1937,

---

118 The instructions were to target all Republican warships, all Republican or Soviet merchant ships, all ships no matter the flag moving at night within three miles of Spanish territorial waters, and all merchant ships no matter the country of origin escorted by Republican convoy. Frank, Jr., "Naval Operations in the Spanish Civil War, 1936–1939," 42.

119 Thomas, *The Spanish Civil War*, 2001, 719; Coverdale, *Italian Intervention in the Spanish Civil War*, 311–13.

120 On the Havock incident, see Thomas, *The Spanish Civil War*, 2001, 719–21.

121 Coverdale, *Italian Intervention in the Spanish Civil War*, 319–20; Frank, Jr., "Naval Operations in the Spanish Civil War, 1936–1939," 55.

122 Frank, Jr., "Naval Operations in the Spanish Civil War, 1936–1939," 43.

Italy rejected a request by Franco for the transfer of submarines because Mussolini

> could not miss the fact that when Italian troops entered Santander on 26 August with all the propaganda trappings of a liberation, the world raised no protest, but the naval actions at the same time brought the threat of a massive international naval reaction. Franco was clamoring for more troops, aircraft, and equipment for the land war, and so Mussolini ordered a major escalation in the levels of his men and material to Spain. But when Franco also called for the transfer of two more submarines to the Spanish flag, Mussolini refused.[123]

The timing of Italy's different phases of naval involvement is also consistent with a limited-war logic. Rome embraced a more cautious role after the 1937 Nyon Agreement which authorized destruction of any state's submarine that threatened merchant vessels.[124] It was, as one historian judges, "the most forceful resistance to Axis moves of the entire prewar period" and surprised Mussolini with its seriousness. The interdiction campaign was immediately canceled and Mussolini subsequently switched to "a quieter operation."[125] Moreover, Italy's decision four months earlier to expand interdiction in the summer of 1937 was preceded by clear signs from the United Kingdom's Prime Minister Chamberlain that indicted London's interest in dialogue.[126] The leading historian of the war concludes, "[Mussolini] may have seen no real cost to Italy in further alienating the British by attacking shipping on the high seas ... he may have been convinced that British passivity and ineffectiveness were so great that he could fly in the face of their interests without doing any serious or irreparable harm."[127] Thus, indicators of low escalation risk from the most important states for any escalation prompted an assertive intervention, and indicators of high escalation risk prompted a return to more caution.

A September 1937 cable from the Italian ambassador to Germany provides a unique internal view into Rome's thinking and the role of escalation in general and domestic politics of escalation-related decisions in particular. The cable notes that British/French promises to use naval force against

---

123 Frank, Jr., "Naval Operations in the Spanish Civil War, 1936–1939," 44.

124 Coverdale, *Italian Intervention in the Spanish Civil War*, 313–14.

125 Frank, Jr., "Naval Operations in the Spanish Civil War, 1936–1939," 43–45; Whealey, *Hitler and Spain*, 59.

126 Coverdale, *Italian Intervention in the Spanish Civil War*, 308–11.

127 Thomas, *The Spanish Civil War*, 2001, 311.

a "pirate" submarine were unlikely to be a bluff. It then notes the French political and diplomatic tone in particular had sharpened and concludes the French may actually want non-intervention to collapse through a militarized incident. The memo then summarizes that, as a result, Italy and Nationalist Spain should pull back on submarine activity to avoid an incident.[128] A similar theme appears in a cable five months later. A German dispatch back to Berlin in February 1938 describes how Italian representatives hoped to participate in the new interdiction program from Nyon "in order not to come under suspicion" that their submarines were responsible for the problem.[129] This suggests how Italy modulated the deniability of its activity in response to activity by outside powers that increased the risk of escalatory incidents.

Detection, Collusion, and the Non-Intervention Committee

Although some foreign participants like Italy were an open secret, secondary accounts and available primary materials suggest much of covert involvement was uniquely visible to the intelligence services of the major European powers. This created a degree of mutual observability among those with access to the "backstage" at the same time that public-facing perceptions of foreign involvement were shrouded in ambiguity and unacknowledged by officials.[130] This section analyzes detection of covert involvement and patterns of collusion that emerged regarding foreign intervention in the Spanish Civil War.

The disjuncture was facilitated by the existence and design of the Non-Intervention Committee. The NIC was intended to improve communication and crisis avoidance among the key European powers. It was specifically intended to protect leaders from domestic political constraints to avoid a repetition of the escalation process prior to World War I.[131] Put differently,

---

128 Ambassador in Italy to the Foreign Ministry, October 8, 1937, DGFP, Doc. 434. Note that Coverdale does not attribute much causal weight to the British/French response (316), instead arguing Italy intended to stop interdiction before the Nyon agreement was reached.

129 Charge d'Affaires in Italy to the Foreign Ministry, February 17, 1938, DGFP, Doc. 530.

130 Frank, Jr., "Naval Operations in the Spanish Civil War, 1936–1939," 25.

131 On the fresh memory of World War I, Edwards notes, "for on the broader stage of Europe the scene was no less disturbed, and while the conflict which had erupted was a bitter tragedy for Spain, it was also to prove a major test for European stability. The Great War, as it was fearfully remembered, had exhausted the victors without improving the lot of lesser powers, and had not noticeably soothed the still ardent passions of nationalism. Above all, two powerful ide-

the NIC was designed to insulate backstage behavior from audience pressures. A Chairman's Sub-Committee, a select subset of members, was charged with handling the vast majority of working activity and served as a kind of gatekeeper and private forum for complaints.[132] Only member states could submit evidence of intervention violations "which effectively ensured that the Committee would not be pestered by either of the belligerents themselves nor by journalists or other private citizens on the spot."[133] As one contemporary analysis noted, "by this clever move the Committee insulated itself against consideration of charges preferred by private individuals, newspaper observers, international organizations, the Madrid Government and the rebels, and governments other than those meeting in London."[134] Member-states agreed that "proceedings should be treated as strictly confidential" and that each NIC meeting would result in a vetted public communiqué.[135] Enrique Moradiellos concludes that the NIC had "a hint of deceptiveness": "its real end was not the one declared (the avoidance of foreign participation in the war) but rather the safeguarding of those established objectives by its mere existence and apparent efficacy."[136] These features reflected a sense among leaders that, given the dangers of another

---

ologies, communism and nationalism." Jill Edwards, *The British Government and the Spanish Civil War, 1936–1939* (London: Macmillan, 1979), 1; regarding domestic politics in particular, Buchanan notes that "The evolution of British opinion towards the war has to be understood within the context of changing public attitudes towards foreign policy more broadly. The First World War had shattered the idea that foreign policy was an elite preserve, beyond the scrutiny of the public." Tom Buchanan, *Britain and the Spanish Civil War* (New York: Cambridge University Press, 1997), 21.

132 Sub-Committee members were France, Portugal, the United Kingdom, Germany, Italy, Belgium, Sweden, Czechoslovakia, and the Soviet Union. The subcommittee would "become the real power-house of non-intervention" at the cost of wider input and judgment; Edwards, *The British Government and the Spanish Civil War, 1936–1939*, 45; the ability of weaker states in the subcommittee to oppose the diplomatic arrangements of the larger powers was, in practice, marginal. As Thomas concludes, "the smaller States even on the Sub-Committee were only too willing to follow the lead of the great Powers, and the real debates were confined to France, Britain, Germany, and Italy." See Hugh Thomas, *The Spanish Civil War*, 1st edition (New York: Harper & Row, 1961), 281.

133 Edwards, *The British Government and the Spanish Civil War, 1936–1939*, 46.

134 Norman J. Padelford, "The International Non-Intervention Agreement and the Spanish Civil War," *American Journal of International Law* 31, no. 4 (1937): 587.

135 "Non-Intervention Committee Portugal Still an Absentee," *The Times*, September 15, 1936.

136 Enrique Moradiellos, "The Allies and the Spanish Civil War," in *Spain and the Great Powers in the Twentieth Century*, ed. Sebastian Balfour and Paul Preston (New York: Routledge, 1999), 106.

war in interwar Europe, "Public opinion was ... to be interpreted and moulded by politicians and journalists."[137]

With the exception of Italy's ground role, effective secrecy combined with ambiguity about foreign "volunteers" led to no clear third-party exposure of the German, Soviet, and Italian naval roles. I therefore code these three cases as "low" and Italy's ground role as "high." A review of coverage in *The Times* (London) from 1936 to the end of 1938 finds significant reporting on international volunteers but rare accounts regarding Soviet, German, and Italian naval interventions. Regarding Soviet involvement, very few stories appear regarding Russian or Soviet crews or personnel. A 1936 story on the battle for Madrid notes rumors of "Russian pilots and aircraft at Barcelona" but refutes these, saying they "lack confirmation" and strain credibility.[138] A December 1936 story on "volunteers" reports that "some claimed that they were the Regular Red Army forces; others that they were Soviet volunteers."[139] This period also saw very few allegations of Italian naval participation. For example, the 1937 peak of Italian submarine activity featured conspicuous circumlocutions referring to unidentified "piracy" rather than Italian activity.[140] Coverage of German involvement frequently identified German arms support and the deployment of naval vessels near Spain.[141] Accounts of German nationals include the German government's claim of "volunteers" and do not dispute it.[142] Two exceptions are worth noting. First, the bombing of Guernica included allegations of German piloting.[143] More-

137 Buchanan, *Britain and the Spanish Civil War*, 22.

138 "Madrid in Danger," *Times* [London, England] October 20, 1936, p. 17. The Times Digital Archive, December 14, 2017.

139 "'Volunteers' in Spain," *Times* [London, England], December 10, 1936, p. 13. The Times Digital Archive, December 14, 2017.

140 See, for example, the account that "attacks upon unarmed merchant ships by armed forces, naval or aerial, whose identity has not been fully established, have occurred with increasing frequency of late in the Mediterranean." In "Piracy in the Mediterranean," *Times* [London, England], August 25, 1937, p. 13. The Times Digital Archive, December 14, 2017. See also "The Pirates," *Times* [London, England], September 3, 1937, p. 13. The Times Digital Archive, December 14, 2017.

141 E.g., "Arms for Spain," *Times* [London, England], August 10, 1936: 10. The Times Digital Archive, December 14, 2017.

142 "German Volunteers in Spain," *Times* [London, England], December 3, 1936, p. 14. The Times Digital Archive, December 14, 2017.

143 As one review notes, "the German air force rushed to his aid, bombing the Basque city of Guernica on 26 April 1937, causing appalling carnage among the civilian population. Accounts of this were quickly given by foreign correspondents staying there, and the event was unanimously condemned in the global press." Jürgen Wilke, "How Nazi Press Instructions Framed

over, an explicit report mentioning the Condor Legion appeared toward the end of the war (1938).[144] In contrast, Italian air and ground operations within Spain were regularly reported and specifically linked to the Italian military.[145]

Recent media-focused studies have shown the role of press censorship in the two most important media locations, the United Kingdom and Germany, in steering public perceptions of the war in Spain. Deacon's systematic review of British Broadcasting Corporation coverage documents how the NIC and censorship in London led to very little coverage of state-sponsored foreign involvement.[146] In contrast, media coverage in the BBC regarding genuine foreign "volunteers" was significant.[147] Wilke's analysis of German press guidance finds clear evidence that public-facing press accounts were sanitized in that "covert assistance to Nationalist troop transports by German battleships was denied or re-interpreted by the Nazi propaganda ministry." There were specific occasions, such as the bombing of a German *Deutschland* in 1937, when German propaganda specifically accused Soviet crews of operating in Spain. Yet more common was attributing Spanish Republican gains to "Bolshevik" or "American communist" support, eliding the question of whether international communist help was volunteers or government-directed.[148]

Given the degree of third-party exposure, the theory expects detecting governments to expose the Italian ground role but to collude regarding Soviet, German, and Italian naval interventions. Interestingly, I find collusion about all four. Rather than expose, both intervening governments and bystanders like the United Kingdom avoided public exposure of intervention

---

German Perceptions of the Spanish Civil War," *Catalan Journal of Communication & Cultural Studies* 8, no. 2 (October 1, 2016): 291.

144 "Foreign Aircraft in Spain," *Times* [London, England], March 22, 1938, p. 15. The Times Digital Archive, December 13, 2017.

145 E.g., "Madrid Government's Allegations," *Times* [London, England], October 28, 1936, p. 11. The Times Digital Archive, December 14, 2017. "Italian Troops in Spain," *Times* [London, England], March 15, 1937, p. 13. The Times Digital Archive, December 14, 2017.

146 Deacon, "A Quietening Effect? The BBC and the Spanish Civil War (1936–1939)," 143–58.

147 Deacon's survey of 1,558 news items finds 18% addressed international intervention issues, with the "largest proportion of these items concerned the decision-making of the Non-Intervention Committee." Stories about Germany and Italy are mentioned from 1938, e.g., "French note to Britain on Barcelona air raids: list of 400 German & Italian planes serving Franco," March 19, 1938.

148 Wilke, "How Nazi Press Instructions Framed German Perceptions of the Spanish Civil War," 288–92.

activity. This took place via the use of the rhetoric of volunteers (bolstered by the NIC's conclusions), via withholding of intelligence, and through press censorship.

BRITAIN AND FRANCE

Throughout the war, British and French leaders prioritized diplomacy and escalation control.[149] Following the initial revolt in Spanish Morocco, the British cabinet, for example, quickly concluded that the initial aim of British policy was to remain "aloof from the conflict," avoid the civil war from "consolidating opposed and conflicting ideological blocs," and thereby "prevent it from growing into a European war."[150] The exposure of Italy's hand in the airlift of the Spanish Army of Africa prompted leaders in London and Paris to urgently secure pledges of non-intervention and engineer the creation of the NIC. Yet the incumbent leaders of Britain and France faced complex domestic pressures. French leaders, for example, faced an active leftist opposition skeptical of the policy of non-intervention and sympathetic to the Republican cause.[151]

British and French intelligence provided their leaders with a surprisingly intimate view of the covert and "volunteer" involvement of foreign military forces. For example, internal British documents describe private bilateral consultation about intelligence on the arrival of German personnel by December 1936.[152] As noted above, French officials cited human source eyewitness reports in their private warnings to German representatives about arrivals in Cadiz. A British intelligence report from January 1937 described a shipment of Italian ground units to Spain including the names of specific vessels and intelligence suggesting few were genuine "volunteers."[153] An-

---

149 While later events (i.e., Munich) would show British and French aversion to war was extreme, Smoke usefully points out that Germany, Italy, and the Soviet Union made calculations about intervention in Spain in 1936 without much greater uncertainty. As he summarizes, "the restraint that Hitler and especially Mussolini showed early in the war was substantially a product of their erroneous expectation that more significant escalations would draw a vigorous, perhaps military, response from the West." Smoke, *War: Controlling Escalation*, 73.

150 Coverdale, *Italian Intervention in the Spanish Civil War*, 92–93.

151 Thomas, *The Spanish Civil War*, 2001, 331–32; 337; 375–76; Edwards, *The British Government and the Spanish Civil War, 1936–1939*, 16–17; Coverdale, *Italian Intervention in the Spanish Civil War*, 310–11; 369.

152 Coverdale, *Italian Intervention in the Spanish Civil War*, 196.

153 Memorandum by Mr. G. A. Fisher on the departure of Italian volunteers for Spain (Naples), January 19, 1937, *Documents on British Foreign Policy, 1919–1939*, Vol. 18, Series 2 (hereafter DBFP), Doc. 90.

other intelligence report around the same time describes internal German debates about whether to provide their own ground troops and the presence of German advisors in Spain.[154] A later report clarified that German military personnel were flying missions and operating antiaircraft equipment.[155] Other primary documents describe intelligence shared by the French regarding "so-called volunteers" that had arrived from Germany and were posing as Spanish Foreign Legion members.[156] German diplomatic cables in March 1937 report that French officials had privately cited "indisputable evidence" that Italian military units under Italian commanders were fighting in Spain.[157] At sea, the British Admiralty was decrypting Italian communications allowing it to track specific Italian submarines engaged in the expanded interdiction campaign in August 1937.[158]

Consistent with theory, British and French leaders prioritized escalation control and managed their privileged view of covert foreign involvement. The NIC was central, offering a private forum for consultations about intervention and a tool to deflect hawkish domestic criticism of restraint. Coverdale notes that British and French leaders "had established the committee in the hope of avoiding direct clashes between the great powers, and preferred to pretend that violations of the agreement did not exist." He quotes a British diplomat who later explained its purpose: "I had thought the Non-Intervention Committee was generally admitted to be largely a piece of humbug but an extremely useful piece of humbug. Where humbug is the alternative to war, it is impossible to put too high a value upon it."[159] The NIC's function drew strength from the deniability of those foreign interventions that were taking place:

> Deception is an uncertain business. Nowhere is this more true than in circumstances in where it has political as well as military significance ... [P]olitically, deception that is only partially revealed may still serve to allow plausible denial, which may add a degree of flexibility in diplomacy.

---

154 Sir E. Phipps (Berlin) to Foreign Office, January 2, 1937, DBFP, Doc. 3.

155 Sir E. Phipps (Berlin) to Foreign Office, January 4, 1937, DBFP, Doc. 7.

156 Mr. Eden to Sir G. Clerk (Paris), No. 60, January 8, 1937, DBFP, Doc. 35.

157 Ambassador in France to the Foreign Ministry, March 25, 1937, DGFP, Doc. 235.

158 "The Admiralty's Operational Intelligence Center, established just a few months before, was decrypting Italian naval messages and tracking Italian submarines as they went about their 'secret' war." Frank, Jr., "Naval Operations in the Spanish Civil War, 1936–1939," 43; Edwards, *The British Government and the Spanish Civil War, 1936–1939,* 118–19.

159 Coverdale, *Italian Intervention in the Spanish Civil War,* 97.

Britain deemed such false but plausible denials by its antagonists useful in its non-intervention and Nyon policies.[160]

The NIC was specifically seen as a way to insulate British and French leaders from domestic pressure to intervene. Jill Edwards maintains the "unpublicized aim" was to use the NIC's "veneer of international respectability ... to sedate internal opposition and take 'the steam out of press insinuations which excite public opinion.'"[161] By endorsing the ambiguous language of "volunteers," the NIC reinforced the unacknowledged status of foreign involvement. This loosened the commitment of interveners and reduced their provocation, echoing the logic in chapter 2.[162] The NIC's deliberations in 1937 and 1938, for example, were dominated by debate over coordinated "volunteer" withdrawals which elided the difference between genuine volunteer foreign fighters (i.e., Abraham Lincoln Brigade; International Brigades) and state-sponsored interventions (especially Italian and German military personnel).[163] Internal German records show Berlin distinguishing in private between foreign personnel under foreign command and genuine volunteers, the value of maximizing the apparent similarity of the two, and improved escalation control from publicly referring to them with the same term.[164]

Moreover, the NIC also encouraged communication about intentions via non-acknowledgment, closely following the logic I develop in chapter 2. Participation in the NIC and its rhetoric of volunteerism were seen as indicators that Germany, Italy, and the Soviet Union remained committed to limited war. Prime Minister Anthony Eden, for example, defended non-intervention diplomacy by arguing that "the knowledge that many governments, despite all discouragement, were working for it, has greatly reduced the risks of a general war."[165] Germany and France appear to have understood this communicative logic as well. In a particularly revealing cable from

160 Frank, Jr., "Politico-Military Deception at Sea in the Spanish Civil War, 1936–1939," 107.

161 Edwards, *The British Government and the Spanish Civil War, 1936–1939*, 199.

162 Edwards, *The British Government and the Spanish Civil War, 1936–1939*, 62. On the use of volunteers rhetoric to refer to military personnel by British leaders, see Thomas, *The Spanish Civil War*, 1st edition (New York: Harper & Row, 1961), 396, 602.

163 Thomas, *The Spanish Civil War*, 2001, 563–64, 726, 774–75, 810, 825.

164 Charge d'Affaires in Great Britain to the Foreign Ministry, February 21, 1938, DGFP, Doc. 533; Memorandum by Head of Political Division IIIa, February 28, 1938, DGFP, Doc. 538.

165 Edwards, *The British Government and the Spanish Civil War, 1936–1939*, 62; Thomas, *The Spanish Civil War*, 2001, 602.

December 1936, Germany's ambassador in Paris relays France's expression of concern after detecting German personnel in Spain ("the urgent necessity for not pouring more oil on the Spanish fire at this time") and its interest in "avoid[ing] the acute danger of war." Furthermore, the cable notes, "France wants to be given proof that we are willing to collaborate in the creation of an atmosphere conducive to peace in Europe and are willing to desist from arbitrary methods." The "atmosphere" refers to non-intervention diplomacy and "arbitrary methods" appears to be a reference to German behavior inconsistent with its pledge to not intervene.[166]

In addition to non-intervention diplomacy, British and French leaders controlled escalation pressures at home via censorship. In response to questions in the House of Commons, for example, Eden denied in November 1936 and again in April 1937 that the Cabinet had decisive evidence that Germany and Italy had organized military units in Spain in violation of their commitments.[167] British leaders also steered coverage by major papers like *The Times*. The government discouraged reporting on suspicions of Germany's role in bombing within Spain, including after the infamous Guernica attacks.[168] They argued this was justified because they "wanted to avoid situations where negative or provocative material might exacerbate international tensions."[169] As Deacon's aforementioned review of British news coverage concludes, the

> core part of the government's strategy for achieving military isolation of the war was to contain discussion of its wider political significance and symbolism. Throughout, senior officials sought to cool the ardour of public debate and deny the wider international and ideological ramifications of the conflict [via] ... effective management of the mainstream media.[170]

Finally, although avoiding public exposure, British and French leaders drew on their intelligence to engage in direct, private warnings to the interveners. As noted above, French private warnings to German officials in Paris were issued after German personnel landed at Cadiz in late 1936. German documents note a similar encounter in March 1937 when the French Foreign Minister privately cited "indisputable evidence" Italy had broken

166 Ambassador in France to the Foreign Ministry, December 24, 1936, DGFP, Doc. 164.
167 Thomas, *The Spanish Civil War*, 2001, 602.
168 Edwards, *The British Government and the Spanish Civil War, 1936–1939*, 196–97.
169 Deacon, "A Quietening Effect? The BBC and the Spanish Civil War (1936–1939)," 145.
170 Deacon, "A Quietening Effect? The BBC and the Spanish Civil War (1936–1939)," 144.

her word regarding Italian units and commanders to the German ambassa-dor.[171] Such collusive behavior reached its height during Italy's naval inter-diction campaign in summer 1937. London issued two private warnings to Italy to avoid attacks against British shipping based on intelligence evi-dence about Italy's sponsoring role.[172] Later the Royal Navy exchanged in-formation with Nationalist naval commanders to avoid incidents at sea that could inflame British domestic opinion.[173] The Royal Navy, in turn, shared information with the Nationalist navy on the location of all British and British-flagged shipping. Such secret coordination avoided the need for "direct action for which the Royal Navy was below strength, and which might easily lead to embroilment with the major powers and further hu-miliation of both Great Britain and her navy."[174]

THE INTERVENERS

The same basic pattern emerged for Germany, Italy, and the Soviet Union. Although documentation is incomplete, all three intervening states appear to have obtained regular and well-informed reports from their respective intelligence services on others' interventions. This information was kept private and only shared within the confines of the NIC. The aggregate effect, along with British and French efforts, was tacit cooperation to co-produce ambiguity. As one historian concludes, "It was tacitly agreed by the powers near the end of November [1936] to refer no more complaints to the com-mittee."[175] This pattern is largely consistent with the theory. Clashes within Spain created clear pathways to large-scale escalation, providing strong motivation for collusion. With the exception of the Italian ground role, col-lusion via the rhetoric of "volunteers," press censorship, and the operations of the NIC reinforced genuine ambiguity about foreign involvement.

The clearest view of these dynamics is available for Germany and indi-rectly for Italy, given the better availability of primary records from the Nazi regime.[176] German intelligence carefully monitored other foreign mil-

---

171 Ambassador in France to the Foreign Ministry, March 25, 1937, DGFP, Doc. 235.

172 Edwards, *The British Government and the Spanish Civil War, 1936–1939*, 118.

173 Thomas, *The Spanish Civil War*, 2001, 774.

174 Edwards, *The British Government and the Spanish Civil War, 1936–1939*, 128.

175 Frank, Jr., "Politico-Military Deception at Sea in the Spanish Civil War, 1936–1939," 91–93.

176 As noted above, German records from this period were among those seized, translated, and published by the British government following World War II.

itary assistance to the opposing Republicans. Between October and December 1936, Germany, Italy, and the Nationalists developed an infrastructure for secure information-sharing and Germany's own intelligence capabilities were expanded to create a network for monitoring naval shipments to Spain from abroad.[177] A pair of messages from September 1936 showcase careful analysis of outside covert aid: one report notes the Republican side had received the support of Russian pilots "disguised as members of the International Red Cross," and a Foreign Ministry analysis based on information in Moscow finds the evidence of official Soviet military aid inconclusive.[178] A month later, telegrams from Moscow and Barcelona noted shipments of Soviet military aid and autonomously organized Russian pilots.[179] An intelligence review late in the war explicitly distinguishes between genuine volunteers supporting the Republican government (i.e., International Brigades) "from the fliers, other officers, and specialists sent by Russia."[180] A memo from the Political Division in the German Foreign Ministry in April 1937 shows German leaders understood the political utility and sensitivity of such information. The memo proposes that, in light of the NIC's review of alleged intervention activity, the embassy in London should receive special dispatches of German intelligence about such activity.[181]

German leaders withheld this information and appear to have done so to help reinforce limits on the war. The same Foreign Ministry memo proposing that intelligence be forwarded to the German staff at the NIC noted such evidence should only be used for "counterattack" should Berlin's involvement be demonstrated by others.[182] Leaders in Berlin appeared to take additional measures to avoid complications from such intelligence, at times refusing to share intelligence with these representatives.[183] An especially revealing Foreign Ministry memo about leaked German intelligence reflects caution about how such information could impact escalation dynamics. The memo laments the unauthorized publication in a German newspaper of inaccurate allegations of French troop participation in the front

177 Frank, Jr., "Naval Operations in the Spanish Civil War, 1936–1939," 32, 36.

178 Consul General in Barcelona to the Foreign Ministry, September 16, 1936, DGFP, Doc. 81; Charge d'Affaires in the Soviet Union to the Foreign Ministry, September 28. 1936, DGFP, Doc. 88.

179 Ambassador in the Soviet Union to the Foreign Ministry, October 26, 1936, DGFP, Doc. 107; Consul General in Barcelona to the Foreign Ministry, October 29, 1936, DGFP, Doc. 112.

180 Memorandum by Head of Political Division IIIa, February 28, 1938, DGFP, Doc. 538.

181 Memorandum by Head of Political Division III, April 21, 1937, DGFP, Doc. 246.

182 Memorandum by Head of Political Division III, April 21, 1937, DGFP, Doc. 246.

183 Thomas, The Spanish Civil War, 2001, 344–46.

lines. The memo notes how the news story had prompted an angry inquiry from the French ambassador. The writer, Ernst von Weizsacker, invokes the need for better censorship, lamenting that "this is in my opinion another instance which shows that a press policy in international matters without the participation of the Foreign Ministry must have unfavorable results."[184]

Italy developed its own intelligence network which, though less extensive than Germany's, carefully monitored events in Spain's war.[185] As with its own intervention, Italy's use of intelligence was less cautious than its German ally. Italy appears to have been the initiator of accusations of foreign intervention by the Soviet government in the NIC's earliest meetings in the fall of 1936. A summary of a November 1936 meeting, for example, notes "Italian charges against Soviet intervention"; yet the committee itself deemed that such claims "were not supportable by the evidence produced and that the Soviet Government could not in consequence be held to have violated its agreement."[186] Although he does not specifically address whether such claims were supported with evidence or featured "volunteer" rhetoric, Coverdale does note that Italian news stories covered French and Russian aid.[187]

Soviet internal documents released after the end of the Cold War, though less extensive, paint a similar picture of rich information on rival outside interventions. Personnel from the Soviet NKVD and GRU intelligence agencies were widely dispersed within the Spanish Republican military and intelligence apparatus as advisors. A review of Stalin-era documents on the Spanish Civil War notes that "agents of the GRU were everywhere" within the Republican military, including in positions of command authority and operational planning; the air forces, navy, and tank groups were "the most heavily penetrated and controlled by the advisers."[188] Soviet intelligence assets outside of Spain also provided useful evidence of external involvement. It even turned up evidence of bystander outside powers

---

184 Minute by the Director of the Political Department, July 24, 1937, DGFP, Doc. 402.

185 "Italian diplomatic espionage was extraordinarily active" during the period and cites an example of a British classified diplomatic report passed by Italian intelligence to Germany early in the war; Coverdale, *Italian Intervention in the Spanish Civil War*, 111; see also Frank, Jr., "Naval Operations in the Spanish Civil War, 1936–1939," 32, 36.

186 Padelford, "The International Non-Intervention Agreement and the Spanish Civil War," 587.

187 Coverdale, *Italian Intervention in the Spanish Civil War*, 265, 277.

188 Ronald Radosh and Mary R. Habeck, *Spain Betrayed: The Soviet Union in the Spanish Civil War* (New Haven, CT: Yale University Press, 2001), 57.

knowing about Soviet involvement. A British intelligence report obtained by Soviet intelligence and sent back to Moscow, for example, includes precise descriptions of its own shipments of "a hundred thousand Mauser rifles... fifty million cartridges."[189] In fact, Ronald Radosh and Mary Habeck argue the deep Soviet penetration of Spanish Republican institutions may have given them the best intelligence capabilities regarding the Spanish Civil War of all of the European powers.[190]

Moscow largely colluded by keeping its intelligence private. Soviet representatives did repeat media reports of German and Italian involvement when accused at the NIC. Yet Soviet leaders never presented evidence based on intelligence to corroborate such claims.[191] Soviet leaders also used other tactics to blunt the seriousness of its complaints, as when its complaint to the NIC about external aid to the Nationalists in October 1936 "refrained from attacking Germany and Italy directly and instead focused on Portugal, a much weaker state which transshipped German and Italian supplies."[192] David Cattell's review of Soviet behavior recounts how "the Soviet Union herself did not contribute one piece of evidence that would put these powers in a bad light" and deems this "surprising" and finds it "difficult to understand the failure." He goes on to suggest either Moscow had no intelligence or Soviet leaders feared "the release of information might lead to its [own] exposure" and thereby unravel non-intervention diplomacy.[193]

Although largely theory-consistent, collusion regarding Italian ground involvement is surprising in light of the escalation dynamics I identify. Because the Italian ground role was widely known to domestic and other audiences, major powers could not meaningfully influence what was known about the intervention through collusion. The theory suggests situations of open secrecy should lead to exposure by rivals as a way to undermine the intervention. In short, there was more collusion than the theory expects. This likely reflects an interesting feature of this case: interdependence. Refuting Italy's public position that its nationals were "volunteers" would also seem to be a refutation of German and Soviet claims that their nationals

189 This is described as "one example of the quality of the material to which the Soviets had access." Radosh and Habeck, *Spain Betrayed*, 99–101.

190 Radosh and Habeck, *Spain Betrayed*, 99–101.

191 On the "general propaganda pattern" of citing media reports but not adding information to them, see David Cattell, *Soviet Diplomacy and the Spanish Civil War* (Berkeley: University of California Press, 1957), 5.

192 Cattell, *Soviet Diplomacy and the Spanish Civil War*, 43.

193 Cattell, *Soviet Diplomacy and the Spanish Civil War*, 48–49.

were "volunteers." The particular method for avoiding acknowledgment for all three external interveners therefore created interdependence or mutual reliance. This is also reflected in the way negotiations at the NIC focused on the interlinked nature of volunteer withdrawal proposals.

Conclusion

The civil war that erupted in Spain in 1936 threatened the powers of Europe with realistic scenarios for another continent-wide war. Geographic limits were central to preventing such an escalation. Major European powers used secrecy and non-acknowledgment regarding foreign intervention to help control the risks of large-scale escalation. Both mechanisms of the theory played a role. Covertness and collusion were believed to help reduce the impact of domestic pressures that could push forward escalation, in particular in Paris and London. Moreover, covertness and collusion, in particular through participation in the NIC, were believed to provide continuous reassurance that even intervening powers sought to limit the war.

Overall, the conflict makes a strong case that limited war produces different secrecy dynamics. Rather than helping build operational military advantages through deception of adversaries (i.e., operational security logic) or insulating leaders from anti-intervention dovish reactions (i.e., domestic dove logic), secrecy and non-acknowledgment were tools to keep the civil war in Spain contained. Moreover, both intervening states and bystanders like the UK were mutually aware of one another's combat roles; that is, backstage behavior was mutually visible. Although domestic politics did play a role, the primary consideration driving manipulation of information and strained references to "volunteers" was hawkish, nationalist reactions. Of particular note in this regard is Germany. Despite Hitler's ultimate strategic goal of hegemony through bellicosity and aggression, Berlin carefully monitored domestic politics in Britain and France and modulated German and Italian visibility to avoid provoking a continental war prematurely.

Two other findings from the chapter are important to highlight. First, direct communication in a formal international institution, i.e., the Non-Intervention Committee, facilitated limited war. Non-intervention pledges were clear and recognizable "thresholds" to localize the violence in Spain. The NIC provided a private space for airing grievances, clarifying backstage behavior, and monitoring one another's commitment to limited war. Even the most brazen intervention—Italian ground forces very visibly participating in key battles in Spain—could be collectively framed as "volunteers" to help minimize tit-for-tat escalation and avoid a larger European war. Second, several cases show factors and dynamics outside the scope of my theory. The Italian ground role was steadfastly denied by Italy as "volunteer" despite being an early mover and localized in its scope. Moscow's value from keeping its role covert was overdetermined, both benefiting its diplomatic relationships with France and Great Britain as well as helping avoid unraveling non-intervention diplomacy.

Finally, the Spanish Civil War laid the foundation for conflicts analyzed in later empirical chapters. It included early examples of effectively concealed military aid and visible-but-unacknowledged clashes among major powers. The direct clashes between Italian volunteers and concealed Soviet tanks crews presage the covert clashes in later conflicts like the Vietnam War. Moreover, specific aspects of the war in Spain would be cited in later conflicts, such as the device of volunteers to render military personnel unofficial and unacknowledged. Later chapters show explicit references to these dynamics in Spain underscoring the role of learning across conflicts.

5

The Korean War (1950–1953)

Two decades after the Spanish Civil War and only five years after World War II, conflict between North and South Korea threatened to again plunge the wider international system into war. The Korean War, fought from 1950 to 1953, grew to include multiple outside interventions. Yet despite Soviet, American, and Chinese combat participation, the war was successfully limited to the Korean peninsula. This chapter focuses on the covert side of the Korean War, showing how escalation control drove leaders to embrace covert behavior and collude when detecting it. This limited war, in turn, became a key reference point for the future encounters in the Cold War. The Korean War would become the paradigmatic case of how great powers in the atomic age could successfully limit war.[1] How force was used on both

---

1 Robert Jervis, "The Impact of the Korean War on the Cold War," *Journal of Conflict Resolution* 24, no. 4 (December 1, 1980): 578–84; John Lewis Gaddis, *The Cold War: A New History* (New York: Penguin Group (USA), 2005), 50–65; Yuen Foong Khong, *Analogies at War: Korea, Munich, Dien Bien Phu, and the Vietnam Decisions of 1965* (Princeton, NJ: Princeton University Press, 1992). Smoke describes the influential concepts of "a war arena and of geographic sanctuaries," important for later Cold War encounters, as specifically emerging from the Korean War. Examples of such sanctuaries in the Korean War include Western use of force near and over the Yalu River and the Chinese and Soviet refusal to endanger American military assets in Japan. Richard Smoke, *War: Controlling Escalation* (Cambridge, MA: Harvard University Press, 1977), 14–16; Brodie too noted the sanctuaries concept emerging from the Korean War and cites its impact later: "as a result, the concept of sanctuary has played an important part in speculations on limited war as well as in certain war games." Bernard Brodie, *Strategy in the Missile Age* (Princeton, NJ: Princeton University Press, 1959), 329.

sides of the Korean War was quickly recognized on both sides as "likely to be a pattern for the future."[2] This chapter sheds new light on the specific ways secrecy and non-acknowledgment played a part in this process.

The Korean War is an important conflict to analyze for both historical and theoretical reasons. Though limited, the war helped launch the Cold War. In the United States, fighting in the Korean War reversed much of the postwar demobilization, helped propel approval of the influential NSC-68 policy strategy, and swelled the nascent national security state.[3] Theoretically, the war featured multiple outside interventions which allow a variety of comparisons and contrasts relevant to the theory's observable implications. Chosen despite similar structural features, this range includes an overt intervention (United States), a covert intervention (Soviet Union), and an unacknowledged "volunteer" intervention (China). Table 5.1 summarizes the cases I analyze in this chapter.

The chapter also features cases of detection. Table 5.2 summarizes collusion and exposure patterns. American leaders, for example, obtained conclusive evidence of covert Soviet participation in air combat through intelligence collection techniques like signals intercepts. Even before its more widely visible entry in late November 1950, US leaders also detected China's quiet participation in combat operations in northern North Korea. Public reporting of Soviet involvement was minimal, while China's ground entry appeared in mainstream news stories by early November 1950. Information

2 Smoke, *War: Controlling Escalation*, 8; Jervis, "The Impact of the Korean War on the Cold War"; Schelling also observed that Korea set precedents for how limited war would be fought in later Cold War encounters. Thomas Schelling, *The Strategy of Conflict* (Cambridge, MA: Harvard University Press, 1960), 130. Osgood notes that Korea in general "served as the great catalyst of limited-war thinking," Robert E. Osgood, *Limited War Revisited* (Boulder, CO: Westview Press, 1979), 6; see also Christopher M. Gacek, *The Logic of Force: The Dilemma of Limited War in American Foreign Policy* (New York: Columbia University Press, 1994), 132. On the Soviet side, see a CIA-translated secret Soviet Ministry of Defense publication, titled "Air Forces in Modern Local Wars," that showed Soviet leaders learning from the experience of the Korean, Vietnam, and other Wars. CIA Intelligence Information Special Report, March 30, 1976, CIA CREST, Doc. 5076e965993247d4d82b67d6.

3 Jervis, "The Impact of the Korean War on the Cold War"; Steven Casey, "Selling NSC-68: The Truman Administration, Public Opinion, and the Politics of Mobilization, 1950–51," *Diplomatic History* 29, no. 4 (2005): 655–90; Steven Casey, *Selling the Korean War: Propaganda, Politics, and Public Opinion in the United States, 1950–1953* (New York: Oxford University Press, 2008); Michael J. Hogan, *A Cross of Iron: Harry S. Truman and the Origins of the National Security State, 1945–1954*, 1st ed. (New York: Cambridge University Press, 2000); William Stueck, *The Korean War: An International History* (Princeton, NJ: Princeton University Press, 1995). Jervis (584–88) also reviews whether other events could have stimulated such a convergence in threat perception and concludes the Korean War was uniquely critical.

TABLE 5.1. Intervention Cases in the Korean War

	Timeline	Location	Timing	Form	Details	Theory support
United States	June 1950 to end	Local (Korean peninsula)	First mover	Overt	Public, acknowledged ground, air units aiding South Korea	Strong
	November 1950 to end	Peripheral (Mainland China)	First mover	Covert	Concealed, unacknowl-edged ground operations supporting KMT remnants	Strong
Soviet Union	November 1950 to end	Local (Korean peninsula)	Subsequent intervener	Covert	Concealed, unacknowl-edged air combat role	Strong
China	October 1950 to end	Local (Korean peninsula)	Subsequent intervener	Covert (open secret by November 1950)	"Volunteer" ground, air operations in North Korea (November 1950–end)	Mixed

TABLE 5.2. Detector Behavior in Korean War

	Detection	Third-party exposure	Expectation	Outcome	Theory support
Covert Soviet (Korea)	Yes: United States	Low	Collusion	Collusion	Strong
Covert Chinese (Korea)	Yes: United States	High	Exposure	Initial collusion, then exposure	Mixed
Covert United States (China)	Yes? China	Low	Collusion	Collusion	Strong

on American covert operations targeting the Chinese mainland is less consistent; it went entirely unnoticed in public reporting but was likely identified by Chinese intelligence sources.

Beyond these core findings, the chapter has additional historiographical and theoretical interest. First, the chapter includes novel historical findings. It details the covert air war between Soviet and American pilots during the Korean War which we discussed in the book's earlier chapters. Although I am not the first to identify and review these encounters, this chapter includes a detailed review of a large number of newly accessed declassified American intelligence documents. This provides an unusually candid view of the anticipation and detailed knowledge of a detected covert intervention as well as powerfully demonstrating the non-trivial role secrecy can play in limiting war. I also review new documentary evidence about the role of covert US military aid to Chinese nationalists. Second, the chapter features an interesting case of open secrecy. China's visible but unacknowledged "volunteers" resembled those used in the Spanish Civil War. I show how this labeling choice was understood by Mao, Stalin, and American observers as a disingenuous but convenient device for controlling escalation. Third, the case shows how alternative logics for secrecy can coexist with the limited-war logic I develop. China's entry also included adversary deception using secrecy. An operational security logic and my own theory therefore provide insight into different aspects of the war.[4] My theory shows how secrecy-related practices helped keep the conflict from escalating further.

I begin here by providing an overview of the conflict and the key escalation features that I argue influence choices about how to intervene and what to do when covert intervention is detected. I then analyze each outside power in turn. The second section analyzes the initial American overt intervention as well as the covert intervention on mainland China later in the war. The next section describes and assesses the Soviet covert intervention in the air; it includes a review of the tacit collusion by the United States as well. The fourth section focuses on China's role in the war, highlighting the importance of tactical surprise in its first phase of covert involvement and limited-war concerns in its second phase.[5]

4 E.g., Branislav L. Slantchev, "Feigning Weakness," *International Organization* 64, no. 3 (2010): 357–88.

5 I rely on a combination of new archival materials on American and Soviet behavior, extant collections of primary materials, and specialists' analysis of original Chinese records. My analysis of the American decision to overtly intervene and its intelligence on Chinese and Soviet

Overview and Context

In coordination with his Soviet and Chinese allies, Kim Il Sung and the Korean People's Army (KPA) launched a surprise attack into South Korea on June 25, 1950.[6] Within two weeks of the invasion, they had captured large swaths of South Korean territory including Seoul. President Truman ordered immediate assistance to South Korea from American forces in occupied Tokyo, authorizing use of air, naval, and US combat troops within four days of the attack. The United Nations Security Council (UNSC) simultaneously passed a resolution demanding the end of hostilities and the assistance of member states to restore the prewar status quo.[7] American-led military support under General Douglas MacArthur's command staved off defeat and, by early August 1950, a stalemate emerged along the outskirts of the southern port city of Pusan. A mid-September amphibious landing

---

intervention draws on published primary collections; most important are the *Foreign Relations of the United States* (hereafter *FRUS*; all references are to Volume 7, "Korea," unless otherwise noted) series and a collection of Central Intelligence Agency documents published in 2010. These were supplemented with new archival materials from the State Department and Congress (from National Archives and Records Administration I and II locations), White House records from the Truman Presidential Library, and intelligence documents from the CREST system. Moreover, an important set of documents on the Soviet side, which also shed some light on Chinese knowledge and decisions, were made available and translated after the Cold War. I mostly draw on a collection of such documents held at the Woodrow Wilson Center's Cold War International History Project as well as related working papers based on these materials. Finally, on the Chinese side, I largely rely on several book-length analyses of China in the Korean War by specialist historians who had access to a collection of primary materials on Mao's decision-making during Korea. Most important are Sergei Goncharov, John Lewis, and Litai Xue, *Uncertain Partners: Stalin, Mao, and the Korean War* (Stanford, CA: Stanford University Press, 1993); Chen Jian, *China's Road to the Korean War* (New York: Columbia University Press, 1994); Shu Guang Zhang, *Mao's Military Romanticism: China and the Korean War, 1950–1953* (Lawrence: University Press of Kansas, 1995).

6 The existence, sequence, and extent of consultation with Stalin and Mao have been the subject of significant attention by historians of the Korean War. New evidence since the end of the Cold War shows significant prior consultation took place at the initiative of the North Koreans and some presence of Soviet advisors in planning and executing the invasion. For a review of the state of debate, see James I. Matray, "Korea's War at 60: A Survey of the Literature," *Cold War History* 11, no. 1 (February 2011): 99–129. The historiography of the war has included significant debate over the relative importance of civil vs. international factors. For representative works of either side, see, respectively, Bruce C. Cumings, *The Origins of the Korean War, Vol. 2: The Roaring of the Cataract* (Princeton, NJ: Princeton University Press, 1990); Stueck, *The Korean War: An International History*.

7 The resolution was not vetoed by the Soviet Union due to their boycott of the Council; the Chinese Communists did not veto because China's seat had not yet been transferred from the Nationalists.

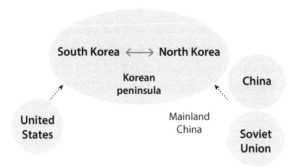

FIGURE 5.1. Structure of Korean War.

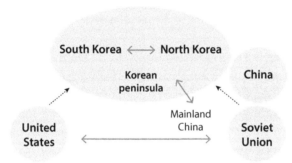

FIGURE 5.2. Key escalation scenarios, Korean War.

at Inchon dramatically reversed the war's momentum, allowing American-led forces to recapture Seoul, threaten North Korea's supply lines, and force a hurried retreat of the KPA. MacArthur's advancing UN forces crossed the 38th parallel into North Korea and continued a northward advance toward the Chinese border. Urgent Sino-Soviet discussions about a now-beleaguered ally led to a rough division of labor: Mao would provide ground troops relabeled as volunteers, while Stalin would secretly provide air support. The resulting counteroffensive nearly destroyed the overextended UN troop columns and allowed recapture of almost all of North Korea by the first months of 1951. Here the shifting tides of the war stopped as the two sides settled into a military stalemate that lasted two years and finally broke with an armistice struck in 1953.

Figure 5.1 identifies the local combatants and local conflict zone (i.e., Korean peninsula). It also notes external intervening powers and the most likely peripheral zone into which the war could expand (i.e., mainland China). Figure 5.2 highlights the two most likely scenarios for large-scale escalation which influenced decision-making: the spread of combat to peripheral areas like mainland China, and the emergence of direct combat between outside interveners. Once American and other Western forces were overtly involved, localization of the conflict to the Korean peninsula was a pressing challenge. Failure to do so could turn the war into a regional conflict involving China or, in the worst case, a global war between American and Soviet forces. Both scenarios were explicitly discussed in internal deliberations. The involvement of both Soviet and Chinese military personnel in late 1950 made geographic confinement especially important. Their role led to clashes between the military forces of major powers inside the Korean peninsula, some publicly observable (i.e., US-China) and some concealed (i.e., US-Soviet). As I argue below, the desire to control escalation and avoid a wider war led to the use of non-acknowledgment and effective secrecy.

Controlling the two escalation problems I identify in chapter 2 was an important concern. The destructiveness of any large-scale war was highly salient for leaders given the recent memory of enormously destructive fighting in World War II and China's own civil war. Beyond this, all three outside powers were eager to rebuild after these conflicts, making escalation control that much more important. The advent of atomic weapons, and the Soviet Union's acquisition in 1949, infused further concern for any larger war.

Regarding domestic politics and hawkish pressure, American leaders in particular wrestled with a volatile domestic climate. The idea of limited war itself was difficult to square with the enormous national effort used in World War II. As Soviet and American trust eroded in the late 1940s, fears of communist subversion and aggression were strong. The Truman White House therefore struggled to mobilize mass public support for the Korea intervention without succumbing to hawkish demands for an early attack on either Communist China or the Soviet Union.[8] While the personalist dictatorships in Moscow and Beijing felt far fewer domestic constraints, Mao and Stalin understood how escalation could be influenced by US domestic political constraints. Miscommunication risks lurked in many of the diplomatic crises of the late 1940s and early 1950. Alliance politics was infused in any clash due to the recent conclusion of the Sino-Soviet mutual defense pact and the North Atlantic Treaty. Moreover, the ideological character of the budding rivalry between Moscow, Washington, and their allies produced

8 Casey, *Selling the Korean War.*

acute concern for reputation as well as uncertainty about strategic goals among the United States, China, and the Soviet Union. Both sides therefore had good reason to seek ways to demonstrate their resolve as well as their restraint to facilitate escalation control.

CROSS-CONFLICT LEARNING

Efforts to compete while controlling escalation were informed by lessons from previous encounters. Overall, the Korean War was underinformed by previous experience. As George and Smoke note, during the war "the concept of limited war was still a novel one and did not enter into the framework of American military-strategic planning."[9] Moreover, the Chinese Communist Party had emerged from its own civil war within a year of the war, meaning little interaction with the West had a chance to develop. Although it did not create a blank slate, I argue below that this early encounter in the Cold War was fertile ground for misunderstanding. This explains one miscommunication failure and instance of exploitation that pushed the war to a larger scale and enabled Chinese tactical surprise.[10]

Decision-makers sought comparisons in evaluating the feasibility of limited war in general and covert or undeclared war in particular. References in primary documents show how past conflicts helped leaders grasp escalation dynamics and state behavior. One example involved reaching back into the nineteenth century. A high-level British intelligence analysis of the risks of war with China, for example, cited the Crimean War. The British Chiefs of Staff urged their American counterparts to exercise caution in early January 1951 by arguing that

> while it may be possible to confine active operations to a sort of "Crimean War" like in Korea, once they cease to be so localised there is in fact no such thing as "limited war." We find it almost impossible to believe that open general war against China in the Far East could fail to spread sooner rather than later to war on a worldwide scale with Russia fully

9 Alexander L. George and Richard Smoke, *Deterrence in American Foreign Policy: Theory and Practice* (New York: Columbia University Press, 1974), 146; Jervis notes that despite occasional references to limited-conflict scenarios in American internal analysis in the two years before the North Korean invasion, "[n]owhere was the belief in the possibility of limited wars spelled out with an analysis of what could cause them, keep them limited, and how they might be fought." Jervis, "The Impact of the Korean War on the Cold War," 572.

10 E.g., Alexander Ovodenko, "(Mis)Interpreting Threats: A Case Study of the Korean War," *Security Studies* 16, no. 2 (April 1, 2007): 254–86.

engaged. It would, in our view, be far too optimistic to assume either that China would not invoke the Sino-Russian Treaty or that Russia would not respond if she did invoke it.[11]

A few other comparisons were made to events from the interwar period. A pair of such references appeared in early November 1950 as part of the attempt to assess the implications of the appearance of Chinese military personnel on the battlefield. For example, the US ambassador in Moscow noted the danger of over-extending American military forces into East Asia and the concern of allies about a widened war. He then describes "a pattern" with reference to several historical analogs to make the case for potentially ignoring undeclared clashes, referencing both the Spanish Civil War and the "Amur River," site of a Soviet-Japanese border incident in 1937:

> We here cannot forget [the] situation which existed between Soviet and Japanese Governments in mid-thirties when actual hostilities were engaged in along Amur River but without an open declaration of war. Also in [the] Spanish Civil War there were German and Italian military units engaged but their presence overlooked or winked at by other great powers. Similarly, we have had recent experience in Greece where Maejos [Markos] guerrillas were equipped with many weapons coming from foreign sources and frontiers were opened to give sanctuary to Andartes. It seems a pattern has developed in such matters.[12]

A third example shows a nascent understanding of the links between how great powers intervene, domestic constraints, and escalation. A top secret State Department memo assessed Soviet intentions given China's entry. Drawing again on the Spanish Civil War and Soviet-Japanese episodes in the 1930s ("Nomanhan Incident" was the name Japan used for border clashes in 1939), John Davies argues on November 7, 1950 that Soviet leaders surely understood that controlling escalation in Korea was more difficult than in past undeclared or "volunteer"-based conflicts because of the Soviet adversary's domestic politics:

> The Kremlin is, of course, alert to the grave and unpredictable [*sic*] risks which flow from Chinese intervention. It may even be inviting them,

---

11 "Vulnerability of China," Memorandum by the British Chiefs of Staff to Joint Chiefs of Staff, January 4, 1951, NARA II, RG 218, Joint Chiefs of Staff, Geographic File 1951–1953, Box 14, CCS 381 Far East Sec. 1, p. 63.

12 The Ambassador in the Soviet Union (Kirk) to the Secretary of State, November 7, 1950, *FRUS*.

seeking to precipitate World War III. What seems more likely, however, more in keeping with the Kremlin's political personality, is that it accepts rather than seeks the risks of general conflict. It cannot believe that the risks do not exist, even though it is twice removed from formal responsibility—itself to Peiping and Peiping to the "volunteers." The Kremlin undoubtedly realizes now that it is not dealing with controlled incidents—as it did with the Axis in Spain and the Japanese at Nomanhan. In this situation it is playing with the volatile fire of American democracy.[13]

One can see several lessons being drawn from the interwar references. One was that clashing major powers could ignore their own incidents. Another lesson referred to the reaction to such incidents: Ambassador Kirk's telegram specifically notes that this kind of behavior can be "overlooked or winked at" as part of his overall recommendation that Washington downplay Soviet and Chinese involvement in the Korean War. A third lesson seems to have been specifically about risk, democracy, and war escalation. The second memo self-referentially cites a volatile democratic decision-making context as something an adversary likely takes into account, especially compared to clashes with Nazi Germany, Fascist Italy, and Imperial Japan that could be more easily manipulated by less accountable leaders. Such comparisons therefore provided important context for intervention decisions, as I describe below.

US Intervention in Korea

Washington reacted swiftly to the rapid advance of North Korea's invading force in late June 1950. Within five days, Truman approved unrestricted use of air and naval assets as well as General MacArthur's request to redeploy ground troops from Japan to protect the crucial Korean port city of Pusan.[14] American leaders coordinated with allies to simultaneously shepherd resolutions condemning the invasion as an act of North Korean aggression through the United Nations Security Council and built multinational contributions for a "police action" to respond.[15] The result was a highly publicized intervention intended to preserve the viability of South Korea and restore

---

13 Draft Memorandum by Mr. John P. Davies of the Policy Planning Staff, November 7, 1950, *FRUS*.

14 The sequence of these decisions is described in detail in Allan R. Millett, *The War for Korea, 1950–1951: They Came from the North* (Lawrence: University Press of Kansas, 2010), 114–27.

15 Stueck, *The Korean War: An International History*, 61–63.

the status quo ante. The US role in conducting the war was dominant; indeed, the "United Nations Command" and its leadership was simply the American military's Far East Command. The US ground, naval, and air roles lasted until the conclusion of armistice talks in 1953.

My theory highlights the importance of timing and location in shaping escalation risk severity and the form of intervention. The US intervention in Korea provides strong support to the mechanisms and conditions I identify. Most importantly, this intervention benefited from being a "first-mover" decision. Drawing on sensitive intelligence and public Soviet statements, American leaders were confident that Moscow sought to carefully distance itself from the North Korean invasion. China too was uninvolved in the initial operations in late June. Moreover, military aid could be confined to the Korean peninsula proper, preserving an unambiguous geographic limit. Following the logic of chapter 2, this meant American intervention, while raising escalation risks, would not eliminate the most important "salient thresholds" preventing large-scale escalation. Later Soviet and Chinese decision-making, in contrast, had to deal with the reality of large numbers of Western combat forces publicly known and acknowledged to be in active combat.

To be clear, Western leaders were aware of the escalation risks in providing military aid to South Korea. Secretary of State Dean Acheson noted Washington decision-making in the first weeks "was taken in the full realization of a risk of war with the Soviet Union."[16] The State Department's top advisor to General MacArthur cabled Secretary Acheson stating that US intervention on behalf of South Korea "risks Russian counter moves."[17] The breadth and depth of limited-war concerns—and a sense of imperfect control over it—is demonstrated by National Security Council (NSC) planning. NSC 73/4, approved in August 1950, noted the geostrategic dangers of a general war "in the light of the Korean situation," the possibility of intentional or intentional pathways to general war ("Global war could come in one of three ways: (a) by Soviet design; (b) by a progression of developments growing out of the present situation; or (c) by a miscalculation on the part of either the U.S. or the USSR") and recommended a rapid de-

---

16 Memo from Secretary of State to Secretary of Defense, June 28, 1950, *FRUS*.

17 Telegram from Sebald to Secretary of State, June 25, 1950, *FRUS*. However, the cable concludes intervention was better than inaction because failure to intervene "would start [a] disastrous chain of events leading most probably to world war."

fense buildup in case it transpired.[18] Moreover, the American strategic priority was in safeguarding Europe and avoiding entanglement in a large war in Asia. The two spheres were seen as linked, given finite military capabilities and postwar demobilization. Escalation in Korea was therefore both costly and diversionary, neither of which were in Washington's geostrategic interests.[19]

Yet internal documents suggest American leaders perceived the escalation problem to be manageable in this first stage. This was due in part to sensitive intelligence that showed Moscow was trying hard to minimize and hide its own role in the first weeks of the invasion. A June 28 cabinet meeting, for example, included President Truman expressing concern about Soviet participation and ordering his national security team to give "special attention ... to obtaining intelligence concerning clear evidence of Soviet participation in Korean hostilities."[20] On the ground and in diplomatic communications, US observers found evidence that Soviet leaders were making clear efforts to distance themselves from the invasion. An intelligence analysis of North Korean POW interrogations reported, "Soviet advisors departed from the NK units before or at the time that the units crossed the 38th parallel" and judged that this "reflects Soviet avoidance of direct involvement in the Korean conflict."[21] Moreover, the American ambassador in Moscow noted how private communications with his Soviet counterparts "avoided direct Soviet implication" by relying on "numerous ambiguities" and giving "no publicity to participation [of] Soviet

18 Report by the National Security Council, August 25, 1950, *FRUS* Volume 1, National Security Affairs; Foreign Economic Policy.

19 Marc Trachtenberg, *A Constructed Peace: The Making of the European Settlement, 1945–1963* (Princeton, NJ: Princeton University Press, 1999); Victor D. Cha, "Powerplay: Origins of the U.S. Alliance System in Asia," *International Security* 34, no. 3 (January 1, 2010): 158–96; Victor D. Cha, *Powerplay: The Origins of the American Alliance System in Asia* (Princeton, NJ: Princeton University Press, 2016).

20 Record of Action by the National Security Council, NSC Action 308, June 28, 1950, Harry S. Truman Presidential Library (hereafter HSTL), President's Secretary's Files (hereafter PSF), National Security Council File 1947–1953, p. 2.

21 Korea Bulletin, HSTL, August 30, 1950. Other raw reports of Soviet advisors in rear areas note, "pilot of a North Korean Yale aircraft, upon interrogation, reported a Soviet colonel as an air base commander, assisted by some 15 Soviet personnel of lower rank" (Joint Morning Sitrep No. 2, HSTL, PSF, Intelligence File); "A Soviet major general is reportedly directing the North Korean attack. Another report placed a Soviet major general in Seoul" as well as "Soviet Military Advisory Group reportedly is using the Banto Hotel or the Mitsui Building in Seoul as a command post" (Joint Morning Sitrep No. 5, HSTL, PSF, Intelligence File).

'volunteers.' "[22] This was the critical evidence that Moscow was "not prepared to risk the possibility of global war."[23] Intelligence analysis echoed
this conclusion, arguing the United States "faced a strong possibility of
global war" but that "the USSR is not yet prepared to risk full-scale war
with the Western Powers." Moscow will "seek to localize the Korean conflict" by "publicly disclaiming any responsibility for the invasion and ...
providing support to North Korea short of open participation by Soviet
forces in an attempt to perpetuate the civil war and maintain North Korean
positions."[24] The impact of this intelligence on judgments of Soviet intentions is consistent with the communication function outlined in chapter 2,
where I argue that an adversary observing secrecy about a rival's role
should infer a desire for escalation control.

At the same time, the operational and symbolic benefits of an overt
US role were routinely cited in early deliberations about intervention,
consistent with the theory's expectations about the benefits of the frontstage. Low-profile, covert aid was seen as impractical given the operational
demands of a beleaguered ally. North Korea's rapid advances created an
urgent need for immediate, large-scale ground support. In the initial transmission of instructions to General MacArthur in Tokyo, for example,
American leaders expressed certainty that leaks regarding American naval
and air assistance would take place.[25] During a closed briefing to members
of Congress on June 30, moreover, General Omar Bradley asked attendees
to treat the briefing as secret. When asked why, he clarified he did not mean
"to keep secret the fact that we were going to send ground troops in. That
fact ... could not possibly be kept secret because there is no effective censorship in Korea."[26]

22 Telegram from Kirk to Secretary of State, June 27, 1950, *FRUS*; Telegram from Kirk to
Secretary of State, June 30, 1950, *FRUS*; Telegram from Kirk to Secretary of State, November
14,1950, *FRUS*.

23 Telegram from Kirk to Secretary of State, June 26, 1950, *FRUS*; Telegram from Kirk to
Secretary of State, June 25, 1950, *FRUS*.

24 Study of CIA Reporting on Chinese Communist Intervention in the Korean War, October 1955, CIA-RDP86B00269R000300040002-2, p. 35.

25 In the exchange, Tokyo asks, "What publicity is being released in Washington regarding
missions and directives enunciated above by the President?" The response from Washington is
no publicity has been given yet but "it is recognized that your action ... may result in leaks from
Korea." Tokyo then responds that a public announcement would be valuable and that "information is certain to leak in next 24 hours" in any case. Washington (CSA) to Tokyo (CINCFE), June
1950, DA TT 3426, HSTL, PSF, Korean War File, pp. 6–7.

26 Memorandum of Conversation, June 30, 1950, HSTL, George M. Elsey Papers, p. 10.

Equally important was concern about signaling resolve and the risks of a deterrence failure. Placing its intervention on the frontstage had significant signaling appeal to leaders in Washington. References to the importance for the United Nations specifically, given the parallels between the Korean scenario and previous cases unaddressed by the League of Nations, appear several times in deliberations in June and July 1950. An early State Department intelligence analysis warned that "hope that the UN might become an effective international organization will have been virtually destroyed" if the organization did not successfully deal with the Korean crisis.[27] Visibly intervening through the United Nations was believed to be an important opportunity to show the new institution's capacity to address aggression and deter future Soviet adventurism. Truman and State Department advisors therefore insisted any US military intervention be repeatedly branded with the UN label.[28] This was supported by Washington's allies. The US ambassador to the United Nations, Warren Austin, reported that delegations from Australia, Sweden, and Italy specifically mentioned the importance of a firm response.[29]

EARLY COLLUSION ABOUT SOVIET PERSONNEL

Soviet efforts to distance itself from the invasion were a key indicator for American leaders that an overt intervention would be unlikely to prompt a larger war. Because many of the signs of Soviet distancing were via intelligence, Washington had unique information. It took concrete steps to reinforce this narrative of Soviet detachedness, a preliminary kind of collusion. Moreover, the internal debates that informed this reaction showcase particularly clear evidence of leaders understanding the potential impact of domestic hawkish reactions on escalation control.

To do this, the United States withheld intelligence indicating Soviet personnel performed advisory roles in the North Korean invasion, and some hints of possible combat participation. Moreover, public-facing official statements from Washington were intentionally geared toward focusing attention on North Korea and bolstering Soviet claims of non-involvement. One diplomatic cable warned that publicly charging Stalin with directing the invasion "might make it difficult for the Soviets to disassociate themselves

27 An Intelligence Estimate Prepared by the Estimates Group, June 25, 1950, *FRUS*.
28 Casey, *Selling the Korean War*, 27, 30.
29 Telegram from Austin to Secretary of State, June 26, 1950, *FRUS*.

from the North Koreans in the face of successful free world counter-action."[30] The British Foreign Office agreed and argued it "might be advantageous not to lay [the] attack at [the] door of [the] Russians in [the] hope that if [the] South Koreans proved strong enough to defend themselves, the Russians might conceivably ditch [the] North Koreans since [the] Russians had not committed their own prestige publicly."[31] The administration also warned congressional leaders against using inflammatory rhetoric. Meeting at the White House with the president and key advisors, a select group of legislators were asked to notice how the president's statement "did not refer in any way to the Soviet government" and explained that "it's best to leave a door wide open for the Soviet Union to back down without losing too much face.... If we publicly say that the Soviets are responsible for the actions of the communists in North Korea then, as a matter of prestige, the Soviet government will be forced to continue supporting the North Korean forces and we will find ourselves with a really tough scrap on our hands."[32]

The frankness of official American commentary about a Soviet role was also influenced by knowledge of a constrained domestic environment in which hawkish voices were a significant concern. Truman repeatedly urged his cabinet advisors and public information officers early in the war to avoid direct accusations of a Soviet role due to "the fear that the domestic mood might suddenly overheat."[33] Paul Nitze, State Department Policy Planning Staff director, identified a dilemma that would influence the American approach to information about Soviet involvement in Korea throughout the war. The more the United States tied the war to the Soviet Union, he argued, the more Washington would be forced to choose between highly visible appeasement and a dangerously escalated war:

30 Telegram from Kirk to Secretary of State, June 26, 1950, *FRUS*. The American ambassador in Paris similarly argued that "we all know, of course, that the Kremlin has set in motion and is directing the Korean operation, but as long as it is not so publicly cited, it would be easier for the Soviets privately to restrain the North Koreans." Telegram from Bruce to Secretary of State, June 26, 1950, *FRUS*.

31 The Swedish and Dutch delegations felt similarly regarding naming the Soviet Union. Other allies felt differently: the Australian and Argentine representatives, for example, were reported as advocating "it time to call things by their right names" by specifying the Soviets as the source of aggression. Telegram from Austin to Secretary of State, June 26, 1950, *FRUS*.

32 Memorandum of Conversation, June 27, 1950, HSTL, George M. Elsey Papers, p. 8.

33 This caution in rhetoric was in stark contrast to rhetoric exaggerating the Soviet threat used by Truman less than a year earlier when building support for the Truman Doctrine. For the contrast and specific examples of restraint regarding the Soviet role, see Casey, *Selling the Korean War*, 29–39.

It is distinctly not to the interest of United States to make any move on its part which would tend to widen the conflict ... Should the U.S. officially denounce the Soviet government as responsible for the aggression, it would be very difficult to avoid the logical consequences of such a position, i.e. branding the Soviet Union as the aggressor through U.N. action. Other steps, such as breaking diplomatic relations, etc., would be almost inescapable once the direct accusation was made. Failure to take these steps which would logically flow from any official position would be a very serious indication of fear of the Soviet Union.[34]

These efforts were framed by concerns about specific ways the Korean conflict could escalate and how best to localize the war given an overt intervention. Through intelligence withholding and official rhetoric, the United States helped reinforce the "frontstage" perception that its own overt involvement was not producing a direct clash with Soviet forces.

Soviet Intervention

COVERT AIR OPERATIONS IN KOREA

General MacArthur's amphibious landing at Inchon in September 1950 created the realistic prospect of a military march all the way to the Yalu River, the northern border between North Korea and China. As part of a coordinated Sino-Soviet response, the Soviet Union covertly deployed an estimated 40,000–70,000 servicemen in air combat, antiaircraft, and support roles to Manchuria and northern North Korea. At their peak in 1951–1952, around 26,000 Russian servicemen served in twelve divisions as fighter pilots, antiaircraft artillery operators, and aviation technicians.[35] As one of the leading researchers on the Soviet role plainly concludes, "Russians took part in every major air battle from late 1950 until spring 1953."[36] Their operational role was anything but cosmetic. Losses from Soviet-flown

---

34 Memorandum from Nitze to Acheson, July 23, 1950, "Checklist of Questions," Congressional 1950–1953, Box 8, Records of the Policy Planning Staff 1947–1953, General Records of the Department of State, Record Group 59, National Archives, College Park, MD. Quoted in part in Casey, *Selling the Korean War*.

35 Jon Halliday, "Air Operations in Korea: The Soviet Side of the Story," in *A Revolutionary War: Korea and the Transformation of The Postwar World*, ed. William J Williams (Chicago: Imprint Publications, 1993), 149–50; Kathryn Weathersby, "The Soviet Role in the Early Phase of the Korean War: New Documentary Evidence," *Journal of American-East Asian Relations* 2, no. 4 (Winter 1993): 438; Xiaoming Zhang, *Red Wings over the Yalu: China, the Soviet Union, and the Air War in Korea* (College Station, TX: Texas A&M University Press, 2002), chap. 6.

36 Halliday, "Air Operations in Korea: The Soviet Side of the Story," 158.

MIG-15s in particular led American air commanders to shift how they used airpower, avoiding flying missions during the day and in northwest North Korea in an important spring 1951 Chinese campaign.[37]

A limited-war logic provides powerful reasons for Moscow to conceal its role. On one dimension, the escalatory dangers of the intervention were low; combat encounters were confined to the Korean peninsula retaining localization of the war. However, the Soviet air entry came after the overt intervention of the United States and its allies. It was almost certainly inviting clashes between major powers within that local conflict. Moreover, the specific mechanisms for loss of escalation control were clear and present. The Soviets could plausibly surmise the response of the United States, and other democracies could be influenced by the visibility and severity of clashes. They also plainly knew that both major powers, and their allies, had significant room for miscommunication.

Soviet records now available shed considerable light on the timing and character of their covert role. An unusually granular view of the covert Soviet air role is provided by the availability of an end-of-war report by the commander of the 64th Fighter Aviation Corps.[38] It reports Soviet air crews shooting down 1,097 enemy aircraft during the war, with 319 Soviet aircraft and 110 pilots lost. The Corps was composed of fighter aviation divisions and antiaircraft artillery battalions. The mission took place in three basic phases. From November 1950 to spring 1951, a smaller contingent of the 64th Corps flew missions to protect "bridges across the Yalu River, airfields in the area of Dandong, and the hydroelectric station in the area of Sinuiju." Dozens of crews were also reserved "to retrain Chinese and Korean pilots to conduct combat operations." A spring offensive and the opening of a new airfield in mid-1951 led to the largest total deployment size and resulted in "heavy losses in bombers, ground attack aircraft, and fighters" during this first phase. A cable from Stalin to Mao in March 1951 references the need for additional fighter divisions "in view of the forthcoming major operations" which will require "the largest possible aviation force at the front."[39] In 1952, alterations in American tactics and the deployment of more advanced fighter jets led to a higher operational tempo with less effec-

37 Zhang, *Red Wings over the Yalu*, 123–26.

38 All data unless otherwise noted from Report from the 64th Fighter Aviation Corps of the Soviet Air Forces in Korea, July 1953, Wilson Center Digital Archive (hereafter WCDA), Document 114963.

39 Telegram from Stalin to Mao or Zhou Enlai via Zakharov, March 15, 1951, WCDA, Doc 112103.

tive Soviet performance. Despite efforts to integrate trained North Korean and Chinese pilots in late 1952, adverse weather conditions and American tactical changes meant the "main burden of performing combat missions laid mainly on the Corps ... until the conclusion of the armistice" in 1953.

Stalin imposed significant restrictions to conceal the Soviet role, ensuring air combat with US pilots would remain on the war's backstage. He was only willing to deploy Soviet personnel in ways that maximized plausible deniability.[40] He gave strict orders to assume the appearance of North Korean or Chinese personnel and to avoid apprehension by the enemy.[41] Planes flown by Soviet pilots bore the markings of North Korea or China. Soviet pilots wore Chinese-style uniforms and were assigned pseudonyms. Bombing and strafing operations were disallowed and flying deep behind enemy lines strictly forbidden. Most challenging, Soviet pilots were instructed to conduct intense aerial dog fights while only communicating with a set of memorized Chinese words. A Soviet veteran of the Korean War, still flummoxed by this obviously impractical order, told American journalists years later that "it worked until the first real fight in the air, when we forgot not only our Chinese commands but Russian words too—except for dirty language."[42]

Consistent with the theory, covertness was favored to allow Soviet combat aid without triggering a wider war. Prior work by historians of the war suggests Stalin was very concerned about conflict escalation even as he supported proactive and risk-raising policy (i.e., North Korea's invasion and China's entry).[43] Xiaoming Zhang concludes, "fearing the conflict might escalate into a full-blown war between the Soviet Union and the United States, Moscow placed security restrictions on Soviet pilots in an effort to conceal their participation in the Korean conflict."[44] Recent studies of the

40 Halliday, "Air Operations in Korea: The Soviet Side of the Story," 152; Weathersby, "The Soviet Role in the Early Phase of the Korean War: New Documentary Evidence," 434.

41 These details are described in Halliday, "Air Operations in Korea: The Soviet Side of the Story," 152–53; Weathersby, "The Soviet Role in the Early Phase of the Korean War: New Documentary Evidence," 436–38.

42 Quoted in Douglas Stanglin and Peter Cary, "Secrets of the Korean War," *U.S. News & World Report*, August 9, 1993.

43 Halliday, "Air Operations in Korea: The Soviet Side of the Story," 152; Stueck, *The Korean War: An International History*, 44.

44 Zhang, *Red Wings over the Yalu*, 139; Weathersby notes this reluctance and concludes Stalin was "extremely reluctant to risk direct confrontation." This represents the most generous interpretation of Stalin's motives and one that seems more consistent with Soviet rejection of the North's invasion and China's entry. Weathersby, "The Soviet Role in the Early Phase of the Korean War: New Documentary Evidence."

Korean War reach the same conclusion drawing on primary materials from all three sides and Chinese and Soviet specialists. Ted Hopf's analysis of Soviet decision-making in the early Cold War, for example, describes a number of foreign policy decisions by Stalin in 1949 and 1950, including concealed pilots in Korea, driven by "fear of provoking the United States."[45] To be fair, documenting Stalin's motivation for covertness is inevitably more difficult than doing so on the American side because the documentary record is comparatively much thinner. Documentation about reasoning rather than factual matters is especially rare.

Soviet strategic priorities reflect the geostrategic and economic constraints Soviet leaders faced in 1950. Stalin's overall strategic priority in the late 1940s and early 1950s was consolidating Soviet influence and advancing geopolitical Soviet ambitions without triggering an early war with the West.[46] Stalin's goal in supporting the North Korean invasion that kicked off the war was to opportunistically revise the territorial status quo while localizing the war.[47] These twin priorities have been noted widely by Cold War historians. William Stueck argues that rhetoric aside, Stalin felt "a deep sense of insecurity" relative to the United States stemming from atomic, air, and naval inferiority as well as a substantial deficit in military-industrial strength if both sides were mobilized.[48] A third world war over Korea—far from the coveted European theater and well before postwar recovery was complete—would be a massive and destructive mistake in Stalin's view.[49] Somewhat different interpretations of Stalin's geostrategic goals that em-

45 Ted Hopf, *Reconstructing the Cold War: The Early Years, 1945–1958* (New York: Oxford University Press, 2012), 122–30; see also Sheila Miyoshi Jager, *Brothers at War: The Unending Conflict in Korea* (New York: W. W. Norton 2013); Millett, *The War for Korea, 1950–1951*.

46 Kathryn Weathersby, "Should We Fear This? Stalin and the Danger of War with America," June 2002, Woodrow Wilson Center Cold War International History Project, Working Paper No. 39.

47 As noted, historians like Weathersby read the primary materials in light of the cautious half of Stalin's goals. Others read primary materials and find evidence of high-stakes gambling. See, for example, Alexandre Mansourov, "Stalin, Mao, Kim, and China's Decision to Enter the Korean War, Sept. 16–Oct. 15, 1950: New Evidence from the Russian Archives," Cold War International History Project Bulletin, Nos. 6/7 (Winter 1995). My own view is that these interpretations are not mutually exclusive and treating them as such ignores that Stalin may have made risky decisions while using tools, like covert intervention, to mitigate the risk of the worst escalation scenarios.

48 Stueck, *The Korean War: An International History*, 44.

49 "Stalin, however, was neither ready nor willing to bring on a direct military confrontation with the United States.... The fate of Korea, while related to the security concerns of the Soviet Union, did not affect the most vital Soviet interests." Chen Jian, *China's Road to the Korean War* (New York: Columbia University Press, 1994), 161.

phasize the more revisionist goals recognize the tradeoff between Europe and Asia, the priority of Europe in that tradeoff, and the undesirability of a large war growing out of Korea for Soviet interests. Vojtech Mastny, for example, argues Soviet goals were to bog down the United States in a war in Asia (i.e., via the Korean War) while building up military capabilities in Eastern Europe to win in the more important European theater.[50] Put differently, a more revisionist Stalin that still sought freedom of action in Europe would value escalation control.

What primary evidence is available supports the limited-war thesis in several respects. Soviet records indicate Stalin was very concerned about limiting the escalatory consequences of Soviet air participation. Early North Korean requests for Soviet air support earlier in the war were declined.[51] Even as Stalin and Mao quietly negotiated a combined response to the advancing Western forces in October 1950, Stalin made an ambiguous commitment to provide air cover.[52] More conclusive is evidence Stalin approved covert air support knowing it would be quickly detected by American intelligence. Even with the constraints he imposed on Soviet pilots, a remarkable cable to Stalin from his top defense advisor in Pyongyang warned that any pilots "will inevitably be discovered by the U.S. troops right after the first air combat, because all the control and command over the combat in the air will be conducted by our pilots in the Russian language."[53] This directly contradicts a logic of surprise, suggesting Soviet leaders knew their role would be detectable but still useful.

In addition, Kathryn Weathersby's review of primary Soviet records concludes that Stalin showed "cautious opportunism" but that "at no point

50 Vojtech Mastny, Sven S. Holtsmark, and Andreas Wenger, *War Plans and Alliances in the Cold War: Threat Perceptions in the East and West* (New York: Routledge, 2013), 18.

51 One telegram features a request for a Soviet YAK-9 fighter regiment to provide air defense of Pyongyang in late September 1950. Telegram from Soviet Defense Minister A. M. Vasilevsky to Stalin, September 21, 1950, WCDA, Doc. 112684. See also Zhihua Shen, "China and the Dispatch of the Soviet Air Force: The Formation of the Chinese-Soviet-Korean Alliance in the Early Stage of the Korean War," *Journal of Strategic Studies* 33, no. 2 (2010): 215–18.

52 A telegram from Stalin in July 1950 notes, "we consider it correct to concentrate immediately 9 Chinese divisions on the Chinese-Korean border for volunteers' actions in North Korea in the event of the enemy's crossing the 38th parallel. We will do our best to provide the air cover for these units." Ciphered Telegram from Stalin to Zhou Enlai via Roshchin, July 5, 1950, WCDA, Doc. 110689. On the October back-and-forth on Soviet air cover, see Chen Jian and Yang Kuisong, "Chinese Politics and the Collapse of the Sino-Soviet Alliance," in *Brothers in Arms: The Rise and Fall of the Sino-Soviet Alliance, 1945–1963*, ed. Odd Arne Westad (Stanford, CA: Stanford University Press, 1998), 253–55; Shen, "China and the Dispatch of the Soviet Air Force," 224–28.

53 Telegram from Vasilevsky to Stalin, September 23, 1950, WCDA, Doc. 112685.

in his deliberations over the situation in Korea was he willing to allow the conflict to draw him into a direct military confrontation with the United States."[54] One specific exchange Weathersby cites is between Stalin and Mao in early October 1950. Even as he emphasizes the manageable risks to China in sending ground "volunteers," Stalin notes that the evidence of a shared fear of escalation in the West should not be overvalued, given that they might attack China or the Soviet Union due to "prestige" considerations.[55] Drawing on Chinese records of Sino-Soviet discussions during the course of the Korean War, Xiaoming Zhang similarly concludes Stalin's persistent fear of widening the war led to secrecy rules as well as other limitations on how Soviet and Chinese air assets were used. Beyond secrecy, Stalin restricted the number of fighter planes provided, where the planes would be stationed, and the roles (air defense vs. bombing) and places (north of the 38th parallel) they could fly to avoid widening the war.[56] An

---

54 Weathersby, "Should We Fear This?," p. 20. Again, Weathersby likely goes too far when she concludes that "at every juncture he took steps to prevent such an escalation." Stalin's approval of the North Korean invasion disproves this singular focus on preventing escalation. Rather, Stalin appears to have had offensive, revisionist, but limited goals and consistently sought to avoid escalation within this context.

55 Sent during negotiations over China's ground entry, Stalin appeals to Mao by downplaying the risk of intentional American expansion of the war ("the USA, as the Korean events showed, is not ready at present for a big war") but notes that "the USA, despite its unreadiness for a big war, could still be drawn into a big war out of prestige, which, in turn, would drag China into the war, and along with this draw into the war the USSR, which is bound with China by the Mutual Assistance Pact." Message from Stalin to Mao, October 5, 1950, WCDA, Doc. 117313. While Stalin's message downplays even this escalation danger, Weathersby rightly notes the message's purpose was to convince Mao to send ground troops and therefore "Stalin's bravado was apparently largely for Chinese consumption." Kathryn Weathersby, "The Soviet Role in the Early Phase of the Korean War: New Documentary Evidence," *Journal of American-East Asian Relations* 2, no. 4 (Winter 1993): 435. For an interpretation that attributes more seriousness to Stalin's cavalier expressions toward escalation, see Mansourov, "Stalin, Mao, Kim, and China's Decision," and Mastny, Holtsmark, and Wenger, *War Plans and Alliances in the Cold War*, p. 18.

56 See, for example, Ziaoming's description that "the Soviet leader agreed to dispatch five antiaircraft artillery regiments to Korea, while asking the Chinese to contribute another five. For fear of escalating the war in Korea, he warned the Chinese not to send their air force across the 38th parallel. Therefore, the air war on the Communist side would continue to concentrate on air defense against American bombardments," and "fearing an escalation of the military conflict between the Soviet Union and the United States, Moscow allowed Soviet planes to be stationed only at airfields inside China, and they had to be disguised with Chinese colors. No more than forty MiGs would be sent into air combat at any one time. Moreover, Soviet pilots were required to wear Chinese uniforms, and they were restricted from flying over enemy-controlled territory and the sea, as well as from speaking Russian over the radio. In case they were captured, they were to say that they were minority Chinese of Soviet extraction." Xiaoming Zhang, "China and the Air War in Korea, 1950–1953," *Journal of Military History* 62, no. 2 (1998): 349, 362–63.

American intelligence cable from August 1950 relayed the sentiments of Soviet military officers in occupied Germany providing some insight into the mood among military elite:

> According to Soviet military personnel the Russians were concerned about the political situation developing from the Korean war. Several officers said that after the outbreak of the Korean war they expected a protest by the Western Powers and, at the most, a UN intervention on paper. They were stupefied by the USA intervention in the Korean war. They also said that should the U.S.S.R. enter the war the Soviet heavy industry would be wiped out by US long-distance bombers against which there was no efficient means of defense. It was the impression that officers who were veterans of World War II were not in the mood for another war.[57]

DETECTION AND REACTION

What did American leaders know about covert Soviet combat participation and how did they react? This section reviews declassified material showing that US leaders predicted and detected covert Soviet participation. Many are reviewed for the first time to the best of my knowledge.[58] They supplement earlier accounts of Soviet air participation based on elite interviews and other sources.[59]

The United States was prepared to detect any Soviet covert entry because they anticipated it. Declassified State Department policy planning records that precede Soviet entry show that US leaders anticipated the most likely Soviet combat role in response to the American overt intervention would be on the backstage. An August 1950 State Department memorandum on the possibility of external intervention, for example, argued, "Soviet or Chinese communist forces might be organized elements of the regular Soviet or Chinese Communist armies fighting under their own banners, or they might masquerade as North Korean forces fighting as an integral

---

57 "Soviet Russian Support and Plans, Korea," CIA Information Report, September 7, 1950, CIA Records Search Tool (hereafter CREST), CIA-RDP82-00457R005700670001-2.

58 The documents come from a variety of collections and archival locations. Most documents appear in the CIA's "Baptism by Fire" collection and CIA's CREST system; other documents come from intelligence files in the Truman Library collection; a few are from Digital National Security Archive and DDRS collections.

59 See sources in footnote 1, chapter 1.

part of the North Korean Army."[60] A draft of the military command instructions similarly notes various covert intervention scenarios by Soviet or Chinese units.[61] The bureaucracy was therefore prepared to identify such a decision once implemented.

Declassified intelligence records provide a basic timeline of American detection. The earliest indications of Moscow's covert entry in the fall of 1950 were circumstantial. Several reports in November report the entry of advanced Soviet MIG-15 jet fighters. Some cite the likelihood of Soviet piloting given the lack of trained North Korean and Chinese jet pilots and, in one case, apparent retreat toward Soviet rather than Chinese territory. These suspicions were strengthened by the clear logic American analysts saw in keeping Soviet participation covert.[62] Yet a formerly "eyes-only" report to President Truman about the issue of Soviet participation in early December 1950 concluded the evidence "does not yet allow conclusion Soviet pilots are flying."[63]

The first half of 1951 marked a turning point. An increasing volume and diversity of information about Soviet military personnel became available. A raw intelligence report from January, for example, reported Soviet anti-aircraft crews had arrived in North Korea and were not permitted to leave specific sites.[64] A July 1951 analysis of this and other raw reports noted the

60 Draft Memorandum by State Department for the NSC, August 30, 1950, *FRUS*.

61 For example, "in the event of the open or covert employment of major Soviet units south of the 38° parallel, you will assume the defense, make no move to aggravate the situation and report to Washington. You should take the same action in the event your forces are operating north of the 38° parallel and major Soviet units are openly employed. You will not discontinue air and naval operations north of the 38° parallel merely because the presence of Soviet or Chinese Communist troops is detected in a target area but if the Soviet Union or the Chinese Communists should announce in advance their intention to reoccupy North Korea and give warning, either explicitly or implicitly, that their forces should not be attacked, you should refer the matter immediately to Washington. In the event of the open or covert employment of major Chinese Communist units south of the 38° parallel, you should continue the action as long as action by your forces offers a reasonable chance of successful resistance. In the event of an attempt to employ small Soviet or Chinese Communist units covertly south of the 38° parallel, you should continue the action." Ambassador in Korea to Secretary of State, September 23, 1950, *FRUS*, Doc. 537.

62 A National Intelligence Estimate in late November 1950 concluded the most likely initial Soviet air role would be "actual participation without identification." "Soviet Participation in the Air Defense of Manchuria," NIE 2/2, November 27, 1950, CIA CREST, Doc. 0000269239.

63 Memorandum from Lay to Truman, December 8, 1950, Digital National Security Archive, Doc. HN00508.

64 "Soviet Activities in Pyongyang," CIA Information Report, January 4, 1951, CIA CREST, CIA-RDP82-00457R006700120004-5.

"presence in AAA role near Pyongyang in small numbers is well established."[65] Regarding Soviet pilots specifically, a top secret "Special Intelligence Estimate" from April 1951 noted Soviet air force personnel would likely continue to advise and participate in combat flights.[66] Especially precise information appears in intelligence reporting starting in July 1951. A formerly top secret CIA Daily Digest from August 1951 reports "two regiments of a Soviet 9th Air Army fighter division have been operating in the Manchuria-Korea border area," noting that "all pilots and ground operators heard on the ground-controlled intercept network have been Russian."[67] This richer picture is reflected in summaries from later 1951 and 1952 that estimate 25,000–30,000 Soviet military personnel "physically involved in the Korean War," more than 150 daily combat missions flown in the northwest of North Korea, and conclude "a de facto air war exists over North Korea between the UN and the USSR."[68]

These records also illustrate the evolution in the intelligence sources that could document a Soviet role. Early intelligence reports were based on eyewitnesses ("Two non-Asiatics in Soviet uniforms reportedly were observed 28 June in tanks on way to the Han River") and enemy interrogation ("Interrogation of a captured North Korean naval officer revealed that many Soviet naval advisors are at Wonsan").[69] The August 1951 CIA Daily Digest cited above, in contrast, is based on signals intercepts. It describes "preliminary analysis of radio-telephone traffic intercepted during the period 19 May–16 July suggests that two regiments of a Soviet 9th Air Army fighter division have been operating in the Manchuria-Korea border area."[70] A May 1952 National Security Agency analysis similarly analyzes communications intercepts. The ratio of languages used in intercepted communications leads to the conclusion that "of the total flights referred to by these nets during the period, 90% were made by pilots flying aircraft whose call

65 "Report of Indications of Soviet-Communist," July 5, 1951, Watch Committee of the Intelligence Advisory Committee, CREST, CIA-RDP91T01172R000400230013-0.

66 "Communist Military Forces in the Korean Area," April 27, 1951, Special Intelligence Estimate, No. 2, CIA CREST, Doc. 0001226087.

67 Untitled intelligence summary (Top Secret Suede), August 14, 1951, HR 70-14, CIA CREST, http://www.foia.cia.gov/sites/default/files/document_conversions/44/1951-08-14b.pdf.

68 "NIE-55/1 Communist Capabilities and Probable Courses of Action in Korea," July 30, 1952, on file with author.

69 Joint Morning Sitrep No. 6, 4 July 1950, HSTL, PSF, Intelligence File; Joint Daily Summary #7, July 4, 1950, HSTL, PSF, Intelligence File.

70 Untitled intelligence summary (Top Secret Suede), August 14, 1951, HR 70-14, CIA CREST, http://www.foia.cia.gov/sites/default/files/document_conversions/44/1951-08-14b.pdf.

numbers equated to 'allied' (Russian) units and were vectored and controlled by Russian speaking operators of stations of the Russian language GCI [Ground Controlled Intercept] net."[71]

The diversity of records about covert Soviet piloting shows this was circulated widely within the government.[72] The drafting of a National Intelligence Estimate draws on civilian and military intelligence sources. Special and National Intelligence Estimates are also circulated to the top positions in the American foreign policy bureaucracy. References to Soviet covert combat participation in such analytic products therefore ensure Russian language and other indications was not tucked inside isolated agencies. A November 1952 report on Far East policy, for example, notes, "in the air war, Chinese and Soviet-piloted MIG-15 jets bear the brunt of the Communist effort in northwestern Korea."[73] Presidential interest in this intelligence is reflected in the aforementioned December 1950 memo. Presidential awareness is confirmed by an April 1951 eyes-only report addressed to Truman on the status of air forces in Manchuria which notes Soviet covert participation ("If they use Russian pilots in their rear areas (over the Yalu bases, for example) as they have been doing").[74] Moreover, the aforementioned NSC policy review was prepared for "the information of the President and the President-elect."[75]

Corresponding to the communication and "conspicuous restraint" concepts developed in chapter 2, several US documents specifically link Moscow's covertness to its larger intentions about escalation and limited war. Intelligence reviews from 1951 and 1952 preface their descriptions of the backstage Soviet combat role by noting that "the Soviet Union has avoided publicly associating itself with the Communist cause in the Korean war" and engaged in "considerable pains to conceal or deny official involvement."[76]

---

71 Letter from Ganey to Lemay, June 20, 1952, Digital National Security Archive, Doc HN00713.

72 Robert Jervis, "Reports, Politics, and Intelligence Failures: The Case of Iraq," *Journal of Strategic Studies* 29, no. 1 (2006): 3–52.

73 "Current Policies of the Government of the United States of America Relating to the National Security," 1 November 1952, National Security Council, Vol. 1 Geographical Area Policies, HSTL, PSF, National Security Council File 1947-1953, p. III-C-2.

74 Memorandum Secretary of Air Force to the President, June 26, 1951, HSTL, PSF, Korean War File.

75 "Current Policies of the Government of the United States of America Relating to the National Security," November 1, 1952, Note by the Executive Secretary, p. 1.

76 "The Soviet Role in the Korean War," December 19, 1951, Current Intelligence Review, Central Intelligence Agency, CIA-RDP79S01060A000100260001-6. See also Current Intelligence Review, November 14, 1951, CIA CREST, CIA-RDP79S01060A000100210001-1.

Two formerly top secret air force reports explicitly cite Soviet interest in localizing the war. One memo notes key features of the air campaign: The Soviets "have been much more scrupulous than the Chinese Communists in avoiding open participation" and MIG-15s have been used for defensive rather than offensive missions. The author argues that Moscow has "good reason to believe that such local fighting would not develop into general war" which echoes "the considered view of all the U.S. intelligence agencies … that the Soviet Union does not want to become involved in a showdown war with the U.S. in the immediate future, although she is prepared to accept some risk of its occurrence."[77] Another air force eyes-only report, sent to the president and mentioned above, argued Moscow was avoiding "use of Russian air force against the UN forces [which] would precipitate world war" by equipping and training Chinese crews and confining any Russian pilots to rear areas.[78] Finally, a CIA assessment of covert Soviet participation in April 1951 noted, "all these indications suggest that the Soviets will continue to enlarge their air effort by stages geared to their assessment of US and UN reactions to each forward move, and the degree of success achieved by the Communist air forces."[79] This same logic was applied to other aspects of Soviet secrecy. In October 1950, for example, American intelligence analysis stated, "there has been little Soviet press comment on the alleged bombing of Siberian territory by a U.S. plane" and concluded that "recent Soviet statements provide no indication that the Soviet people are being prepared psychologically for an overt involvement in Korea."[80]

How did the United States use this intelligence? In chapter 2, I argued that collusion is especially likely when the detector has unique information. This depends on the degree of third-party exposure, which I code here as "low." There was almost no public reporting on *Soviet* air participation in a

77 The memo also describes various reasons Soviet and Chinese leaders should perceive Western escalation fears and complaints that giving them a Manchurian sanctuary gives them an opportunity to inflict damage on the United States without a wider war (they can avoid "kick[ing] over traces"). Memorandum from C. F. Cabell, "Current Situation in Korea," November 21, 1950, NARA II, RG 341, Top Secret Control & Cables Section, Box 53.

78 This "would give the Communists an extremely strong military position, presumably without serious risk of precipitating world war." Memorandum Secretary of Air Force to the President, June 26, 1951.

79 "Communist Military Forces in the Korean Area," April 27, 1951, Special Intelligence Estimate, No. 2, CIA CREST, Doc. 0001226087, pp. 13–14.

80 "Report of Indications of Soviet-Communist," October 29, 1950, Joint Intelligence Indications Committee, CREST, CIA-RDP91T01172R000400200016-0.

review of news reporting from November 1950 to the end of the war.[81] Several issues related to Soviet air assistance were publicly reported, such as arms shipments to North Korea and a buildup of Soviet air assets within the Soviet Union.[82] Regarding the identity of air crews, the public reporting often referred to "Chinese," used the more ambiguous "communist pilots" designation, included official clarifications that denied Soviet involvement or mischief, or some simply admitted that "who pilots these modern planes is not known."[83] As noted below, American censorship and press guidance appear to have helped produce this outcome.

Recall that US leaders withheld evidence of a Soviet advisory role in the initial invasion and carefully tailored their public language to avoid accusations of Soviet participation. Once Moscow's combat entry was detected, a similar response followed. As noted above, the command instructions to General MacArthur in the field were to ignore unannounced Soviet military personnel.[84] This basic formulation was repeated in revised instructions to the UN commander as forces approached the 38th parallel and again after MacArthur was relieved of his command in 1951.[85] American

81 Review is based on a search of all *New York Times* reporting in this period using keywords such as "MIG," "fighters," "Russia(n)" and "Soviet."

82 A typical example is Hanson W. Baldwin, "The Manchuria Build-Up." *New York Times*, November 16, 1950. The reporter does hint at Soviet piloting when writing that they "are not Chinese Community aircraft, because Peiping only has four or five pilots qualified to fly jets."

83 On attribution to Chinese pilots, see "MIG-15 Is Downed over North Korea," *New York Times*, February 19, 1952. On "communist" pilots, see "Communists had seriously challenged Allied air superiority ... Communist air strength in Korean operations at 1,400 planes, including the 700 MIG's." Austin Stevens, "Reds in Korea Challenge U.N. in Air, Vandenberg Declares," *New York Times*, November 22, 1951. On denying Soviet participation, see the clarification that "it was learned from sources of the highest responsibilities that actual Soviet military activities portend nothing extraordinary at this time." Austin Stevens, "Russians Massing, Rayburn Declares," *New York Times*, April 10, 1951. On unknown identity of pilots, see "Russo-China Split on Korea Reported," *New York Times*, December 25, 1950.

84 Interestingly, the State Department insisted "determination [of] whether major Soviet combat units have entered Korean hostilities or have clearly indicated their intention of engaging in hostilities, and the decision to initiate the actions contemplated by NSC 76 should be made only by the President." See State Department Consultant's Comments on NSC 76, July 25, 1950, HSTL, PSF, National Security Council Meetings File (1943–1953).

85 MacArthur was instructed that "bombing operations north of the 38th parallel should not be discontinued merely because the presence of Soviet or Chinese communist troops is detected in a target area" and that "[i]n the event of an attempt to employ Soviet or Chinese Communist units covertly south of it, the United Nations Commander should continue the action as long as he believes his forces capable of successful resistance." Memo for approval Marshall to the President, September 27, 1950, HSTL, http://www.trumanlibrary.org/whistlestop/study_col lections/korea/large/documents/pdfs/ki-18-3.pdf. These commands about covert Soviet entry

THE KOREAN WAR 169

journalists reporting on the Korean War were censored; one journalist who reportedly heard Russian spoken while on a military plane had his story rejected by censors.[86] Three months after signals intercepts had revealed detailed information on the size and extent of Soviet piloting, the Air Force Chief of Staff, General Hoyt Vandenberg, made the misleading public remark that "Communist China has become one of the major airpowers of the world."[87]

All of this resulted in a frontstage narrative in striking contrast with what was known about backstage clashes through intelligence. The key consideration for collusion was concern about controlling escalation and domestic hawkish pressure in particular. A revealing internal debate, ostensibly about the legality of undeclared war, shows American leaders understood that reactions to covert Soviet participation would influence the risk of inadvertent escalation. State Department planning in the summer of 1950, including private commentary by noted Sovietologist George Kennan, analyzed the two basic ways Soviet forces could enter. Kennan, for example, wrote that Russian units "using the uniforms or insignia of the Soviet Union" in Korea "would create an entirely new situation, requiring a complete re-examination of our position" since hostilities would be "much more difficult to isolate than the present one and obviously might easily lead to general Soviet-U.S. hostilities."[88] Yet covert clashes could be handled differently. History showed that "extensive hostilities can be carried on by the United States without a formal declaration of a state of war."[89]

---

were reiterated to MacArthur's replacement, General Matthew Ridgeway: "In event of open or covert employment of major Soviet units in Korea (including "Volunteers") you will, subj to security of your forces, assume the defensive, make no move to aggravate situation, and report to JCS. This is not to be interpreted as a restriction on conduct of air and naval operations in Korea. If Soviet Union announces in advance its intention to reoccupy North Korea and gives warning either explicitly or implicitly that their forces should not be attacked, you will refer the matter immediately to JCS; In event of an attempt to employ small Soviet units covertly in Korea you should continue your current action." Secretary of State to the Embassy in the United Kingdom, *FRUS*, 1951, Part 1 Korea and China, Doc. 267.

86 Halliday, "Air Operations in Korea: The Soviet Side of the Story," 60.

87 On his underplaying the Soviet role for public consumption, see Zhang, *Red Wings over the Yalu*, 133.

88 Untitled memorandum from George Kennan, June 27, 1950, NARA II, RG 59, Policy Planning Staff, Country and Area Files, Box 20, Korea 1947–50 [4]. Cover notes indicate the paper was shared with Secretaries of State and Army and Truman's White House aid (Jessup).

89 Memorandum from Savage to Nitze, "Possible Generalization of Hostilities," August 3, 1950. NARA II, RG 59, Policy Planning Staff, Country and Area Files, Box 20, Korea 1947–50. A cover note indicates the memo "embodies suggestions made by George Kennan and he concurs in the conclusions and recommendations."

Moreover, "since it is not Communist practice to issue a declaration of war" and given American unpreparedness for general war,

> we should use the device of recognition of a state of war only as a final resort. We should not thus generalize hostilities and restrict our freedom of action unless the Soviet Union affronts us in such manner that no other course is possible, or unless we decide that a generalization of hostilities is in our National interest. We should leave ourselves free to take limited military action against Soviet forces without a declaration, if this seems advisable. We have considerable maneuverability for this purpose.[90]

The specific idea that backstaging Soviet involvement would provide face-saving ways for Moscow to remain restrained was also noted. An intelligence assessment after the initial detection of Chinese ground forces noted that "since the USSR has scrupulously maintained the thin fiction of having no responsibility ... the Kremlin can afford to write off the Korean venture and try to minimize the tactical defeat it has suffered."[91] American decision-making recognized that Soviet leaders may be influenced by behavior which threatened their prestige despite Stalin's dominant position domestically. Moreover, a private November exchange between Secretary Acheson and his British counterpart included Acheson noting that "we have officially ignored Sov[iet] arms and advisers, 'volunteers' from Manchuria and other assistance in the past even though whole world know facts. We did so in order to leave other side a way out."[92]

Domestic hawkish sentiment was an important condition influencing this response. In tense November debates following detection of Chinese military personnel, Secretary Acheson argued that Washington would confront a dilemma if it linked Soviet leaders to the war. Although he and his fellow cabinet members knew "the Soviet Union is behind this ... we shouldn't say so—we shouldn't say so because we can't do anything about it now and to say that this is the Soviet Union and not to do anything about it would weaken us in world opinion."[93] Ambiguity about whether Soviet

90 "Memorandum from Savage to Nitze, August 3, 1950," 1950, 2–3, "Possible Generalization of Hostilities," Korea 1947–50, Box 20, Country and Area Files, Records of the Policy Planning Staff, 1947–53, General Records of the Department of State, Record Group 59, National Archives, College Park, MD.

91 Study of CIA Reporting on Chinese Communist Intervention in the Korean War, October 1955, CIA-RDP86B00269R000300040002-2, p. 80.

92 Telegram from Acheson to Foreign Secretary Bevin, November 6, 1950, FRUS.

93 Meeting Transcript, National Security Council, November 28, 1950, HSTL, George M. Elsey Papers, p. 12.

pilots were involved was understood to provide important political cover for restraint. A formerly top secret State Department policy planning memo, for example, states that "it is assumed that any airpower used by the Chinese Communists will not be so readily identifiable as Soviet as to raise the question of bombing Soviet bases, at least until after a decision is taken about action against Chinese bases."[94] Stephen Casey's review of American primary documents similarly concludes that "because Truman and his advisers were so keen to stop the fighting spilling out of the Korean peninsula, they had faced obvious constraints on what they could say and do. Not wanting to provoke the Soviets or inflame domestic opinion, they had … invariably shied away from ratcheting up the rhetoric."[95]

Later interviews with participants also indicates domestic politics, and a particular fear of hawkish public sentiment, played a role for American leaders as well. Paul Nitze recounted that a key consideration driving the American concealment of Soviet combat participation was that "the public would expect us to do something about it and the last thing we wanted was for the war to spread to more serious conflict with the Soviets."[96] Jon Halliday also interviewed Eisenhower's attorney general and close advisor Herbert Brownell who stated that "we had to keep that under the carpet. If that had ever gotten out, there would have been tremendous pressure to have a war with Russia."[97] Based in part on confidential interviews, Matthew Aid's history of US signals intelligence similarly concludes that evidence of Soviet involvement was handled with extreme care "in order to prevent the leakage of this highly sensitive intelligence to right-wing members of Congress, such as Senator Joseph McCarthy, who would no doubt have used (or misused) the information to drum up public support for war with the USSR at a time when the US government was trying to prevent that from happening."[98] John Gaddis's summary of new insights into the

94 Emphasis added. Memorandum from Hooker to Nitze, February 28, 1951, "U.S. Policy toward Bombing Chinese Bases in China and Manchuria if Next Chinese Communist Offensive in Korea is Supported by Considerable Air Power." NARA II, RG 59, Policy Planning Staff 1947–53, Country and Area Files, Box 20, Korea 1947–50.

95 Casey, *Selling the Korean War*, 122. On hawkish public opinion outpacing the Truman administration in late 1950 and early 1951, see 35–36, 75–77, 84, 100, 109–111. On the administration's intentional strategy to prevent overheating public opinion and its influence on everything from opting against seeking congressional authorization to minimalist presidential addresses, see 30–33, 34–39, 71–72, 89, 215.

96 Halliday, "Air Operations in Korea: The Soviet Side of the Story," 160.

97 Halliday, "Air Operations in Korea: The Soviet Side of the Story," 160.

98 Matthew M. Aid, *The Secret Sentry: The Untold History of the National Security Agency* (New York: Bloomsbury, 2009), 35.

Cold War from post–Cold War research concludes, "the Soviet Union never publicized its involvement in these air battles, and the United States, which was well aware of it, chose not to do so either. The two superpowers had found it necessary but also dangerous to be in combat with one another. They tacitly agreed, therefore, on a cover-up."[99]

China's Intervention

Along with Soviet air support, North Korea in fall 1950 desperately needed ground reinforcements to forestall the northern march of MacArthur's forces. China provided these units. After weeks of negotiations with Stalin, on October 14, Mao ordered the newly christened "Chinese People's Volunteers" (CPV) to cross the Yalu River border. This initial deployment featured carefully concealed night marches, false North Korean uniforms, and instructions to pose as ethnically Korean volunteers.[100] Two weeks of limited operations against UN forces followed. After a mysterious break in contact, a well-organized counteroffensive using more than 200,000 Chinese personnel was launched on November 25. This surprise counteroffensive reversed the war's momentum, turning back MacArthur's northward march. Several panicked weeks followed, after which UN forces recovered and an eventual stalemate near the original border settled in. Chinese "volunteers" conducted ground and air operations up through the war's armistice negotiations in 1953 and CPV representatives participated in those negotiations. This section reviews the role of secrecy and non-acknowledgment in its intervention. Doing so requires distinguishing between two phases: the first month, in which China's role was effectively concealed from all but Western intelligence ("first phase"), and the much longer period from late November 1950 until the end of the war ("second phase"). The latter featured a widely visible but unacknowledged intervention, rendered unofficial via the label "volunteers."

China's intervention has received much scholarly attention from diplomatic historians and IR scholars. Other scholars have focused on the diplomatic signaling from Beijing to Washington prior to China's entry as a case of failed deterrence.[101] The evidence I present here largely does not address

99 Gaddis, *The Cold War: A New History*, 60.

100 Shu Guang Zhang, *Mao's Military Romanticism: China and the Korean War, 1950–1953* (Lawrence: University Press of Kansas, 1995), 93–99.

101 Thomas C. Schelling, *Arms and Influence*, New Ed (New Haven, CT: Yale University Press, 1966), 55; Alexander L. George and Richard Smoke, *Deterrence in American Foreign Pol-*

this question; my focus is on how China intervened once American leaders did not heed its warnings. Regarding secrecy specifically, Branislav Slantchev most recently has argued that, during the first phase, China used secrecy to "feign weakness" to generate a powerful surprise counter-attack.[102] Evidence I present corroborates this story, suggesting effective secrecy in the first phase followed an operational security logic of deceiving the adversary to gain tactical advantages via surprise. In contrast, I argue the second phase exemplifies how covert-but-visible (i.e., "open secret") interventions are motivated by limited-war concerns and can help do so. By China not formally recognizing its involvement in Korea, it gave the United States flexibility to not expand the war to mainland China in response to hawkish pressure at home to confront Chinese involvement. My findings therefore substantiate O'Neill's hypothesis that China's intention in using the language of volunteers "may have been that the war was not a fully official act of the Chinese government. Mao's worry, one that he had discussed with Stalin, was that the United States would attack China with nuclear weapons. The new name may have been meant to diminish the pressure on the United States for a stronger response."[103]

A SURPRISING ENTRY

China's goals in the war have been the subject of considerable debate. Some attribute a defensive motive; China's troops entered only at the last minute to help avoid a North Korean collapse. Others see offensive goals as well. China's decision to cross the old border (38th parallel) and occupy South Korea's capital, for example, suggests Mao's interest in potentially pushing South Korea and its external patrons off the peninsula entirely. Still others point to domestic politics and the opportunity a war provided for consolidation of Communist Party power.[104] As I argue in chapter 2, my theory does not rely on strong assumptions about positive intervener goals. Whether Mao was defensive-minded, revisionist, or merely concerned with domestic

---

icy: *Theory and Practice* (New York: Columbia University Press, 1974); Thomas J. Christensen, "Threats, Assurances, and the Last Chance for Peace: The Lessons of Mao's Korean War Telegrams," *International Security* 17, no. 1 (1992): 122–54; Jonathan Mercer, "Emotional Beliefs," *International Organization* 64, no. 01 (2010): 1–31.

102 Slantchev, "Feigning Weakness," 357–88.

103 Barry O'Neill, *Honor, Symbols, and War* (Ann Arbor: University of Michigan Press, 1999), 126.

104 Jian, *China's Road to the Korean War.*

politics, a desire to avoid large-scale conflict only a year after winning the Chinese Civil War was a serious concern.

Instead of limited-war goals, Mao's use of secrecy in this first phase was deception and battlefield advantage. Recognizing the technological inferiority of his forces vis-à-vis those in the UN Command, Mao believed his best chance for reversing the war's direction was to use the principles of surprise and guerilla-style tactics honed during the Chinese Civil War.[105] The operational advantages of deception were strengthened by MacArthur's aggressive march northward which had extended Western supply lines beyond what could be defended and separated key elements of the attacking force. Chinese historians with access to select records from this period conclude Mao prioritized tactical surprise in China's initial entry and insisted on strict secrecy to enable this.[106]

The deception was successful in part because American leaders and its key allies, picking up early signs of ethnic Chinese on the battlefield, misinterpreted China's behavior. Prior American intelligence estimates explicitly analyzed China's likely form of entry. Such analysis linked the expected covert Chinese role to limited war, arguing it would seek to avoid "further antagonizing of the UN and reduce [the] risk of war with the US ... continued covert aid would offer most of the advantages of overt intervention, while avoiding its risks and disadvantages."[107] Chinese nationals fighting in Chinese-only units appeared at the end of October 1950.[108] A National Intelligence Estimate on November 8 urged clarification of the "scale and purpose of Chinese Communist intervention" and concluded elements of the Chinese Fourth Field Army were being reassembled into a "regular Chi-

---

105 Zhang, *Mao's Military Romanticism*, 87–93.

106 Zhang (1992) describes how Mao felt a clash with US forces was inevitable in late October due to MacArthur's rapid advances. To maximize combat effectiveness, Mao "stressed that the first assault should be by surprise. When he was told that the presence of Chinese forces in Korea was still unknown to the enemy, Mao urged the CPV to exploit this 'secrecy' further" (p. 100). Jian (1994) reviews similar documents and describes how "[i]n order not to reveal prematurely the CPV's movement into Korea, Mao ordered the entire country, especially the public media, to adopt a policy of 'only act and not talk.' ... Mao also ordered CPV soldiers to dress in the uniforms of the Korean People's Army in the initial stage of their operations, so that they would be in a position to take the UN forces by surprise when the first encounter occurred" (pp. 208–9).

107 "Memorandum by the Central Intelligence Agency, November 12, 1950," *FRUS* 1976, 933–36, http://digital.library.wisc.edu/1711.dl/FRUS.

108 Telegram from Drumright to Secretary of State, November 1, 1950, *FRUS*. Memorandum from Clubb to Rusk, November 1, 1950, *FRUS*.

nese Communist division."[109] As Chinese forces mysteriously pulled back from contact one week into November, US intelligence detected some ominous signs (i.e., military buildups in Manchuria) but missed the carefully concealed flow of supplies and personnel across the Yalu River.[110]

The role of limited war in secrecy decisions in this first phase is therefore mixed. For China, secrecy helped deceive an adversary and made its intervention on behalf of North Korea more effective. This was not about limiting war. For the Americans and British, escalation control was a key reason for colluding after detecting China's first phase entry. Keeping another major power's entry "backstage" made further escalation to a larger regional war less likely, consistent with the theory. Interestingly, the misalignment of secrecy motives here underscores one risk of the limited-war logic. As I argue in chapter 2, the ambiguity of covert behavior can breed mistakes, especially if adversaries have little previous experience. China's entry illustrates this well. The nature of China's intentions, based on its covert entry into combat, was difficult to establish. Because its role was effectively hidden from domestic audiences, it was plausible to observers like the United States and United Kingdom that China was using secrecy to keep the war limited. However, this was a misunderstanding that actually aided China's efforts at building a short-term tactical advantage. Although misapplied in this case, detector behavior in this case provides evidence that (a) escalation concerns can drive detector collusion even when inaccurate, and (b) this can create a misunderstanding that is operationally advantageous for the covert intervener.

"VOLUNTEERS" AND LIMITED WAR

The second phase of China's intervention began with a dramatic counteroffensive that reversed the West's military gains.[111] China's deployment of more than 200,000 well-organized and visible ground troops changed the course of the war. The motive(s) and timing of Chinese decisions have been the subject of considerable historiographical debate. What prompted Beijing's intervention? When exactly was the final decision? How much agency

---

109 Memorandum by the Central Intelligence Agency (forwarding National Intelligence Estimate), November 12, 1950; Millett, *The War for Korea, 1950–1951*, 313.

110 The disparity was significant: CIA estimates immediately before China's counteroffensive put the number of Chinese in North Korea at 30,000–40,000; in reality it exceeded 200,000.

111 Millett, *The War for Korea, 1950–1951*, 313–16.

did Mao exercise compared to his Soviet ally or rivals in the Chinese Communist Party?[112] My specific theoretical questions about the form of China's intervention sidestep many of these issues.[113]

Broad knowledge of China's entry was unavoidable because of North Korea's beleaguered battlefield status. Zhang, for example, describes how the rapid northward advance of MacArthur's UN forces led Mao to shift from a gradual buildup to a near-term counteroffensive. Exchanges between Mao and Stalin cite urgent manpower needs that are significantly revised upward in light of mounting KPA losses in the weeks preceding final approval.[114] Yet China had a choice: what *form* of visible intervention would it adopt? Beijing debated and opted to describe its forces as "volunteers" to create some deniability, however implausible. This, I find, was driven by a desire to control the risks of a wider war and reflects the link between acknowledgment, intervention, and escalation.

Whether a large-scale Chinese ground entry would lead to a wider war against the United States and its allies was a critical consideration and explicitly debated in internal messages. Cables between Mao and Stalin in the final October negotiations discuss this general possibility (it might "provoke an open conflict between the USA and China") and the specific possibility that escalation will be encouraged by outside audience reactions and issues like prestige ("despite its unreadiness for a big war, could still be drawn into a big war out of prestige"). This concern is also reflected in China's acute concern for Soviet agreement to provide air defense for Man-

112 The conventional answer has been that China's entry was reluctant, defensive, and prompted by the crossing of the 38th parallel by UN forces, subsequent seizure of Pyongyang, and rapid advance toward the Chinese border. Defensive motives: distrust of the West after their support for Kuomintang Nationalists during and after the Chinese Civil War, an acute military vulnerability due to non-existent air and naval capabilities, and, should the North Korean army collapse, the nightmare scenario of a long-term American military presence in Japan and on its Manchurian border. See, for example, Zhang, *Mao's Military Romanticism*; Chen Jian foregrounds domestic benefits of war mobilization for the Chinese Communist Party and dates some important decisions to enter earlier. See Jian, *China's Road to the Korean War*, 143–54, and the discussion in the preface to the paperback edition (xi–xii).

113 That is, whatever the specific motive and timing of the decision, and whatever the degree of autonomy China had vis-à-vis Stalin, Mao and those in his inner circle saw secrecy in the first phase as helpful for operational advantage and non-acknowledgment in the second phase as helpful for controlling escalation.

114 See, for example, Mao's reply to Stalin on October 3 that five to six Chinese infantry divisions would not be sufficient; Stalin's reply (October 5) that this figure was a minimum; Mao's reply (October 7) that nine infantry divisions and Soviet-supplied artillery, construction equipment, and vehicles would be needed to avoid North Korea's total defeat. All in WCDA, Korean War 1950–1953 collection.

churia and China's coastal cities.[115] The solution was to avoid official acknowledgment by using the label of "volunteers," just as interveners in Spain had done. Once the Chinese counteroffensive was launched, centralized direction was obvious given the coordinated tactical maneuvers using all-Chinese units.[116] Despite its implausibility, the terminology of volunteers was no accident: it was discussed in Sino-Soviet negotiations and enshrined in Chinese bureaucratic policy; even North Korean leaders were specifically advised to use "volunteers" in their public statements.[117] Maintaining this diplomatic device led to unusual measures. For example, Stalin cabled Mao to clarify that the Chinese representatives to the first armistice talks in 1951 could not be from the People's Liberation Army but instead from Chinese People's Volunteers representatives in Korea.[118] Echoing the proposals for removing "volunteers" in the Spanish Civil war, ceasefire proposals featured clauses in which China would assume responsibility for and extract their volunteers.[119]

The primary goal in avoiding official acknowledgment through the volunteerism language was localizing combat to the Korean peninsula. This is the conclusion of each historian that has assessed primary Chinese materials on this issue. It supports the theory's expectations from chapter 2 where later interveners are likely to prefer a covert form to control escalation

115 On China's vulnerability to US airpower and the "special attention to the issue of aviation" in the final notes exchanged about its intervention, see Telegram from Soviet Ambassador to China N.V. Roshchin, October 7, 1950, WCDA, Doc. 117314.

116 Secretary of State Acheson complained the visibility of the counteroffensive made it "impossible to pretend that this is not an openly aggressive move by the Peiping regime." Telegram to Embassy in London, November 28, 1950, *FRUS*. MacArthur too noted "no pretext of minor support under the guise of volunteerism or other subterfuge now has the slightest validity." Telegram to Joint Chiefs of Staff, November 28, 1950, *FRUS*.

117 Sino-Soviet intervention planning that mentions the issue of calling Chinese (and Soviet) personnel "volunteers" appears in Ciphered Telegram, Filippov (Stalin) to Mao Zedong and Zhou Enlai (via Roshchin), October 1, 1950, WCDA, Doc. 113729, and Letter from Zhou Enlai to Stalin, October 14, 1950, WCDA, Doc. 114216. On Mao's internal policy guidance regarding "volunteers," see Zhang, *Mao's Military Romanticism*, 109. On Chinese instructions to North Korea regarding the terminology of "volunteers," see Telegram from Zhou Enlai to Chai Junwu, November 8, 1950, WCDA, Doc. 114220.

118 Mao informs Stalin that "these representatives must be from the command of the corresponding military units, and not representatives of the governments. Thus, from the Chinese side a representative of the volunteer troops must participate and not a representative of China, as a warring state." In Ciphered Telegram, Mao Zedong to Filippov (Stalin), June 30, 1951, WCDA, Doc. 110372.

119 Stueck, *The Korean War: An International History*, 155, 157; Telegram from Henderson to Secretary of State, January 24, 1951, *FRUS*, 1951, Vol. 7, Part 1.

dangers. For example, Chen Jian's review of the original documentary record concludes that Mao and other members of the CCP believed that "by calling Chinese troops in Korea volunteers, they would be able to better convince the Chinese people of the moral justification of the intervention, while at the same time alleging that Chinese troops were organized on an unofficial basis, thus reducing the risk of a formal war with the United States and other Western countries."[120] Shu Guang Zhang cites cables between Mao and the Chinese military in early October ordering a name change to "Chinese People's Volunteers" and concludes the Chinese leaders hoped by doing this they "could control the political risks of a general war" and avoid "the appearance of declaring war against the United States."[121] William Stueck's review concludes Mao chose the label "in the hope this would reduce prospects for a U.S. declaration of war against the PRC."[122] Finally, citing both Soviet and Chinese sources, a trio of historians conclude:

> It appears, for example, that like Zhou and Stalin, Mao was acutely aware of the importance of avoiding a formal declaration of war. Ever since the creation of the NFF [Northeast Frontier Force] on July 13, Mao had fretted about the name of the force to be sent to Korea. He resisted calling it the People's Liberation Army because this would make the Chinese expeditionary troops official and could be interpreted as tantamount to the formal declaration that he sought to avoid. Such a declaration would trigger the provisions under the Sino-Soviet alliance that required the Soviet Union to render China assistance "by all means at its disposal." Direct Soviet involvement in the conflict, Mao believed, would carry the potential for touching off a third world war. With all this in mind, he first had the idea of referring to the men as "support troops" but in the end accepted the recommendation to call them "volunteers."[123]

Moreover, internal documents on the American side show this device worked as planned. Moreover, the documents explicitly note the implau-

120 Jian, *China's Road to the Korean War*, 187.

121 Shu Guang Zhang, *Deterrence and Strategic Culture: Chinese-American Confrontations, 1949–1958* (Ithaca, NY: Cornell University Press, 1992), 108.

122 Stueck, *The Korean War: An International History*, 100.

123 Sergei Goncharov, John Lewis, and Litai Xue, *Uncertain Partners: Stalin, Mao, and the Korean War*, 1st ed. (Stanford, CA: Stanford University Press, 1993), 175. According to Goncharov et al., the shift from "supporters" to "volunteers" came at the suggestion of a high-level advisor who believed supporters still implied central direction (339).

sibility of the volunteerism label and the message this sent. The American ambassador in Moscow noted with some concern sharpening Chinese public statements acknowledging Chinese volunteers in the Korean War. However, he concluded, "we are still inclined [to] feel that CPG [Beijing] is not in fact inviting war with US and UN" in part because the "emphasis thus far has been on [the] service of 'volunteers.' While the nature of this type intervention misleads no one, in [the] realm international relations it retains significance and [the] CPG has not chosen to go beyond this. It provides [the] CPG with [a] way out."[124] A State Department analysis from November on Chinese intentions noted the important role of Soviet leaders in determining its scope and form, concluding, "this assumption that the Moscow aim in the present move is limited in immediate scope is supported by the circumstance that there seems to be some effort to disguise the intervention, if only nominally."[125] Importantly, US leaders interpreted China's continued use of the language of "volunteers," rather than official acknowledgment of People's Liberation Army personnel, as an effort to keep the door open to a settlement or Chinese withdrawal (i.e., "have avoided committing selves publicly to total war by referring to Chinese Communists troops as 'volunteers'").[126]

DETECTION AND REACTION

As noted above, the United States and some close partners detected China's first phase entry. The second phase, while under the fig leaf of "volunteerism," was widely visible such that all publics and states were aware. I argue in chapter 2 that collusion or exposure is influenced by the uniqueness of information. China's ground involvement was an open secret by the first week of November. A review of reporting in the *New York Times* finds multiple, unambiguous reports of Chinese military personnel in combat with UN forces as early as November 5.[127] The start of China's major counteroffensive in late November, moreover, received generous news coverage,[128]

124 Chargé in Korea (Drumright) to the Secretary of State, November 13, 1950, *FRUS*.

125 Memorandum by the Director of the Office of Chinese Affairs (Clubb) to the Assistant Secretary of State for Far Eastern Affairs (Rusk), November 4, 1950, *FRUS*.

126 Telegram from Wilkinson to Secretary of State, November 9, 1950, *FRUS*.

127 E.g., Associated Press, "Chinese Reds Slice Behind British Unit in Western Korea," *New York Times*, November 05, 1950; "Chinese Troops in Korea," *New York Times*, November 5, 1950; Lindesay Parrott, "4 Armies Involved," *New York Times*, November 10, 1950.

128 E.g., Lindesay Parrott, "China's Reds Stall U.N. Push in Korea; Aim to Split Front," *New York Times*, November 27, 1950.

even as the Chinese government refuted claims of its nationals being centrally directed and instead asserted their "volunteer" status.[129] I therefore code China's ground and air role as an "open secret," widely visible to both publics and other states.[130] The theory expects exposure by the United States and its allies. I find mixed support for the theory. Initial attempts to collude in ignoring and withholding intelligence were followed by attempts to actively expose and refute China's claims.

Despite these major newspaper headlines, private communications in the first month of China's entry focused on shaping public reporting in a collusive manner. While this is at odds with the theory's expectation given the public reporting noted above, the reasons given for collusion do track well with the theory's logic. Advocates argued that downplaying China's role could help make restraint on both sides easier. A November 4 message from the British Foreign Secretary, for example, argued, "there was everything to be said for ignoring limited Chinese intervention" and that publicizing China's role in the Security Council "might make it more, rather than less, difficult for the Chinese to climb down and avoid open commitment … forcing the Chinese into a position from which they cannot withdraw."[131] Secretary Acheson's reply agreed, adding the allies should "do everything we can not to spread the hostilities."[132] He also cautioned that "just as we pretended Moscow was not committing aggression in N[orth] K[orea] so it may be necessary for us not to overplay the new factor of Chi[nese] intervention in N[orth] K[orea] until our combined political-military interests require that action."[133] These discussions show how leaders believed collusion could meaningfully impact the degree of political flexibility on both sides and thereby the scope of subsequent hostilities.

Washington and London shifted the approach once China's large counteroffensive in late November was underway. This change reflects the reality that American or British collusion would no longer influence the degree of mobilization in hawkish domestic audiences. Consistent with the theory's logic, the more publicly visible Chinese role in the second phase empow-

129 E.g., "The spokesman said that Peiping regime had no reason to prevent Chinese 'volunteers' from entering the Korean war 'to fight under the unified command of the Korean Democratic People's Government in the great war of resistance against American aggression,'" *New York Times*, "Peiping Denounces M'rthur Report," November 12, 1950.

130 Note again that, while China's entry was clear, key operational details were effectively concealed in the October/November period which enabled its tactical surprise.

131 Telegram from Bevin (UK) to Department of State, November 3, 1950, *FRUS*.

132 Telegram from Acheson to Embassy in London, November 6, 1950, *FRUS*.

133 Telegram from Acheson to US Mission to UN, November 13, 1950, *FRUS*.

ered hawkish domestic audiences in the United States. These actors heavily criticized the Truman administration's refusal to attack China directly and helped push the White House to take a tougher stand in its diplomacy.[134] In response, official statements and diplomacy at the United Nations featured the United States drawing attention to China's entry into the war and lobbying allies and other governments to condemn it. This was symbolized by lobbying member governments to expand UN resolutions to include a claim of Chinese aggression rather than just North Korea. As Casey summarizes, "in sharp contrast to the summer, neither Truman nor Acheson was willing to mask this fact from the public."[135] In doing so, American leaders were specifically taking aim at China's claims of volunteerism.

US Intervention in China

Even as Chinese military forces flowed south, the United States redoubled its efforts to maintain geographic limits on the combat with Chinese forces within Korea. Hawkish elites in the United States advocated direct action against China, such as imposition of a naval blockade, conducting air strikes against "sanctuary" targets in Manchuria or other parts of Chinese territory, and declaring war against China. Each of these steps would eliminate the geographic limits on the war. Instead, the United States chose covertness as a form of retaliation. A little-known aspect of this strategy was covert intervention outside the Korean Peninsula. Occasionally referenced in histories of the Korean War but rarely analyzed, the Truman administration rejected calls for overt and direct military attacks against parts of mainland China. Instead, the White House authorized a boost to covert operations helping Chinese Nationalists seeking to retake China from the Communist Party. This produced a backstage widening of the war beyond the Korean Peninsula while preserving geographic limits on the frontstage.

Early advocacy appears in top secret State Department exchanges in December 1950. A series of memos wrestled with how to address the threat of China beyond the war itself given that "heavy sustained fighting in Korea between Chinese Communist and UN forces" was likely. The recommendation was for "cold-war tactics" including to "encourage, strengthen, support, and coordinate existing guerrilla and anti-Communist forces in South

---

134 See also Casey, *Selling the Korean War*.

135 Casey, *Selling the Korean War*, 130–31; on linking this to the NSC-68 policy of mobilization, see Steven Casey, "Selling NSC-68: The Truman Administration, Public Opinion, and the Politics of Mobilization, 1950–51," *Diplomatic History* 29, no. 4 (2005): 655–90.

China. This would probably be largely a covert operation."[136] Such covert support could eventually lead to the fragmentation of the Chinese communist regime and at minimum could draw military assets away from Korea.[137] The National Security Council approved this approach in January 1951.[138] This covert substitution logic was invoked later in the war; a summer 1951 memo, for example, noted that "while continuing to seek to avoid precipitating general war" the United States should "support a vigorous campaign of covert operations designed ... [t]o aid effectively anti-Communist guerrilla forces in Communist China and Korea."[139]

Several distinct covert initiatives targeting Chinese territory were included.[140] One was a covert aid program to support Nationalists in Burma. Operation Paper was managed by the first covert action organization (Office of Policy Coordination) with guidance from the Central Intelligence Agency and State Department.[141] It covertly supplied material and personnel to General Li Mi, a high-ranking former Nationalist general who maintained a small surviving military force on the Burmese side of the border with China. From early 1951 until late 1952, Operation Paper delivered thousands of weapons and ammunition, and hundreds of trained Nationalist volunteers from Taiwan largely via the CIA-supported Civil Air Transport firm. Thailand was the intermediary, receiving secret shipments and

---

136 Memorandum Clubb to Stuart, December 9, 1950, NARA II, RG 59, Office of Chinese Affairs, Top Secret Subject File 1945-1950, Box 18.

137 Memorandum Merchant to Clubb, 4 October 1950, NARA II, RG 59, Office of Chinese Affairs, Top Secret Subject File 1945-1950, Box 18. The same goal is cited in a memo written during the first phase of China's entry that provided recommendations should China deepen its combat role without a declaration of war. Memorandum Rusk to Clubb, November 17, 1950, NARA II, RG 59, Office of Chinese Affairs, Top Secret Subject File 1945–1950, Box 18.

138 Draft Report by the National Security Council (101/1) "U.S. Action to Counter Chinese Communist Aggression," *FRUS*, 1951, Vol. 1, Part 1, Doc. 62.

139 Memorandum Prepared in the Department of State, August 18, 1951, *FRUS*, 1951, Vol. 7, Part 1, Doc. 523.

140 In addition to Burma, the United States boosted covert propaganda and guerilla operations in Chinese Manchuria and covert support for guerilla raids against Chinese coastal Chekiang and Fukien provinces from nearby islands. For overviews, see William Leary, *Perilous Missions: Civil Air Transport and CIA Covert Operations in Asia*, 2nd ed. (Washington, DC: Smithsonian, 2002); Frank Holober, *Raiders of the China Coast: CIA Covert Operations During the Korean War*, 1st ed. (Annapolis, MD: US Naval Institute Press, 1999).

141 The State Department and CIA roles are reflected in discussions of State's authorization for CIA covert sabotage attempts on Chinese vessels, overflights of Chinese mainland to supply guerillas, and clandestine support for Li Mi in the form of currency. See Director's Logs, Central Intelligence Agency, September–December 1951, http://www.foia.cia.gov/sites/default/files/document_conversions/1700319/1951-09-01.pdf.

ferrying them across the Thai-Burma border to Li Mi's forces.[142] While US assistance "dramatically improved effectiveness" of the units, American leaders were "anxious to see Li Mi move quickly into Yunnan"; at one point, OPC representatives threatened to cut funding unless Li Mi moved into China.[143] Li Mi and his forces launched incursions into China's southern province in June 1951 and August 1952. However, even with its improvements, effective Chinese Communist counter-attacks destroyed Li Mi's forces and the goal of diverting Chinese materiel and personnel from the Korean theater was largely unfulfilled.[144]

Thus, American strategic priorities remained stable. Tense debates in the Truman administration about China's major counteroffensive led to agreement that even the most limited overt US military strikes against Chinese bases or territory would risk a general war. Instead, policymakers embraced "extensive covert operations on mainland China."[145] The goal was to "force the Chinese Communists to drain forces from the Korean conflict in the north in order to meet threats elsewhere."[146] Safeguarding Europe and avoiding a larger entanglement in Asia was critical. Even as their rhetoric about Chinese "volunteers" sharpened, the paramount goal of US policy remained confining combat to the peninsula. Yet keeping all of China as an unmolested sanctuary would make progress, let alone success, in the Korean War difficult. Covert military intervention to aid dissident Chinese groups could avoid a wider war but also pressure China. In contrast, heeding calls for overt bombing of Manchuria or the mainland coastal line would risk igniting a full-scale, geographically unbounded war with China.

This relatively unknown facet of the war underscores the multiple ways in which the backstage facilitated a geographically bounded conflict. As I

---

142 Daniel Fineman, *A Special Relationship: The United States and Military Government in Thailand, 1947–1958* (Honolulu: University of Hawaii Press, 1997), 137–41.

143 Fineman, *A Special Relationship*, 141; Richard Michael Gibson, *The Secret Army: Chiang Kai-Shek and the Drug Warlords of the Golden Triangle* (Hoboken, NJ: Wiley, 2011), 69.

144 "At the end of 1951, the KMT, with US help, opened a runway at Mong Hsat in northern Burma ... Quickly, the United States began transporting more powerful weapons [and] seven hundred regular KMT soldiers from Taiwan landed at the Mong Hsat airstrip. Thus fully equipped, Li Mi attempted one more desperate invasion in August 1952. As before, however, his offensive went nowhere. His forces made it only sixty miles into Yunnan, and the Red Army easily repulsed him. Never again would Li Mi—or the CIA—attempt a largescale invasion of southern China. Operation Paper had ended." Fineman, *A Special Relationship*, 142–43; see also Gibson, *The Secret Army*, 78–81.

145 Stueck, *The Korean War: An International History*, 134.

146 "Civil Air Transport (CAT): A Proprietary Airline, 1946–1955," Central Intelligence Agency Clandestine Services History, Vol. 1 of 4, Doc. 52371fe2993294098d51762b, p. 88.

argue in chapter 2, peripheral interventions that expand the spatial location of combat have severe escalation risks that reward covertness. The Truman White House quietly opted for covert methods to put pressure on Beijing outside the peninsula. Escalation concerns were paramount in this choice of covert over overt means.

DETECTION AND REACTION

Beyond declassified American records, there is very little documentation on these military aid efforts in public reporting and regarding Chinese or Soviet intelligence detection. On the one hand, it is clear this covert intervention case was not widely exposed. A review of *New York Times* reporting during the relevant period (December 1950 to end of war) features no discussion of covert or otherwise unofficial activities like Operation Paper. Mainstream news stories did report on related discussions involving Formosa. Some reports in 1951 and 1952 noted internal American debates about the possible use of Chinese Nationalist personnel based in Formosa within the Korean theater, and others hinted that US naval forces might cease preventing Formosa-based raids into mainland China. [147] The theory therefore expects any Chinese or Soviet intelligence detection to be followed by collusion given that any insight into such operations was unique and the risks of escalation were high.

On the other hand, describing and assessing the degree of detection and exposure/collusion is difficult. Although it is clear American leaders expected China's leaders to detect greater resistance on its borders, it is not clear that they expected Washington's hand to be apparent in this. Moreover, evidence of Chinese or Soviet detection of these operations is not available given documentary constraints. That being said, it is certain that the United States was aware that Chinese Communist intelligence assets had deeply penetrated the Chinese Nationalist forces in Formosa and presumably elsewhere. This penetration was identified as early as the Chinese civil war.[148] Though circumstantial, it is worth noting that Washington used other policy tools besides intervention with the expectation that its adver-

---

147 E.g., William S. White, "Gen. Barr Defends U.S. China Policy," *New York Times*, June 23, 1951. See also "the United States Seventh Fleet ... may no longer prevent Nationalist raids against the mainland," Hanson W. Baldwin, "Formosa Move Big Step to Put Heat on China," *New York Times*, February 01, 1953.

148 Panagiotis Dimitrakis, "US Intelligence and Chinese Spies in the Civil War," *Journal of Intelligence History* 13, no. 1 (January 2, 2014): 62–75.

sary's intelligence would identify without wide public knowledge. Ding-man documents Eisenhower's secret repositioning of atomic-related assets in 1953 as an attempt to quietly signal and coerce Soviet leaders.[149]

Conclusion

North Korea's invasion of South Korea in the summer of 1950, only five years after World War II had concluded, threatened to turn a budding Cold War rivalry into a regional or even global war. The US-Soviet covert air war that developed in late 1950 was a striking example of the way in which limits were transgressed but the war remained contained via secrecy and non-acknowledgment. The Korean War also featured an open secret inter-vention by China which drew on the language of "volunteers" to keep the war limited, mirroring tactics used in the Spanish Civil War. Although the Korean War would become a critical limited-war precedent itself, its con-duct was shaped by lessons from previous conflicts.

The public side of the conflict holds important insights as well. The ini-tial overt American intervention follows the basic logic developed in chap-ter 2. Leaders in the United States perceived a tolerable level of escalation risk and chose to privilege the operational and symbolic advantages of a public, multilateral intervention. The United States also shifted from a pos-ture of collusion regarding China's initial covert entry to one of exposure once China's role was widely visible and reported by international media. This is also consistent with the theory, showing that collusion to limit war is not without its own limits.

Finally, the Korean War underscores the potential for mistakes and ex-ploitation. One communication problem is that, under some conditions, secrecy and non-acknowledgment can have multiple motives. As discussed in chapter 2, this can create possibilities for ambiguous messaging. China's actions show a deeper danger: mimicry and exploitation. China's initial co-vert entry appeared to reflect escalation control practices. American and British intelligence reached exactly this conclusion when first detecting Chinese personnel. In reality, China was effectively concealing the quiet in-troduction of many additional military units to enable a surprise attack. The surprise offensive in late November 1950 was a classic case of the opera-tional security logic, generating temporary tactical advantages via effective deception of the enemy. Importantly, all three major powers successfully

---

149 Roger Dingman, "Atomic Diplomacy during the Korean War," *International Security* 13, no. 3 (1988): 50.

restored geographic limits on the conflict in the aftermath, in part through covertness and collusion regarding other aspects of the war. Each of these episodes would prove important a decade later as these same three governments struggled to compete while limiting another war in Asia. I explore the conflict in Vietnam in the next chapter.

6

The Vietnam War (1964–1968)

With the division of Europe settled, the center of gravity in the middle period of the Cold War shifted to Vietnam.[1] The fate of the former French colony of Indochina became an ideological and geopolitical struggle over the larger trajectory of Asia. Since the late 1950s, American-backed South Vietnam struggled to thwart a well-resourced and aggressive insurgency. In North Vietnam, Ho Chi Minh's Chinese- and Soviet-backed regime enjoyed greater stability and, at least by 1960, supported the insurgency to the south. South Vietnam's military struggles drew in outside support from the United States, which prompted corresponding aid from China and the Soviet Union to North Vietnam. After nearly a decade of counterinsurgency and conventional warfare, the Paris Peace Accords of 1973 ended an active American role. By 1975, Saigon had fallen and South Vietnam was absorbed in a final North Vietnamese offensive.

The war's historical importance is difficult to overstate. Vietnam shaped the course of the Cold War toward détente, fueled the Sino-Soviet split, undermined American willingness to intervene in other conflicts for a generation, and inflicted tremendous death and destruction on populations in Southeast Asia. The war also has important value for theoretical analysis. As in the conflicts discussed in the previous two chapters, the Vietnam War features multiple interventions that both showcase the interactive nature

---

1 Marc Trachtenberg, *A Constructed Peace: The Making of the European Settlement, 1945–1963* (Princeton, NJ: Princeton University Press, 1999).

of escalation dynamics and facilitate theoretically useful comparisons. The Vietnam War also features puzzling forms of collusion among the major adversaries as part of an overall effort to control the escalation process and avoid a larger war in Asia.

This chapter focuses on the covert side of the Vietnam War, focusing on the 1964–1968 period. As previous scholarship has shown, secrecy played a role in justifying initial US military strikes against North Vietnam during the 1964 Gulf of Tonkin incident and helped Nixon cope with anti-war protests after the 1968 period.[2] Nothing I present here contradicts these well-established findings. Rather, I argue that covertness and collusion helped limit the war in the interim. To do so, I analyze secrecy and non-acknowledgment regarding the interventions listed in table 6.1.

The United States, China, and the Soviet Union each engaged in covert military interventions that exceeded the generally recognized limits of the Vietnam War. In North Vietnam, Chinese and Soviet covert air defense participation led to direct encounters with American pilots conducting the air war against Hanoi. In Laos, American covert air and ground operations spread the zone of combat beyond the political borders of Vietnam. Over time, its role became an "open secret," but non-acknowledgment was thought to preserve the fig leaf of Laotian neutrality and contain the war. In all three cases, secrecy and non-acknowledgment were used by leaders on both sides to control escalation. This, along with more well-known tactics

---

2 John M. Schuessler, *Deceit on the Road to War: Presidents, Politics, and American Democracy* (Ithaca, NY: Cornell University Press, 2015); see also Robert J. Hanyok, "Skunks, Bogies, Silent Hounds, and the Flying Fish: The Gulf of Tonkin Mystery, 2–4 August 1964," *Cryptologic Quarterly* 19, no. 4/20, no. 1 (Winter 2000–Spring 2001): 1–55; Reiter, skeptical of the deception that Schuessler identifies, notes that "the only clear case of democratic deception to open the door to war is the Johnson administration's treatment of the Gulf of Tonkin Incident"; Dan Reiter, "Democracy, Deception, and Entry into War," *Security Studies* 21, no. 4 (2012): 605. On domestic doves and secrecy regarding operations like Cambodia, see Ray Locker, *Nixon's Gamble: How a President's Own Secret Government Destroyed His Administration* (Guilford, CT: Rowman & Littlefield, 2015), 28; Christopher Andrew, *For the President's Eyes Only: Secret Intelligence and the American Presidency from Washington to Bush* (New York: Harper Collins, 1996), 360–61; on the role of antiwar views and secrecy regarding nuclear mobilization under Nixon, see Scott D. Sagan and Jeremi Suri, "The Madman Nuclear Alert: Secrecy, Signaling, and Safety in October 1969," *International Security* 27, no. 4 (2003): 150–83; William Burr and Jeffrey Kimball, "Nixon's Secret Nuclear Alert: Vietnam War Diplomacy and the Joint Chiefs of Staff Readiness Test, October 1969," *Cold War History* 3, no. 2 (January 2003): 113–56; on the role of secrecy in facilitating peace negotiations under Nixon, see Pierre Asselin, *A Bitter Peace: Washington, Hanoi, and the Making of the Paris Agreement* (Chapel Hill, NC: University of North Carolina Press, 2002), 24–32.

TABLE 6.1. Intervention Cases in the Vietnam War

	Dates	Location	Timing	Form	Details	Theory Support
US intervention	1964–1973	Local (Vietnam)	First mover	Overt	Public, acknowledged ground, air units	Strong
	1964–1973	Peripheral (Laos)	First mover	Covert (open secret)	Concealed, unacknowledged air and ground operations	Strong
Chinese intervention	1965–1969	Local (North Vietnam)	Subsequent intervener	Covert	Concealed, unacknowledged air defense role	Strong
Soviet intervention	1965	Local (North Vietnam)	Subsequent intervener	Covert	Concealed, unacknowledged air defense role	Strong

like the US "gradualist" air campaigns, kept the war localized.[3] In contrast, the initial American intervention took place before other major powers were involved and was localized to Vietnam. Consistent with the theory, escalation control concerns were subordinated to the operational and symbolic benefits of overt involvement. Because I focus on covertness and collusion issues, my findings do not directly address debates about counterinsurgency strategy, casualty sensitivity, regime change strategy, politicized intelligence estimates, airpower, military effectiveness, or why North Vietnam ultimately defeated such a strong opponent.[4]

3 On other tactics of limited war used in Vietnam, see Stephen Peter Rosen, "Vietnam and the American Theory of Limited War," *International Security* 7, no. 2 (1982): 83–113.

4 Regarding counterinsurgency strategy, see, e.g., Jonathan D. Caverley, "The Myth of Military Myopia: Democracy, Small Wars, and Vietnam," *International Security* 34, no. 3 (January 1, 2010): 119–57; James McAllister, "Who Lost Vietnam?: Soldiers, Civilians, and U.S. Military Strategy," *International Security* 35, no. 3 (2010): 95–123. Regarding casualty sensitivity, see, e.g., Christopher Gelpi, Peter D. Feaver, and Jason Reifler, *Paying the Human Costs of War: American Public Opinion and Casualties in Military Conflicts* (Princeton, NJ: Princeton University Press, 2009). For regime change strategy, Elizabeth N. Saunders, *Leaders at War: How Presidents Shape Military Interventions* (Ithaca, NY: Cornell University Press, 2011); Lindsey A. O'Rourke, *Covert Regime Change: America's Secret Cold War* (Ithaca, NY: Cornell University Press, 2018). Regarding intelligence estimates, Joshua Rovner, *Fixing the Facts: National Security and the Politics of Intelligence* (Ithaca, NY: Cornell University Press, 2011). For more on airpower, see, e.g., Robert A. Pape, "Coercive Air Power in the Vietnam War," *International Security* 15, no. 2 (1990): 103;

TABLE 6.2. Detector Behavior in the Vietnam War

	Detection	Third-party exposure	Theory expectation	Outcome	Theory support
Covert United States in Laos	Yes: China, Soviet Union	High	Exposure	Collusion (Soviet Union) and exposure (China)	Mixed
Covert China in Vietnam	Yes: United States	Low	Collusion	Collusion (United States)	Strong
Covert Soviet in Vietnam	Yes: United States	Low	Collusion	Collusion (United States)	Strong

The responses to covert activity in Vietnam also suggest the importance of escalation, though support for the theory is mixed. Table 6.2 summarizes the collusion and exposure patterns during the period I analyze. For each covert intervention, detection by rival major powers took place, as my theory expects and contrary to theoretical expectations if secrecy were used to deceive an adversary (operational security logic). For the Chinese and Soviet covert intervention, my theory receives strong support, as US leaders carefully managed intelligence to avoid boxing themselves into retaliation and a possible escalatory spiral. For the American covert intervention in Laos, the support is mixed. China's decision to publicly draw attention to US bombing operations in Laos is consistent with the theory's expectation of how open secret interventions are handled. Soviet collusion to avoid drawing public attention, while drawing on the escalation control mechanisms in the theory, takes place under unexpected conditions.

Finally, the covert side of Vietnam holds three broader lessons. First, the chapter makes clear that, rather than a proxy conflict, overlapping overt and covert interventions created pockets of direct combat between the United States and China and between the United States and the Soviet Union. These casualties were expected and known privately. The lack of

Robert Pape, *Bombing to Win: Air Power and Coercion in War* (Ithaca, NY: Cornell University Press, 1996); Phil Haun and Colin Jackson, "Breaker of Armies: Air Power in the Easter Offensive and the Myth of Linebacker I and II in the Vietnam War," *International Security* 40, no. 3 (January 1, 2016): 139–78. For military effectiveness, see, e.g., Caitlin Talmadge, *The Dictator's Army: Battlefield Effectiveness in Authoritarian Regimes* (Ithaca, NY: Cornell University Press, 2015). And for North Vietnam's victory over its opponent, see e.g., Andrew Mack, "Why Big Nations Lose Small Wars: The Politics of Asymmetric Conflict," *World Politics* 27, no. 2 (1975): 175–200; Ivan Arreguin-Toft, "How the Weak Win Wars: A Theory of Asymmetric Conflict," *International Security* 26, no. 1 (Summer 2001): 93–128.

publicity and acknowledgment, however, kept these incidents from triggering larger escalation. Second, it offers a contrasting narrative about secrecy in the war. The Nixon administration infamously used secrecy to cope with antiwar dissent, hoping that covertness would blunt the outrage from incursions like "Operation Menu" in Cambodia. Analyzing covert military operations during the early and middle periods of the war reveals different secrecy dynamics. Secrecy's role in the larger Vietnam War was therefore both broader and more complex. Leaders of a democracy used it not only to downplay the costs of war and cope with young protestors in the streets but also to control escalation dynamics via what one US leader called "persistent prevarication."[5] Third, the theory makes sense of variation among different elements of a single major power's military operations. American leaders were overtly involved in Vietnam and covertly involved in Laos. I show that distinct escalation risks and limited-war dynamics led to different kinds of decisions regarding military operations in Vietnam and Laos.

The chapter is structured as follows. First, I provide an overview of the Vietnam War and its escalation context, highlighting salient escalation scenarios and evidence of the value of lessons from previous conflicts like the Korean War. I then assess the three covert interventions. The second section analyzes American covert intervention in Laos, the third addresses the covert Chinese combat role in North Vietnamese air defense, and the fourth focuses on Soviet missile defense operators. Each section includes analysis of the detectors and their reaction. The final section addresses the broader context, analyzing the initial overt American intervention and shift in intervention behavior and domestic politics that occurred in 1968.[6]

---

5 "Telegram from the Embassy in Laos to the Department of State," November 29, 1965, in *Foreign Relations of the United States* (hereafter *FRUS*), 1964–1968, Volume 28 Laos, Doc. 207. The turning point, as I explain below, was 1968. By the time Richard Nixon took office, hawkish Vietnam voices in Congress and the wider public remained, but the intensity of antiwar protests had eclipsed them as sources of presidential concern. After 1968, moreover, Chinese and Soviet combat participation in North Vietnam's air defense had been phased out. Many of the covert Laos operations were maintained under Nixon but on a different basis.

6 Regarding sources, available declassified primary materials on the American intervention are vast. I draw in particular on the complete versions of formerly top secret internal histories by the US Defense Department ("United States–Vietnam Relations 1945–1967," completed January 15, 1969, hereafter "Pentagon Papers") and State Department ("Vietnam 1961–1968," completed Spring 1969, hereafter "State INR Retrospective"); records from the Lyndon Johnson Presidential Library, the Central Intelligence Agency's CREST document repository, and recently declassified Presidential Daily Briefs. On China, I largely rely on analysis by Chinese specialists, drawing on primary materials regarding Mao's decision-making during Vietnam, in particular Qiang Zhai and Chen Jian. For the Soviet Union, I rely on Soviet specialist Il'ia Gaiduk's book on

Overview and Escalation Context

The defeat of French forces at Dien Bien Phu in 1954 led to independence for the new states of Laos, Cambodia, and a partitioned North and South Vietnam. A decade of political consolidation by Ho Chi Minh's communist government in Hanoi and the anti-communist Ngo Dinh Diem government in Saigon followed. The impetus for the Vietnam War was a nascent insurgency in South Vietnam.[7] In response to questionable performance by the South Vietnamese army and the illegitimacy of Diem's rule, US leaders gradually embraced an increasingly active combat role. Increased American aid to South Vietnam for counterinsurgency operations started in 1961 in the Kennedy-approved Operation Farmgate air missions. Under President Johnson, US leaders embraced an overt American ground counterinsurgency and bombing role in 1965, and the highly publicized, gradualist Rolling Thunder bombing campaign. Figure 6.1 identifies the local combatants, local conflict zone, external intervening powers, and relevant peripheral zones. The existing conflict into which external powers intervened was within the borders of North and South Vietnam. The peripheral areas included neighboring Laos and Cambodia. Figure 6.2 highlights the two key scenarios for large-scale escalation: widening to all of Southeast Asia via Laos or Cambodia, or the emergence of direct combat between outside interveners.

These peripheral areas were especially dangerous because of simmering civil wars within Laos and Cambodia. Moreover, both neighbors served as conduits for aid from North to South Vietnam, complicating strategic planning for both sides. Laos was the lynchpin. Its long border with North

Soviet policy in Vietnam, which draws on primary materials accessible in the early 1990s but no longer available to researchers.

7 Though not a major power intervention, North Vietnam also concealed its role in South Vietnam but was detected by South Vietnamese and American intelligence. Some in Washington interpreted North Vietnam's covert posture as escalation-driven. One internal American report invokes the theory's key claims when arguing "the final, and probably major, reason that North Vietnam chooses to hide its actual part in the rebellion is fear of retaliation against its own territory. International awareness of the DRV's involvement in the southern insurgency would create a climate of opinion in which South Vietnam and perhaps the United States might take direct action against North Vietnam, an escalation of the conflict that is greatly feared by the northern leadership.... The northern leaders, though clearly desirous of guiding the insurgents toward victory, are equally eager to contain the war." Joseph J. Zasloff, "The Role of North Vietnam in the Southern Insurgency," Rand Corporation, p. 91, in Lyndon B. Johnson Presidential Library (hereafter LBJL), National Security Files (hereafter NSF and same years/country unless noted), 1963–1969, Vietnam, accessed via Proquest History Vault (hereafter PHV), Folder 002791-006-0672.

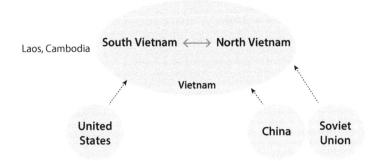

FIGURE 6.1. Structure of Vietnam War.

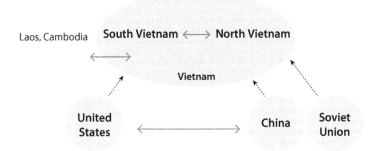

FIGURE 6.2. Key escalation scenarios, Vietnam War.

Vietnam made it an essential transmission belt for supplies moving south via the Ho Chi Minh Trail. This was encouraged by its status as neutral. At the Geneva Conference of 1962 to resolve its own civil war between the royalist central government and communist-allied Pathet Lao, major powers agreed to treat Laos as neutral and avoid a militarized presence.[8] This neutrality status was never fully observed; North Vietnamese troops never left northern Laos.[9] Yet Laotian neutrality was observed vis-à-vis major

---

8 Timothy Castle, *At War in the Shadow of Vietnam: United States Military Aid to the Royal Lao Government, 1955–75* (New York: Columbia University Press, 1995), chap. 2.

9 As noted below, an initial breach of the withdrawal commitment at Geneva was an unacknowledged North Vietnamese troop contingent in Laos that never withdrew after the 1962 neutrality agreement. Publicly North Vietnam claimed its troops in Laos "have all been withdrawn." Privately, CIA estimates noted 7,000 unacknowledged North Vietnamese army regulars in Laos. While I do not analyze North Vietnam's role in detail, the US reaction echoes the backstage collusion mechanism in the theory: the United States did not make an issue of these troops because it expected Hanoi to "keep this military presence small and inconspicuous" and that they

powers. Undermining that neutrality, as I show below, would eliminate a key firewall preventing a wider regional war evolving from Vietnam. Laotian neutrality was therefore seen by all involved as a war-limiting device. Regarding clashes between the major powers, the overt American bombing campaign in North Vietnam created numerous opportunities for clashes. Once Chinese and Soviet personnel joined the conflict, as described below, such combat encounters were not unusual but were kept on the "backstage." An especially pressing concern for both Chinese and American leaders was a repeat of the Korean War scenario in which operations in a neighboring country had led to air and ground combat.

The broader conditions surrounding the Vietnam War also made escalation dynamics a serious concern. The war unfolded within a polarized international environment with enormous American, Soviet, and Chinese conventional and nuclear capabilities. With the vivid memory of the destructiveness of even localized US-Chinese combat in the Korean War, a conventional land war was considered extremely costly. Recent events sharpened the threat of the largest form of escalation, especially the near-escalation to nuclear war during the Cuban Missile Crisis in 1962 and the successful detonation of a nuclear weapon by China in 1964. Moreover, the First Indochina War had already been influenced by outside involvement, as the insurgency against French leaders in the 1950s had benefited from Chinese weaponry and military training.[10] Washington assumed the burden of state-building from the French and a legacy that made clashes with China or its Soviet ally plausible.[11]

Escalation-control problems were significant. Leaders of all three external powers governed amid meaningful—and at times decisive—domestic political constraints. Changes in Beijing and Moscow were significant in this regard. While the democratic constraints of US presidents were similar to those in Korea and the early Cold War, China and the Soviet Union underwent domestic political changes that increased their vulnerability to disagreements among "hawks" and "doves."[12] Stalin's death in 1953 and the

---

"would use the infiltration routes circumspectly." In Castle, *At War in the Shadow of Vietnam*, 49–50.

10 Chen Jian, "China and the First Indo-China War, 1950–54," *China Quarterly*, no. 133 (March 1, 1993): 85–110.

11 Mark Atwood Lawrence, *Assuming the Burden: Europe and the American Commitment to War in Vietnam*, 1st ed. (Berkeley: University of California Press, 2005).

12 For a recent and detailed analysis of the evolution in Cold War consensus and the growing hawk/dove split during Vietnam, see Ronald R. Krebs, "How Dominant Narratives Rise and

tumultuous tenure of Nikita Khrushchev made contestation for power within the Soviet Politburo significant.[13] Similarly, Mao's grip on power slipped and then reemerged between 1964 and 1968.[14] A significant leadership fissure within the Chinese Communist Party had developed that was ultimately resolved through the brutal purges related to the Cultural Revolution. The Democratic Johnson White House was consistently concerned with criticism by Republican lawmakers regarding weakness.[15] While antiwar sentiment dominates the modern memory of Vietnam, American public opinion was strongly supportive throughout the 1964–1968 period.[16] The result was that adversaries on both sides had room for uncertainty about the domestic political landscape, both among the masses and elites, and the potential for constraints on leader decisions regarding escalation.

Also important was the swelling Sino-Soviet rivalry and its potential to contribute to escalation via miscommunication. The competition between China and Soviet leaders to support North Vietnam and other communist allies added to the risks of misunderstanding and was fertile ground for outbidding that could fuel tit-for-tat escalation.[17] At the same time, clashes with either China or the Soviet Union could snowball to include both. As

---

Fall: Military Conflict, Politics, and the Cold War Consensus," *International Organization* 69, no. 04 (September 2015): 809–45.

13 Seweryn Bialer, *Stalin's Successors: Leadership, Stability and Change in the Soviet Union* (New York: Cambridge University Press, 1982).

14 Chen Jian, *Mao's China and the Cold War* (Chapel Hill: University of North Carolina Press, 2001), 238–45.

15 For example, a striking memo from Vice President Humphrey to Johnson opposing overt bombing in February 1965 notes the problem of domestic hawkish criticism and compares it to the Korean War: "In Vietnam, as in Korea, the Republicans have attacked the Democrats either for failure to use our military power to 'win' a total victory, or alternatively for losing the country to the Communists. The Democratic position has always been one of firmness in the face of Communist pressure but restraint in the use of military force; it has sought to obtain the best possible settlement without provoking a nuclear World War III; it has sought to leave open face-saving options to an opponent when necessary to avoid a nuclear show-down." Memorandum from Vice President Humphrey to President Johnson, February 17, 1965, *FRUS*, Vol. 2, Vietnam, January–June 1965, Doc. 134.

16 On the power of hawkish views on Vietnam before 1968, see Daniel C. Hallin, *The "Uncensored War": The Media and Vietnam* (Berkeley: University of California Press, 1989); a more recent analysis of polling data and hawkishness up through 1968 is in Caverley, "The Myth of Military Myopia."

17 Lorenz M. Lüthi, *The Sino-Soviet Split: Cold War in the Communist World* (Princeton, NJ: Princeton University Press, 2010), chap. 10; Nicholas Khoo, "Breaking the Ring of Encirclement: The Sino-Soviet Rift and Chinese Policy toward Vietnam, 1964–1968," *Journal of Cold War Studies* 12, no. 1 (January 1, 2010): 3–42.

one American analysis noted, the ostensible obligation to defend China in Laos under the Sino-Soviet alliance would create significant pressure to intervene ("pose a painful dilemma for the USSR which it would choose to avoid if at all possible"). Lower-level escalation in Laos was especially problematic given Moscow's concern for "its leadership position in the Communist world.... [It] cannot afford to appear to have abandoned support for Communist movements in Asia or to appear less interested in this regard than China."[18]

CROSS-CONFLICT LEARNING

One factor working in favor of escalation control, however, was availability of lessons from previous encounters. The evidence of cross-conflict learning in Vietnam is quite striking. The Korean War was "by far the most often cited" historical analogy during Vietnam.[19] Often these comparisons were used to make sense of covertness and limited war. In Washington, leaders referenced Korea as they analyzed forms of potential Chinese intervention. An internal memo by Vice President Hubert Humphrey in 1965 mentioned "the 'lessons' of 1950–53," which he interpreted to mean that "if we begin to bomb further north in Vietnam, the likelihood is great of an encounter with the Chinese Air Force operating from sanctuary bases across the border. Once the Chinese Air Force is involved, Peking's full prestige will be involved as she cannot afford to permit her Air Force to be destroyed."[20] A well-known memo from presidential advisor George Ball in January 1966 warned of "grave danger of precipitating a war with China" in part based on the fact that "Peiping has steadily increased its covert cooperation" with North Vietnam, including sending "army engineer units." He then notes that the risk of expanding US bombing in North Vietnam is that "we may miscalculate the threshold of Chinese intervention as we did in Korea." In

---

18 "U.S. Negotiating Position Concerning Laos," unsigned (originally classified "Top Secret"), undated (folder label "5 EE (1) Laos October 1967–December 1968"), LBJL, NSF, accessed via PHV, Folder 002793_013_0421.

19 Yuen Foong Khong, *Analogies at War: Korea, Munich, Dien Bien Phu, and the Vietnam Decisions of 1965* (Princeton, NJ: Princeton University Press, 1992), 99; see also Hallin, *The "Uncensored War*," 28–38.

20 Memorandum from Vice President to President Johnson, February 17, 1965, *FRUS*, 1964–1968, Vol. 2: Vietnam, Doc. 134. The memo expressed Humphrey's reservations about an expanding American commitment in Vietnam based on the domestic and international political implications.

rebutting the claim that China's absence of overt intervention thus far meant that it was staying out permanently, Ball retorts that

> one should never forget the behavior of the Chinese during the first five months of the Korean War. No Chinese troops came to give North Korea the punch necessary to push UN forces from their toe hold at Pusan. The Chinese erected no defenses along the 38th parallel to stop a UN invasion when the Inchon landing turned the tide. Even Pyongyang was sacrificed, as was virtually all of the industrial and agricultural area of North Korea. The general estimate in Washington by October 1950 was quite logical: if Peiping had intended intervention it would have done so by then. Yet Chinese Communist troops crossed the Yalu October 14, engaged UN forces October 26, and massively counterattacked General MacArthur's armies November 26. Today only the most reckless will assure you that we know when Peiping will feel it necessary to intervene to safeguard its own military and political interests.[21]

Parallel reasoning influenced the Chinese. Chen Jian's review of Chinese records finds several instances when the Korea precedent was invoked. Early in the war, for example, Mao clashed with other Communist Party leaders over the degree of caution China should exercise with respect to North Vietnam's behavior. A 1962 report by the head of the Communist Party's international liaison department notes that in its management of the Vietnam crisis, Beijing should "learn from the lessons of the Korean War" and warned "that Khrushchev was repeating Stalin's trick by pushing China into another confrontation with the United States in Vietnam."[22] Later Sino-Vietnamese negotiations included specific references to the "Andong model" and "volunteer" pilots, a reference to the Andong Province in northeast China from which Soviet- and Chinese-flown aircraft operated during the Korean War. As Chen Jian describes, the two sides agreed that

> if the Chinese air force was to enter the war, the first choice would be to use Chinese volunteer pilots and Vietnamese planes in operations; the second choice would be to station Chinese pilots and planes on Vietnamese air fields, and enter operations there; and the third choice would be to adopt the "Andong model," that is, when engaging in military

---

21 Memorandum from the Under Secretary of State (Ball) to President Johnson, January 25, 1966, *FRUS* 1964–1968, Vol. 4, Vietnam, 1966, Doc. 41.

22 Chen Jian, "China's Involvement in the Vietnam War, 1964–69," *China Quarterly*, no. 142 (June 1, 1995): 362.

operations, Chinese pilots and planes would take off from and return to bases in China. If Chinese land forces were to be used in operations in Vietnam, they would basically serve as a reserve force; but if necessary, Chinese troops would participate in fighting.[23]

Wars prior to Korea were occasionally referenced as well. For example, communist leaders publicly offered "volunteer" military personnel to North Vietnam in 1965 and 1966. Analysts in the US intelligence community extrapolated from the precedent of the Spanish Civil War to make sense of these promises. In one especially revealing analysis in July 1966, the head of the State Department's intelligence analysis bureau noted that "we cannot exclude the possibility that the Warsaw Pact members will send military technicians, as distinct from foot soldiers, labeled as volunteers." The author specifically notes that "the parallel was drawn between the Spanish civil war and Vietnam—with mention of the fascist role in sending military personnel and equipment to Spain for testing" during public rallies on the anniversary of the Spanish Civil War. He even goes further, interpreting the timing as a kind of warning-by-historical-analogy ("Moscow may intend the references to the International Brigade as a warning to the US").[24]

US Covert Intervention in Laos

This section analyzes American covert military activities in Laos. Backstaging American intervention allowed Washington to slow the supply of men and materiel through Laos while protecting the frontstage image of a geographically bounded conflict in Vietnam. This, in turn, helped control the escalation process by making it less likely the war in Vietnam would spill into Laos and trigger a larger regional war. Neutrality was a legal device that kept a lid on a fragile balance of forces and low-level combat within Laos. Neutrality created a special concern about evidence of American involvement. For example, military personnel were stripped of identifying markers when US covert ground operations into Laos (Operation Brass Tacks) started in March 1965. Shultz, for example, notes a critical concern in ground operations was that "U.S. military personnel would be captured

---

23 Jian, "China's Involvement in the Vietnam War, 1964–69," 369.

24 Thomas Hughes, "Volunteers for Vietnam—A Status Report," Research Memorandum, Department of State Intelligence and Research, RSB-72, July 27, 1966, LBJL, NSF, 1963–1969, Vietnam, accessed via PHV, Folder 002795-004-0273. The International Brigade was the name for the foreign volunteer military force in Spain.

during these operations and paraded as flagrant violators of the 1962 Geneva Accords."[25] His history of the military's covert operations group finds that "paralleling the enthusiasm for covert operations was apprehension over possible unintended consequences," specifically "upsetting the situation in Laos."[26] As Castle's history of the US program concludes, North Vietnamese use of Laos for infiltration routes and American covert air operations against those routes could have expanded the Vietnam War:

> Both sides wisely avoided a full-scale war in Laos. The North Vietnamese army and their Pathet Lao allies could have struck back at many of the important Laotian river sites, including Luang Prabang. Washington could have ordered American troops inserted into Laos and placed along the Trail. In either case the result would have been an immediate and bloody escalation of the war. Both countries refrained from direct confrontation and precipitous military action, so this "nonattributable war" exacted relatively few American casualties.[27]

LAOS: OVER THE BORDER

At its peak, covert US programs in Laos involved a sprawling set of programs involving the Department of Defense, Central Intelligence Agency, USAID, and the State Department.[28] The sensitivity of these missions given Laotian neutrality led to the subordination of military leaders' operational decisions to the US ambassador's judgment, who was given "a mandate from the president to hold the line on US military activity in Laos."[29] Ambassadors like William Sullivan (1964–1969) therefore assessed military requests for more aggressive missions in light of diplomatic sensitivities. Indeed, Sullivan's role in "presid[ing] over a considerable air and ground campaign" led to the Laotian theater becoming known as "Sullivan's war."[30]

---

25 Richard Shultz Jr., *The Secret War Against Hanoi: Kennedy's and Johnson's Use of Spies, Saboteurs, and Covert Warriors in North Vietnam* (New York: HarperCollins, 1999), 215.

26 Shultz Jr., *The Secret War Against Hanoi*, 71–72.

27 Castle, *At War in the Shadow of Vietnam*, 136.

28 Castle, *At War in the Shadow of Vietnam*, 98.

29 Castle, *At War in the Shadow of Vietnam*, 93; on Sullivan's prioritization of avoiding Geneva violations and its impact on covert ground operations in particular, see Shultz Jr., *The Secret War Against Hanoi*, 214.

30 For example, the title of chapter 6 is "Sullivan's War" in Castle, *At War in the Shadow of Vietnam*.

This included embassy-imposed restrictions on tempo of operations, the distance into Laos ground raids could travel, targets of air strikes, and so on.[31]

Modest American covert support for the Royal Lao government by the CIA was initiated under President Kennedy in 1962. The CIA programs were surveillance-focused. American kinetic military activity within Laos was approved only later, under the Johnson administration, as part of the expansion of US activity in Vietnam more broadly in late 1964 and early 1965. In the air, the Johnson administration approved covert American piloting of bombing runs in Laos in mid-1964. By late 1964, covert bombing missions managed by the embassy and administered by the air force and navy targeted the Pathet Lao insurgency in northern Laos (codenamed Barrel Roll) and the Ho Chi Minh Trail in the south (codenamed Steel Tiger). On the ground, the White House approved secret cross-border surveillance and interdiction missions from South Vietnam in March 1965 targeting the Ho Chi Minh Trail. Operations Shining Brass and later Prairie Fire were cross-border missions into Laos administered by a new wing of the US military assistance group in Saigon (Military Assistance Command, Vietnam—Studies and Observations Group, or MACVSOG).[32] Covert military operations in Laos were terminated in 1973 with the Paris Peace Accords.[33]

The primary goal US leaders sought to achieve with covert operations in Laos was interdiction. An August 1965 cable from the American ambassador in Vientiane urged Washington to "define our objectives as best we can" within the three broad categories of "interdiction, harassment, and intelligence." Interdiction was "the ideal end result" but, Sullivan argued, would require "large numbers of ground forces moving into Lao territory from Vietnam in order to occupy the terrain ... which would involve the overt violation of the 1962 agreements on Laos."[34] Harassment was, in essence, making movement along the Ho Chi Minh trail more difficult. Covert cross-border operations also sought to gather intelligence on the kinds of units and equipment passing into South Vietnam. Especially early in the intervention, Washington also hoped that its covert actions would convince

31 Shultz Jr., *The Secret War Against Hanoi*, 215.

32 Shultz Jr., *The Secret War Against Hanoi*, 214–24.

33 In response to congressional scrutiny and prohibitions following exposure in the Pentagon Papers and elsewhere, Nixon banned US military personnel from entering Laos in 1972 and terminated air operations as part of the Paris Peace Accords in 1973.

34 Telegram Embassy Laos (Sullivan) to Secretary of State, August 9, 1965, LBJL, NSF, accessed via PHV, Folder 002787_009_0625.

Hanoi to reduce support for the insurgency and negotiate.[35] Invoking the themes of detection and communication in chapter 2, the State Department's intelligence bureau judged that, while unlikely to be decisive, covert actions against North Vietnam and Laos approved by Johnson in late 1964 and early 1965 "might be viewed in Hanoi as evidence that the US was more willing to take 'whatever militant, active measures might be necessary to win its objectives in Laos and South Vietnam.'"[36] The Pentagon Papers history further describes that late 1964 approval of Air Force-Navy armed reconnaissance missions in Northern Laos "were not publicized and were not expected to have a significant military interdiction effect. They were considered useful primarily for their political value as another of a long series of signals to Hanoi to the effect that the US was prepared to use much greater force to frustrate a communist take-over in South Vietnam."[37]

EXPOSED BUT UNACKNOWLEDGED

The logistics of the Laos intervention were challenging. In the air, some American covert missions in Laos were flown by pilots from a private front company often used for covert action in East Asia (called Air America) and received false documents by the Laotian government to appear as contractors.[38] On the ground, MACVSOG's cross-border missions were crafted to ensure "plausible deniability in the event they were captured." American military personnel wore "Asian-made uniforms with no insignia or other identifying marks, and carried so-called 'sterile' weapons and other equipment that could not be traced back to the United States."[39] These constraints led to micromanaging by the program leadership against which military leaders often chafed.[40] The American ambassador in Vientiane, for example, carefully limited the distance US ground forces could operate within Laos to minimize the risk of capture (which would be "extremely embarrassing to [the] US politically") and kept the use of airlifts to rescue cross-border teams (which could "jeopardize the secrecy of their locations by

35 Rosen, "Vietnam and the American Theory of Limited War."

36 State INR Retrospective, Part A, Section 3, 1969, p. 10.

37 Pentagon Papers, Part IV. C. 3, "Evolution of the War: ROLLING THUNDER Program Begins," p. 6.

38 Castle, *At War in the Shadow of Vietnam*, 69.

39 William Rosenau, *Special Operations Forces and Elusive Enemy Ground Targets: Lessons from Vietnam and the Persian Gulf War*, MR-1408-AF (Santa Monica, CA: RAND Corporation, 2001), 14.

40 This is a recurring theme in Shultz Jr., *The Secret War Against Hanoi*.

conspicuous airlifts") to a bare minimum.[41] In another example, the ambassador described how US-marked helicopters could aid search-and-rescue missions within Laos only if they operated from airfields that "are isolated and in areas closed to ordinary tourists, including journalists.... [W]e regard risks of exposure [as] minimal."[42]

Despite these efforts, covert operations in Laos were an open secret by late 1965. This is clear from contemporary press accounts as well as the candid assessments of decision-makers at the time.[43] As early as December 1965, National Security Advisor Mac Bundy described "an almost constant stream of press leaks on our operations in Laos" and admitted that the "Press is already concentrating on [the] Laos story as [a] major feature of Viet-Nam reporting."[44] These measures were paired with careful efforts to influence how international and US-based press covered events in Laos. American press policy sought to avoid acknowledgment of any reported activity and minimize the precision and certainty of anything that did get reported.[45]

Yet the US response was to refuse acknowledgment. A high-level meeting in Washington on the risk of "leakage of our planning and program"

41 Telegram Embassy Laos (Sullivan) to Secretary of State, August 9, 1965, LBJL, NSF, accessed via PHV, Folder 002787_009_0625; Telegram Embassy Laos (Sullivan) to Secretary of State, April 19, 1965, LBJL, NSF, accessed via PHV, Folder 002787_009_0625.

42 Telegram Embassy Laos (Sullivan) to Secretary of State, July 22, 1965, LBJL, NSF, accessed via PHV, Folder 002787_009_0625.

43 To assess this, I surveyed news coverage in *Washington Post*, *New York Times*, *Los Angeles Times*, and *Chicago Tribune* between June 1, 1964 and December 31, 1968 using keyword search terms that linked Laos with any form of US military operations. These newspapers represent each of the major geographic media markets and span the political spectrum. Coverage of activities in Laos began in early 1965. Whereas only one of the most relevant twenty news articles in 1964 alleged American covert involvement, thirteen of twenty (65%) of the most relevant twenty articles from 1965 and 1966 reference such operations. Headlines such as "U.S. Bombing Raid on Red Aid Route in Laos Reported" (*NYT*/AP, 3/4/1965), "Air Raids Fail to Cut Off Viet Cong Supplies Over Ho Chi Minh Trail," (*LAT*, 12/8/1965), and "U.S. Raids in Laos Called Effective" (*NYT*, 1/9/1966) were common by 1965. Articles in 1966 specifically referred to "700 Aircraft Operating Daily in Laos, Vietnams" (*WP*, 7/11/1966), the "officially denied but well-known American bombing of the Ho Chi Minh Trail," and described that "American Strategy Carefully Avoids Second Front in Laos" (*LAT*, 3/7/1966). One July 1966 *New York Times* article specifically characterized American and North Vietnamese activities in Laos as "an open secret here" ("Gains for Regime Seen in Laos War," *NYT*, 7/26/1966).

44 Telegram Department of State (Bundy) to Embassy Laos (Sullivan), December 24, 1965, hereafter LBJL, NSF, accessed via PHV, Folder 002787_009_0625.

45 William M. Hammond, *Public Affairs: The Military and the Media, 1968–1973* (Washington, DC: GPO, 1996), 133–35.

decided that "the USG would continue a stonewall 'no comment' response to any Hanoi propaganda blast as a result of the above missions."[46] Other declassified documents on US press strategy regarding Laos show American leaders attentive to the unique problem of evidence. A series of cables about a March 1968 battle in which the Pathet Lao overran a site used covertly by the United States is especially revealing. In one cable, the American ambassador reports that there were no American casualties but urges White House silence about a recent battle, warning of a "most serious problem" if the Pathet Lao or North Vietnam "make [a] major propaganda issue out of this event and publish damaging evidence such as documents left behind."[47] A second cable summarizes Sullivan's consultation with Prime Minister Souvanna in which Souvanna "winced" at the prospect of the American role being publicized ("the enemy would be able, if he chose, to make some pretty damaging disclosures") but was reassured that much evidence had been destroyed by a US Air Force bombing run.[48] A reply from State Department headquarters instructs Sullivan to issue a typical denial about later Pathet Lao public claims of American casualties and documents ("standard reply to press queries referring to such allegations is that we do not comment on communist propaganda") unless "confronted with strong evidence of U.S. presence and/or deaths.... [T]hen and only then do we believe our contingency press guidance should be used."[49] Moreover, a cable from Secretary of State Dean Rusk to the embassy in Vientiane describes White House approval of cross-border ground operations but warns to adopt "maximum effort to avoid acknowledgment." This could be done either by "declining comment on communist propaganda charges, if such were original source," or by "citing apparent navigational error."[50]

46 "Memorandum for the Record: Meeting of Principals on Vietnam," December 19, 1964, in *FRUS*, 1964–1968, Vol. 28 Laos, Doc. 152.

47 Telegram Embassy Laos (Sullivan) to Secretary of State, March 1968 (cable VIENTIANE 5118), LBJL, NSF, accessed via PHV, Folder 002787_010_0664.

48 Telegram Embassy Laos (Sullivan) to Secretary of State, March 1968 (cable VIENTIANE 5119), LBJL, NSF, accessed via PHV, Folder 002787_010_0664.

49 Telegram Secretary of State to Embassy Laos (Sullivan), March 1968 (cable STATE 132391), LBJL, NSF, accessed via PHV, Folder 002787_010_0664.

50 "Telegram from the Department of State to the Embassy in Laos," February 24, 1967, in *FRUS*, 1964–1968, Vol. 28 Laos, Doc. 277.

ESCALATION AND COVERTNESS

Why use a covert form in Laos? Why not embrace the operational simplicity and stronger signaling potential of an overt intervention? Why, in particular, was covertness useful even after wide exposure? The primary motive for covertness was protecting neutrality and the war limitation function it provided. To be clear, this was not driven by legalism per se. Neutrality in Laos was the legal codification of a fragile set of mutual restraints that helped limit fighting outside Vietnam's borders to a low level. As Ambassador Sullivan summarized in a cable, "the probable military results" of using American ground forces to more effectively interdict the Ho Chi Minh trail "have to be measured against the predictable political costs" of overtly violating Laotian neutrality. This "would involve far more than just a question of principle. There would be very real practical consequences as well," and "these same considerations applied to all measures proposed against the corridor which entailed overt, conspicuous violation of Lao territory and the 1962 Agreements."[51] The reality was that unraveling Laos's neutrality could widen its civil war and open a new front in US-North Vietnamese combat. It could also invite Chinese military deployments in northern and central Laos near its border, American military deployments to protect Thailand, and draw in a Soviet presence.[52] A memorandum by John McNaughton argued that American troops in Laos would be matched unit-for-unit by the North Vietnamese, leading to an expanding black hole for precious US ground units.[53]

Specifically, visible and acknowledged violations of neutrality by the United States were thought to invite broader North Vietnamese involve-

---

51 Telegram Embassy Laos (Sullivan) to Secretary of State, July 22, 1965, LBJL, NSF, accessed via PHV, Folder 002787_009_0625.

52 See the escalation scenarios described in "Reactions to a Certain US Course of Action in Southeast Asia," September 10, 1965, SNIE 10-10-65, in *FRUS*, 1964–1968, Vol. 28 Laos, Doc. 196.

53 McNaughton forecasts that "a brigade will beget a division and a division a corps, each calling down matching forces from North Vietnam into territory to their liking and suggesting to Hanoi that they take action in Northern Laos to suck us further in." Pentagon Papers, Part IV. C. 6. b., Vol. II, "U.S. Ground Strategy and Force Deployments, 1965–1967," p. 159 [all Pentagon Papers section information is based on the official National Archives and Records Administration index listing]. He continued by citing wider regional consequences, arguing that "it might become necessary to deploy additional forces to Thailand and expand operations further to protect South Vietnam. To counter large-scale [Chinese] overt intervention in northern Laos, it would be necessary to establish a strategic defense. Invocation of the SEATO Treaty would be indicated. In the event the [Chinese] attack Thailand, use of nuclear weapons against LOCs and supply bases in southern China might be required." Pentagon Papers, Part IV. C. 6. b., Vol. II, p. 168.

ment and possible Chinese or Soviet entry. American managers of the covert program linked the integrity of neutrality to Soviet leaders' decision-making. The role of Soviet prestige in the American preference for secrecy and non-acknowledgment echoes themes in chapter 2 on the other-regarding logic of covertness. A cable from 1965 analyzed the dilemmas of Soviet policy in Laos and the link to American decisions about official acknowledgment. Sullivan noted "a very limited community of interest between the USSR and ourselves in [Southeast Asia] may be slowly emerging. It is one that neither we nor they need acknowledge, but which in time may become tacitly understood." Both superpowers hoped to contain the degree of violence in Laos; avoiding embarrassment of Soviet leaders by overt violation of the Geneva Agreement was essential:

> [A] sudden change in the internal political situation or overt American military intervention might seriously embarrass the USSR and lead to a basic reassessment of its strategy in this area. We assume that a chief Soviet concern is [the] possibility a rightist group at some point might oust Souvanna and denounce the Geneva accords, thereby seriously undercutting the Soviet position in Laos. Overt American military intervention or official acknowledgment of it could also seriously restrict Soviet room for maneuver. Either eventuality might force the USSR to come out four square for the P[athet] L[ao] and involve the Soviets far more deeply economically and militarily than they or we wish. But as long as there are fair prospects for avoiding these shoals, the USSR is in a good position to sit back patiently and wait for the breaks to come its way.[54]

American diplomatic consultation with its allies, such as the British, helped inform this view. A late 1965 cable from the US ambassador William Sullivan, for example, complained to headquarters about "a recent tendency on part of press to zero in more closely than usual upon possibility of US air and ground operations in Laos" and that "responses to press inquiries by senior officials are beginning to skirt away from our policy of persistent prevarication." This increasing exposure and precision of information had diplomatic implications:

> [The] British Ambassador ... is becoming most sensitive to recent press stories, especially because Soviets are trying to get British to subscribe

---

54 Telegram Embassy Laos (Sullivan) to Secretary of State, December 4, 1965, LBJL, NSF, accessed via PHV, Folder 002787_009_0625.

to condemnation of U.S. actions. [The British] will stoutly deny they are taking place; but [they] will be hard put to it if some official U.S. spokesman slips over the line and admits what we are doing here.... Therefore, I would urge once again that all responsible officials be cautioned to be wary of press probing on U.S. operations in Laos and that all consciences be collectively steeled against the continuing need to dissemble.[55]

A volatile and polarized domestic environment back in the United States created a potent mix that could drive escalation forward. A detailed memo for President Johnson written in April/May 1967 by the defense secretary's closest advisor, John McNaughton, reflects this.[56] As described and quoted at length in the Pentagon Papers history, this memo featured a set of arguments about further escalation in ground troop levels in Vietnam. By 1967, the domestic mood had shifted to a combination of vociferous antiwar doves and frustrated pro-war hawks. McNaughton's memo describes how these forces could combine to create acute pressure for a fast victory through significant escalation, including major ground actions in Laos. McNaughton considered a key question ("Will the factors ... generate such impatience in the United States that 'hawk' pressures will be irresistible to expand the land war into Laos, Cambodia and North Vietnam and to take stronger air and naval actions against North Vietnam, with consequent risks of a much larger war involving China and Russia?") and provided a pessimistic answer:

The addition of the 200,000 men, involving as it does a call-up of Reserves and an addition of 500,000 to the military strength, would, as mentioned above, almost certainly set off bitter Congressional debate and irresistible domestic pressures for stronger action outside South Vietnam. Cries would go up—much louder than they already have—to "take the wraps off the men in the field." The actions would include more intense bombing—not only around-the-clock bombing of targets already authorized, but also bombing of strategic targets such as locks and dikes, and mining of the harbors against Soviet and other ships. Associated actions impelled by the situation would be major ground actions in Laos, Cambodia, and probably in North Vietnam—first as a

55 "Telegram from the Embassy in Laos to the Department of State," November 29, 1965, in FRUS, 1964–1968, Vol. 28 Laos, Doc. 207.
56 Pentagon Papers, Part IV. C. 6. b., Vol. II, "U.S. Ground Strategy and Force Deployments, 1965–1967," pp. 146–65.

pincer operation north of the DMZ and then at a point such as Vinh. The use of tactical nuclear and area-denial radiological- bacteriological-chemical weapons would probably be suggested at some point if the Chinese entered the war in Vietnam or Korea or if US losses were running high while conventional efforts were not producing desired results.[57]

The second escalation-control mechanism that covertness can address is miscommunication. Several documents suggest that American leaders saw covertness, sometimes simply referred to as deference to the neutral status of Laos, as expressing restraint and a continued interest in limiting the war. One US diplomatic cable made this point in reverse, seeking approval from Laos for "public mention of escorts" because of a desire to "reinforce [the] signal to Hanoi and Peking which would not be as strong if we appeared [to] be trying to suppress this information."[58] This suggests a high-level American perception that *how* it crossed the line of military action in Laos was being observed by key adversaries. Especially powerful evidence is found in a widely circulated Special National Intelligence Estimate that drew on intelligence inputs from across the US government. The SNIE analyzed possible reactions to hypothetical "sustained ground operations" by US forces in southern Laos. It notes that while American and South Vietnamese "have operated in Laos for years," these activities "remain largely unacknowledged—in deference to the 'neutral' status of the Lao government." An overt ground operation, however, would be different; "crossing this political threshold would be read in Peking as US willingness to contemplate a far more activist course in Indochina in search of a military decision."[59] The term "activist" clearly suggests that US leaders believed unacknowledged operations conveyed a restrained political goal.

DETECTION AND REACTION

While careful to avoid acknowledgment of covert operations in Laos, US leaders understood well that North Vietnam, China, and the Soviet Union would detect them. The most obvious reason that US adversaries were

57 Pentagon Papers, Part IV. C. 6. b., Vol. II, "U.S. Ground Strategy and Force Deployments, 1965–1967," pp. 154.

58 "Telegram from Embassy in Laos to the Department of State," June 11, 1964, in *FRUS*, 1964–1968, Vol. 28 Laos, Doc. 92.

59 "Chinese Reactions to Possible Developments in Indochina," May 28, 1970, SNIE 13-9-70, CIA CREST, Doc. 0001166445, p. 6.

likely aware of covert Laos operations is because they were meant to see it. As noted above, American leaders in several instances explicitly hoped that covert operations in Laos would help to communicate a message about American willingness to do more to North Vietnam than previously in the war. Moreover, the internal records of the US military's own covert action arm, MACVSOG, concluded that North Vietnamese intelligence agents had penetrated South Vietnamese partners and tipped them off about covert ground operations into Laos.[60] This was later confirmed when, during peace talks to end the war, North Vietnamese representatives specifically referred to MACVSOG activities.[61] Further, cables from Ambassador Sullivan in Vientiane occasionally reference the Pathet Lao or North Vietnamese enemy seizing documentation that would demonstrate the nature of American covert operations.[62]

Moreover, to the extent that insights can be made into the intelligence available to leaders in Hanoi, Moscow, and Beijing, it appears that all three carefully monitored developments in Laos and knew that the US public position was inaccurate. Chinese and Soviet intelligence deeply penetrated the North Vietnamese security state. Advisors from both external powers had a close view of North Vietnamese sources. This was because of their critical role in building up Hanoi's intelligence infrastructure. Merle Pribbenow reviews Vietnamese materials recently made available, which show the depth of entanglement with Soviet Air Defense, GRU, and KGB intelligence representatives. He notes that the GRU in particular "obtained valuable and rather detailed technical and tactical information from the interrogation of American prisoners of war in North Vietnam."[63] Information from these and other sources was shared in accordance with a standing intelligence-sharing agreement between Hanoi and Moscow.[64] China also

60 The intelligence leaks were precise enough to disclose a map of one forward operating base; Shultz reports that Hanoi's sources included a cook and a driver. Shultz Jr., *The Secret War Against Hanoi*, 243–46.

61 Shultz Jr., *The Secret War Against Hanoi*, 126.

62 See, for example, Telegram Embassy Laos (Sullivan) to Secretary of State, March 1968 (cable VIENTIANE 5119), LBJL, NSF, accessed via PHV, Folder 002787_010_0664.

63 Merle Pribbenow, "The Soviet-Vietnamese Intelligence Relationship during the Vietnam War," *CWIHP Working Paper No. 73*, December 10, 2014, 10–11. This was because "results of these interrogations were shared with the GRU and Soviet Air Defense (PVO) officers, and that on several occasions Soviet military officers personally participated in the interrogation of American prisoners of war" (11).

64 Pribbenow, "The Soviet-Vietnamese Intelligence Relationship during the Vietnam War," 5–8.

appears to have been privy to North Vietnamese military intelligence. Prib-benow finds evidence of close cooperation between Chinese military advi-sors and North Vietnamese military intelligence units. The North Vietnam-ese, moreover, used interrogations, human sources, and signals to learn extensive information about some aspects of US military operations and activity.[65] Lastly, specialists on China's role in the Vietnam War have dis-cussed in passing the likely detection of at least the basic contours of US covert operations like those in Laos. James Hershberg and Chen Jian, for example, report that Chinese primary materials mention intelligence monitoring of the US covert naval intelligence-gathering missions that were involved in the Gulf of Tonkin incident.[66] Qiang Zhai specifically notes that China carefully monitored the evolution of US covert activity in Laos as well.[67]

How did the two major power detectors react? The answer depends. Chinese official press and radio statements echoed their North Vietnamese counterparts in routinely accusing the United States of intervention in Laos. In contrast, Soviet leaders exercised far more restraint. Especially striking are the direct and explicit conversations, always in private, between American and Soviet representatives pressuring the United States to tamp down the visibility of its covert operations in Laos. This constitutes a rare case of explicit coordination among adversaries regarding covert activity in war. This divergence between Soviet and Chinese reactions is not ex-pected by my theory. While the American expansion into Laos created se-vere escalation risks by undermining geographic limits, the covert inter-vention was widely known by 1965 due to exposure by third-party sources. As developed in chapter 2, open secret situations should prompt exposure by adversaries. China's reaction is therefore consistent with my theory's

65 Pribbenow reports that North Vietnamese intelligence successes in specific efforts to intercept signals (5-6) and tap foreign embassies, the latter of which "produced thousands of foreign-language 'documents' that revealed the 'plans and intentions' of the Americans and their allies." Pribbenow, "The Soviet-Vietnamese Intelligence Relationship during the Vietnam War," 8.

66 "After he told Mao that the local Vietnamese commander was responsible for the initial attack on a US destroyer on August 2, Mao told him that, according to China's intelligence, the alleged second incident on the 4th, during which US officers on two ships believed they had been fired upon, was 'not an intentional attack by the Americans,' but the result of 'mistaken judg-ment' and misleading information, a statement that appears to be correct." James G. Hershberg and Chen Jian, "Reading and Warning the Likely Enemy: China's Signals to the United States about Vietnam in 1965," *International History Review* 27, no. 1 (March 1, 2005): 61.

67 Qiang Zhai, "Reassessing China's Role in the Vietnam War: Some Mysteries Explored," in *China and the United States: A New Cold War History*, ed. Xiaobing Li and Hongshan Li (Lan-ham, MD: University Press of America, 1998), 102, 104.

expectations. The more cautious approach by Moscow is not, though the rationale supports the theory's mechanisms.

Regarding China, American diplomatic cables and the Pentagon Papers feature passages in which American leaders vent about the routine accusations of meddling on Radio Hanoi and Radio Peking. North Vietnam is described as accusing the United States of "armed interference" in Laos and "gross violations of the General Agreements" of Geneva.[68] The US intelligence community did interpret this exposure in ways that echo the theory's signaling mechanisms: Chinese and North Vietnamese accusations about Laos operations were seen as warnings. A CIA intelligence memo carefully analyzed the adversary reaction to the earliest covert air strikes in late 1964. It linked propaganda blasts about American covert action to "pledges of support for North Vietnam in the event of US attacks," reporting that "the Chinese repeated their earlier warning that US use of Laotian territory to expand the war in Vietnam could spread the 'flames of war' throughout Indochina."[69] Whiting's review of US intelligence notes that American leaders believed Chinese foreign ministry references to "wanton bombings in Laos" were linked to warnings that the Chinese would not "stand by idly" if the Geneva agreements were violated. American leaders surmised that China was issuing an important deterrence warning about more overt and ambitious involvement.[70]

Moscow, in contrast, conspicuously and consistently ignored US activity in public. This possibility was noted by US leaders and helped motivate their use of secrecy in Laos in the first place. A State Department telegram, for example, suggested that the "Soviets, so long as we do not excessively advertise our actions, are willing in general to ignore them. However, we

---

68 Pentagon Papers, Part IV. C. 2. c, "Evolution of the War: Military Pressures Against NVN, November–December 1964," p. 62. See also Telegram State Department to Embassy Saigon, January 5, 1965, "Assessment Barrel Roll Missions," LBJL, NSF, accessed via PHV, Folder 002791-010-0264. An earlier intelligence analysis of North Vietnam's reaction to US activity from June 1964 also mentions "charges of current US bombing missions in Laos, which Hanoi has attacked without saying that they constitute a threat to North Vietnamese security." Memorandum from Hughes to Secretary of State, June 5, 1964, "Hanoi Threatens 'Retaliatory Blows' if North Vietnam Attacked," LBJL, NSF, accessed via PHV, Folder 002787_007_0894.

69 "Communist Reactions to BARRELL ROLL Missions," Intelligence Memorandum, December 29, 1964, LBJL, NSF, accessed via PHV, Folder 002795_002_0609; "Communist Military Posture and Capabilities vis-à-vis Southeast Asia," Intelligence Memorandum, December 31, 1964, LBJL, NSF, accessed via PHV, Folder 002795_002_0609.

70 Allen S. Whiting, *The Chinese Calculus of Deterrence* (Ann Arbor: University of Michigan Press, 1975), 173–74.

consider maximum effectiveness [of] this total program will involve continued willingness [to] act quietly, eschew publicity, and turn aside press or
diplomatic queries."[71] Similarly, Castle's history of covert US activity in
Laos notes that Soviet leaders valued the low-visibility, deniable nature of
American operations. Indeed, the Geneva agreement on Laotian neutrality
and subsequent covert activity in Laos resulted in a superpower sleight-of-
hand. Moscow, unable to enforce Pushkin's pledge to halt North Vietnamese
trespass of Laos, decided to turn a blind eye to the kingdom. Washington—
increasingly concerned with Vietnam and confident Moscow would not
intervene in Laos, as long as US ground forces did not enter the country—
embarked with Thailand on a complex, covert military assistance program
to Laos. Unquestionably, in late 1962, with good reason, the United States
and Thailand were in direct violation of the Geneva agreements. But, as
long as the US-Thai activity was conducted "quietly," the superpowers chose
to ignore the obvious.[72]

In fact, declassified documents show evidence of direct, private consultations between Soviet and American leaders about the visibility of the US
covert intervention in Laos. These also hint at the dilemma Moscow faced
as leaks became more and more common. During a December 1964 meeting of their representatives on the sidelines of the United Nations, Soviet
representatives stated that they "believed and continued to believe that it
would be best if the United States withdrew from Laos all of its forces, both
military and para-military, and particularly the air force now stationed in
that country," as a way to rectify the "discrepancy between US words and
deeds." American leaders steadfastly refused to acknowledge "so-called US
military personnel in Laos."[73] An even more remarkable exchange took
place during a June 1967 private dinner with the secretary of state and Soviet
Foreign Minister Gromyko. Gromyko noted his regret about "US behavior
in Laos," warning that it "weakened Soviet arguments for maintaining the
Laos agreements." He specifically lamented change over time, stating that
"The US is not only present, but it is present in a new way.... At one time,
the US was not in Laos openly. We had military personnel there but they

71 Telegram Embassy Saigon to Secretary of State, January 7, 1965, LBJL, NSF, accessed via
PHV, Folder 002791-010-0264.

72 Castle, *At War in the Shadow of Vietnam*, 61.

73 "Memorandum of Conversation: Secretary's Delegation to the Nineteenth Session of
the United Nations General Assembly," December 5, 1964, in *FRUS*, 1964–1968, Vol. 28 Laos,
Doc. 147.

were in civilian clothes. Now the US military operates openly. The US is present, and this weakens the Soviet position as co-Chairman, and makes it difficult to use its influence positively."[74]

These private exchanges, in turn, influenced Washington's larger perception of Soviet caution. The June 1967 dinner followed a private exchange of demarches about Laos six weeks earlier in April.[75] During this exchange, internal American assessments of the Soviet message concluded that its private warnings about Laos operations were "another signal from Moscow that they cannot let further intensification or escalation of our bombing of North Vietnam go without reaction on their part." Echoing the theory's key mechanisms, leaders on both sides seemed attentive to the need to retain flexibility and control in any tit-for-tat sequence. One American memo notes that "we should undertake as a matter of urgency a new line of discussion with the Soviet leaders, particularly before they get further involved in Vietnam. The closer they come to confrontation with us, the more difficult it will be for them to retreat, and the harder it will be to achieve a settlement."[76]

The diverging approaches to American covert intervention in Laos therefore provide mixed support for the theory. In general, this feature of the conflict underscores the more cautious approach of the Soviet leaders compared to their Chinese counterparts. Despite the "open secret" of American involvement, Moscow privately lobbied American leaders to reduce their visibility and abstained from drawing attention to it. This is consistent with the theory's mechanisms—i.e., collusion to limit war—but takes place under conditions that the theory suggests should prompt exposure. In contrast, China seized on the propaganda advantage of highlighting its rival's presence in Laos. This corroborates the intuition of the theory that third-party exposure erodes the value of collusion and shifts a detector's priority to seizing the diplomatic advantages of exposure.

---

74 "Memorandum of Conversation: Secretary's Dinner for Foreign Minister Gromyko," June 21, 1967, in *FRUS*, 1964–1968, Vol. 28 Laos, Doc. 293.

75 "Telegram from the Department of State to Secretary of State Rusk at the American Chiefs of State Conference, Punta del Este, Uruguay," April 13, 1967, in *FRUS*, 1964–1968, Vol. 28 Laos, Doc. 280. See also "Memorandum from the Ambassador at Large (Harriman) and the Under Secretary of State for Political Affairs (Rostow) to Secretary of State Rusk," April 17, 1967, in *FRUS*, 1964–1968, Vol. 28 Laos, Doc. 281.

76 "Telegram from the Department of State to Secretary of State Rusk at the American Chiefs of State Conference, Punta del Este, Uruguay," April 13, 1967, in *FRUS*, 1964–1968, Vol. 28 Laos, Doc. 280.

Chinese Covert Intervention in North Vietnam

China's intervention was prompted by the initiation of American air strikes within North Vietnam. China's role was significant and impactful; the leading historian of China's covert military aid concludes that without it, "the history, even the outcome, of the Vietnam War might have been different."[77] While China's role as an advisor and weapons supplier to Hanoi was long-standing and well-known, its introduction of combat-involved personnel took the form of military construction units and antiaircraft artillery (AAA) crews.[78] These units were based in North Vietnam. In total, sixteen divisions of Chinese AAA cycled through North Vietnam between 1965 and 1969 at a total strength of 150,000.[79] Chinese military construction crews rebuilt bombed roads and railways but also, in the process, fired on American aircraft. These crews also sped construction of airfields in North Vietnam. Chinese government statistics, reviewed by Chinese specialists since the end of the Cold War, tally participation in more than 2,000 combat encounters and responsibility for 1,700 American planes shot down.[80]

Chinese combat participants first arrived in the summer of 1965 and all units departed by March 1969.[81] The deployment of Chinese military personnel over the border and in combat roles was not publicized or acknowledged. As Qiang Zhai describes, China "did not openly acknowledge its sizable presence in North Vietnam."[82] Whiting similarly reports that Chinese troops "remained publicly unacknowledged."[83] North Vietnam also conspicuously refrained from publicizing the sizable boost to its air defense and logistics capabilities in its official broadcasts.[84] China's goals were twofold: improve air defense of North Vietnam in light of intensifying American air strikes, and deter American leaders from more aggressively

77 Jian, "China's Involvement in the Vietnam War, 1964–69," 380.

78 Because of my focus on combat participation rather than outside aid for non-combat duties like road construction, the discussion that follows focuses on antiaircraft artillery crews specifically.

79 Jian, "China's Involvement in the Vietnam War, 1964–69," 376.

80 Jian, "China's Involvement in the Vietnam War, 1964–69," 371–75.

81 Jian, *Mao's China and the Cold War*, 223–29.

82 Zhai, "Reassessing China's Role in the Vietnam War: Some Mysteries Explored," 111.

83 Indeed, the only reference to Chinese personnel in North Vietnam was in a single short news item in a 1968 North Vietnamese publication. Whiting describes how American intelligence monitored these official publications for indications of acknowledgment of an outside role. Whiting, *The Chinese Calculus of Deterrence*, 187.

84 Whiting, *The Chinese Calculus of Deterrence*, 187.

destabilizing North Vietnam, which would threaten or endanger the Chinese border. Although Beijing agreed to quietly send construction and AAA units, it declined to provide "volunteer" pilots despite requests from Hanoi, agreeing only to supply flyers if US leaders supported a South Vietnamese invasion northward.[85] Qiang Zhai's review of these Chinese records specifically links its refusal to provide pilots to China's larger desire to avoid a direct confrontation with the United States, a scenario created by a rival's "first-mover" intervention.[86]

ESCALATION AND COVERTNESS

An overarching goal in Vietnam was opposing the American intervention while controlling the risk of a larger war. Fredrik Logevall notes that early in the war, neither Soviet nor Chinese leaders were "keen to see an Americanized war in Vietnam" given that such a development "could confront them with difficult choices and potentially bring them into direct contact with the US Seventh Fleet." Therefore, Beijing and Moscow had "advised the DRV to go slowly, and to avoid provoking Washington."[87] Lumbers also notes that even after the American overt intervention in 1965, "China's interest in a victory in Vietnam was tempered by its fear of a Great Power collision" and that "Mao's determination to launch the Cultural Revolution, even as early as January 1965, made this a particularly inopportune time for another Korea-like clash."[88] Another influential study of Chinese

---

85 Jian summarizes transcripts of Beijing-Hanoi consultations in April 1965 in which North Vietnam's representatives solicited such "volunteers" while "the Chinese were reluctant." The agreement also stipulated a second, deeper level of air participation should this provision fail: China would allow its pilots and planes to participate in the air war from airfields on the Chinese side of the border, referred to as the "Andong model" in reference to the Korean War. Jian, "China's Involvement in the Vietnam War, 1964–69," 369; Zhai, "Reassessing China's Role in the Vietnam War: Some Mysteries Explored," 107.

86 Qiang notes that "Beijing's intention to avoid a direct confrontation with the United States may have also played a role" (and that this disappointed North Vietnam by leaving it exposed to US airpower and played a role in their turn to the Soviet Union for air defense); Qiang Zhai, *China and the Vietnam Wars, 1950–1975* (Chapel Hill: University of North Carolina Press, 2000), 107.

87 Fredrik Logevall, "The Indochina Wars and the Cold War, 1945–1975," in *The Cambridge History of the Cold War*, ed. Melvyn P. Leffler and Odd Arne Westad, Volume 2: Crises and Détente (New York: Cambridge University Press, 2012), 295.

88 Michael Lumbers, *Piercing the Bamboo Curtain: Tentative Bridge-Building to China During the Johnson Years* (New York: Manchester University Press, 2008), 117.

deterrence practices cites its behavior in Vietnam as providing clear signs of "Chinese concern over a possible Sino-American war."[89]

Historians citing Chinese primary material substantiate the importance of limited war and fears of inadvertent escalation. Qiang Zhai describes Mao's concern that the Vietnam War would spread to Chinese territory in the key period of mid-1965 (Mao "feared that the enemy might deploy para-troop assault forces deep inside China").[90] He also cites private remarks by Zhou Enlai, which noted that "war had its own law of development, usually in a way contrary to the wishes of people." He specifically drew attention to "a common pattern in warfare: accidents and miscalculations rather than deliberate planning often lead to war between reluctant opponents."[91] Hershberg and Jian note that "Mao agreed with him about the need to avoid a direct confrontation with the United States" but also sought to warn Washington about endangering North Vietnam's stability. This nuanced message supports limited war. As Hershberg and Jian note, "it was no easy matter to compose and convey a subtle mixed message that would blend resolve—and readiness for military confrontation—with limited objectives that would at least preclude an unnecessary clash brought on by misunder-standing, misperception, or miscommunication."[92]

Primary evidence now available specifically suggests that China's covert intervention was made visible to US military and intelligence assets inten-tionally. As Zhai notes, the Chinese presence in Vietnam "was not carried out under maximum security against detection by Washington," which in-dicates that Beijing expected its role to be detected by the Americans, given its "aerial photography and electronic intercepts."[93] Whiting states that China's intervention clearly appeared to be "carried out in such a manner as to be certain of detection by United States intelligence but not by general

---

89 Whiting, *The Chinese Calculus of Deterrence*, 189.

90 Zhai, *China and the Vietnam Wars, 1950–1975*, 143–44.

91 Zhai, *China and the Vietnam Wars, 1950–1975*, 144; Qiang also notes China opposed a North Vietnamese military offensive against South Vietnam cities. A low-intensity war was pref-erable for Beijing in order to ensure North Vietnam's reliance on Chinese rather than Soviet aid and because it "would reduce the incentive for the United States to expand the war, thus avoiding a potential Sino-American confrontation" (178–79).

92 James G. Hershberg and Chen Jian, "Informing the Enemy: Sino-American 'Signaling' and the Vietnam War, 1965," in *Behind the Bamboo Curtain: China, Vietnam, and the World Be-yond Asia*, ed. Priscilla Mary Roberts (Stanford, CA: Stanford University Press, 2006), 218.

93 Zhai, "Reassessing China's Role in the Vietnam War: Some Mysteries Explored," 108–9.

audiences at home or abroad."[94] China could be confident of US detection because it was aware of Taiwan-based reconnaissance flights; moreover, Beijing did not consistently force Chinese military personnel to alter their appearance.[95] Detection meant that the covert intervention could communicate a blend of restraint and resolve. Drawing on transcripts of Mao's talks with North Vietnam following the Gulf of Tonkin incidents, Hershberg and Jian note that Mao stated that showing Washington "the Chinese also have legs, and legs are used for walking" would be possible by "mov[ing] another air division and half an airborne division to Kunming and Simao and we will do this openly."[96] The blend of resolve and restraint was also conveyed through intermediaries, seemingly a response to the difficulty in signaling that surrounded the Korean War.[97]

Moreover, the message was received. One US intelligence review analyzed China's role and made inferences that parallel both mechanisms of the theory. First, it noted that "the concealment of such information was well within Peking's capability." It then interpreted the conspicuous but covert involvement as escalation control: China had sent its covert support troops in a way that would be "deliberately made known … so as to be credible without appearing provocative by publicly confronting the United States."[98] Whiting's analysis concludes that Chinese "covert deployment of troops to the DRV for construction and combat against American bombing" was designed to send "signals [that] were consistent and credible" and which "communicated a feasible Chinese response."[99] Yet by refraining from wider publicity, China hoped to gain "maximum private credibility with

---

94 Whiting, *The Chinese Calculus of Deterrence*, 172.

95 Whiting, *The Chinese Calculus of Deterrence*, 177, 186.

96 Hershberg and Jian, "Reading and Warning the Likely Enemy," 62. Note that in context, it is clear Mao's reference to "openly" refers to the visibility of Chinese military movements to its adversary rather than wider publicity. This is consistent with China's complete absence of publicity for its deployments in Chinese state media.

97 For example, a message of cautious resolve was conveyed in strict secrecy by Chinese Foreign Minister Yi Chen via a British diplomat in April 1965. See discussion of simultaneous restraint message ("China will not provoke war with the United States") and deterrent warning message ("what China says counts" and "if the United States bombs China that would mean war and there would be no limits to the war") in Zhai, *China and the Vietnam Wars, 1950–1975*, 138–39; Hershberg and Jian, "Informing the Enemy: Sino-American 'Signaling' and the Vietnam War, 1965." Both describe US receipt analysis of this particular message and their understanding of some putative red lines which, if observed, would avoid Chinese entry.

98 Whiting, *The Chinese Calculus of Deterrence*, 186.

99 Whiting, *The Chinese Calculus of Deterrence*, 193.

minimum public embarrassment or provocation for the United States."[100] The message of limited war via both restraint and resolve was highlighted in a particularly striking memo to the secretary of state by his chief intelligence analyst, Thomas Hughes. It notes the "generally accepted" perception in the intelligence community "that the Chinese Communists want to avoid a confrontation with the United States over the Vietnam issue."[101] Hughes then argues that details of Chinese military aid provide "signs of caution," interpreting these actions as more "a contribution toward keeping Hanoi in the war than a sign of Chinese willingness or preparation eventually to share the actual fighting." Expanded Chinese aid, moreover, would be guided by "caution in its approach," given that "it desires to maintain the conflict at the 'protracted people's war' level."[102] He specifically predicts that China could boost its role by engaging only in deniable clashes ("If the missile came from North Vietnam's territory or from a patrol boat even only ostensibly operated by the North Vietnamese, the Chinese might expect no more of a confrontation with us than occurs between the USSR and the US when a Soviet-made SAM shoots down a US airplane").[103] Another intelligence report suggested China might expose its role (give "publicity to Chinese AAA units") as a way to send a stronger signal of resolve.[104]

100 Whiting, *The Chinese Calculus of Deterrence*, 172; another study predating access to Chinese records concludes that China's behavior in Vietnam involved "careful maneuvering to avoid an unnecessary war with the United States ... Beijing also signaled that it hoped to avoid a Sino-American war." Specifically, Garver argues China "intended to convey to Washington the seriousness of China's intent to stand firm behind North Vietnam" and that, in order "[t]o avoid locking itself into a situation that might escalate into a direct confrontation with the United States, Beijing did not officially acknowledge its military presence in North Vietnam." John W. Garver, "The Chinese Threat in the Vietnam War," *Parameters* 22, no. 1 (1992): 78.

101 Memorandum from Thomas Hughes to Secretary of State, December 16, 1967, "China's Scope for Augmented Vietnam Participation," LBJL, NSF, accessed via PHV, Folder 002793-012-0001. Notably, Hughes points out evidence of Chinese interest in limited war includes both observable indicators in Vietnam and the general belief that China learned from the Korean War that a large ground conflict with the United States was exceedingly costly ("The Chinese are believed to have learned their lesson during the Korean War about the enormous power of the United States and can hold no doubt that, in direct and full-scale confrontation, China could not hope for success").

102 Memorandum from Thomas Hughes to Secretary of State, December 16, 1967, "China's Scope for Augmented Vietnam Participation," pp. 2, 4.

103 Memorandum from Thomas Hughes to Secretary of State, December 16, 1967, "China's Scope for Augmented Vietnam Participation," p. 4.

104 State INR Retrospective, 1969, p. 179. To be clear, the nature of China's military presence in North Vietnam was one of several behavioral indicators US intelligence and other government analysis mentions. Other issues scrutinized included the tone and specific claims of

DETECTION AND COLLUSION

Given these assessments of China's intent, it is clear that American leaders detected covert Chinese combat participation. Declassified intelligence material provides unique insight into just how closely this was tracked. Early in the war, the United States expected that China's desire to keep the war limited would lead to a covert or "volunteer" role, if any developed.[105] The first signs of People's Liberation Army military units in North Vietnam appear to have arrived in July 1965, only weeks after their dispatch from Chinese territory and within three months of American combat operations in South Vietnam. The section on China in a July 23, 1965, Special National Intelligence Estimate notes that "they are already stepping up their military assistance, including the introduction of some rear service elements into North Vietnam, and would give more aid if requested by the DRV."[106] By October 1965, a semi-regular series of intelligence memoranda on the swelling Chinese military presence in North Vietnam started. The October report notes, "Chinese Communists in June 1965 began deploying a limited number of military support units into North Vietnam" in the northeast region of the country which "marked the first time that Chinese troops had been stationed outside China since 1958."[107] It estimates that as many as 19,000 military personnel were deployed, with an additional 20,000 on the Chinese side of the border.[108] Confirming combat participation took more time, though unexcised portions of an October 1965 report note that Chi-

---

Chinese propaganda, internal military and civil defense preparations within China, and the private diplomatic messages relayed to Washington.

105 See, for example, the prediction that "China would in fact be cautious about becoming involved," China would only make available antiaircraft and perhaps planes to North Vietnam, and the possibility that "unacknowledged Chinese Communist units might make deep incursions into Laos." In Special National Intelligence Estimate, May 25, 1964, "Probable Consequences of Certain US Actions with Respect to Vietnam," 50-2-64, CIA CREST, Doc. 0001166401. Nine months later a similar report predicted "limited numbers of Chinese ground forces as 'volunteers.'" In Special National Intelligence Estimate, February 18, 1966, "Communist Reactions to Possible US Courses of Action against North Vietnam," 10-3/1-65, FRUS Vol. 2, Vietnam, Jan.–June 1965, Doc. 139.

106 "Communist and Free World Reactions to a Possible US Course of Action," July 23, 1965, SNIE 10-9-6, CIA CREST, Doc. 0001166393.

107 Intelligence Memorandumhttp://www.foia.cia.gov/sites/default/files/document_conversions/89801/DOC_0000475033.pdf, "Chinese Communist Military Presence in North Vietnam," October 20, 1965, CIA CREST, Doc. 0000475033.

108 Intelligence Memorandumhttp://www.foia.cia.gov/sites/default/files/document_conversions/89801/DOC_0000475033.pdf, "Chinese Communist Military Presence in North Vietnam," October 20, 1965, 6–7.

nese personnel "appear to include a possible [anti-aircraft artillery] division," which likely explains why American pilots reported "unusually heavy flak; two US aircraft were downed by ground fire" in a recent bombing mission.[109]

By September 1966, intelligence reports on China's role described "seven major Chinese units in North Vietnam, all of them probably of division size." Of those seven divisions, the report notes, "one is known to be an air force anti-aircraft artillery (AAA) division" and one "an army AAA division."[110] The precision of estimates further sharpened into 1967. Records of top White House deliberations also mention covert Chinese involvement, as when National Security Advisor Walt Rostow noted in 1966 that "Hanoi has already permitted a substantial number of Chinese Communist engineering and anti-aircraft forces to enter North Viet Nam."[111] Rostow later cautioned Johnson that new bombing would probably lead China "to introduce many more engineering and anti-aircraft forces along the roads and rail lines between Hanoi and China in order to keep the supplies moving."[112] A CIA memo on Sino-Vietnamese relations in June 1967, for example, describes a stable Chinese presence featuring four more divisions than were known in September 1966:

> There has been no evidence of change in the level or type of support provided by the Chinese. The strength and composition of Chinese forces in North Vietnam have been constant during the past four months. There are still a total of between 26,000 and 48,000 Chinese soldiers in North Vietnam. Units tentatively identified include four anti-aircraft artillery (AAA) divisions, a railway engineer division, and four suspect special engineer divisions.... The AAA units are deployed to defend these construction projects. Peking has rotated units in and out of Vietnam on a regular six-to-eight-month cycle since February 1966.

109 Intelligence Memorandumhttp://www.foia.cia.gov/sites/default/files/document_con versions/89801/DOC_0000475033.pdf, "Chinese Communist Military Presence in North Vietnam," October 20, 1965, 5. One sentence in this paragraph is excised. Based on context, it is plausible this sentence refers to some sort of signals-related intelligence gathered during the strike which led to two downed US aircraft.

110 Intelligence Memorandumhttp://www.foia.cia.gov/sites/default/files/document_con versions/89801/DOC_0000475033.pdf, "Chinese Communist Military Presence in North Vietnam," September 29, 1966, CIA CREST, Doc. 0000854558, p. 1.

111 Memorandum from the President's Special Assistant (Rostow) to President Johnson, November 30, 1966, *FRUS*, Vol. 4 Vietnam, 1966, Doc. 319.

112 Memorandum from the President's Special Assistant (Rostow) to President Johnson, May 6, 1967, *FRUS*, Vol. 5 Vietnam, 1967, Doc. 162.

The most recent rotations took place between 30 May and 3 June, at which time the AAA unit at Lang Son and another at Yen Bai were replaced by new units from China.[113]

A more granular level of detail—including information derived from signals intercepts that is rarely made public—is available in recently declassified Presidential Daily Briefs (PDB). Briefs from July 1965, for example, capture the initial entry of Chinese troops. President Johnson is told that intercepted communications show a buildup on the Chinese side of the border on July 1 and, two weeks later, "a Chinese military entity continues to communicate from northeastern North Vietnam, but clarification of its role is still lacking."[114] Most important, Johnson is briefed in February 1966 on intercepted communications of the 103rd Anti-Aircraft Division showing its movement toward the border and crossing into North Vietnam. The PDB notes the significance: "This marks the first time a Chinese Communist tactical unit has deployed into North Vietnam. Previous Chinese units were engineer and logistic, although some of them may have had antiaircraft elements attached. The 103rd is one of 12 antiaircraft divisions attached to Peking's air force. It would have, at a minimum, three regiments for a total of just over 3,100 men."[115]

My theory expects the decision to expose or collude regarding China's involvement to be influenced by the uniqueness of this information due to the level of third-party exposure. Even as US intelligence tracked Chinese combat involvement, public reporting on this aspect of the war was highly unusual and almost always linked to a non-combat role. A review of *New York Times* reporting from the key period of analysis confirms this.[116] Much of the public reporting about China's role in Vietnam noted its importance for military supplies, linked Chinese personnel to an engineering/labor role while denying a combat role, or attributed stiff air defense to North Vietnam rather than Chinese (or Soviet) forces.[117] This sometimes led to con-

---

113 Intelligence Memorandumhttp://www.foia.cia.gov/sites/default/files/document_con versions/89801/DOC_0000475033.pdf, "Sino-Vietnamese Frictions," June 21, 1967, LBJL, NSF, accessed via PHV, Folder 002789-017-0694.

114 "The President's Daily Brief 1 July 1965" and "The President's Daily Brief 16 July 1965," CIA CREST, Documents 0005967760 and 0005967784 respectively.

115 The President's Daily Brief 2 February1966," CIA CREST, Doc 0005968131.

116 I analyzed reporting from June 1965 to late 1969 using search terms like "anti-aircraft" and "aid" linked to "China/Chinese" or "Peiping."

117 On military supplies, see Seymour Topping, "Red China Denies Balking Hanoi Aid," *New York Times*, January 16, 1966. On engineering/labor role, typical clarification stated that "there

spicuous mysteries, as when an American Air Force source was quoted in a story saying, "the North Vietnamese air defense is the most sophisticated ever put to the test of combat."[118] Given this pattern, the theory expects the American leaders to collude in keeping China's role on the backstage as a way to effectively supplement other limits on the war.

As expected, the American reaction was a clear case of collusion rather than exposure. Consistent with the theory, the clearest discussion of the overall American reaction to China's entry, and the logic for tacitly colluding, appears in the account of former US intelligence analyst Allen Whiting. He first describes China's logic for avoiding publicity about its participation in the war over North Vietnam. He notes that, while "Peking accepted a modest propaganda loss" by not advertising its support for the Vietnamese, "the Chinese leadership apparently appreciated the difference between credible deterrence and a provocative 'lock-in' of enemy escalation. Under the circumstances a low profile was preferable to publicity."[119] American leaders were not completely silent and informed select journalists that Chinese military units were in North Vietnam. However, in Whiting's account, US leaders carefully sought to minimize escalation risks through managing the optics of the situation:

> American officials carefully couched their revelations in such a manner so as to minimize attention and reaction in congressional and press circles.... [T]he Johnson administration had no desire to arouse American concern over the prospects of war with China and had no intention of stumbling inadvertently into that war. Its unobtrusive release of information revealing the PLA presence avoided alarm while alerting Peking it was aware of Chinese activity in the DRV and intended to abide by its implications.[120]

---

are no Chinese combat units in North Vietnam, intelligence sources believe, but an estimate total of 11,000 or 12,000 Chinese Army engineers and horde of laborers are working constantly to rebuild bridge and to keep the rail from Hanoi to Nanning in China operating." Hanson W. Baldwin, "China's Entry into Vietnam War Held Unlikely," *New York Times*, December 22, 1965. On attribution to North Vietnam, see an article noting "a high Defense Department official has acknowledged that North Vietnam's MIG jet fighters and antiaircraft missiles have cut down the effectiveness of United States bombing." "U.S. Aide Asserts MIG's Curb Raids," *New York Times*, April 20, 1967.

118 Sam Butz, "Our Pilots Call Hanoi 'Dodge City,'" *New York Times*, October 16, 1966. The article mentions Russian-made SA-2 systems without identifying operators.

119 Whiting, *The Chinese Calculus of Deterrence*, 187.

120 Whiting, *The Chinese Calculus of Deterrence*, 188.

Sensitivity about publicizing China's role also created problems with US allies. In July 1964, public accusations that China had a military presence in Vietnam led to urgent messages of restraint by the United States. Then-Prime Minister of South Vietnam Nguyen Khanh alleged that the "Chinese had moved a regiment of their troops into North Vietnam."[121] American representatives immediately demanded that South Vietnam withdraw its accusation by issuing a communique that there was "no confirmed action" by Chinese communist forces. Although this dispute occurred before US intelligence had concluded that Chinese units were in North Vietnam, it shows the political sensitivity of allegations about China's entry for Washington.[122] Another example comes from later. Even as US intelligence confirmed Chinese combat participation in air defense, President Johnson sought to reassure China that expanded US bombing in North Vietnam was not directed at Beijing.[123] Describing the public relations strategy for a Johnson trip to Asia in October 1966, Lumbers notes:

> The Johnson team made a conscious effort to ensure that the meeting in Manila did not assume anti-Chinese overtones or exacerbate tensions. William Bundy insisted to LBJ's speechwriters that any "references to aggression [in Vietnam] should focus on North Vietnam, with Communist China being referred to only in a supporting role and no implication that the [Manila] group is a new alliance to combat the over-all menace of Communist Chinese aggression." Keeping the war limited depended as it had before on projecting restraint to Beijing.

Soviet Covert Intervention in North Vietnam

Concurrent with China's entry was Soviet participation in North Vietnamese air defense. Although advisory personnel were present in North Vietnam for the duration of the 1964–1968 period, Soviet participation in combat operations lasted for a period of only six months. It began in the summer of 1965 as preparations for SA-2 missile systems near Hanoi concluded; by late fall 1965, their North Vietnamese counterparts were sufficiently trained to take over operations. Given the larger US-Soviet rivalry, its combat participation carried particularly explosive implications. Covertness allowed Moscow to support North Vietnam's air defense but avoid forcing combat

---

121 William M. Hammond, *Public Affairs: The Military and the Media, 1962–1968* (Washington, DC: GPO, 1989), 96–97.

122 Hammond, *Public Affairs: The Military and the Media, 1962–1968*, 97–100.

123 Lumbers, *Piercing the Bamboo Curtain*, 149–53.

incidents that could widen the war. A low-visibility, unacknowledged role helped its ally, sent a message to the Americans, and retained control over subsequent escalation. Each of the key mechanisms of the theory played a role: Soviet and American leaders using secrecy and non-acknowledgment to control escalation; the perceived value of both limited knowledge and non-acknowledgment; and inferences about an interest in limited war based on observing covertness. As one history of the Soviet role concludes:

> Despite Soviet interest in and concern for North Vietnam, Moscow did not desire a confrontation with the United States precipitated by North Vietnam.... To minimize the possibility of confrontation with the United States, the presence of Soviet personnel at the North Vietnamese missile sites was not publicized. In effect, the Soviet Union signaled the United States that it did not desire a Soviet-American confrontation. At the same time, the lack of official American comment on the Soviet technicians was a U.S. signal to Moscow that the U.S. similarly did not desire a confrontation.[124]

The turning point for Soviet involvement came in February 1965. Moscow publicly announced provision of new air defense weapons to North Vietnam and an offer of "volunteers."[125] The aid was in response to increased American bombing of North Vietnam and not long after the original Gulf of Tonkin incident. Smaller in scope than the Chinese intervention, the Soviet Union sent highly advanced surface-to-air missile systems and Soviet technicians to operate and maintain them. Estimates based on Soviet records and American intelligence at the time suggest around 2,000 Soviet military personnel were in-country at any given time servicing SA-2 missile systems from mid-1965 to as late as 1967.[126]

The first combat engagement involving Soviet personnel took place in late July 1965 and resulted in the shootdown of an American F-4C.[127]

124 Daniel S. Papp, *Vietnam: The View from Moscow, Peking, Washington* (Jefferson, NC: McFarland, 1981), 68–70.

125 Ilya V. Gaiduk, *The Soviet Union and the Vietnam War* (Chicago: Ivan R. Dee, 1996), 24–27.

126 US intelligence estimated 1,500–2,500 Soviet military personnel in Vietnam in September 1965 but did not detail what proportion were involved in SAM operations. Gaiduk cites a Soviet embassy report from 1967 putting the figure at 1,165, which apparently includes both missile operators and maintenance crews. "Status of Soviet and Chinese Military Aid to North Vietnam," CIA Special Report, September 3, 1965, CIA CREST Doc. 0000652931; Gaiduk, *The Soviet Union and the Vietnam War*, 61.

127 Merle L. Pribbenow, "The 'Ology War: Technology and Ideology in the Vietnamese Defense of Hanoi, 1967," *Journal of Military History* 67, no. 1 (2003): 177.

Soviet personnel moved out of an active role in firing the missiles as they trained their Vietnamese comrades in operating the SAM systems. However, Pribbenow notes that "Soviet soldiers continued to participate in combat missile launches for some time" and advisors and technicians remained on site—and vulnerable to US air strikes—even after transitioning out of operational roles.[128] Ilya Gaiduk cites a Soviet embassy report from 1967 that estimates 1,165 Soviet military experts in maintenance and operator roles for surface-to-air missiles and mentions that they took part in combat missions, "suggesting a more active role" than conventionally acknowledged.[129] English-language news reports from the 1989–1991 period describe Soviet operation of missile systems in mid-1965 and phasing out by the end of 1966 as Vietnamese took over operations.[130]

While leaders in Moscow generally sought to support their North Vietnamese ally and not fall behind in the Sino-Soviet rivalry, covertly supplied missile systems were meant to limit the damage from US air superiority and air attacks on Hanoi.[131] Yet the weaponry that could do so was prohibitively technical. As Papp notes, "the only personnel who were trained in their use were Soviet technicians, who therefore had to be sent to the D.R.V."[132] Soviet leaders therefore sent regiments of missile-related personnel in secret. Gaiduk describes Soviet leaders as "eager to avoid publicizing this aid."[133] Western media reports from 1989–1991 also note the intense secrecy for these personnel. Moscow's public acknowledgment was limited to vague calls for Eastern bloc volunteers in 1965 and 1966, which served as "a propaganda ploy, as a means of putting pressure on the United States, and in some respects as a smoke screen for the introduction of Soviet advisers into Vietnam."[134] To be clear, the dearth of primary documents leaves many aspects of this covert deployment unknown, including the logistical arrangements Soviet leaders made to avoid publicity.

128 Pribbenow, "The 'Ology War," 177–78.

129 Gaiduk, *The Soviet Union and the Vietnam War*, 61.

130 See, for example, Francis Clines, "Russians Acknowledge a Combat Role in Vietnam," *New York Times*, April 14, 1989. See also the Associated Press story "Soviet Involvement in the Vietnam War," at http://historicaltextarchive.com/sections.php?action=read&artid=180.

131 Gaiduk, *The Soviet Union and the Vietnam War*, 59; Papp, *Vietnam*, 68.

132 Papp, *Vietnam*, 68–70.

133 Gaiduk, *The Soviet Union and the Vietnam War*, 62.

134 Gaiduk, *The Soviet Union and the Vietnam War*, 64.

ESCALATION AND COVERTNESS

While primary documentation on Soviet considerations is unavailable, scholars of Soviet policy regarding Vietnam consistently link its covert posture to escalation. Moscow was generally not "keen to see an Americanized war in Vietnam, one that could confront them with difficult choices and potentially bring them into direct contact with the US Seventh Fleet."[135] Moreover, escalation caution was evident in how Soviet leaders handled deepening American activity in Vietnam. Gaiduk describes how Soviet documents repeatedly express limited-war concerns at each major pivot point in the expanded American intervention. As Washington expanded its air and ground war, he notes that "the danger of global conflict and a showdown with the United States was in the back of Soviet leaders' minds. Consequently they were anxious to avoid any turn of events that might lead to such a disaster."[136] This consideration led Moscow to play an off-and-on role as intermediary between Hanoi and the United States and to encourage their Eastern European allies to do the same.[137] To be clear, Gaiduk also observes that Soviet leaders viewed the likelihood of something like a "general war" erupting from Vietnam as remote.[138] Still, Gaiduk notes that Soviet leaders did find it plausible that American leaders might use tactical nuclear weapons out of desperation. They also worried about what, if any, Chinese guarantees were given to North Vietnam should this nuclear threshold be crossed.[139]

The perception in Washington was that Moscow sought to avoid large-scale escalation of the Vietnam War but had imperfect control over that process. American policymakers specifically saw the Sino-Soviet rivalry as an important source of unpredictability in Soviet policy. They noted indications of deepening Soviet involvement in North Vietnam in 1965 as an effort to "deprive Peking of exclusive credit for having backed this crucial 'national liberation struggle'" and "offset the Chinese charges of Soviet lukewarmness toward such efforts, long one of the key issues in the dispute."[140]

135 Logevall, "The Indochina Wars and the Cold War, 1945–1975," 295.

136 Gaiduk, *The Soviet Union and the Vietnam War*, 73.

137 Gaiduk, *The Soviet Union and the Vietnam War*, 73–75, 82–92, 95. These initiatives included "Marigold" and "Sunflower."

138 Gaiduk, *The Soviet Union and the Vietnam War*, 74.

139 Gaiduk, *The Soviet Union and the Vietnam War*, 47, 74.

140 Memorandum Prepared in the Policy Planning Council, "Soviet Policy in the Light of the Vietnam Crisis," February 15, 1965, *FRUS*, Vol. 14 Soviet Union, Doc. 96.

Similarly, an early 1966 intelligence assessment of Soviet interests in North Vietnam noted that a Soviet delegation seemed selected "to underscore Moscow's contention that the defense of the Communist bloc essentially depends on the USSR's power. This line is aimed as much at Peking as at Washington and the Soviet leaders have demonstrated that they consider it an effective tool in the context of intensive Sino-Soviet rivalry for influence and credit both in Hanoi and throughout the Communist movement."[141] Finally, a 1968 memo argued, in response to growing Chinese aid to Hanoi, "[the] Soviets would read into this wider implications related to the Sino-Soviet quarrel." The tendency to outbid one another was thought to be an important determinant of their response to US actions: the "nature of Soviet action would be affected by what Chinese communists did. [The] Soviets would not wish to be in [a] position of doing less."[142] This dynamic could rob Moscow of its control. One memo from February 1965, for example, noted the "agonizing" dilemma for Moscow if a " 'wider war' develops" in Vietnam. For Moscow "to appear to renege would be extremely costly in the struggle with Peking. On the other hand, the Soviets must see one particularly dangerous feature in this crisis; they will not be in full charge, but can have their hand forced by Hanoi and perhaps also by Peking."[143] The embassy in Moscow articulated the same concern. Ambassador Foy Kohler noted that "while I continue to believe that [the] Sov[iet]s are anxious to avoid escalation of hostilities in Vietnam," Moscow could adopt a more active and dangerous role in Hanoi given "their obvious interest in demonstrating their reliability as a socialist ally in face of goading commentary by [Chinese Communists]."[144]

DETECTION AND COLLUSION

Declassified American records make clear that covert Soviet combat participation was expected and linked to escalation dynamics. Even before Moscow entered the war, American leaders predicted it as a likely Soviet

141 "Role of Tolubko in the Shelepin Delegation," CIA-DIA Memorandum, January 7, 1966, CIA CREST, CIA-RDP82R00025R000500250002-2.
142 Pentagon Papers, Part IV. C. 7. b, "Evolution of the War: Air War in the North, 1965–1968," Vol. 2, Part IV. C. 2. c, "Evolution of the War: Military Pressures Against NVN, November–December 1964," pp. 161–62.
143 Memorandum Prepared in the Policy Planning Council, "Soviet Policy in the Light of the Vietnam Crisis," February 15, 1965, *FRUS*, Vol. 14 Soviet Union, Doc. 96.
144 Telegram from the Embassy in the Soviet Union to the Department of State, February 11, 1965, *FRUS*, Vol. 14 Soviet Union, Doc. 93.

reaction to US bombing in the North. The Joint Chiefs of Staff anticipated Soviet provision of SA-2 missile systems in response to aggressive, overt US bombing in North Vietnam. In debates in February 1965 that led to the initiation of US bombing of North Vietnam, the JCS assessed that "the chances are about even that the Soviets would agree to provide some SA-2 defenses."[145] This estimate was supported by the wider intelligence community in a Special National Intelligence Estimate from the same time.[146] However, the consensus view was that any Soviet missile assistance would be covert, reflecting a US belief in Moscow's caution about escalation. The JCS argued that Moscow "would do so in ways calculated to minimize the initial risks to them. By providing the necessary Soviet personnel in the guise of 'technicians,' the USSR could preserve the option of ignoring any Soviet casualties."[147] The intelligence community used almost identical language, predicting Soviet leaders would use a form of intervening directly in combat operations that would preserve escalation control:

> If the Soviets should provide SA-2s, we believe that they would do so in ways calculated to minimize the initial risks to them. One likely way of doing this would be to deploy some SA-2 defenses for the key Hanoi-Haiphong area, hoping that this degree of involvement would serve to restrain the US and still not engage Soviet personnel in actual fighting. SA-2s deployed in this area, however, probably would be used if attacking US aircraft came within their range. By providing Soviet personnel in the guise of "technicians," the USSR would preserve the option of ignoring any Soviet casualties. This would be a fairly limited Soviet involvement, but it would represent a greater commitment to North Vietnam than has obtained in the past. In this situation of increased risks, we believe that the USSR would be seeking means to curb the conflict.[148]

145 Memorandum from the Joint Chiefs of Staff to Secretary of Defense McNamara, February 11, 1965, *FRUS*, Vol. 2, Vietnam, Jan.–June 1965, Doc. 109.

146 Special National Intelligence Estimate, "Communist Reactions to Possible U.S. Actions," SNIE 10–3–65, *FRUS*, Vol. 2, Vietnam, Jan.–June 1965, Doc. 111. The estimate analyzed Soviet reactions and assessed that there was "an even chance that some SA-2 installations would be provided."

147 Memorandum from the Joint Chiefs of Staff to Secretary of Defense McNamara, February 11, 1965, *FRUS*, Vol. 2, Vietnam, Jan.–June 1965, Doc. 109.

148 Special National Intelligence Estimate, "Communist Reactions to Possible U.S. Actions," SNIE 10–3–65, *FRUS*, Vol. 2, Vietnam, Jan.–June 1965, Doc. 111. The estimate analyzed Soviet reactions and assessed that there was "an even chance that some SA-2 installations would be provided."

These predictions were affirmed when US intelligence detected Soviet missile site construction in the spring of 1965. Multiple intelligence sources provided a detailed view to American government observers once Soviet SA-2s and associated personnel began to arrive. The Pentagon Papers summary notes that in early April 1965, US reconnaissance photography revealed "the first SA-2 SAM site under construction" near Hanoi.[149] Notes from a briefing by the director of central intelligence in July 1965 state that US intelligence had "photographed five SA-2 surface-to-air missile sites forming a ring 10 to 15 miles out from Hanoi" built by Soviet technicians.[150] A similar briefing one month later assessed that each site required technicians and other staffing of around 1,000 people, some of whom would take close to a year to be fully trained.[151] By September 1965, a special intelligence report on Soviet aid to North Vietnam estimated "1,500 to 2,500 Soviet military personnel. . . . The bulk of Soviet military personnel in Vietnam are SAM operators."[152] The Presidential Daily Briefs given to Johnson at this time show how sensitive signals intercept information helped confirm these suspicions. A September report to the president noted that "communications intelligence indicates that Soviet and Vietnamese personnel are jointly manning the communications complex that was involved in the launch of one or more missiles on 6 September. Overall control apparently is still in Soviet hands."[153]

Reflecting the communication function described in chapter 2, US leaders viewed Soviet missile aid as a cautious warning to Washington. One intelligence analysis concluded that "the Russians meant their action as a warning that further escalation risked counterstrikes against targets in the South or US carriers."[154] The head of the State Department's intelligence

149 Pentagon Papers, Part IV. C. 3, "Evolution of the War: ROLLING THUNDER Program Begins," p. 110.

150 "DCI Mahon Briefing (North Vietnam)," July 9, 1965, CIA CREST, CIA-RDP82R 00025R000500250002-2.

151 "Background Material DCI Briefing of Stennis Subcommittee," August 6, 1965, CIA CREST, CIA-RDP82R00025R000500290005-5. The logic for estimates was as follows: "Soviet SA-2 launch sites typically require 140–150 men. A four-site regiment with headquarters and technical support elements totals close to a thousand men. Individual sites cannot operate independently for any length of time without support. Many of the equipment operators need only a few months' training, but maintenance and missile assembly require a large number of skilled technicians with much more extensive training—up to 10 months."

152 Special Report, "Status of Soviet and Chinese Military Aid to North Vietnam," September 3, 1965, CIA CREST, Doc 0000652931, p. 4.

153 "The President's Daily Brief 10 September 1965," CIA CREST, Doc. 0005967883.

154 State INR Retrospective, Part A, Section 5, 1969, p. 32.

arm noted that Soviet leaders "almost certainly assume that we are aware of their action." He argued that "Moscow is undoubtedly seeking to impress the US with the seriousness of its determination to help the DRV" and that air defense supplies were likely thought to "help deter the US from bombing that field … especially if Soviet personnel are involved."[155] A third intelligence assessment interpreted the new Soviet role in North Vietnam's air defense in 1965 as an indication that "the Soviet leadership was willing, for the sake of possible gain in its struggle with Peking for leadership in the Communist movement and the Afro-Asian world, to put its relations with the US in serious jeopardy."[156]

Yet American analysts interpreted the form of Moscow's combat role as an indicator of continued concern about larger escalation. A fall 1965 intelligence memo on Soviet aid to North Vietnam observed that "Moscow has taken great pains to avoid allowing its assistance to lead to a direct Soviet-US confrontation and continues to emphasize the defensive nature of its aid."[157] A Special National Intelligence Estimate from 1966, for example, observed that "the Soviets have shown themselves keenly aware of the dangers of escalation and reluctant to become deeply involved in the war," noting that "up to now, the Russians have not emphasized their role in Hanoi's air defense," though they may adopt "more overt participation of personnel or improvement of defense weapons systems" should US activity intensify.[158] The estimate stated that even if Hanoi accepted its offer of volunteers, "the Soviet leaders would try to avoid the appearance of direct US-Soviet combat."[159] An intelligence estimate of likely Soviet reactions to new American measures in 1967 referenced both resolve and restraint themes, predicting that "Beyond supplying equipment, the Soviets could take certain other actions to bolster the North Vietnamese and warn the United States. They might believe, for example, that the provision of limited numbers of volunteers, or of crews for defense equipment

155 Memorandum from Intelligence and Research (Hughes) to the Secretary, "Soviet Delivery of IL-28s to North Vietnam," May 26, 1965, LBJL, NSF, accessed via PHV, Folder 002791_015_0482.

156 Memorandum Prepared in the Policy Planning Council, "Soviet Policy in the Light of the Vietnam Crisis," February 15, 1965, FRUS, Vol. 14 Soviet Union, Doc. 96.

157 Special Report, "Status of Soviet and Chinese Military Aid to North Vietnam," September 3, 1965, CIA CREST, Doc. 0000652931, p. 7.

158 Special National Intelligence Estimate, "Current Soviet Attitudes Toward the U.S.," July 29, 1966, SNIE 11-16-66, FRUS, Vol. 14 Soviet Union, Doc. 169.

159 Special National Intelligence Estimate, "Current Soviet Attitudes Toward the U.S.," July 29, 1966, SNIE 11-16-66, FRUS, Vol. 14 Soviet Union, Doc. 169.

or possibly aircraft, would serve as a warning without leading to a serious confrontation."[160]

As with China's involvement, there was a conspicuous absence of public news reporting on Soviet combat involvement in Vietnam. A review of stories in the *New York Times* during 1965 suggests that reporting on Soviet military supplies was common.[161] Although site construction for the SA-2 missiles was publicly reported, the identity of any crews operating those missile sites was left ambiguous. The comment in one contemporary report is typical as it reported that "neither could sources confirm that Soviet technicians were at work on the projects. However, it was assumed that this was probably so, as the North Vietnamese are not believed capable of doing the job alone."[162] Given this pattern of absent or ambiguous identification of Soviet participation, the theory expects the American leaders to collude in keeping its role on the backstage.

Indeed, the American response to detecting covert Soviet entry was collusion. This was in combination with a high-level decision to attack the missile sites despite the certainty of inflicting Soviet casualties. Attacking the Soviet-manned missile sites was critical to minimize aircraft losses, enable reconnaissance, and disrupt supplies entering North Vietnam.[163] Moreover, attacks would show that insertion of Soviet personnel was not a trump card. As one participant noted, "if they think SAMs can protect their industry, they have won an important element.... If Soviets put their men and material into a situation that knocks down American planes, they must expect retaliation."[164] This was approved knowing that Russians would die. A November 9, 1965, Presidential Daily Brief informed Johnson that "yesterday's US air strike against a surface-to-air missile site near Haiphong apparently led to Soviet casualties. An intercepted conversation from the site made reference to 'one comrade killed and four wounded.' Soviet tech-

---

160 Special National Intelligence Estimate, "Soviet Attitudes and Intentions Toward the Vietnam War," May 4, 1967, SNIE 11-11-67, CIA CREST, Doc 0000272968, p. 2.

161 E.g., Seymour Topping, "South Vietnam Planes Hit North; U.S. Then Calls a Halt to Strikes; Soviet Pledges Red Defense Aid," *New York Times*, February 9, 1965.

162 Robert F. Whitney, "Hanoi Is Building Sites for Missiles," *New York Times*, April 16, 1965.

163 See detailed analysis of loss of photographic intelligence of key ports in Hanoi Haiphong area if SA-2s were effective. Memorandum from Joint Chiefs of Staff (Wheeler) to Secretary of Defense, "Air Operations Against North Vietnam," JCSM-615-65, Annex B "Intelligence," LBJL, NSF, accessed via PHV, Folder 002791_015_0482.

164 Notes of Meeting, July 26, 1965 (6:10–6:55 pm), *FRUS* 1964–1968, Vol. 3, Vietnam, June–December 1965, Doc. 90.

nicians have been called 'comrade' in earlier voice intercepts."[165] The intelligence community recognized that geographically widening US bombing to industrial areas in North Vietnam "would inextricably involve industrial and civilian losses beyond the objectives deliberately targeted, as well as almost certain Soviet and Chinese casualties."[166]

However, covertness was an essential enabler for these US-Soviet clashes. The Soviet choice to send their personnel secretly made American strikes easier to contemplate. As General Wheeler noted toward the end of this July 26 session, "if they announce that there are Russians in the site, it would make your decision more anxious."[167] In the debates over whether to approve the bombings, Ambassador Llewellyn Thompson specifically noted managing the optics of the strike to ensure mild reactions by the North Vietnamese and Soviet Union, stating that "as long as it looks as if the sites are all not Hanoi we are going after, I think their reaction will be mild. We should not say they are manned by Soviets—need to fuzz that up. It would be good if we can tie it in with something else."[168] Declassified notes from White House deliberations of the strike illustrate the concern for escalation, Russian casualties, and the role of secrecy in managing those risks. One especially revealing exchange during a meeting of principal national security advisors and the president on July 26, 1965, proceeded as follows:

> *President*: Where does your intelligence tell you Russians are operating?
> *Wheeler*: In 6 and 7.
> *President*: Are you sure they are Russians?
> *Wheeler*: [less than 1 line of source text not declassified]—that is the weight of our evidence.

---

165 "The President's Daily Brief 9 November 1965," CIA CREST, Doc 0005967987.

166 Special National Intelligence Estimate, "Probable Communist Reactions to a U.S. Course of Action," September 22, 1965, SNIE 10-11-65, *FRUS*, Vol. 3, Vietnam, June–December 1965, Doc. 148. Some in the intelligence community believed bombing in such areas would leave Soviet leaders "specifically affronted" and "would be likely to regard the US action as a direct challenge to themselves … since it would probably result in Soviet casualties. They would be unlikely to place any credence in assurances that US intentions were still limited." (Quotes from dissenting comments to SNIE 10-11-65 by the Director of Intelligence and Research, Department of State.) However, this was a minority viewpoint; the rest of the intelligence community predicted Soviet leaders would redouble efforts to stop the war and pressure North Vietnam.

167 Notes of Meeting, July 26, 1965 (12:30–3:15 pm), *FRUS* 1964–1968, Vol. 3, Vietnam, June–December 1965, Doc. 87.

168 Notes of Meeting, July 26, 1965 (6:10–6:55 pm), *FRUS* 1964–1968, Vol. 3, Vietnam, June–December 1965, Doc. 90.

Rusk: I would not hit one of the sites close in to Hanoi. Only reason to hit 6 and 7 is to give warning to NVN. Very important if we strike that nothing be said about Russians being there. Political effect of hitting 6 and 7 is a warning to not move sites farther out from Hanoi. Not at all sure we'll hit anything—they may have moved them out from there. Intensify reconnaissance to see if we can pick up anything.

...

President: How provocative will this be?

Wheeler: When they sent up the missiles, they expected something.

President: What would be our reaction to the Russians bombing our sites?

Rusk: Various indications that if Russians and US collide, it would be dangerous. Killing the first Russians—[1-1/2 lines of source text not declassified].

(Here president admonished the group NOT to speak to anyone about this. "This is a war—and the stakes are high.")[169]

Regarding the distinct theoretical mechanisms I develop, these internal American deliberations include some hints of a role for both knowledge and acknowledgment. White House decision-makers appear to have been aware that media reporting would include speculation but not confirmation of US-Soviet casualties. In a revealing comment by Vice President Hubert Humphrey, for example, he notes that "all the press knows the Russians are in the site business."[170] At a later White House meeting that same day, the director of the US Information Agency noted that a strike against missiles sites "will increase the 'crisis atmosphere.' Every European newspaper takes it for granted that Russians shot down our plane."[171] Despite these reports, however, White House officials believed joint non-acknowledgment of such casualties would facilitate restrained reactions.

Finally, managing the optics of strikes went beyond White House silence about Soviet casualties. These same discussions included decision-makers struggling to find ways to frame the strikes as defensive and any Russian casualties as incidental. Under Secretary of State George Ball, a consistent

---

169 Notes of Meeting, July 26, 1965 (12:30–3:15 pm), *FRUS* 1964–1968, Vol. 3, Vietnam, June–December 1965, Doc. 87. General Wheeler was the Chairman of the Joint Chiefs of Staff, Rusk, the Secretary of State, and McNamara, the Secretary of Defense.

170 Notes of Meeting, July 26, 1965 (12:30–3:15 pm), *FRUS* 1964–1968, Vol. 3, Vietnam, June–December 1965, Doc. 87.

171 Notes of Meeting, July 26, 1965 (6:10–6:55 pm), *FRUS* 1964–1968, Vol. 3, Vietnam, June–December 1965, Doc. 90.

voice of caution, noted in the July 26 discussions that it "will be viewed as a decision break-through—this will be a world impression" but the severity of international reactions will be influenced if "taking out [a] SAM site with [the] purpose of taking out [a] military target—SAM only incidental."[172] Moreover, attentiveness to the optics of the July 1965 SAM strikes was part of a larger attempt by the United States to manage the optics of its growing military operations in South Vietnam. As Secretary of State Dean Rusk argued:

> There appear to be elements of caution on the other side—in Hanoi as well as in Moscow. Our purpose is to keep our contacts open with the other side in the event that they have a new position to give us.... The U.S. actions we are taking should be presented publicly in a low key but in such a way as to convey accurately that we are determined to prevent South Vietnam from being taken over by Hanoi. At the same time, we seek to avoid a confrontation with either the Chinese Communists or the Soviet Union.[173]

US Overt Intervention in Vietnam

Discussion up to now has focused on three covert interventions. For three interventions that transgressed the most important limiting thresholds of the Vietnam War, escalation considerations were critical and covertness was seen as valuable for avoiding large-scale escalation. Moreover, except for China's exposure of American bombing operations in Laos, detection of these covert interventions was followed by collusion as a way to further reinforce escalation control.

Yet these escalation problems were partially derived from the initial decision by one major power to intervene overtly. As noted in chapter 2, my limited-war theory suggests that major powers should value the logistical and symbolic benefits of an overt form. When escalation risks are mild rather than severe, those overt benefits tend to dominate as escalation control is deprioritized. I translate this to two features: timing and location. That is, an intervention should be overt if it precedes any other major power

---

172 Notes of Meeting, July 26, 1965 (12:30–3:15 pm), *FRUS* 1964–1968, Vol. 3, Vietnam, June–December 1965, Doc. 87.

173 Summary Notes of the 553d Meeting of the National Security Council, "Deployment of Additional U.S. Troops to Vietnam," July 27, 1965, *FRUS* 1964–1968, Vol. 3, Vietnam, June–December 1965, Doc. 93.

entry ("first mover") and is tailored to the local ongoing conflict rather than beyond it ("local").

Such was the case with the United States within Vietnam. The initial overt intervention consisted of two distinct but related decisions in early 1965. The Johnson White House approved overt military participation in ground and air counterinsurgency operations within South Vietnam as well as a public bombing campaign within North Vietnam. The considerations driving the decision to overtly intervene correspond well to the theory's mechanisms. First consider operational benefits. The overt American entry followed signs that its local ally urgently needed more robust help. A memo from National Security Advisor Bundy on February 7, for example, argued that "without new US action, defeat appears inevitable" and recommended a program of "graduated and continuing reprisal" as the best option.[174] Similarly, intelligence assessments in April during debates about US participation in the ground war "could find no evidence that the Viet Cong were weakening" and pointed to increasing terror attacks to show that determination was likely strengthening. Military assessments in South Vietnam cited a growing gap between insurgent and South Vietnamese military capabilities, warning that the war effort "might collapse completely if US forces were not deployed."[175] The Pentagon Papers further note that opponents of expanded overt operations in mid-1965 relented in light of desperate battlefield conditions ("a series of disastrous defeats in the spring of 1965 which convinced a number of observers that a political-military collapse within [South Vietnam] was imminent).[176] The State Department's retrospective on intelligence assessments marks the turning point in mid-1964, when coup threats and bogus data on the counterinsurgency "swung the pendulum of Washington opinion from guarded optimism to pessimism regarding the outcome of the war.... [P]rospects in the South had grown so dim that some authorities in the US Government felt the situation could be salvaged only with a respite from Communist attacks."[177]

This urgency turned sentiment in Washington against the operational constraints that accompanied covert tools.[178] This included specific critiques

---

174 State INR Retrospective, Part A, Section 4, 1969, p. 44.

175 State INR Retrospective, Part A, Section 5, 1969, pp. 9–10.

176 Pentagon Papers, Part IV.C.1, "Evolution of the War: U.S. Programs in South Vietnam, November 1963–April 1965," p. vii.

177 State INR Retrospective, Part A, Section 4, 1969, pp. 18–19, 25.

178 American military personnel had covertly participated in air (both bombing and transport roles) and ground combat (shifting from advisory to combat operations) since the late Ken-

of secret, deniable methods as insufficient. The Pentagon Papers review of decision-making about bombing the North, for example, cites an important "shift of emphasis" in mid-1964. Advocates for overt military involvement—who had not yet won agreement from their colleagues—argued that the scope of needed action in South Vietnam was too great for covert methods to be effective. It quotes a cable from Secretary of State Dean Rusk weighing the pros and cons of larger air attacks against North Vietnam:

> It is our present view here that substantial initial attacks without acknowledgment would simply not be feasible. Even if Hanoi itself did not publicize them, there are enough ICC [International Control Commission] and other observers in North Vietnam who might pick them up and there is also the major possibility of leakage at the South Vietnam end. Thus, publicity seems almost inevitable to us here for any attack that did significant damage.[179]

Symbolic benefits of a narrow intervention within Vietnam also factored in. The earlier invocation of domino logic created serious reputational and credibility problems should South Vietnam fall. Logevall's summary of war expansion notes that "Vietnam, in this way of thinking, was a 'test case' of Washington's willingness and ability to exert its power on the international stage" and to teach Soviet/China that "indirect aggression could not succeed.... [I]t was also the administration's domestic political credibility and officials' own personal credibility."[180] Finally, and crucially, debates about American overt intervention in 1964 and 1965 were in the context of a less dangerous environment than Soviet, Chinese, and American leaders themselves would face later. The United States was the first-mover outside power. The intervention created a fait accompli for other states and raised the escalation dangers in Vietnam; covertness would therefore be more important for limiting the war as Moscow and Beijing weighed their own interventions and Washington looked to expand its own into places like Laos.

---

nedy administration. This earlier covert American role had been the result of incremental expansion, an "Americanization" of the war that would eventually give way to "Vietnamization" under Nixon. By 1964, however, intelligence agencies and policymakers agreed these approaches were failing badly. On covert air role, see Robert F. Futrell, *The United States Air Force in Southeast Asia: The Advisory Years to 1965* (Washington, DC: Office of Air Force History, 1981); on the covert ground role, see Shultz Jr., *The Secret War Against Hanoi.*

179 Pentagon Papers, Part IV. C. 2. a, "Evolution of the War: Military Pressures Against North Vietnam, February–June 1964," pp. 21–22.

180 Logevall, "The Indochina Wars and the Cold War, 1945–1975," 297–98.

Conclusion

This chapter focuses on the 1964–1968 period. I began with an explicit admission to well-established findings that secrecy helped generate public support for the initial US overt intervention and waiting to deal with anti-war sentiment later. In short, the domestic dove alternative logic explains these features of the war. Rather than refute this, I focus on the ways in which secrecy and non-acknowledgment were used to control escalation dynamics and limit war during the critical four years that followed US overt intervention within Vietnam.

After 1968, changes in the political and strategic context led to major changes in the war, including the issues impacting secrecy and non-acknowledgment. With the American shift to Vietnamization and threat of invasion or broad destabilization of North Vietnam gone, China and the Soviet Union had either withdrawn or were on their way out by 1968. This reflected no change in escalation features but, instead, the completion of their original strategic goal of ensuring North Vietnamese viability. That year also represented a turning point in domestic politics in the United States. As Daniel Hallin and others have noted, sympathetic news coverage and a difficult hawks/dove split persevered until the symbolic loss caused by the Tet Offensive in January 1968.[181] There was still reason for covertness, but the basis shifted. While the domestic problem for the Johnson White House was primarily hawkish criticism, the Nixon White House faced broad and vocal antiwar sentiment after 1968. Secrecy about Laos, peace negotiations, and other issues was then a key tool for dealing with domestic dovish opposition.[182] Reflecting this shift, leaks about covert activity in Laos that were tolerable earlier in the war became fatal under Nixon. Press reports about "American paramilitary activity in Laos" prompted congressional inquiry and "led Missouri Senator Stuart Symington to conduct formal congressional hearings on US involvement in the Far East."[183] These

---

181 Hallin, *The "Uncensored War"*; Caverley, "The Myth of Military Myopia."

182 This did not completely extinguish the older logic for secrecy and non-acknowledgment. Even as the Nixon White House was disclosing Laos operations details, internal critics worried that "a more open policy would serve mainly to freeze the two sides [US and North Vietnam] into positions harder than ever before.... By admitting the nature of our air operations in Laos, we risk making explicit something the NVN / PL [North Vietnamese and Pathet Lao] may prefer to remain ambiguous, thereby reducing their flexibility as well as ours." Hammond, *Public Affairs*, 265.

183 Castle, *At War in the Shadow of Vietnam*, 97–98, chap. 7.

hearings led to sustained national debate about Laos for the first time and, along with the revelations in the Pentagon Papers, signaled the beginning of the end of the intervention.[184]

184 Hammond, *Public Affairs*, 265; domestic dovish resentment led to congressionally imposed restrictions on US operations in Laos, as Castle notes: "The military situation in Laos began to change in the late 1960s. America's covert paramilitary war in Laos was fast escalating into a conventional conflict with enormous human and financial costs. The increased aggressiveness of the North Vietnamese dry-season campaigns, a new administration in Washington, and a growing antiwar feeling in the American Congress brought change, albeit slowly, to America's Lao policy … public revelations about the true extent of America's involvement in the kingdom brought about stiff reductions, mandated by the US Congress, in Lao military aid." Castle, *At War in the Shadow of Vietnam*, 133–34.

7

The War in Afghanistan (1979–1986)

During the 1980s, Afghanistan played host to interventions by the United States and Soviet Union. Long a peripheral concern for Washington and Moscow, a pro-communist coup in 1978 thrust Afghanistan into the center of the Cold War rivalry. A growing insurgency eventually forced Soviet leaders to intervene militarily, first covertly and then overtly. In response, Washington worked with a local partner, Pakistan, to provide significant covert aid to Afghan rebels. During nine years of occupation, the Soviets maintained an occupation force of more than 75,000 combat troops, with 600,000 military personnel spending time in the country at least once. Soviet leaders also provided thousands of civilian, intelligence, and military advisors, suffered a total of 13,000 dead and more than 40,000 wounded, and spent in excess of 10 billion rubles.[1] This chapter assesses how concerns over the risk of escalation to a wider regional war influenced decisions about intervention and how to react to detected covert involvement.

This conflict plays a useful role in the book's overall research design by allowing an initial assessment of two generalizability questions. First, the

---

1 Overall data from Raymond L. Garthoff, *Detente and Confrontation: American-Soviet Relations from Nixon to Reagan*, Revised (Washington, DC: Brookings Institution Press, 1994), 989–90, 1021–23; Artemy Kalinovsky, *Long Goodbye: The Soviet Withdrawal from Afghanistan* (Cambridge, MA: Harvard University Press, 2011), 1, 42.

war in Afghanistan was fought without a plausible scenario for escalation to global conflict. Instead, the specter of a regional war—specifically encompassing Pakistan—was the salient and large-scale escalation scenario that dominated deliberations about intervention form and how to handle intelligence about covert aspects of the war. Put differently, it is a less likely place for large-scale escalation concerns to be relevant compared to more explosive periods like the 1950s. Second, it features a covert intervention with a minimal role for personnel. The US covert aid program primarily relied on Pakistani intermediaries to deliver arms to Afghan rebels. Finding evidence that escalation control influenced covertness is less likely given that the risk of direct Soviet-American casualties was lower than in Vietnam or other wars. If covert dynamics are influenced by escalation dynamics in this kind of conflict, it suggests the theory has purchase for other conflicts with only regional escalation risks and which feature minimal personnel involvement. I return to this issue in my analysis of Iran's covert intervention during the American occupation of Iraq (2003–2011) in chapter 8.

Tensions caused by events in Afghanistan had an outsized impact on international politics. In 1979, the Soviet Union was widely believed to be at the height of its power and ambition yet, by the end of its intervention in 1988, it was visibly crumbling from within. Similarly, détente was fatally wounded by the Soviet overt invasion. Moreover, Afghanistan accelerated the Soviet dissolution that ended the Cold War by contributing to domestic popular dissatisfaction and harming the economic fruits of détente.[2] The covert collaboration between Pakistan and the American Central Intelligence Agency (CIA) forged a lasting, though often tense, cooperative partnership that continues today. Within Afghanistan, Soviet occupation and American aid fueled the rise of provincial warlords, undermined the central government, and unleashed centrifugal forces that would later descend into civil war and create a sanctuary for al Qaeda and Osama Bin Laden.[3] As with previous empirical chapters, Afghanistan featured multiple interventions with important differences among interveners and changes over time

---

2 On the impact on détente, Garthoff describes the Afghanistan invasion as "sharply dividing the previous decade of détente … from the ensuing years of containment and confrontation." Garthoff, *Detente and Confrontation*, 922; on the link to dissolution of the Soviet Union, see Rafael Reuveny and Aseem Prakash, "The Afghanistan War and the Breakdown of the Soviet Union," *Review of International Studies* 25, no. 04 (1999): 693–708.

3 On the connection between the occupation, covert aid network, and the rise of terrorist organizations in Afghanistan, see Steve Coll, *Ghost Wars: The Secret History of the CIA, Afghanistan, and Bin Laden, from the Soviet Invasion to September 10, 2001* (New York: Penguin, 2004).

TABLE 7.1. Intervention Cases in the War in Afghanistan

	Dates	Location	Timing	Form	Details	Theory support
Soviet Union	1979	Local (Afghanistan)	First mover	Covert	Concealed, unacknowledged ground, air forces	Weak
	1979–1988	Local (Afghanistan)	First mover	Overt	Public, acknowledged ground and air intervention including occupation	Strong
	1982–1987	Peripheral (Pakistan)	First mover	Covert	Concealed, unacknowledged air strikes and ground raids	Strong
United States	1979–1986	Local (Afghanistan)	Subsequent intervener	Covert (open secret by about 1984)	Concealed, unacknowledged weaponry to rebels	Strong
	1986–1988	Local (Afghanistan)	Subsequent intervener	Overt	Shift to providing uniquely identifiable weaponry (Stinger)	Mixed

(see table 7.1) allowing me to deconstruct the conflict in a way that helps expand analysis of overt/covert choices.[4]

The chapter also features three instances in which covert intervention is detected. I find clear evidence that both Soviet and American intelligence services carefully tracked their rival's covert activity. Table 7.2 summarizes collusion and exposure patterns. American intelligence, for example, de-

4 I do not analyze Chinese and Iranian aid to Afghan rebels, both mentioned in American intelligence materials. One reason is that coding Iran as a major power in the years following the revolution is suspect. Regarding China, the reason is because their role appears to have been minor and there is an acute lack of documentation. One clue that escalation and limited war played a role for the former is a Defense Intelligence Agency memo which mentions Beijing's own concerns about Soviet retaliation against Pakistan ("sensitivity to Pakistani concerns about possible Soviet reprisal"). See "China and Afghanistan: PRC Concerns and Ability to Influence Events," March 1983, Defense Intelligence Estimates Memorandum, National Security Archive, Doc. AF01435.

TABLE 7.2. Detector Behavior in Afghanistan

	Detection	Third-party exposure	Expectation	Outcome	Theory support
Covert Soviet in Afghanistan	Yes: United States	Low	Collusion	Collusion	Mixed (over-determined)
Covert Soviet in Pakistan	Yes: United States	Low	Collusion	Collusion	Strong
Covert United States in Afghanistan	Yes: Soviet Union	High (after 1983)	Exposure	Exposure	Strong

tected early covert Soviet involvement in Afghanistan in 1979 and covert Soviet cross-border operations into Pakistan in the mid-1980s. Soviet intelligence kept tabs on the flow and character of weapons through Pakistan. Reactions to this information provide some support for the theory but also showcase the attractions of exposure under some conditions. The resulting pattern of exposure and collusion largely supports the theory given the nature of wide exposure via mainstream news sources.

Beyond the core findings, this chapter has three additional lessons. First, it features new descriptive details. Although the overt Soviet invasion and American covert aid program are well known, I review documents on the earlier Soviet covert involvement (mid-1979) as well as Soviet military operations inside Pakistan (primarily 1984–1987). The latter specifically shows a dangerous regional dimension of the war. Sensitivity to publicity about cross-border incidents in Pakistan also bears a striking resemblance to post–9/11 debates about covertness in American drone attacks in the same part of Pakistan.[5] Second, Afghanistan hosted an extreme case of open secrecy. The US covert weapons supply program was widely known and discussed by 1984. Yet for two years, the Reagan administration refused to officially acknowledge these reports and rejected calls for overt forms of military aid (i.e., the Stinger missile proposal). This shows how covertness in an intervention can take on symbolic meaning that is relevant even after wide exposure. Third, the conflict features deviant and mixed cases. The early Soviet covert involvement was overdetermined, influenced by both fears of provoking a local nationalist backlash and considerations somewhat related to escalation. Soviet exposure of the US covert aid program is

---

5 E.g., "Secret Memos Reveal Explicit Nature of U.S., Pakistan Agreement on Drones," *Washington Post*, October 23, 2013.

unexpected by the theory and does not seem related to escalation dynamics. I discuss the factors that produce these anomalies.

The rest of the chapter is structured as follows. I first assess the key escalation-related issues influencing the conflict, including how previous Cold War encounters had produced a basic code of conduct for superpower involvement and shaped the way interventions were undertaken and interpreted. I then focus on the Soviet role in Afghanistan, first assessing its covert intervention in mid-1979 and then its transition to an overt intervention in late December 1979. This section also addresses detection of the Soviet covert combat role by American intelligence and the US response. A third section unpacks the American military aid program. I assess the covert phase and the role of escalation considerations as well as the transition to an overt posture with the provision of Stinger missiles in 1986. I also review evidence that Soviet intelligence detected the covert program and Soviet leaders regularly and publicly drew attention to this kind of outside meddling. I conclude by assessing the Soviet covert involvement in neighboring Pakistan, drawing on newly assessed US intelligence documents to describe and analyze the covertness and collusion surrounding this facet of the war.[6]

Overview and Context

For much of the Cold War, Afghanistan was non-aligned, receiving economic aid from both American and Soviet patrons though with a tilt towards its Russian neighbor. A coup in 1978 empowered the Afghan communist party and Soviet leaders quickly embraced a new ally. In part because of détente, escalation dynamics functioned somewhat differently in Afghanistan. Compared to Vietnam and especially the Korean War, decisions about Afghanistan took place in the shadow of accumulated experience, regular US-Soviet diplomatic contacts, and détente-related agreements on cooperation in trade and strategic arms. Along with its landlocked, remote location,

---

6 I rely primarily on now-accessible archival materials on both American and Soviet decision-making. Several specific collections provide an unusually clear picture of several aspects of the war. One especially useful collection from both Washington and Moscow resulted from an international conference in 2002 organized by the Wilson Center's Cold War International History Project. I supplemented this with findings from an unusually large collection of analytic documents released by the Central Intelligence Agency (see http://www.foia.cia.gov/), curated American primary document collections from the Digital National Security Archive and Digital Declassified Reference System, and archival research in the CIA's Records Search Tool (hereafter CREST) at the US National Archives.

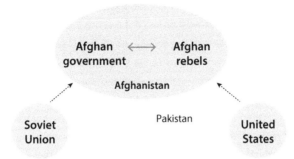

FIGURE 7.1. Structure of Afghanistan war.

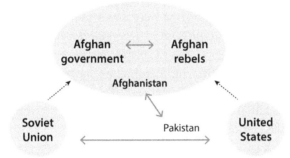

FIGURE 7.2. Key escalation scenarios, Afghanistan EST.

Afghanistan did not feature a credible scenario for evolving into a global US-Soviet conflagration. Figure 7.1 identifies the local combatants, local conflict zone, external intervening powers, and relevant peripheral zones. The ongoing conflict was between the government of Afghanistan and Afghan rebels. The most salient peripheral area was Pakistan. Figure 7.2 highlights the two key scenarios for large-scale escalation: widening to include Pakistan and South Asia more broadly, or the emergence of direct combat between outside interveners. As noted, the latter was largely off the table.

Even though World War III was unlikely, the other large-scale escalation scenario still loomed and was likely to be highly damaging. Both sides found the spread of the war to include Pakistan, Iran, and even India as plausible and dangerous. Such a scenario was made especially plausible by the porous Afghanistan-Pakistan border, Pakistan's own active support for rebels, and the Soviet-Indian cooperative relationship.[7] Indeed, the risk of

7 See review of CIA intelligence estimates below.

the war growing to include Pakistan and its territory was regularly assessed by American intelligence and embassy reporting.[8] Moreover, regional war would pose tough questions regarding an even larger conflict. Especially delicate was the nature of Washington's 1959 Agreement of Cooperation with Pakistan which, albeit vaguely, seemed to obligate protection from Soviet military forces. In the eyes of a few analysts, this security guarantee did mean Afghanistan had a plausible connection to global war ("a scenario for the outbreak of World War III, with all of its horrifying potential for nuclear escalation").[9] In general, however, the US-Pakistan link was seen as part of the geopolitical complexity and risks of a regional war rather than a trigger for global war.

Escalation-control problems were significant. Concern about domestic reactions and miscommunication were highly relevant in Afghanistan. Regarding the former, domestic hawkish reactions remained a concern in both Washington and Moscow. American presidents remained vulnerable to criticism from conservative, anti-communist, hawkish voices, particularly under Democratic President Carter (i.e., through January 1981).[10] Leadership disputes within the Soviet Politburo, meanwhile, continued to feature the post-Stalin factionalism which was often split along hawk/dove lines.[11] Although strategic stability was greater as a result of détente, considerable uncertainty about regional geostrategic ambitions remained. The Soviet invasion of Afghanistan, for example, prompted significant internal debates in Washington about its expansionist ambitions into the Middle East. More-

---

8 See, for example, Telegram Embassy Afghanistan to Secretary of State, December 16, 1982, Digital National Security Archive, Doc. AF01410; Department Press Briefing, December 17, 1982, Digital National Security Archive, Doc. AF01411.

9 To be clear, this view is not representative and the references to war involving South Asia outnumber this reference by a factor of ten or more. Reported in Coll, *Ghost Wars*, 43.

10 Under Carter, the role of domestic hawks in the rival Republican party was an ever-present concern. This influenced decisions to publicize potentially explosive intelligence about Soviet covert behavior. Under Reagan, an administration itself more hawkish than the previous White House, such concerns were less acute. However, hawkish voices in Congress played a critical role in swelling the size of the covert aid program in the mid-1980s and in lobbying for overt assistance despite the risks of Soviet retaliation. While less contentious, this demonstrates their continued relevance for Washington decision-making.

11 Dimitri K. Simes, "The Soviet Succession: Domestic and International Dimensions," *Journal of International Affairs* 32, no. 2 (1978): 211–21; Seweryn Bialer, *Stalin's Successors: Leadership, Stability and Change in the Soviet Union* (New York: Cambridge University Press, 1982); on the hawks/doves split in the Politburo and the relevance of international events and American policy to that balance, see Jack Snyder, "International Leverage on Soviet Domestic Change," *World Politics* 42, no. 1 (October 1989): 1–30.

over, the fear of appearing too aggressive and provocative to Soviet leaders influenced American covert aid throughout the life of the program, especially because weaponry was being used to directly kill Russian soldiers rather than a proxy's troops.

A final clarification about a specific scenario that mattered early in the conflict: insulating détente. My definition of "large-scale escalation" in chapter 2 does not include milder but still disruptive outcomes like a serious decline in diplomatic cooperation among major powers. This is for good reason: if such scenarios were sufficient to push states onto the "backstage," the theory would seem to always expect covertness. Yet, as I describe below, the superpowers' shared interest in insulating détente's fruits in 1978 and 1979 from a diplomatic crisis affected decisions about collusion and covertness in Afghanistan. I do not consider this strong support for the theory. I do, however, consider it consistent with the basic mechanisms and describe it below in some detail. There is close conceptual similarity between using secrecy to avoid crises and using it to control and avoid large-scale conflict escalation. Moreover, specific mechanisms of the theory—such as empowerment of hawkish domestic voices—play a role.

CROSS-CONFLICT LEARNING

One escalation-control enabler in Afghanistan was the accumulated lessons of previous encounters. The conflicts followed decades of competition during the Cold War. This produced a set of unusually thick and explicit rules for how two major power adversaries could compete while keeping war limited. American and Soviet leaders solidified a kind of "code of conduct" regarding intervention by the superpowers, symbolized by the 1972 Basic Principles Agreement.[12] These tactics included tacit rules about avoiding

---

12 The language of the BPA includes that "[b]oth sides recognize that efforts to obtain unilateral advantage at the expense of the other, directly or indirectly, are inconsistent with these objectives. The prerequisites for maintaining and strengthening peaceful relations between the USA and the USSR are the recognition of the security interests of the Parties based on the principle of equality and the renunciation of the use or threat of force." For an interpretation of the agreement as an example of mutual misunderstanding, see Eric Grynaviski, *Constructive Illusions: Misperceiving the Origins of International Cooperation* (Ithaca, NY: Cornell University Press, 2014). See also Joanne S. Gowa and Nils H. Wessell, *Ground Rules: Soviet and American Involvement in Regional Conflicts* (Philadelphia, PA: Foreign Policy Research Institute, 1982), 7–8, 12; Alexander L. George, "Crisis Prevention Reexamined," in *Managing U.S.-Soviet Rivalry: Problems of Crisis Prevention*, ed. Alexander L. George (Boulder, CO: Westview Press, 1983), 376–90.

overt intervention in a rival's spheres of influence, use of proxy forces, and the need for direct communication (i.e., hotlines; notification of military maneuvers).[13] These rules could "regulate the competitive pursuit of their interests" and "impart some stability and predictability to their actions," which would make it easier to avoid regional conflagrations and any kind of global or nuclear war.[14] Experience had shown that publicly visible commitments, threats, and direct involvement—typified by the very public brinkmanship of the Cuban Missile Crisis—could engage prestige, boost domestic constraints, and make compromise more difficult.[15] Despite these efforts, intense debates within Washington and Moscow about the nature of the "code of détente" remained as did disputes between the two sides about application and interpretation of such rules.[16]

Lessons from specific encounters were also important. As Jervis notes, geographic and other limits in past conflicts like Vietnam "seems to have affected at least the western perceptions of the guerilla war in Afghanistan." Even as the trappings of détente collapsed with the overt Soviet invasion, "the West seems to have understood that the sanctuaries in Pakistan would be respected as long as the military aid being funneled through that country was sharply limited. But if this restraint were loosened, so probably would be that on attacking the bases in Pakistan."[17] Vietnam was a particularly salient reference point. For example, a formerly top secret transcript of a March 1979 meeting between top Soviet leaders and the Afghan president includes Soviet Premier Alexei Kosygin drawing on Vietnam. He makes the case that Soviet intervention at that stage was unwise ("the best way is that which would preserve the authority of your government among the people") by citing "the example of Vietnam ... The Vietnamese people

13 Roy Allison and Phil Williams, "Crisis Prevention: Patterns and Prospects," in *Superpower Competition and Crisis Prevention in the Third World*, ed. Roy Allison and Phil Williams, Ford/Southampton Studies in North/South Security Relations (Cambridge: Cambridge University Press, 1990), 250–55; Gowa and Wessell, *Ground Rules*, 15. Alexander L. George, "US-Soviet Global Rivalry: Norms of Competition," *Journal of Peace Research* 23, no. 3 (September 1, 1986): 247–62.

14 Roy Allison, "The Superpowers and Southwest Asia," in *Superpower Competition and Crisis Prevention in the Third World*, ed. Roy Allison and Phil Williams (Cambridge: Cambridge University Press, 1990), 177.

15 George, "Superpower Interests in Third Areas," 115–19.

16 See, for example, the split in the Carter administration between Cyrus Vance and Zbigniew Brzezinski, as described in Keren Yarhi-Milo, "In the Eye of the Beholder: How Leaders and Intelligence Communities Assess the Intentions of Adversaries," *International Security* 38, no. 1 (2013): 23. Grynaviski, *Constructive Illusions*, 69–72.

17 Robert Jervis, "Security Regimes," *International Organization* 36, no. 2 (Spring 1982): 372.

withstood a difficult war with the USA and are now fighting against Chinese aggression, but no one can accuse the Vietnamese of using foreign troops. The Vietnamese are bravely defending by themselves their homeland against aggressive encroachments." Kosygin specifically invokes the form of aid in Vietnam, arguing that "we have helped and are helping Vietnam a great deal, but they never asked us to send them our pilots. They only asked for technical specialists. We are training 400 Afghan officers. Choose the people you need, and we will expedite their training."[18]

On the American side, confidential cables from Kabul and private advice from President Carter's national security team referenced Vietnam before and during the Soviet invasion. For example, a cable from Ambassador Bruce Amstutz in August 1979 compared the deepening Soviet involvement in Kabul's counterinsurgency operations ("military advisors ... have become steadily more numerous—perhaps totaling more than some 2,000—and they have been entering into direct command roles") to the United States in South Vietnam, noting that "the nature of the Soviet commitment appears to be evolving through stages not too unlike those the [United States Government] went through in Vietnam."[19] A memo from the National Security Council staff to then-National Security Advisor Zbigniew Brzezinski specifically addressed the "increasing tendency in the news media and around town generally to make an analogy between Afghanistan and Vietnam." Stephen Larrabee's memo goes on to admit some similarities but highlighted differences in geographical distance, local logistics, Soviet media environment, and Soviet domestic constraints ("they are not likely to face many of the constraints that the US faced in Vietnam"). Importantly, however, one difference cited in the memo directly implicated American intervention policy ("The North Vietnamese could count on outside aid and weapons in large quantities; this is not (yet) the case in Afghanistan"), with Larrabee concluding that the fate of the Soviet occupation would be influenced by "our ability to work effectively with Pakistan and other countries to aid the insurgents."[20]

18 Record of Meeting A. N. Kosygin, A. A. Gromyko, D. F. Ustinov and B. N. Ponomarev with N. M. Taraki, March 20, 1979, in "Documents on the Soviet Invasion of Afghanistan," November 2001, Cold War International History Project (CWIHP), e-Dossier No. 4, p. 71.

19 Ambassador Bruce Amstutz to Department of State, "An Evaluation of the Bala Hissar Mutiny," August 6, 1979, Digital National Security Archive, Doc. AF00606.

20 Stephen Larrabee to Zbigniew Brzezinski, "Soviet Policy in Afghanistan," December 31, 1979, in "Towards an International History of the War in Afghanistan, 1979–1989," Wilson Center CWIHP Document Reader, Volume 1: US Documents, April 29–30, 2002.

An especially revealing, high-level comparison to Vietnam by Brzezinski himself in the immediate wake of the invasion used Vietnam to motivate American covert intervention. He wrote to Carter on December 26, 1979, that while the invasion "could become a Soviet Vietnam, the initial effects of the intervention are likely to be adverse for us" and worried that, unlike North Vietnam, the Afghan rebels "have no sanctuary, no organized army, and no central government." Brzezinski's memo specifically addresses the issue of military weaponry and outside intervention, recommending that "it is essential that [the] Afghanistani resistance continues. This means more money as well as arms shipments to the rebels, and some technical advice" because rebels in Afghanistan "have limited foreign support, in contrast to the enormous amount of arms that flowed to the Vietnamese from both the Soviet Union and China." He further recommends that the United States "concert with Islamic countries both in a propaganda campaign and in a covert action campaign to help the rebels."[21]

Soviet Union in Afghanistan

INITIAL COVERT SOVIET INTERVENTION IN AFGHANISTAN

Soviet combat activities in Afghanistan began in a covert form six months before the well-known invasion. The impetus was an especially threatening uprising in western Afghanistan in March 1979 and requests from Afghanistan's co-leaders Nur Muhammad Taraki and Hafizullah Amin. The Soviet Politburo reviewed its Afghanistan policy and approved covert deployment of several units of Russian combat troops to perform base security near Kabul, protect Soviet personnel in Kabul, fly air transport flights to move Afghan Army units to areas of rebellion, and, in some reports, fly aerial combat missions. Soviet goals were defensive. Moscow sought to avoid an embarrassing counter-revolution against an allied government in a state on its own border and its replacement with a regime helpful to the United States' intelligence and geostrategic goals.[22]

Pockets of dissent against Kabul spread in the Afghan countryside throughout the winter of 1978–1979 in reaction to communist land reforms,

21 Memorandum from Zbigniew Brzezinski to the President, "Reflections on Soviet Intervention in Afghanistan," December 26, 1979, in "Towards an International History of the War in Afghanistan, 1979–1989," Volume 1.

22 See discussion of "basically defensive nature of Soviet intentions" and the threat of an American partner on the Soviet border in particular. David N. Gibbs, "Reassessing Soviet Motives for Invading Afghanistan: A Declassified History," *Critical Asian Studies* 38, no. 2 (2006): 255–57.

secularization efforts, and socialist education initiatives which threatened local ways of life.[23] In March 1979, the Herat uprising in the third largest city in the country sharpened the threat to the central government, especially after most of an Afghan Army division defected and turned their weapons against regime loyalists. Four days of brutal fighting left hundreds of Afghans and dozens of Soviet advisors and their families dead. Control of Herat was wrested from the rebellion only after loyal military units from elsewhere in Afghanistan arrived, enabled by Soviet consultations and transport aid.[24]

The Herat uprising prompted urgent requests to Moscow for a more direct military role in countering the rebellion. Over the phone and in person, Taraki urged Soviet leaders to deploy a division or more of combat troops. When Soviet leaders balked, he suggested sending Soviet troops with equipment in Afghan markings, Afghan uniforms, and using personnel from Central Asian Soviet republics.[25] He was especially keen to have trained Soviet personnel, or at worst Vietnamese or Cuban personnel, to operate sophisticated Soviet tanks and helicopters.[26] Although the Politburo initially refused to provide Soviet military units, a larger review of its Afghanistan policy completed in June led to approval of covert military deployments to Afghanistan. One Soviet airborne battalion (600 men) was flown to protect Bagram Air Force Base, the primary airfield supplying Kabul and a critical air link enabling Soviet leaders to airlift equipment on short notice.[27] The unit was to be deployed wearing "aviation-technical maintenance uniforms" to disguise their purpose. A second contingent of KGB special forces personnel (125–150 men) were to be deployed to Kabul

23 Garthoff, *Detente and Confrontation*, 990.

24 Garthoff, *Detente and Confrontation*, 991; Odd Arne Westad, "Prelude to Invasion: The Soviet Union and the Afghan Communists, 1978-1979," *International History Review* 16, no. 1 (February 1, 1994): 57–58; Coll, *Ghost Wars*, 39–40.

25 Garthoff, *Detente and Confrontation*, 991–94; Westad, "Prelude to Invasion," 57. See also Meeting of Kosygin, Gromyko, Ustinov, and Ponomarev with Taraki in Moscow, March 20, 1979, Wilson Center Digital Archive (hereafter WCDA), Document 113263.

26 See the exchange about helicopter crews from the Soviet Union, Cuba, or North Vietnam in Meeting of Kosygin, Gromyko, Ustinov, and Ponomarev with Taraki in Moscow, March 20, 1979.

27 Sarah E. Mendelson, *Changing Course: Ideas, Politics, & the Soviet Withdrawal from Afghanistan* (Princeton, NJ: Princeton University Press, 1998), 47; Garthoff, *Detente and Confrontation*, 998. See also Top Secret Excerpt from CC CPSU Politburo Minutes, June 29, 1979, "Towards an International History of the War in Afghanistan, 1979-1989," Wilson Center CWIHP Document Reader, Volume 2: Russian and East European Documents (hereafter CWIHP Reader Vol. 2), April 29–30, 2002, Doc. 156.

to provide security for Soviet personnel in case of emergency. They were instructed to wear civilian dress and pose as support staff to the embassy.[28]

Soon after, rivalry within the ruling People's Democratic Party of Afghanistan peaked when Amin activated loyal factions of the Afghan military to crack down on Taraki's supporters and executed Taraki. Leaders in Moscow including Brezhnev were shocked.[29] Amin's rise in September 1979 prompted them to begin quiet steps to locate a replacement.[30] A post-Amin Politburo policy review provides further confirmation of the details of Moscow's covert military personnel. The policy review authorizes Soviet "subunits" in Afghanistan to continue their existing missions, mentioning a parachute battalion (presumably those at Bagram), fixed-wing and helicopter transport squadrons, and a security detachment (presumably those in Kabul).[31] Additional deployments appear to have been added as well. Another KGB special forces unit was likely sent to protect Amin in late November.[32] Two additional battalions were deployed to Bagram Air Force Base along with several other "subunits" in early December, bringing the total Soviet combat personnel at the base to 2,500, according to one estimate.[33]

What considerations influenced Soviet decision-making? Because Moscow would be the first outside power and tailored its involvement to the territory of Afghanistan, my theoretical expectation is an overt form. I argue in chapter 2 that escalation risks for this kind of intervention scenario are mild; this allows interveners to privilege the operational and symbolic benefits of publicly acknowledged involvement. Here the Soviet leaders chose

28 Gromyko Andropov Ustinov Ponomarev Report to CPSU CC on the Situation in Afghanistan, June 28, 1979, in "The Cold War in the Third World and the Collapse of Détente in the 1970s," Wilson Center CWIHP Bulletin, Issues 8–9, 1996, 152–53.

29 Garthoff, *Detente and Confrontation*, 1004–6.

30 The leader in exile who was later installed after the invasion, Babrak Karmal, was relocated from Czechoslovakia to Moscow on October 10; Amin had Taraki executed on October 9. Garthoff, *Detente and Confrontation*, 1009–10.

31 Excerpt from Minutes of CC CPSU Politburo, October 31, 1979, in CWIHP Reader Vol. 2. As the order appears in Lyakhovskiy, "[t]he Soviet subunits located in Afghanistan (communications centers, the parachute battalion, the fixed-wing and helicopter transport squadrons) and also the Soviet institutions' security detachment are to continue to perform the assigned missions." Aleksandr Lyakhovskiy, "Inside the Soviet Invasion of Afghanistan and the Seizure of Kabul, December 1979," Working Paper No. 51, Cold War International History Project, January 2007, p. 10.

32 Described (but no other mention) in Garthoff, *Detente and Confrontation*, 1010.

33 Mendelson, *Changing Course*, 53; Aleksandr Antonovich Lyakhovskiy, "Inside the Soviet Invasion of Afghanistan and the Seizure of Kabul, December 1979," Working Paper No. 51, Cold War International History Project, January 2007, 15, 30–32, http://www.wilsoncenter.org/sites/default/files/WP51_Web_Final.pdf.

a covert form. Why? Available evidence suggests the Soviet preference for covertness was due to two basic reasons, only one of which, I believe, can be said to be related to escalation dynamics.

One important motivation for using a covert form of intervention, unrelated to my theoretical claims, was to protect the communist brand. This had two forms. Keeping Soviet combat aid to Kabul on the "backstage" was valuable within Afghanistan. Doing so avoided undermining the legitimacy of Kabul while allowing Moscow to shore up the operational military side. A recurring concern for Soviet leaders was preserving the domestic credibility of the communist party in Afghanistan. A related concern was external: reactions from outside Afghanistan to a visible role. As Raymond Garthoff recounts, the Sino-Soviet rivalry for prestige in the communist world played a role in Moscow's thinking in the summer and fall of 1979. Leaders in Moscow believed putting a Russian face on the fight against Afghan rebels would be a propaganda boon to the Chinese, creating an image of foreign meddling rather than national liberation.[34] Soviet Premier Alexei Kosygin refused Afghan requests for more aggressive assistance because "as soon as our troops cross the border, China and all other aggressors will be vindicated."[35] American intelligence analysis similarly predicted a covert Soviet role because a "more visible commitment" would have "adverse political consequences ... in South Asia and the Middle East."[36] This closely parallels the findings of Alexander Downes and Mary Lilley, in which fears of stimulating a local or regional nationalist backlash drove American covertness in the overthrow of Chile's Allende.[37]

A second factor, related to but not strictly involving escalation control as I define it, was avoiding a diplomatic rupture with the West. Soviet leaders specifically hoped to insulate détente and the fruits of East-West cooperation. Confining Soviet combat involvement to the backstage could reduce the global diplomatic blowback. Soviet Prime Minister Kosygin and Taraki engaged in a revealing exchange at the height of the Herat uprising in March 1979.[38] In reaction to Taraki's proposal to have Soviet equipment

---

34 Garthoff, *Detente and Confrontation*, 992–94.

35 http://digitalarchive.wilsoncenter.org/document/113263.

36 Interagency Intelligence Memorandum, "Soviet Options in Afghanistan," September 28, 1979, CIA CREST, Doc. 0000267105, p. 3.

37 Alexander B. Downes and Mary Lauren Lilley, "Overt Peace, Covert War?: Covert Intervention and the Democratic Peace," *Security Studies* 19, no. 2 (2010): 266.

38 Top Secret Transcript of Telephone Conversation Between A. Kosygin and Taraki, March 18, 1979, in CWIHP Reader Vol. 2.

and personnel airlifted to Kabul and deployed to Herat under the guise of the Afghan Army, Kosygin replies that "it will not be possible to conceal this. Two hours later the whole world will know about this. Everyone will begin to shout that the Soviet Union's intervention in Afghanistan has begun." A relatively rare opportunity to glimpse Politburo debates is also available for the Herat uprising period. Soviet specialists who accessed these records in the early years after the Cold War report that Soviet Foreign Minister Andrei Gromyko criticized a proposed overt intervention by saying, "all that we have done in recent years with such effort in terms of a détente in international tensions, arms reductions, and much more—all that would be thrown back."[39] Prime Minister Kosygin similarly opposed the overt use of Soviet troops due to the crisis in relations with the West it would likely prompt (it "would immediately arouse the international community and would invite sharply unfavorable multipronged consequences").[40] Sarah Mendelson's interviews in the early 1990s with members of the Soviet General Staff that had opposed an overt intervention also mention the crisis in relations with the West as a key concern, noting that the opposition of military generals was because "the international consequences of the intervention included the worsening of relations with the United States."[41]

DETECTION AND US REACTION

American intelligence assets in the region provided regular and reliable reporting on Moscow's covert military role. This was taken as consistent with the larger "rules of the road" under détente in which both superpowers restrained their involvement in conflicts in "third areas." The reaction was a classic case of collusion. This provides qualified but valuable support for the theory. The escalation risks of exposing this intervention were mild for the United States because it was a first mover and localized covert intervention. Although not the same as large-scale conflict escalation, a diplomatic rupture would be a significant casualty of exposure. Moreover, the theory notes that the degree of third-party exposure is important to decisions about collusion. In this case, careful intelligence tracking was the means by

---

39 Gromyko's statement to Politburo, quoted in Garthoff, *Detente and Confrontation*, 993.

40 Meeting of Kosygin, Gromyko, Ustinov, and Ponomarev with Taraki in Moscow, March 20, 1979, WDCA, Document 113263.

41 Mendelson, *Changing Course*, 56.

which the United States discovered covert Soviet combat participation. As a result, the United States could effectively insulate détente through collusion.

A relatively robust record of American intelligence judgments from 1979 show that US leaders did, in fact, possess clear evidence of Soviet covert combat units in Afghanistan. The available declassified embassy cables, intelligence analysis, and NSC documentation provide an intriguing timeline. The earliest available reports of suspected covert military units appear in embassy reports in May and June. For example, a May 8 cable from the Moscow embassy summarizes a conversation with a Pakistani diplomat in which they allege Soviet pilots were flying helicopters to suppress an uprising in Jalalabad.[42] A July cable similarly reports on helicopter crews arriving in Afghanistan.[43] By early September, embassy cables were reporting the Bagram airborne battalion as well.[44] Isolated reports had crystallized into a surprisingly accurate description of covert Soviet military intervention no later than September 1979. As noted in previous chapters, an especially important milestone for any intelligence judgment is its inclusion in an interagency assessment. Just such a report on Afghanistan, entitled "Soviet Options in Afghanistan," was completed in late September. The report described that "the Soviets increased the numbers and expanded the counterinsurgency role there of what now are at least 2,500 of their military personnel." It alleged the Soviets had allowed helicopter and tank crews to operate advanced Soviet equipment and described the Soviet airborne battalion at Bagram Air Force Base. It also recognized the likelihood of underestimation, noting that incremental covert deployment of small battalion-sized units "could be accomplished without immediate detection."[45]

At roughly the same time, field reports from the Kabul embassy were becoming far more precise about the covert Soviet military presence. The top American diplomat in Kabul, Bruce Amstutz, sent cables on October 1 and 3 to State Department headquarters and other embassies describing a conservative estimate of 4,200 Soviet combat personnel in Afghanistan,

42 Cable from Embassy Kabul to Secretary of State, May 8, 1979, "Pakistani Diplomat Discusses Soviet-Pakistan Relations, Afghanistan (Moscow 11355)," in "Towards an International History of the War in Afghanistan, 1979–1989," Wilson Center CWIHP Document Reader, Vol. 1: US Documents (hereafter CWIHP Reader Vol. 1), April 30, 2002.

43 Cable from Embassy Kabul to Secretary of State, July 18, 1979, CWIHP Reader Vol. 1.

44 Garthoff, *Detente and Confrontation*, 1002.

45 Interagency Intelligence Memorandum, "Soviet Options in Afghanistan," September 28, 1979.

including 600 guarding Bagram air field, 500–1,000 armored corps vehicle operators at a tank base near Kabul, and a number of advisors with actual operational roles.[46] Amstutz's cables are especially important for two reasons. He is careful to define what he means by "Soviet combat troops."[47] In addition, his analysis draws on multiple intelligence sources: he reports his assessment is based on the "best information currently available to US, including data confirmed by other sensitive USG sources." Amstutz's estimate therefore offers a window into other intelligence sources outside the embassy rumor mill. American interpretations of Soviet caution in Afghanistan aligns in general with the theory's mechanisms. For example, the September interagency review notes that "Moscow's unwillingness to acknowledge the Afghan regime publicly as a Communist government has suggested that the Soviets have wished to leave open a line of propaganda retreat in case the Khalqis collapse."[48]

How well known was this information within the government? In addition to the interagency intelligence analysis cited above, a National Security Council report on the "Soviet Position in the Third World" in August mentions a known Soviet combat role as well.[49] The National Security Advisor, Zbigniew Brzezinski, took a special interest in the issue in late September, and memos document his requests for clarification about just what the Soviets were covertly doing in Afghanistan.[50] Equally revealing is the warning sent by the top American intelligence leader, the director of Central Intelligence. Stanfield Turner circulated a warning to top-level cabinet members and the president in mid-September that a Soviet invasion was a strong possibility, in part because Soviet combat units were already in-country.[51]

What did the United States do with its intelligence? My theory expects exposure or collusion to depend on the uniqueness of the detector's infor-

46 Cable from J. Bruce Amstutz to US Department of State, October 1, 1979, Digital National Security Archive, Doc. AF00677; Cable from J. Bruce Amstutz to US Department of State, October 3, 1979, Digital National Security Archive, Doc. AF00682.

47 Amstutz includes four groups: clearly distinct Soviet military units providing internal defense of fixed positions; Soviet combat specialists such as armored vehicle operators; clandestine Soviet personnel with clear Slavic features providing some kind of security function in Kabul; and Soviet technicians doing anything more than advising.

48 Interagency Intelligence Memorandum, "Soviet Options in Afghanistan," September 28, 1979, p. 15.

49 National Security Council Paper, August 1979, CWIHP Reader Vol. 1.

50 Memorandum from Thomas Thornton to Zbigniew Brzezinski, September 17, 1979, in Digital National Security Archive Electronic Briefing Book No. 396, Doc. 6.

51 Memorandum from Stanfield Turner for the National Security Council, September 14, 1979, CWIHP Reader Vol. 1.

mation. In this case, wide public exposure of the covert Soviet combat role in Afghanistan did not take place. My review of *New York Times* reporting from March to December 1979 includes, at most, speculation about possible Soviet military involvement. However, it is apparent that the Carter administration used public reporting to indicate its intelligence about a possible Soviet intervention and to amplify its attempts to deter Soviet entry.[52] A press conference in August 1979, for example, included a warning that "we expect others similarly to abstain from intervention and from efforts to impose alien doctrines on deeply religious and nationally conscious peoples."[53] Given the absence of public reporting, the theory expects American leaders to collude in keeping the Soviet role on the backstage to avoid the risk of a larger regional war.

After some debate, the White House elected to keep its intelligence private. This was a somewhat overdetermined outcome. In part, collusion was useful because the public release of intelligence was expected to undermine Soviet cooperation on other issues such as the Iranian hostage crisis. In part, it was the larger danger: provoking the Soviets and empowering domestic hawks in the United States risked undermining détente itself. The question of publicity was the subject of active bureaucratic debate from October to mid-December. Carter's foreign policy team was split: although the National Security Council staff under Brzezinski urged publicizing American evidence to pull the Soviets onto the frontstage, other departments feared prompting a larger strategic crisis. In preparation for possible approval by his colleagues and the president, Brzezinski ordered his staff to compile information and produce a plan for public showcasing of the evidence.[54] Yet as Brzezinski himself describes, this initiative was blocked

---

52 E.g., "Western intelligence reports indicate that the Soviet Union has assembled several hundred of its armed advisers around an airfield outside Kabul." Hedrick Smith, "U.S. Is Indirectly Pressing Russians to Halt Afghanistan Intervention," *New York Times*, August 3, 1979. Another report at the time noted that, "there are signs that Moscow is moving toward direct, broad military intervention." Michael T. Kaufman, "Soviet Role in Afghan Clash Shows Signs of Toughening," *New York Times*, September 6, 1979.

53 Smith, "U.S. Is Indirectly Pressing Russians to Halt Afghanistan Intervention."

54 The initiative is described in Zbigniew K. Brzezinski, *Power and Principle: Memoirs of the National Security Advisor 1977–1981* (Farrar, Straus and Giroux, 1983), , 429; Garthoff, *Detente and Confrontation*, 1052–53; primary material from the initiative includes Memorandum from Thomas Thornton to David Aaron, October 2, 1979, CWIHP Reader Vol. 1; Memorandum from Thomas Thornton to Zbigniew Brzezinski, September 17, 1979, Digital National Security Archive, Doc. AF00685; Memorandum from Zbigniew Brzezinski to Cyrus R. Vance, October 4, 1979, Digital National Security Archive, Doc. AF00682. The public relations plan included diplomatic consultations with regional countries and allies, requests to those states to publicly

by others, most importantly the State Department, for several months.[55]
Brzezinski's requests for public statements from the State Department and
International Communications Agency in early October had no tangible
results.[56] Brzezinski recounts in his memoir how State Department leaders below Secretary Vance stalled the proposal citing détente:

> The State Department [was] still reluctant to press the matter ... As late
> as mid-December, a senior State Department official, Under Secretary
> David Newsom, objected to a proposed press backgrounder on the So-
> viet intervention in Afghanistan, prepared by the NSC, on the grounds
> that this might be seen by the Soviets as U.S. meddling in Afghanistani
> affairs.[57]

Records of these deliberations specifically note concern about face-
saving and restraint. The State Department and other critics of publicizing
intelligence argued the frontstage ensured humiliation of Soviet leaders
while downplaying the intelligence would help both sides protect the overall strategic relationship. Transcripts of a high-level meeting assessing what
to do about intelligence regarding the Soviet role in Afghanistan in mid-
December concluded, "we will continue our diplomatic demarches to the
Soviets on a private basis. There is no benefit in going public at this time."
Specifically, Soviet help with the ongoing Iran hostage crisis was an important complication. Rather than submitting evidence of Soviet covert
involvement in Afghanistan to something like the United States, the committee "felt that it would be better to wait until the hostage problem was
resolved before such a move since we want to maintain maximum Soviet
cooperation at that issue."[58]

However, new intelligence indicating clear Soviet plans to invade shifted
the debate within the administration and prompted an embrace of the

---

express concern or condemnation, publicity via Voice of America, press backgrounders, and
statements of condemnation at international forums like the United Nations. Memorandum
from Thomas Thornton to David Aaron, October 2, 1979.

55 Brzezinski notes that "the State Department [was] still reluctant to press the matter"
and that "[a]s late as mid-December, a senior State Department official, Under Secretary David
Newsom, objected to a proposed press backgrounder on the Soviet intervention in Afghanistan, prepared by the NSC, on the grounds that this might be seen by the Soviets as US meddling in Afghanistani affairs." Brzezinski, *Power and Principle*, 428.

56 Garthoff, *Detente and Confrontation*, 1052–53.

57 Brzezinski, *Power and Principle*, 428.

58 Special Coordination Committee Meeting, December 17, 1979, in CWIHP Reader Vol. 1.

frontstage in the two weeks leading up to the invasion.[59] The shift in American policy from collusion to exposure is consistent with a limited-war logic: a rival maintained a policy of collusion until it was clear that the covert intervener was preparing to enter overtly, which would moot the value of staying quiet. The White House reached agreement in mid-December on providing classified intelligence to reporters via background briefings.[60] This led to newspaper reports of a Soviet combat presence on the border of Afghanistan on December 22.[61] Moreover, as the invasion unfolded and the avoidance of a crisis was rendered moot, the Carter administration shifted to a public relations campaign that highlighted the Soviet frontstage role in Afghanistan. Staffers compiled lists of possible data points to emphasize in public statements ("various themes which need to be documented and elaborated on in order to stress the basic policy points that the President has made").[62] A three-pronged publicity strategy was developed involving press backgrounders to journalists, diplomatic consultations with allies and other governments, and statements at international forums.[63] One memo describes organizing a background press gathering in which a CIA white paper on the Soviet presence in Afghanistan is provided to help shape news coverage.[64]

THE OVERT SOVIET INTERVENTION

The cautious Soviet approach throughout 1979 was forced aside as its covert assistance proved insufficient and the stability of the government in Kabul deteriorated. The transition from a quiet, covert role to a more overt intervention is consistent with key claims of the theory. First, overtness was essential if Moscow was to salvage the regime and restore political

---

59 Garthoff, *Detente and Confrontation*, 1053–54.

60 Brzezinski describes the vote in favor of publicity being reached "with considerable opposition from the State Department." *Power and Principle*, 428.

61 Richard Burt, "U.S. Voices Concern Repeatedly to Moscow Over Afghan Buildup," *New York Times*, December 23, 1979.

62 Memorandum from Jerry Schecter to Zbigniew Brzezinski, January 14, 1980, CWIHP Reader Vol. 1.

63 Memorandum from Thomas Thornton to David Aaron, October 2, 1979, CWIHP Reader Vol. 1.

64 "The CIA is preparing a briefing on Saturday morning for about ten journalists on the Soviet consolidation of the invasion of Afghanistan." Memorandum from Jerry Schecter to Zbigniew Brzezinski, January 30, 1980, CWIHP Reader Vol. 1.

order inside Afghanistan. As I argue in chapter 2, logistical advantages of overtness are a critical draw of the frontstage. Second, an exogenous change reduced the downsides of a diplomatic disruption. Western strategic arms decisions created pessimism about the viability of détente regardless of an invasion.

In the early morning hours of Christmas Day in 1979, the first Soviet airlifts landed in and around the capital. Over the next week, thousands of Soviet military personnel entered Afghanistan through the air and over the Amu Darya River dividing Afghanistan and the southern Uzbek republic of the Soviet Union. More than 250 flights in three days brought 7,700 troops and their weaponry to Kabul alone. Two days after the first units arrived in Kabul, a clandestine brigade of KGB special forces seized Amin's palace and executed him. A coordinated message on Radio Kabul announced the arrival of a former PDPA leader, Babrak Karmal, to lead the country after Amin's bloody rule.[65] At its conclusion in January, the total invasion force of four-plus divisions placed 80,000 Soviet boots on the ground in all major urban areas in Afghanistan.[66]

The Soviet decision to overtly intervene was adopted quickly, quietly, and with an unusually small amount of Politburo or policy expert input. The goal remained preservation of the regime in Kabul by installing a more reliable and competent leader and directly administering counterinsurgency operations. This goal resembled the American goal in its intervention to assume counterinsurgency operations in South Vietnam; the parallel was obvious and widely noticed.[67] Soviet Defense Minister Ustinov and KGB head Andropov, members of the Politburo committee on Afghanistan policy, were the primary advocates. Along with Andropov, Ustinov lobbied and convinced the increasingly frail General Secretary Leonid Brezhnev on December 8. Formal Politburo approval was secured without a full Politburo debate and vote; rather, authorization for the invasion was given in a secluded room with no typists or aids and was recorded in a handwritten note filled with oblique language (Afghanistan was simply "A"). Only the signatures of Ustinov, Andropov, foreign minister Andrei Gromyko, Polit-

---

65 Karmal was in exile in Czechoslovakia since the 1978 revolution but had been in Moscow for weeks prior to the invasion.

66 Garthoff, *Detente and Confrontation*, 1017–20.

67 See discussion of the "increasing tendency in the news media and around town generally to make an analogy between Afghanistan and Vietnam," including detailed analysis of the differences and similarities in Memorandum from Stephen Larrabee to Zbigniew Brzezinski, "Soviet Policy in Afghanistan," December 31, 1979, CWIHP Reader Vol. 1.

buro secretary Andrei Kirilenko, and the unsteady hand of Brezhnev appeared on the authorization.

The Soviet decision to overtly intervene in Afghanistan invasion came in light of several new developments. First, détente had been dealt blows between March and December 1979. Two decisions in the West about arms control were interpreted by Soviet leaders as signs that the West itself may not be serious about détente. One was the US Senate declining to consider the Carter administration's submission of the SALT II treaty for ratification, seen by some in Moscow as "heralding a turn away from détente on the part of the United States."[68] The December 1979 NATO approval of Pershing II medium-range ballistic missiles and ground-launched cruise missiles also seemed to indicate abatement of the arms race might be ending regardless of Afghanistan. These measures in mid- to late 1979 "removed the concerns of some Politburo-members over the effects a Soviet intervention might have on détente."[69]

Also important was the scale of intervention and the logistics of responding to the insurgency in Afghanistan. Soviet policy was specifically influenced by Amin's attempts at power consolidation which damaged trust and prompted additional dissent within Afghanistan. Politburo meetings in September, October, and November show repeated frustration with Amin along two specific lines: his demonstrated unwillingness to share power and his dangerous diplomatic openings to the United States. On the one hand, Amin's purges and repression failed to heed Soviet advice to broaden his political base.[70] On the other hand, Soviet intelligence in Afghanistan detected at least one closed-door meeting between Amin and the United States in the fall. Soviet leaders saw Amin as exploring a more "balanced policy" and, in other meetings, had blamed his Moscow patrons for policy mistakes.[71] Given that Afghanistan shared a long border with the

---

68 Artemy Kalinovsky, "Decision-Making and the Soviet War in Afghanistan: From Intervention to Withdrawal," *Journal of Cold War Studies* 11, no. 4 (October 1, 2009): 50.

69 Odd Arne Westad, "Concerning the Situation in 'A': New Russian Evidence on the Soviet Intervention in Afghanistan," in "The Cold War in the Third World and the Collapse of Détente in the 1970s," Wilson Center CWIHP Bulletin, Issues 8–9, 1996, 130.

70 See the transcripts of the Politburo meeting on November 29 in Aleksandr Antonovich Lyakhovskiy, "Inside the Soviet Invasion of Afghanistan and the Seizure of Kabul, December 1979," Working Paper No. 51, Cold War International History Project, January 2007, 9, http://www.wilsoncenter.org/sites/default/files/WP51_Web_Final.pdf.

71 "Recently there have been noted signs of the fact that the new leadership of Afghanistan intends to conduct a more 'balanced policy' in relation to the Western powers. It is known, in particular, that representatives of the USA, on the basis of their contacts with the Afghans, are

southern Soviet republics, a possible turn toward the West—worst of all, expulsion of Soviet advisors and a full embrace of Americans just as Anwar Sadat had done in Egypt—had profound security implications.[72] A personal memorandum from Andropov to Brezhnev in early December 1979 captures these sentiments. He argues, "the situation in the party, the army and the government apparatus has become more acute, as they were essentially destroyed as a result of the mass repressions carried out by Amin." This domestic decay was combining with signs of wavering Afghan loyalty to create "the danger of losing the gains made by the April [1978] revolution."[73]

In short, a more cautious and covert effort from mid-1979 was cast aside when Soviet leaders were forced to choose to either cut their losses or double down with an overt intervention. Two factors combined to shape the preference for a public, acknowledged role: the urgent and large logistical demands of supporting Kabul by late December 1979 as well as mild escalation risks. As a result, the United States faced a fait accompli of a publicized and acknowledged Soviet military presence. This, in turn, infused Washington's decisions with far greater escalation risks.

United States in Afghanistan

In reaction to the Soviet invasion, President Jimmy Carter approved a broad package of responses in early 1980. Along with the public speeches, press backgrounders, consultation with allies, and symbolic gestures (i.e., Olympics boycott), President Carter authorized a new covert aid program to encourage rebel groups to resist the Soviet presence. Within days of the Soviet airlifts, Carter had authorized secret provision of weapons and related assistance to Afghan insurgent groups. The $30 million CIA-led covert aid program in 1979 would grow to $250 million per year by 1985, "eventually coming to consume the vast majority of its covert action budget" and adopt an overt posture with the provision of Stinger missiles.[74] The program re-

---

coming to a conclusion about the possibility of a change in the political line of Afghanistan in a direction which is pleasing to Washington." In Lyakhovskiy, "Inside the Soviet Invasion of Afghanistan and the Seizure of Kabul," 9–11.

72 Personal Memorandum from Andropov to Brezhnev, Undated (approx. early December 1979), in Wilson Center CWIHP Bulletin, Issues 8–9, 1996, pp. 159–60; on the Sadat scenario, see Westad, "Concerning the Situation in 'A'," p. 130.

73 Personal Memorandum from Andropov to Brezhnev, Undated (approx. early December 1979), in Wilson Center CWIHP Bulletin, Issues 8–9, 1996, p. 159.

74 Alan J. Kuperman, "The Stinger Missile and U.S. Intervention in Afghanistan," *Political Science Quarterly* 114, no. 2 (1999): 223; more than 80% of the CIA's annual expenditures for co-

lied on a local administrator and collaborator, Pakistan. The American covert aid program would become "the largest CIA military support operation since Vietnam" and play an important role in enabling a loose coalition of Afghan rebel commanders to force Soviet withdrawal in 1988.[75] I divide the case into two phases. First, I analyze the covert period, which includes both effective secrecy (1980–1984) and an open secrecy period (1984–1986). I then analyze the overt period (1986–1988) marked by the provision of US-made advanced missile systems (i.e., the Stinger).

American decision-makers were stunned by the Soviet Union's brazen violation of the rules of restraint worked out between the two superpowers.[76] The overt invasion was described internally as "outrageous and unprecedented" and leaders complained that the "speciousness and bald-faced arrogance of the Soviet action can hardly be exaggerated."[77] Invoking the inflammation of hawkish domestic critics, a memo from Brzezinski to the president notes that because the invasion "will have been so naked" in the eyes of domestic audiences, SALT II was possibly damaged irreparably and the administration may be "attacked by both the Right and the Left."[78] Although early covert Soviet activity could be concealed, an NSC staff memo argues, "we have no real option of downplaying the significance of the Soviet action. We need a clear, sharp and unequivocal response, which

---

vert operations, according to one source cited in Bob Woodward and Charles R. Babcock, "U.S. Covert Aid to Afghans on the Rise: Rep. Wilson Spurs Drive for New Funds, Antiaircraft Cannon for the Insurgents U.S. Aid Increasing to Afghan Rebels Fighting Soviets," *Washington Post*, January 13, 1985, A1.

75 Kirsten Lundberg, *Politics of a Covert Action: The US, the "Mujahideen," and the Stinger Missile*, Kennedy School of Government Case Study Program HKS295, 1999, 21.

76 Some American leaders may have not been stunned. One account claims the United States baited the Soviet Union into invading through some form of disinformation which was not widely known even within the US government, but apparently known to Brzezinski. Jonathan Haslam, *Russia's Cold War: From the October Revolution to the Fall of the Wall* (New Haven, CT: Yale University Press, 2011), 319–26; Gibbs, moreover, claims early American non-lethal covert aid and overtures to Amin were seen as offensively motivated and provocative. See David N. Gibbs, "Reassessing Soviet Motives for Invading Afghanistan: A Declassified History," *Critical Asian Studies* 38, no. 2 (2006): 239–63.

77 Memorandum from Marshall Brement for Zbigniew Brzezinski and David Aaron, "Response to the Soviets Regarding Afghanistan: A Menu of Possible Actions," December 27, 1979, CWIHP Reader Vol. 1.

78 Memorandum from Zbigniew Brzezinski to the President, "Reflections on Soviet Intervention in Afghanistan," December 26, 1979, in Digital National Security Archive Electronic Briefing Book No. 396, Doc. 12.

should be given full play by all our communications media."[79] Echoing the themes in chapter 2, the public nature of Soviet intervention boosted domestic constraints and communicated a brazen and aggressive course of action. The goals of the American program evolved. In its first five years, aid was intended to reassure allies and ensnare Soviet military forces in a quagmire. Later, the Reagan administration embraced a goal of forcing Soviet withdrawal.[80]

COVERT INTERVENTION

The theory provides a clear logic for preferring the backstage. With Soviet military forces openly and deeply engaged in Afghanistan, any subsequent intervention would create real risks of a direct clash. American leaders therefore had strong reasons to respond in ways that showed a willingness to resist Soviet expansionism while also limiting the resulting war. This same escalation-control motive also makes sense of the open secrecy phase. Even as covert weapons supply was widely exposed, the theory would expect the United States to use non-acknowledgment to indicate continued value for limited war and avoid provoking Soviet leaders.

Carter's initial approval led to delivery of lethal assistance, including Soviet-origin rifles and rocket-propelled grenades acquired from former Soviet allies like Egypt.[81] Weapons would arrive via a complex network of suppliers. Egypt and China provided Soviet-made weaponry. This concealed the American role and increased the plausibility of denial should such weapons be captured. Saudi Arabia helped finance the operation with an agreement to match American aid dollar for dollar.[82] Yet no partner was as important as Pakistan. Pakistan served as the host of rebel training and weapons distribution and was in charge of physical transport. The result was a multistate, multiyear effort maintained through private intelligence liaison relationships and parallel efforts at concealment. Although other aspects of the covert weapons program would eventually become common knowledge, many details of the supply chain remained secret throughout

---

79 Memorandum from Marshall Brement for Zbigniew Brzezinski and David Aaron, December 27, 1979, 1.

80 See discussion of NSDD-166 below.

81 Coll, *Ghost Wars*, 58–59.

82 For overviews of the supply chain, see Lundberg, *Politics of a Covert Action*; Coll, *Ghost Wars*.

the program.[83] The first shipments of rifles arrived in Afghanistan in mid-January 1980.[84]

The Reagan administration inherited the covert aid program when it took office in January 1981. In the first few years, the Reagan foreign policy team, including Director of Central Intelligence William Casey, did not greatly expand the size and scope of the program compared to its Carter-era origins.[85] The program continued providing strictly delimited military and logistical assistance at a comparable annual level ($60 million) even as late as 1983. The quality and variety of weaponry improved marginally by 1983 to include bazookas, mortars, grenade launchers, and mines of Soviet origin.[86] By 1984 the program was expanding rapidly, partly due to Casey's advocacy and partly from steady advocacy by a member of Congress, Representative Charles Wilson (D-Texas). Wilson used his position on key budget committees to quietly increase the size of the program three times in 1984. Congressional allocation for the 1985 fiscal year further expanded the program. Together, these funding increases quadrupled the size of the program compared to 1983, to $250 million annually.[87]

Casey led a high-level interagency policy review in mid-1984 that resulted in National Security Decision Directive 166 (NSDD-166) in March 1985.[88] It authorized more sophisticated weaponry (i.e., plastic explosives and high-powered sniper rifles) and delivery of advanced American intelligence to rebels. The policy goal also shifted from harassment to forcing a Soviet withdrawal. By 1985, the fact of a large American covert aid program was well-known, constituting a classic "open secret" covert intervention.

---

83 "Secrecy shrouded the logistics pipeline," according to Steve Coll. "In CIA's Covert Afghan War, Where to Draw the Line Was Key: Last of Two Articles," *Washington Post*, July 20, 1992; the role of specific states in the covert aid network was especially sensitive; for example, "the extent of China's role has been one of the secret war's most closely guarded secrets." Steve Coll, "Anatomy of a Victory: CIA's Covert Afghan War: $2 Billion Program Reversed Tide for Rebels," *Washington Post*, July 19, 1992.

84 Charles G. Cogan, "Partners in Time," *World Policy Journal* 10, no. 2 (Summer 1993): 76.

85 Robert M. Gates, *From the Shadows: The Ultimate Insider's Story of Five Presidents and How They Won the Cold War* (New York: Simon & Schuster, 2007), 251; Lundberg, *Politics of a Covert Action*, 10.

86 James M. Scott, *Deciding to Intervene: The Reagan Doctrine and American Foreign Policy* (Durham, NC: Duke University Press, 1996), 50.

87 On Wilson's role in the reprogramming of DOD appropriations for the CIA Afghanistan program, see Scott, *Deciding to Intervene*; Lundberg, *Politics of a Covert Action*, 19; Coll, *Ghost Wars*, 103; on the program swelling to $250 million, see Lundberg, *Politics of a Covert Action*, 21.

88 Coll, *Ghost Wars*, 127–28; Lundberg, *Politics of a Covert Action*, 25.

Some details of Afghan covert aid appeared in media reports as early as 1981; more were disclosed in a mid-1983 *New York Times* story on Reagan's decision to expand the program.[89] By 1984, however, the growth of congressional involvement, led by Charlie Wilson's advocacy in the House, led to leaks from congressional staff sources. Two news stories on the program in 1984 and 1985, for example, cited "congressional" or "committee" sources to describe details about new funding increases.[90] By 1985, covert aid to Afghanistan was "being talked about openly" and in real time.[91] Moreover, an internal CIA assessment by Robert Gates in 1984 noted that Soviet leaders had a history of using American media accounts about the covert aid program to learn about new details and future plans.[92]

ESCALATION RISKS AND LIMITING WAR

Why provide assistance covertly? Why keep American and Pakistani assistance to rebel groups on the backstage? Moreover, as the program evolved from little to no exposure (1980–1983) to wide exposure (1984/1985), did covertness continue to serve a purpose and why? A recurring, high-level concern in managing the form of intervention was the risk of a wider regional war involving Pakistan. Specifically, American leaders worried that an overt posture would directly and nakedly challenge Soviet leaders in a way that made retaliation against Pakistan unavoidable. American intelligence estimates cited several specific ways regional conflict could occur: via a covertly induced collapse of the Pakistani government, an opportunistic military attack by India, and/or a direct militarized dispute between Pakistan and the Soviet Union. Although general war between the United States and Soviets was far down the line of escalation, a regional conflict

89 Carl Bernstein, "Arms for Afghanistan," *New Republic*, July 18, 1981; Leslie Gelb, "U.S. Said to Increase Arms Aid for Afghan Rebels," *New York Times*, May 4, 1983.

90 Margaret Shapiro, "More Aid Voted for Afghan Rebels," *Washington Post*, July 28, 1984; "Congress Is Said to Approve More Aid to Afghan Rebels," *New York Times*, October 10, 1985.

91 Terry Atlas, "U.S. Aid Pipeline to Afghan Rebels Springing Leaks," *Chicago Tribune*, February 3, 1985.

92 Gates remarks in passing that "significant increases in aid to the insurgents that are projected for the next year or so, increases that the Soviets are likely to learn about through leaks as they did the $50 million increase earlier this year." Memorandum from Robert Gates to Director Soviet Analysis, "USSR-Afghanistan Exploring Options," October 17, 1984, in Volume 2, Hearings on the Nomination of Robert Gates to be Director of Central Intelligence, Select Committee on Intelligence, U.S. Senate, September–October 1991, pp. 449–50, https://www.loc.gov/law/find/nominations/gates/023_v2.pdf.

was especially challenging due to the existence of the 1959 US-Pakistan Agreement of Cooperation which, while vague on details, seemed to oblige American leaders to come to Pakistan's aid.

The limited-war function of covertness was so deeply ingrained in the program that a recurring metaphor—the "boiling pot"—was used in private discussions and became a kind of policy mantra.[93] Pakistan's president Muhammad Zia-ul-Haq repeatedly invoked the comparison of boiling water in a pot to describe his concerns about being the recipient of Soviet retaliation from the weapons program. Zia argued quiet forms of aid to Afghan rebels could keep the heat on Moscow, but more extreme forms of aid, especially overt Western weaponry, would cause the pot to boil over ("provoke them to massively escalate the level and intensity of their commitment ... [or] retaliate against Pakistan").[94] Zia's metaphor of a boiling pot became shorthand for the value of intervening while limiting a war in Afghanistan.

More specifically, the danger of Soviet retaliation against Pakistan in response to US covert intervention played a key role in shaping the initial choice to give aid covertly. An embassy cable from mid-1978—more than a year prior to the first lethal assistance from the United States was approved—expressed concern that Pakistan's role in providing weaponry could lead to Soviet retaliation in the form of support for separatism and destabilization within Pakistan.[95] A memo from a staff member of the National Security Council in September 1979—two months before the Soviet invasion—argued proposed covert American aid should be supplied carefully lest it "evoke a more direct Soviet threat to Pakistan."[96] Only weeks after lethal aid was approved in December 1979, CIA analysis in January 1980 cautioned

93 The metaphor of "boiling water" became Zia's "Afghan policy mantra" in which the goal was to irritate and undermine the Soviets but not "provoke them to massively escalate the level and intensity of their commitment" or "retaliate against Pakistan." Lundberg, *Politics of a Covert Action*, 13. Coll also notes that hardly a meeting went by without Zia using the metaphor of hot water that doesn't boil over; Coll, *Ghost Wars*, 70.

94 Lundberg, *Politics of a Covert Action*, 13.

95 E.g., the description of Soviets playing their Pashtunistan or Baluchistan "cards" in Cable from Embassy Kabul to Secretary of State, June 13, 1978, Digital National Security Archive Electronic Briefing Book No. 396, Doc. 1.

96 Memorandum from Thomas Thornton to Zbigniew Brzezinski, September 24, 1979, in CWIHP Reader Vol. 1; see also Gates, *From the Shadows*, 145; Coll notes that debates in mid-1979 about possible covert aid featured concerns that the Soviet retaliation may follow if "they saw an American hand in their Afghan cauldron." Coll, *Ghost Wars*, 43.

that covert aid by the United States, Pakistan, and China could provoke the Soviets to retaliate against Pakistan by supporting tribal separatism.[97]

As the program grew, the value of the backstage over frontstage forms of aid shaped debates about an expanding covert aid program. The possibility of Soviet retaliation was the top concern during meetings between American and Pakistani intelligence officials in 1982 and 1983. Coll reports that in meetings during this period, "the core questions they discussed were almost always the same: How much CIA weaponry for the Afghan rebels would Moscow tolerate? How much would Zia tolerate?"[98] For example, the 1981–1982 expansion to include new weapons such as bazookas or mines hinged on whether such an expansion of covert US military aid could be done "without prompting Soviet retaliation against Pakistan."[99]

Any Soviet clash with Pakistan had significant escalatory risks because of complex domestic politics in Pakistan and alliance dynamics. American intelligence concluded visible Soviet retaliation for Pakistan's role in the covert aid program would have to be met with strength by Pakistan or there would be "severe political consequences for any government in Islamabad" and, for Zia specifically, would "endanger his regime."[100] It also concluded that US-Pakistani security commitments meant a Pakistani-Soviet clash could create a difficult alliance dilemma for American leaders. If Soviet retaliation led to a clash with Pakistan, US leaders would be forced to choose between supporting its security commitment to Pakistan (risking escalation to direct US-Soviet conflict) and abandoning Pakistan (jeopardizing its reputation for alliance reliability). The CIA report specifically argued that states in the Middle East threatened by the Soviet invasion were especially watchful of American responses to Soviet retaliation. Failure to uphold the security commitment to Pakistan might "shake their confidence in the credibility of US commitments."[101]

American leaders also believed their backstage role in the war communicated a measure of resolve to Soviet leaders, especially at the start of the

97 An Intelligence Assessment, "The Invasion of Afghanistan: Implications for Soviet Foreign Policy," January 1980, CIA CREST, Doc. 0000969767, pp. 3–4.

98 Coll, *Ghost Wars*, 65.

99 Coll notes discussions of the risk of Soviet retaliation against Pakistan and Pakistan's fears as a key issue in earliest expansions of the program; *Ghost Wars*, 59; the quote is from Scott describing debates over expanding aid in 1982; Scott, *Deciding to Intervene*, 51.

100 An Intelligence Assessment, "Pakistan: Tough Choices on Afghanistan," July 1982, p. 7.

101 An Intelligence Assessment, "Pakistan: Tough Choices on Afghanistan," July 1982, p. 10.

program in 1979.[102] Early in the covert aid program, advocates articulated their support by arguing it would help communicate American willingness to act. As summarized by intelligence assessments at the time, Washington believed it was "imperative that we not only act to counter what the Soviets have done in Afghanistan, but that we are perceived as having done so."[103] Carter's advisors argued in the wake of the initial invasion that the United States had to make "a concerted effort to teach Moscow that aggression does not pay." To do so, the United States had to "make this a costly effort for the Soviets" through "covert arms supply to Afghan insurgents."[104] A pre-invasion National Security Council memo suggested an early proposal for covert aid would be useful in "showing our determination to become involved in Gulf security" and serving "as a global signal to the Soviets."[105] Rather than communicating weakness (if, say, no form of resistance was used) or communicating reckless aggression and inviting retaliation (if various forms of overt aid were embraced), covert intervention could communicate US resolve to resist Soviet military expansionism while avoiding large-scale escalation.[106]

Further expansion of the program in 1984 and 1985 prompted similar questions. In the interagency debates that resulted in NSDD-166, several specific elements of the expanded program were rejected on the grounds that they would provoke Soviet retaliation and a possible conflict spiral. A proposal to provide sniper rifles for purposes of assassinating Soviet military leaders was rejected for fear of Soviet retaliation.[107] A proposal to drop supplies via American C-130 transport flights over Afghanistan was also rejected because it risked a direct American-Soviet incident that could escalate.[108] Moreover, CIA intelligence analysis in 1984 and 1985 continued

---

102 Austin Carson and Keren Yarhi-Milo, "Covert Communication: The Intelligibility and Credibility of Signaling in Secret," *Security Studies* 26, no. 1 (January 2, 2017): 124–56.

103 Memorandum by G. Matthews, December 29, 1979, CWIHP Reader Vol 1., p. 5; Memorandum from Brement for Brzezinski and Aaron, December 27, 1979, CWIHP Reader Vol 1, p.1.

104 Memorandum from Oksenberg for Brzezinski, 28 December 1979, CWIHP Reader Vol. 1.

105 Note the memo ultimately opposed covertly arming the rebellion at this stage for other reasons. Memorandum from Thornton to Brzezinski, September 24, 1979, CWIHP Reader Vol. 1.

106 Roy Allison, "The Superpowers and Southwest Asia," in *Superpower Competition and Crisis Prevention in the Third World*, ed. Roy Allison and Phil Williams (New York: Cambridge University Press, 1990), 177; Carson and Yarhi-Milo, "Covert Communication."

107 Coll reports that sniper rifles were provided but without the intelligence necessary to allow targeting of Soviet officers for assassination. Coll, "In CIA's Covert Afghan War, Where to Draw the Line Was Key."

108 Coll, *Ghost Wars*, 128.

to show concern for Soviet retaliatory actions against Pakistan. One reported increased Soviet cross-border raids and interpreted them as punishment for earlier expansions in the covert aid program.[109] A five-year assessment of Soviet occupation policy assessed the risk of an outright invasion of Pakistan as very low but warned that Soviet leaders could double down within Afghanistan and expand the war into parts of Pakistan if rebel groups threatened the Soviet presence in Kabul itself.[110]

As noted above, the US intervention was an open secret by 1985 due to repeated leaks. Yet American leaders continued to refuse to acknowledge its role, including rejection of exclusively American-made weapons. Why? Putative covertness allowed US and Pakistan officials to officially deny the program. This had a symbolic rather than practical function: it gave Soviet leaders face-saving space to continue to abstain from retaliation.[111] In other words, placing the US-Soviet competition in Afghanistan fully on the front-stage would make it difficult for Moscow not to react. As Berkowitz and Goodman argue,

> [t]here are only two legitimate reasons for carrying out an operation covertly rather than overtly. One is when open knowledge of U.S. responsibility would make an operation infeasible.... The other valid reason for carrying out an operation covertly is to avoid retaliation or to control the potential for escalation. The fact that covertness is sometimes no more than a fig leaf does not necessarily alter the fact that it is a useful fig leaf. In the 1950s, for example, the Soviet government knew that the CIA was supporting resistance fighters in the Ukraine, since Soviet intelligence had penetrated most of the groups. Similarly, the Soviet leadership knew that the United States was supporting the Afghan mujaheddin in the 1980s. If U.S. leaders had admitted responsibility, Soviet leaders would have felt it necessary to retaliate, as was the case when President Eisenhower owned up to U-2 overflights in 1960.[112]

109 SNIE 11/37-2-85/L, March 1985, p. 3.

110 An Intelligence Assessment, "The Soviet Invasion of Afghanistan: Five Years After," May 1985, CIA CREST, Doc. 0000496704.

111 As a contemporary writer observed, "these programs are covert in name only. The Administration appears to want to retain that fig leaf partly for reasons of international etiquette and law and partly to give itself room to maneuver on the amount of commitment." Leslie Gelb, "The Doctrine/Un-Doctrine of Covert/Overt Aid," *New York Times*, February 21, 1986.

112 Bruce D. Berkowitz and Allan E. Goodman, "The Logic of Covert Action," *National Interest*, 1998.

Deniability helped avoid a situation in which "an aggrieved enemy moved to recover prestige and redress its injury" through retaliatory actions.[113] Coll explains how the focus shifted from effectively hiding American weapons to avoiding provocation of the Soviets:

> By 1985 the Soviet leadership had already learned the outlines of the CIA's Afghan program from the press reports, captured fighters, intercepted communications, and KGB-supervised espionage operations carried out among the rebels. Even the American public knew the outlines of Langley's work from newspaper stories and television documentaries. Increasingly, as the CIA and its gung-ho adversaries argued over the introduction of more sophisticated weapons, the issue was not whether the existence of an American covert supply line could be kept secret but whether the supply of precision American arms would provoke the Soviets into raiding Pakistan or retaliating against Americans.[114]

To be clear, providing American-made weapons both improved the effectiveness of the Afghan rebels and constituted a more humiliating challenge by the United States. Thus, its provocativeness was a function of increasing the lethality of aid and crossing a potentially important "salient threshold." Although these effects are difficult to disentangle, several accounts of the covert dynamics in Afghanistan highlight the particular importance of the symbolism of the covert/overt threshold. Allison argues that crossing the threshold to American-made weapons would be seen by the Soviets as a "qualitatively new stage"; Rodman references the "symbolism of a major US political commitment—embodied in crossing the 'plausible deniability' threshold"; and Lundberg refers to the line-crossing and symbolic nature of crossing this threshold as it "could no longer be thought of as a covert action in the traditional sense."[115] In addition, there is considerable debate about the significance of American-made weapons like the Stinger missiles in terms of rebel effectiveness, with internal voices and outside skeptics arguing it had little practical effect on rebel success.[116]

---

113 Lundberg, *Politics of a Covert Action*, 9.

114 Coll, *Ghost Wars*, 129–30.

115 Allison, "The Superpowers and Southwest Asia," 179. Peter W. Rodman, *More Precious than Peace: The Cold War and the Struggle for the Third World* (New York: Charles Scribner's Sons, 1994), 340. Lundberg, *Politics of a Covert Action*, 36.

116 Skeptics of the impact of the Stinger include Mendelson, *Changing Course*, 99–100; "Stingers, Blowpipes Had 'No Impact' on Afghan War," Foreign Broadcast Information Service, July 23, 1987, Digital National Security Archive, Doc. AF02023. For a view that they had a big

Moreover, provision of highly lethal, non-American weaponry was seen as qualitatively less risky, suggesting that staying below the symbolic threshold of deniability was doing important work. The symbolic threshold of deniable weaponry was an important gesture to show restraint and allow the Soviet Union to save face rather than retaliate.

SOVIET DETECTION AND REACTION

Given the comparative lack of documentary availability, describing and analyzing the Soviet detection of and reaction to covert American intervention is difficult. Available material shows that Soviet intelligence assets in Afghanistan were substantial, as was the potential battlefield importance of weaponry supplied over the Pakistan/Afghanistan border by outside states. Moscow was therefore well informed of the fact of American covert aid and changes therein. Intelligence reports to Moscow from Kabul warned of a substantial increase in covert aid in January 1980 and described specific training and equipment coming via Pakistan in September 1980.[117] Reports in 1981 predicted increases in covert aid by the new Reagan administration and carefully described weapons flows.[118] Later in the program, US policymakers debating whether to provide the Stinger missile presumed it would be quickly discovered in the field and countermeasures would be taken by Soviet commanders in the field within days.[119] This was likely in part because Soviet advisors were deeply embedded in Kabul's ministries from the 1978 revolution; after the Soviet invasion, infantry reports from the field and other military intelligence fine-tuned their knowledge.[120]

How did Soviet leaders react? The theory would expect collusion given the escalation risks in exposing a covert intervention that followed a major

---

impact, see "Afghanistan: AFP Views Importance of 'Stinger' Missiles," Foreign Broadcast Information Service, September 27, 1987, Digital National Security Archive, Doc. AF02053.

117 Excerpt from Bogomolov, January 20, 1980, CWIHP Reader Vol. 2; unsourced document [presumably from intelligence sources], September 1980, CWIHP Reader Vol. 2.

118 Report from Gen. Mayarov et al., May 10, 1981, CWIHP Vol. 2; Report by Military Intelligence Representatives, September 1981, CWIHP Reader Vol. 2.

119 Two former participants note that the Soviet "40th Army headquarters began closely documenting the effectiveness of the new American missile, noting how many rebel groups were being equipped with Stingers, how many had been fired, and how many Soviet or DRA aircraft had been struck." Milton Bearden and James Risen, *The Main Enemy: The Inside Story of the CIA's Final Showdown with the KGB* (New York: Random House Digital, 2003), 252.

120 Political Letter from USSR Ambassador to Afghanistan A. Puzanov to Soviet Foreign Ministry, "About the Domestic Political Situation in the DRA," May 31, 1978 (notes), in "The Cold War in the Third World and the Collapse of Détente in the 1970s," Wilson Center CWIHP Bulletin, Issues 8–9, 1996, 133.

power's overt entry and therefore risked a direct clash. Yet Moscow did not collude, instead highlighting the role of outside powers like the United States in aiding and training the insurgency. One key reason was the search for a justification for the Soviet invasion in the first place. To blunt the damage to Soviet reputation and its defense of communist-led self-determination, Soviet leaders had long been claiming outside meddling helped fuel the insurgency in Afghanistan. Beyond the political benefit of justifying the Soviet invasion, it is difficult given the absence of documentation to assess why collusion was rejected.

This started almost immediately following the coup in 1978, well before the start of the covert military aid program by the United States and its partners. As Mendelson recounts, Soviet leaders "publicly and privately stated that resistance was driven by external force" and claimed the Americans could create an "imperialist military beachhead on the southern border of our country" through its involvement.[121] Nine months before the Soviet invasion, an American intelligence memo noted that "Soviet media were accusing the United States, Pakistan, and Egypt of supporting the insurgents." Robert Gates recounts that in the following month Moscow was "stepping up accusations that the United States and China were instigating the rebellion."[122] In 1983, a "rare feature article" in *Pravda* on Afghanistan is described in an American diplomatic cable as including "the usual charges about being trained by the US and others at bases in Pakistan."[123]

As leaks about the program appeared in Western media, Soviet media claims began to incorporate these details. An American cable report on a *Pravda* article noted "the US has long provided political, military, and moral support for the mujaheddin, citing [a] *Washington Post* report that annual allocations are 300 million dollars and that over 300 Stingers have already been transferred."[124] A Soviet *Pravda* article in 1981 repeated the "facts" from an American journalist's account of covert aid to Afghan rebels, but "provides little commentary ... other than concluding that the *New Republic* article 'opens up the curtain of secrecy under whose cover American imperialism and its allies commit crimes on Afghan territory.' "[125]

---

121 Mendelson, *Changing Course*, 60–61.

122 The intelligence memo is described in Gates, *From the Shadows*, 144. The Gates quote about April 1979 is from p. 132.

123 Cable from Embassy in Moscow to Secretary of State, "Pravda Article on the Improving Situation Inside Afghanistan," June 30 ,1983, Digital National Security Archive, Doc. AF01481.

124 Cable from Embassy in Moscow to Secretary of State, "Soviet Coverage of Rabbani Visit," June 18, 1986, Digital National Security Archive, Doc. AF01743.

125 Cable from Embassy in Moscow to Secretary of State, "Pravda Reports on New Republic's 'Arms for Afghanistan' Article," August 3, 1981, Digital National Security Archive, Doc. AF01247.

THE STINGER: EMBRACING AN OVERT ROLE

The Stinger missile system was a cutting-edge weapon developed for the American military by General Dynamics and first produced only in 1983. It drew on sensitive technology and had only been shared with select NATO allies in late 1985. The Stinger was considered a potential game-changing capability in the mountains of Afghanistan because it promised to potentially end the threat of helicopter-led counterinsurgency.[126] Since 1984, Soviet leaders had relied heavily on helicopter gunships for raids against Afghan rebel groups and had experienced substantially improved outcomes over other tactics. Other missile systems had proven ineffective. Throughout internal deliberations, the Stinger missile was treated by the White House and intelligence community as abandonment of a covert posture in favor of overt support for the rebels.[127] Many considered this an asset; others saw it as a central drawback of providing Stingers. Debate about whether to provide the Stinger missile began only two months after the president signed NSDD-166 in March 1985. After a lengthy interagency debate, the Reagan cabinet approved provision of the missiles. Echoing the theory's points about operational advantages of an overt posture, Stinger proponents argued that providing this kind of weapon would substantially improve operational effectiveness, allowing rebel groups to more effectively shoot down Soviet helicopters. Opponents cited the risk of Soviet retaliation and regional war.[128] The Stinger system was thought to be symbolic.[129] American leaders thought approval of the Stinger system would be seen as a major qualitative shift; the "covert would be overt."[130] Moreover, absten-

---

126 Lundberg, *Politics of a Covert Action*, 29.

127 Because the Stinger was to be supplied without official acknowledgment or public announcement, the intervention technically remained covert according to my definition. With this definitional caveat noted, the remainder of this discussion treats the Stinger in the terms decision-makers applied to it, i.e., as a decision between covert and overt intervention.

128 One additional concern that motivated opposition to the Stinger in the Joint Chiefs of Staff was the risk of technology leakage. The JCS feared the Soviets would quickly acquire a Stinger missile system which would allow countermeasures and copycat attempts to advance more quickly. This concern was overcome in February 1986 after it was discovered that a Greek spy had given the designs of the Stinger to the Soviets as early as 1984. See discussion in Rodman, *More Precious than Peace*, 338–39; Lundberg, *Politics of a Covert Action*, 60.

129 Rodman, *More Precious than Peace*, 340; the internal bureaucratic term to refer to this change was Stinger missiles were not "battlefield credible" (i.e., credibly sourced from somewhere other than the US government). See Cogan, "Partners in Time," 81.

130 The program "could no longer be thought of as a covert action in the traditional sense." Lundberg, *Politics of a Covert Action*, 2, 36.

tion from providing American-made weapons had been a "constantly reiterated Pakistani theme, at all levels of government" and Pakistan's Zia was "very, very worried about introducing at that time blatant, undeniable evidence of superpower involvement and rivalry into the subcontinent."[131]

Why didn't the need to control escalation prevent the Reagan White House from approving provision of the Stinger in 1986? Because the core escalation features of the conflict remained the same, my theory would not expect this transition. The key was the exogenous shock of a new leader atop an adversary that was clearly and credibly committed to withdrawal. This provides mixed support for the theory. On one hand, Gorbachev's rise meant Soviet retaliation was extremely unlikely (i.e., escalation risks fell significantly) and this was a key reason opponents to the Stinger changed their view. On the other hand, the outcome was a result of a domestic leadership change, which is not a factor my theory links to the magnitude of escalation danger.

An important shift that preceded the Stinger issue was approval of NSDD-166 in March 1985. This directive captured a desire to more aggressively push for Soviet military withdrawal from Afghanistan rather than a "bleed them dry" strategy.[132] This reflected greater US confidence in its position in the strategic balance as well as a broader desire to roll back Soviet gains in third areas.[133] Yet whether a more expansive strategic goal necessitated overt weaponry like the Stinger was a separate discussion. Escalation concerns initially blocked such a step. The CIA's Operations directorate staff believed providing the Stinger could lead to retaliation against Pakistan, risking a much larger war.[134] At the State Department, regional experts worried that the Stinger "might provoke the Soviets into retaliation against Pakistan directly" and would create a superpower crisis that would undermine the diplomatic efforts to secure Soviet withdrawal through the

---

131 Lundberg, *Politics of a Covert Action*, 39–40.

132 This shift took the form of a new Presidential finding (NSDD 166) shifting the goal for aid from harassing Soviet occupiers to prompting a withdrawal; Gates, *From the Shadows*, 339; see also Coll's description of NSDD 166 as using all available means to encourage withdrawal. Coll, *Ghost Wars*, 125–28.

133 On rollback generally and congressional enthusiasm driving the expansion of covert aid in Afghanistan, see Scott, *Deciding to Intervene*; on the shifting strategic balance in the 1980s, the lagging US perception of it, and its role in Gorbachev's desire for cooperation and reform, see Raymond Garthoff, *The Great Transition: American-Soviet Relations and the End of the Cold War* (Washington, DC: Brookings Institution Press, 2000), especially 528–38.

134 Lundberg, *Politics of a Covert Action*, 2.

United Nations.[135] Even proponents of giving Stingers noted that, in 1985, those in "Langley and in Foggy Bottom" believed that "if pushed too far, the Soviets might overreact and strike back at Pakistan."[136] Fred Ikle, leading advocate for Stinger missiles internally, later admitted that "one of the things I always worried about was the possibility of escalation on the Soviet side."[137]

An "exogenous" shock of a change to Soviet leadership, and early signs of its policy priorities, changed the terms of the debate. The rise of Mikhail Gorbachev to General Secretary and his appointment of Eduard Shevardnadze to Foreign Minister prompted a shift toward exiting Afghanistan rather than winning. This prompted changes in rhetoric and policy in late 1985 and early 1986 which provided clear indicators that Moscow sought withdrawal. Gorbachev and Shevardnadze sent subtle but significant signals in late 1985 and early 1986 which seemed to indicate Soviet interest in moderation on Afghanistan and even withdrawal. Specifically, private meetings between Secretary of State Shultz and Shevardnadze in early August 1985 left the former "struck by the new Soviet Foreign Minister's different tone and approach."[138] In November 1985, Gorbachev's comments to Reagan on Afghanistan included discussion of withdrawal of Soviet troops as part of a general political settlement. Shultz's memoirs claim, "I thought I saw the beginning of an opening ... [in] Gorbachev's lightly veiled hint about pulling out of Afghanistan."[139] Last, Gorbachev's address to the 27th Party Congress in February 1986 was his first and included unusual language that described the situation in Afghanistan as a "bleeding wound."[140] The reference was seen by many as a sign that Gorbachev differed from previous leadership in his level of seriousness about withdrawal.

Opponents of the Stinger, primarily based in the State Department, changed their views about escalation risks. As one former participant in the debates describes it, "thus the balance in State was tipped, and with it the balance in the government."[141] Ex-participants in these debates note

---

135 Lundberg, *Politics of a Covert Action*, 37; Kuperman, "The Stinger Missile and U.S. Intervention in Afghanistan," 224.

136 Bearden and Risen, *The Main Enemy*, 215.

137 Interview reviewed by Lundberg, *Politics of a Covert Action*, 42.

138 Gates describes the Helsinki meeting in *From the Shadows*, 341.

139 George Shultz, *Turmoil and Triumph: My Years as Secretary of State* (New York: Scribner's, 1993).

140 Gorbachev would have great difficulty in finding a face-saving way of withdrawing; despite these hints in late 1985, the first divisions did not leave Afghanistan until more than two years later. See Kalinovsky, "Decision-Making and the Soviet War in Afghanistan."

141 Rodman, *More Precious than Peace*, 338.

that Gorbachev and Shevardnadze specifically changed how the issue of escalation was perceived. Alan Kuperman describes Ikle as saying that the most important reason skeptics eventually came on board the Stinger missile proposal was that "some US officials perceived the Soviets were 'tired of the war,' so the Red Army was unlikely to increase its commitment of troops sufficiently to invade Pakistan."[142] As one former participant remembers, "what decided the issue was the vigorous entry of the State Department on the pro-Stinger side."[143] Shultz's conversion was critical. As one review describes, "Shultz's decision ... led to vigorous support by the State Department for the introduction of the missile, which broke the deadlock.[144] The link between Gorbachev, retaliation risks, and the adoption of the Stinger is echoed by Abramowitz himself. As Kuperman describes,

> the Stinger decision was a reaction to Gorbachev's ascension to power ... According to Mort Abramowitz, however, Gorbachev was the key. The administration's assessment of the new general secretary as a moderate, not personally committed to the war, led it to conclude that escalating the war would compel withdrawal rather than counter-escalation. "If it had been another Stalin, you might have thought about it differently," he explains.[145]

Overall, a limited-war theory makes sense of the covertness in US military aid from 1980 through 1985. Time and again, fears of Soviet retaliation against Pakistan and a possible regional war steered the United States into expansions in volume but not a change in its covert posture. This rationale held even after the wide exposure of the program around 1984. The theory has less purchase on the transition to an overt posture as triggered by providing the Stinger missile. New Soviet leadership altered how opponents of the overt transition perceived the risks of escalation. Yet this kind of domestic political change is outside the scope of the theory. Structurally, the conflict remained one in which an overt American role would risk a direct clash with the Soviet occupying forces. Thus, the overt period (1986–1988) only provides mixed support for the theory.

142 Kuperman, "The Stinger Missile and U.S. Intervention in Afghanistan," 227.
143 Rodman, *More Precious than Peace*, 338.
144 Scott, *Deciding to Intervene*, 61.
145 Kuperman, "The Stinger Missile and U.S. Intervention in Afghanistan," 243.

Soviet Union in Pakistan

A lesser-known facet of the Afghanistan conflict was significant, covert Soviet military operations into Pakistani territory. Soviet military forces in Afghanistan engaged in cross-border military operations in response to the swelling covert weapons pipeline to Afghan rebels. Relying primarily on air attacks, Moscow sought to disrupt the flow of materials and warn Islamabad and Washington. These air strikes were neither publicized nor acknowledged by Soviet leaders and often attributed to Afghan pilots. Limited-war dynamics provide clear reasons for this preference for the backstage. Intervention in Pakistan was a transgression of a key geographic boundary on the war in Afghanistan. The severe escalation risks of operations into Pakistan therefore provided compelling reasons to prioritize escalation control and use covertness. These same features shaped how American intelligence interpreted these operations when detected, and influenced the American reaction.

Many details of Soviet cross-border operations inside Pakistan remain shrouded in secrecy. Its own records on the Afghanistan invasion are more transparent, yet few documents about Moscow's activities in and decision-making about operations in Pakistan are available. By far the most precise material to make inferences is declassified American intelligence assessments. These are admittedly indirect. Specifically, they display what American leaders perceived and inferred. However, their content supports the logic of the theory well and provides a basis for tentative conclusions.

Covert cross-border operations as a response to covert aid were discussed as early as January 1980 during high-level American and Pakistani bilateral meetings.[146] By 1982, a regional Pakistani governor complained about "a number of incidents in the tribal areas in the recent past" which, he believed, were used by the Soviets "to demonstrate to Pakistanis that the [Government of Pakistan]'s Afghan policy and continued harboring of the refugees entailed great dangers."[147] American intelligence estimates also referred to Soviet efforts to "continue to put heat on Pakistan's President Zia by covert assistance to Zia's political opponents and tribal insurgents."[148]

---

146 Zia mentions Soviet troop incursions into Pakistan in hot pursuit as early as January 1980. See Cable from Embassy Islamabad to Department of State, January 16, 1980, Digital National Security Archive, Doc. AF00802.

147 Telegram Under-Secretary Eagleberger's Call on NWFP Governor Fazle Haq, November 23, 1982, Digital National Security Archive, Doc. AF01403.

148 National Intelligence Estimate, "Andropov's Approach to Key US-Soviet Issues," August 1983, NIE 11-9-83, CIA CREST, Doc. 19830809.

Other high-level intelligence assessments from later in the war note intentional Soviet cross-border operations into Pakistan, anticipate increases in response to intensified covert weapons supplies, and link it to efforts to both interdict and coerce.[149]

These analyses specifically monitored trends in covert Soviet activity into Pakistan and linked it to Soviet desires to achieve operational and political goals while keeping the war limited. For example, a dedicated intelligence analysis by the CIA, entitled "Pakistan: Tough Choices on Afghanistan," was compiled in 1982 to assess such scenarios.[150] The report notes that Pakistan's participation in the covert aid program "risks greater Soviet pressure that could threaten Pakistan's security and stability" and describes ways Soviet leaders could retaliate. Importantly, American intelligence analysis dismissed the idea that Soviet cross-border activity that had already taken place was accidental. There were "occasional bombing and strafing attacks" in 1980 and 1981 but "few of the violations were deliberate"; yet by 1982, the "aerial mining and bombing and strafing incidents ... seemed deliberate, however, and appeared aimed at intensifying pressure on Islamabad to come to terms with the Soviet-dominated government in Kabul."[151] Soviet KGB officers were known to have extensive links with Pashtun and Baloch separatist groups. One scenario was for Moscow to encourage rebellion, undermine support for Zia's regime, and possibly splinter Pakistan. Soviet military raids across the Pakistani border which intentionally raised the risk of clashes with Pakistan's air force or army units and a military crisis were also described. Such actions, especially if paired with pressure by Pakistan's rival India, could result in "Islamabad's worst nightmare ... dismember[ing] Pakistan into ethnically based vassal states in Pashtunistan, Baluchistan, Sind and the Punjab."[152]

149 See, for example, Special National Intelligence Estimate, "Soviet Policy Toward the United States in 1984," August 1984, SNIE 11-9-84, CIA CREST, Doc. 19840814; Special National Intelligence Estimate, "Soviet Problems, Prospects, and Options in Afghanistan in the Next Year," March 1985, SNIE 11/37-2/85/L, CIA CREST, Doc. 0000518057; An Intelligence Assessment, "The Soviet Invasion of Afghanistan: Five Years After," May 1985, CIA CREST, Doc 0000496704; "Current Soviet Strategy on Afghanistan," September 2, 1987, CIA CREST, Doc. 0001475990.

150 An Intelligence Assessment, "Pakistan: Tough Choices on Afghanistan," July 1982, CIA CREST, Doc. 0000534961.

151 An Intelligence Assessment, "Pakistan: Tough Choices on Afghanistan," July 1982, CIA CREST, Doc. 0000534961, pp. 5–6.

152 On the India scenario, see discussion in Special National Intelligence Estimate, "Soviet Policy Toward the United States in 1984," August 9, 1984, SNIE 11-9-84, CIA CREST, Doc. 19840814.

The clearest picture of the sharp increase in Soviet cross-border activity is a 1986 Central Intelligence Agency assessment.[153] It describes a shift in the fall of 1984. After four years of Soviet efforts "largely contained within the country's borders," Moscow had chosen to adopt a strategy that would "combine military pressure on the insurgents with military pressure and subversion in the North-West Frontier Province."[154] They adopted a three-pronged pressure strategy: cross-border air operations, Afghan secret police infiltration of Pakistani tribes, and covertly supported terror bombings within Pakistan. Air violations "escalated rapidly" in the first half of 1986 with "about 500" violations of the border "by Soviet or Afghan aircraft."[155]

Consistent with the theory, American intelligence analysis linked covertness and other policy choices to Soviet interest in controlling escalation. A 1982 report, for example, predicts that in approving increased cross-border activity, "we believe the Soviets would probably try to control the escalation by limiting their attacks to insurgent bases and supply lines not striking deeply into Pakistan, and trying to avoid clashes with the Pakistan Army that could trigger a larger conflict and provoke sharp international censure."[156] Moscow was unlikely to approve larger overt cross-border operations because "gross violations of Pakistan's territory would provoke greater US political and military involvement in South Asia."[157]A Special National Intelligence Estimate in 1985 notes the possibility of greater covert cross-border activity and the simultaneous desire to keep the war limited. It notes that although the Soviet system could tolerate a tough war indefinitely, Soviet leaders sought to avoid "the prospect of a very protracted war with potentially large domestic and international costs." This translated into caution about pushing Pakistan too far, as the report concludes that "we also believe that Moscow is not yet ready to face the military risks and consequences of a significant expansion of hostilities into Pakistan ... [which] would require extensive logistic preparations, including securing

153 An Intelligence Estimate, "Pakistan: Trouble Along the Afghan Border," November 1986, CIA CREST, CIA-RDP06T00412R000606330001-2.

154 An Intelligence Estimate, "Pakistan: Trouble Along the Afghan Border," November 1986, CIA CREST, CIA-RDP06T00412R000606330001-2, p. 1.

155 An Intelligence Estimate, "Pakistan: Trouble Along the Afghan Border," November 1986, CIA CREST, CIA-RDP06T00412R000606330001-2, pp. 1–2.

156 An Intelligence Assessment, "Pakistan: Tough Choices on Afghanistan," July 1982, CIA CREST, Doc. 0000534961, p. 6.

157 An Intelligence Assessment, "Pakistan: Tough Choices on Afghanistan," July 1982, CIA CREST, Doc. 0000534961, p. 6.

of supply lines."[158] The 1986 CIA assessment predicted "the Soviets will continue" their cross-border operations because it was a "relatively low-cost operation that can be carefully calibrated, keeps the Pakistanis on edge, and has not prompted significant international reaction."[159]

How did the United States use—or not use—its detailed intelligence on raids into Pakistan? Public reporting on Soviet-sponsored raids into Pakistan was sporadic and ambiguous.[160] Some of the more detailed reports on such raids maintained ambiguity about their sponsorship. One story in mid-1985 on attacks inside Pakistan using "Soviet-built aircraft," for example, notes that "officials are not certain whether they are Soviet Air Force planes or Afghan planes since both come from the same bases."[161] Another simply refers to "attacks coming from Afghanistan" and quotes an American official discounting the hundreds of cross-border raids in 1986 as "planes accidentally straying across the border."[162] Recall that the intelligence assessments cited above explicitly refute the "accidental" nature of raids by 1985 and 1986. One exception is worth noting. A report from 1985, citing a Pakistani source and unnamed American officials, describes increased Soviet artillery and air attacks within Pakistan that are intended to cut off supplies and deter Pakistan.[163] The theory therefore expects severe escalation risks and an absence of third-party exposure to dominate considerations given that the intervention eroded the geographic bounds of the war in Afghanistan.

Collusion was indeed the American response. As early as 1979, US leaders recognized that exposing Soviet covert activities within Pakistan could inflame geopolitics in the region and "have [a] negative impact on Soviet relations with Iran as well as Pakistan."[164] Moreover, for Pakistani leaders,

158 Special National Intelligence Estimate, "Soviet Problems, Prospects, and Options in Afghanistan in the Next Year," March 1985, SNIE 11/37-2/85/L, CIA CREST, Doc. 0000518057, pp. 2–3.

159 An Intelligence Estimate, "Pakistan: Trouble Along the Afghan Border," November 1986, CIA CREST, CIA-RDP06T00412R000606330001-2, p. 10.

160 I reviewed *New York Times* reporting from 1983 to 1987 using search terms like "attacks" and "raid(s)" regarding Pakistan.

161 Bernard Gwertzman, "U.S. Rushing Missiles to Pakistan; Cites Air Raids from Afghanistan," *New York Times*, July 12, 1985.

162 John H. Cushman Jr., "Pakistan Says It May Request Air Patrols by U.S.," *New York Times*, October 16, 1986.

163 Steven R. Weisman, "Russians Said to Step Up Air and Artillery Attacks Inside Pakistan," *New York Times*, May 15, 1985.

164 Stephen Larrabee to Zbigniew Brzezinski, "Soviet Intervention in Afghanistan," December 31, 1979, in "Towards an International History of the War in Afghanistan, 1979–1989," Wilson Center CWIHP Document Reader, Vol. 1: US Documents, April 29–30, 2002.

drawing attention to Soviet activities would give more ammunition to critics of the government in the frontier areas. American leaders noted the Pakistani reluctance to publicize these incidents in 1982 when a cable noted that some early cross-border incidents "have not been publicized" because of their difficult political implications.[165] Five years later, at the height of concern about Soviet raids, another embassy cable noted that Zia had made an unplanned reference to the Soviet role in terror attacks and other incidents inside Pakistan. This speech grabbed attention within Pakistan and fueled hardline critics and was quickly dealt with. The 1986 intelligence assessment noted above described a series of shootdown incidents, including through the use of American-supplied Stinger missiles. Only one, in May 1986, is noted as being publicly acknowledged by Pakistan.[166] However, the public media reporting on this incident quoted Pakistani officials as describing MIG jets flown by Afghan, not Soviet, pilots.[167]

This material supports three conclusions. First, Soviet leaders appear to have modulated the frequency and visibility of their cross-border raids. This was one tool of coercive pressure on Pakistan which simultaneously retained control of subsequent escalation, helping to avoid a larger regional war. Second, American intelligence carefully tracked these trends and inferred that the reason Soviet leaders kept their involvement low-profile was to continue keeping the war within limits. Third, both Pakistani and American leaders elected not to publicize these events, and even the occasional publicized clash was attributed to Afghan rather than Soviet pilots. The result was several years of cross-border activity shrouded in ambiguity and controlled in its escalation dangers.

165 Telegram Under-Secretary Eagleberger's Call on NWFP Governor Fazle Haq, November 23, 1982, Digital National Security Archive, Doc. AF01403.

166 An Intelligence Estimate, "Pakistan: Trouble Along the Afghan Border," November 1986, CIA CREST, CIA-RDP06T00412R000606330001-2: "Islamabad publicly acknowledged shooting down an Afghan aircraft that crashed inside Pakistani territory in May 1986. Pakistani F-16s shot down at least two intruding aircraft—and possibly another—with five AIM-9L missiles in two incidents in April and May 1986."

167 "Government officials in Parachinar said four Afghan MIG-21's crossed the border just after dawn ... when they were met by two F-16's. Two of the Afghan jets immediately raced back into Afghan airspace as the Pakistani jets homed in on the other two." Interestingly, the same article quotes anonymously from other sources that "Western diplomats said four MIG-27's, believed flown only by Soviet pilots, were seen landing at Kabul airport on April 27, according to Reuters." "Pakistanis Shoot Down an Afghan MIG," New York Times (1923–Current file); May 18, 1986, p. 3.

Conclusion

A limited-war logic for the employment of covertness in external intervention activity nicely captures some of the critical factors in the decade-long
Afghanistan conflict. Fears of wrecking détente influenced Soviet decision-
making in mid-1979 against overt involvement. Avoiding Soviet retaliation
against Pakistan and a larger regional war, moreover, influenced how American leaders provided weaponry to Afghan rebels after the Soviet invasion.
I also find evidence of tacit backstage collusion and the role of escalation
in that process. American leaders, for example, handled intelligence about
detected Soviet combat involvement carefully to avoid creating a diplomatic crisis prior to the Soviet overt invasion. The value of deceiving an
adversary and generating strategic or tactical advantage does not appear to
have been a significant factor, in part because both sides could monitor one
another's covert and overt involvement.[168] Dovish opposition to military
intervention in the United States, moreover, was almost nonexistent after
the overt Soviet invasion in December 1979.[169] In fact, Reagan officials were
pressured by hawkish domestic elites for more aggressive forms of aid to
Afghan rebels rather than less.

The conflict also featured two covert-to-overt transitions which appear
to capture the basic tradeoffs identified in chapter 2 between covert and
overt forms of military involvement. The Soviet overt invasion only came
in reaction to desperation in Kabul, the failure of covert alternatives, and
without other outside powers already militarily involved. This supports
the theory's claims about the role of logistical demands and "first-mover"
advantages in overt intervention. Support for the American provision of
Stinger missiles coalesced only after a change in Soviet leadership and the
overall strategic balance removed escalation as a credible downside. The
rise of Gorbachev encouraged skeptics of the Stinger proposal to embrace
what was seen as overt weaponry because of his clear indications of a desire
to withdraw and not escalate against Pakistan. Other aspects of the cases suggest additional factors outside the scope of the theory. Another consideration driving Soviet value for a covert role in 1979 Afghanistan, for example,

168 Regarding the case of American covert aid, a memoir from one former program participant concludes that the Soviets were "undoubtedly aware that outside aid was coming to the
rebels" even prior to the invasion. Rodman, *More Precious than Peace*, 208.

169 Rodman notes "consistent bipartisan support in Congress"; Rodman, *More Precious
than Peace*, 217; Another scholar notes "virtually unanimous agreement" in both the Carter and
Reagan administrations about the importance of US aid. Scott, *Deciding to Intervene*, 40.

was the desire to avoid the appearance of a failed communist state and Soviet meddling in allied affairs. The American embrace of Stinger missiles was also influenced by a strategic shift in 1985 from bogging down Moscow to expelling it from Afghanistan. This more aggressive goal helped put policy options on the table that had previously been dismissed due to concerns about escalation.

Two other distinguishing features of this chapter are worth noting. First, the Afghanistan conflict underscores the importance of conceptualizing the key variable in this study—"large-scale escalation"—in a capacious and context-specific way. Although the discussion of escalation in chapter 2 makes this point in several ways, the discussion in previous chapters has tended to focus on scenarios of large-scale warfare in Europe, Asia, or globally. This chapter features similar covertness dynamics in a conflict where the primary scenarios were a diplomatic crisis short of an actual military encounter (i.e., 1979 and détente) and a more modestly sized regional war (i.e., 1980s and some kind of war involving Pakistan). Although it stretches my concept of large-scale escalation, the similarities with previous chapters suggest a broader notion of "crisis avoidance" is worth considering.[170] A second feature of the war is inclusion of an intervention case in which only weaponry was provided by the outside power. The fact that large-scale escalation—specifically, retaliation against a cooperating partner, i.e., Pakistan—influenced the choice for covertness regarding a weapons supply program suggests the theory's relevance to a wider scope of cases.

Finally, the Afghanistan conflict completes the historical narrative of the Cold War. Only a year after its military forces withdrew, the unraveling of the Soviet bloc in Eastern Europe and the Soviet Union itself was in process. Superpower confrontations in "outside areas" or "peripheral conflicts" were informed by a long track record by this point in the Cold War. Finding leader views of the links between covertness, outside audience reactions, and mutual understanding of interest in limited war underscores the presence of threads connecting earlier conflicts in the bipolar rivalry (i.e., Korea; Vietnam) with the conflicts at the end of it. In general, the three Cold War–era chapters show that covert intervention as a tool for both geostrategic influence and limited war evolved into a key part of the repertoire of two major powers competing in the shadow of industrialized, even nuclear, warfare.

---

170 Giovanni Sartori, "Concept Misformation in Comparative Politics," *American Political Science Review* 64, no. 4 (December 1, 1970): 1033–53.

8

Conclusion

This book assesses the covert side of modern war, offering a novel perspective on how ignorance and non-acknowledgment regarding foreign military involvement is used by leaders to control escalation and keep wars limited. From Nazi Germany's intervention in interwar Spain to the United States' intervention in late Cold War Afghanistan, I argue that leaders cope with conflict escalation risks in part by using covertness in their own behavior and by colluding to avoid exposure of others' covert involvement. Doing so retains a measure of escalation control, both insulating leaders from domestic hawkish constraints and communicating to one another an interest in limited war. The empirical chapters make clear that important facets of some of the most significant conflicts in the twentieth century unfolded on a kind of "backstage." This backstage helped obscure the erosion of geographic limits including direct, hostile clashes between major powers. Overall, the book suggests that such covert tactics emerged as a response to escalation-control problems in the modern era and that adversaries often tacitly cooperate in secrecy to limit war.

The book also provides a different framework with which to view secrecy in general. We often assume secrecy is used solely to alter the distribution of knowledge, that it is effective, and that it is deployed to benefit one leader or state at the expense of others. This is most obvious in theories that view secrecy as a tool insecure states use to deceive possible adversaries about their bargaining strength and battlefield maneuvers. This book shows the value of loosening these assumptions. My limited-war theory allows secrecy to alter both what is known and what is acknowledged. It explicitly incorporates partial and complete exposure in the theory's logic. These two moves help us understand why even widely exposed, or "open secret," state behavior can still be politically useful. My claims also emphasize how concealment and non-acknowledgment contribute to situational stability rather than merely serving selfish goals. This stabilizing function gives rise to shared incentives, even among adversaries, and tacit collusion to control worst-case outcomes like large-scale escalation. These ideas have implications for the study of secrecy in other contexts.

It is equally important to be clear what the book does not attempt to do. It is not a general theory of secrecy in war. States may also use secrecy to protect operational military movements or avoid dovish domestic criticism. Conflicts that lack pressing escalation risks or have already escalated to a large scale may still feature secrecy to conceal gruesome battlefield images, protect sensitive peace negotiations, and so on. As I describe in chapter 3, covertness as an escalation management strategy first emerged in the wake of the destruction of World War I and drew on technological innovations like airpower that helped obfuscate foreign involvement. The Cold War hosted the refinement of this practice as the lessons of repeated clashes in third areas accumulated. As I detail in this chapter, post–Cold War conflicts and new technologies like cyber suggest that these lessons will not soon be forgotten.

This chapter first summarizes key empirical findings and assesses overall support for the theory. The second section analyzes covert dynamics in Iraq after 2003, building on the Spanish Civil War case (chapter 4) to further suggest the book's findings are not an artifact of the Cold War. The third section considers two extensions of the theory: cyber warfare and intrastate violence. The fourth section addresses lingering questions about the initial motive for intervention rather than its form, exploitation and miscommunication about covert activity, and the impact of social media and leaks. The penultimate section discusses implications for policy, and the final section reviews the book's significance for scholarship on secrecy, war, and broader debates in International Relations (IR).

Summary of Key Findings

The covert sphere routinely features important facets of modern war that provide a different window into historically and theoretically influential conflicts. A consistent theme of the book is that the backstage of war sometimes features direct combat encounters by outside powers that were publicly understood to have avoided such entanglements. Declassified records suggest that, for example, Nazi Germany tracked Soviet covert involvement carefully, assessed how covert German combat participation would affect the balance of hawks and doves in London and Paris, and so on. Chapter 5 reviews unusually candid declassified American records in which US leaders anticipated the covert involvement of Chinese and Soviet personnel in the Korean War and detected their presence after entry. Newly reviewed archival material on the US covert intervention in Laos shows that leaders foresaw media leaks, debated how to respond to leaks, and found diplomatic value in continuing official denials of leaked information.

A broader finding is about the character of modern war itself. Analyzing the backstage provides new insight into how great powers have avoided conflict since World War II. Three of the four empirical chapters describe events unfolding in the shadow of two world wars and nuclear weapons. As I note in chapter 1, conventional explanations for the post-1945 absence of great power war cite the advent of nuclear weapons, the spread of democracy, or the stability of bipolarity. These changes clearly mattered. However, my findings underscore that local conflicts are common and periodically raise the risk of large-scale escalation. Tactics in the covert sphere—both secret, unacknowledged interventions and the collusion that often followed—have helped to control the escalation risks in such encounters. Secrecy and escalation dynamics therefore shed new light on an arguably less violent modern world.

My limited-war theory of covert conflict dynamics receives substantial support. Consider each research question in turn. First, does the *form* of intervention correspond with the expectations of the theory for the overall outcome? I argue that escalation-control concerns should dominate decision-making and produce a choice for covert if (a) the intervention is after another major power has intervened, or (b) it widens the war beyond the prior geographic localization. A second form of evidence is process-related. When covert is chosen, do leaders see their form of involvement as likely to influence the risk of large-scale escalation? If overt is chosen, do leaders discount the risk of escalation and cite the operational and symbolic benefits of public, acknowledged involvement? Table 8.1 summarizes the overall strength of support for the cases of intervention in chapters 4–7. Most cases (12 of 16) feature interventions that are consistent in both outcome and process-related evidence.

TABLE 8.1. Theory Support in Intervention Cases

	Case	Dates	Covert/Overt Form	Support for Theory?
Spanish Civil War (1936–1939)	Germany	1936–1939	Covert	Strong
	Italy	1936–1939	Mixed (ground vs. naval)	Mixed and Strong
	Soviet Union	1936–1938	Covert	Strong but over-determined
Korean War (1950–1953)	United States	1950–1953	Overt	Strong
		1951–1953 (China)	Covert	Strong
	Soviet Union	1950–1953	Covert	Strong
	China	1950–1953	Mixed	Mixed
Vietnam War (1964–1968)	United States	1964–1973	Overt	Strong
		1964–1973 (Laos)	Covert	Strong
	China	1965–1969	Covert	Strong
	Soviet Union	1965	Covert	Strong
Afghanistan (1979–1986)	Soviet Union	1979	Covert	Weak
		1979–1988	Overt	Strong
		1982–1987 (Pakistan)	Covert	Strong
	United States	1979 1986	Covert	Strong
		1986	Overt	Mixed

My second research question focuses on whether covert intervention is detected and how detectors react. Table 8.2 summarizes the strength of support for detector cases in chapters 4–7. Support for the theory again comes in two forms: the observed outcome for the detector (i.e., collude vs. expose) and any evidence about the process of choosing that outcome. I find strong but not uniform support for the theory. Some cases of collusion despite widespread exposure are not expected by the theory, though I find an escalation control often drives such efforts.

An additional finding is evidence of cross-conflict learning. Learning-related evidence provides a distinct form of support for the theory. It is not clear what learning alternative logics for secrecy (i.e., operational security; domestic doves) would expect. Most important, the *content* of such learning would differ from what I find in my cases. Chapters 3–7 feature evidence that the emergence and refinement of covert intervention as an escalation-control tool was a product of experience, experimentation, and learning. In the wake of lessons about controlling escalation and its devastation from World War I, interwar leaders experimented with new ways of

TABLE 8.2. Theory Support in Collusion/Exposure Cases

	Covert Interveners	Collusion/Exposure	Support for Theory?
Spanish Civil War (1936–1939)	Germany, Soviet Union, Italy	Collusion for all: interveners and third-party states (UK, France) withheld information and adopted "volunteers" label. Collusion about Italy (ground) unexpected.	Strong (three of four)
Korean War (1950–1953)	Soviet Union, China, United States (China)	US colludes regarding Soviet air intervention. US attempts collusion then exposes Chinese role. Chinese collusion re: US unclear. Collusion about China unexpected.	Mixed to Strong (two of three)
Vietnam War (1964–1968)	United States (Laos), China, Soviet Union	US colludes regarding Soviet, Chinese. Soviets collude regarding US. China exposes US. Collusion by Soviet Union unexpected.	Mixed to Strong (two of three)
Afghanistan (1979–1986)	Soviet Union, United States	US colludes regarding Soviets in Afghanistan (1979) and Pakistan (1981–1985). Soviets expose US. Collusion regarding early Soviet intervention overdetermined.	Mixed to Strong (two of three)

using force that better coped with domestic hawkish pressures and communication problems regarding interest in limited war. The civil war in Spain (chapter 4), for example, unfolded in the shadow of widespread fears of another continental or even global war. Chapter 5 includes evidence showing that US leaders specifically referenced the Spanish precedent to understand Soviet diplomacy, uses of secrecy, and Chinese "volunteers" and undeclared war during the Korean War. Chapter 6 notes that leaders in China and the United States drew close parallels between the deepening Vietnam War and the Korean War precedent, citing specific references to replicating covert air participation (the "Andong Model") when Chinese leaders sought to intervene covertly without triggering a larger war. Finally, in the twilight of the Cold War, Afghanistan hosted interventions by both the Soviet Union and the United States and again featured explicit references to a previous conflict (e.g. Vietnam).

A Cold War Story? US-Occupied Iraq, 2003–2011

Does this basic pattern apply in the modern, post–Cold War world? In some respects, the appeal of covertness and collusion may be higher in a post–Cold War world. The spread of democracy and hybrid regime types would seem to increase leaders' vulnerability to hawkish domestic nationalism. Moreover, challenges in communicating intentions regarding limited war have been present in post–Cold War conflicts like Bosnia and the Syrian Civil War. Indeed, the Obama White House reportedly studied the history of Cold War covert intervention as it deliberated how to intervene in the Syrian Civil War.[1] Moreover, reports of a "shadow war" between Israel and Iran in the Middle East suggest that covert activity and escalation control continue to be linked, even when rivalries are regional.[2]

The US occupation of Iraq and the Iranian covert intervention that followed suggest the links between limited war, covertness, and collusion continue to be relevant. Though conclusions about the case are necessarily preliminary,[3] this section reviews this conflict to illustrate how the claims of the theory travel to a more recent case.

The invasion and overthrow of Saddam Hussein by the United States and its coalition partners in 2003 was followed by a long, bloody struggle for power. The American-led occupation was highly public and soon con-

---

1 Mark Mazzetti, "C.I.A. Study of Covert Aid Fueled Skepticism About Helping Syrian Rebels," *New York Times*, October 14, 2014, http://www.nytimes.com/2014/10/15/us/politics/cia-study-says-arming-rebels-seldom-works.html?nytmobile=0; see also Paul R. Pillar, "Echoes of Afghanistan in Syria," *National Interest*, October 9, 2015, http://nationalinterest.org/blog/paul-pillar/echoes-afghanistan-syria-14050.

2 Nicholas Kulish and Jodi Rudoren, "Murky Plots and Attacks Tied to Shadow War of Iran and Israel," *New York Times*, August 8, 2012, http://www.nytimes.com/2012/08/09/world/middleeast/murky-plots-and-attacks-tied-to-shadow-war-of-iran-and-israel.html.

3 Regarding documentation, primary evidence on the American side is largely unavailable and awaits eventual declassification. Documents on the Iranian side may never be released so insights into the concerns and motives of Tehran are even harder to obtain. Despite these important limitations, the enormous interest in the Iraq War during and after the conflict produced a considerable literature assessing Iran's covert program and even American detection of it through intelligence collection and sharing. The section draws on these materials to make the best inferences possible about the covert side of the conflict and the role of escalation.

fronted active resistance from both Sunni and Shiite groups.[4] Shiite insurgents sought the covert support of Iraq's neighbor, Iran. Tehran advised, trained, and armed Shiite militia participating in the Iraqi insurgency. Coordination between Iran and Shiite militias in Iraq appears to have begun in 2003, immediately following the fall of Hussein and the start of the US-led occupation.[5] Iran's Islamic Revolutionary Guard Corps (IRGC) played the leading role in organizing the program, with its Quds Force specifically managing operations within Iraq.[6] Over time, Iran and its partners refined a covert arms pipeline from sites in Iran to Shiite militias specializing in improvised explosive devices (IEDs) and drawing on Iran's experience smuggling weapons into Iraq under Saddam Hussein's rule.[7] Iran's goals in covertly supporting the Shiite militia are difficult to establish without better access to internal documents.[8] Some outside analysts attribute defensive goals, given the presence of a hostile US military force on its border, while others find Iran's goals more opportunistic and revisionist.[9]

4 An overt intervention is consistent with the theory given that the invasion was localized to Iraq and preceded other external power interventions. What follows focuses on the covert dimension for reasons of space.

5 Joseph Felter and Brian Fishman, "Iranian Strategy in Iraq: Politics and 'Other Means,'" Occasional Paper Series (Combating Terrorism Center at West Point, October 13, 2008), 62–63, https://www.ctc.usma.edu/posts/iranian-strategy-in-iraq-politics-and-%E2%80%9Cother-means%E2%80%9D.

6 Hezbollah likely played a role as well, but I do not address it because information is less reliable. As one account notes, "[s]ome evidence indicated that the Iranian-backed terrorist group Hezbollah was training insurgents to build and use the shaped IEDs, at the urging of the Iranian Revolutionary Guard Corps." Bob Woodward, *State of Denial: Bush at War* (New York: Simon & Schuster, 2007), 414–15.

7 As Gordon and Trainor note, weapons were "brought into Iraq via the same covert arms distribution network that the Quds Force had relied on before 2003 against Saddam, only now the arms were going to units of the Mahdi Army and other Iran-backed militias." Michael R. Gordon and Bernard Trainor, *The Endgame: The Inside Story of the Struggle for Iraq, from George W. Bush to Barack Obama* (New York: Random House LLC, 2012), 152.

8 On Iran's use of covert subversion to further goals in general, see Colin H. Kahl, Melissa Dalton, and Matthew Irvine, "Risk and Rivalry: Iran, Israel and the Bomb" (Washington, DC: Center for New American Security, June 2012), http://www.cnas.org/files/documents/publications/CNAS_RiskandRivalry_Kahl_0.pdf.

9 Kenneth Pollack, *Unthinkable: Iran, the Bomb, and American Strategy* (New York: Simon & Schuster, 2013), 28–29. Menashri, for example, notes the same regional influence-by-proxy initiatives and concludes Iran "diligently sought out opportunities, in areas, or in movements, that seemed ripe to respond to Iranian influence." David Menashri, "Iran's Regional Policy: Between Radicalism and Pragmatism," *Journal of International Affairs* 60, no. 2 (2007): 159.

Iran's role in the Iraqi insurgency was covert. Tehran regularly denied it, as did Shiite militia leadership.[10] Moreover, the practical manifestations of a covert intervention were present. Iran reportedly removed identifying markings from weapons and other equipment (i.e., "where Farsi markings have existed, attempts have been made to remove them, ... This process, known as 'sanitisation,' has no purpose other than to prevent identification").[11] Was the value of covertness, compared to openly aiding the Shiite militias, at least partially informed by escalation dynamics?

Primary sources on Tehran's logic are unavailable, so I make inferences about motives from secondary accounts and publicly available information from American intelligence. One analysis, based in part on detainee interrogation reports, concludes that Iran sought to keep its training and other support for Shiite militia covert because it "offer[ed] Iran a way to influence the rate and scope of violence in Iraq without risking direct involvement."[12] David Crist argues that the covert aid program resulted after Supreme Leader Khamenei consented to a policy that, "where feasible and without risking war, the Quds Force would create trouble for the Americans in order to prevent Iraq from becoming a staging base against Iran."[13] Another analyst linked Iran's program to its broader use of proxy groups and identified a patient and cautious motive: "It does so, at least in part, to manage risk and thereby reduce the potential for escalation. And it seeks to achieve its goals and to prevail over its adversaries through incremental steps and small victories, rather than rapid progress and decisive victories."[14] American intelligence similarly believed that escalation control was a key goal. Michael Gordon and Bernard Trainor recount a Department of Defense strategy document from 2006 that concluded, "Iran sees deniable terrorist operations as a low-cost way to project power while seeking to

10 Menashri, "Iran's Regional Policy"; Sudarsan Raghavan, "Iran Said to Support Shiite Militias in Iraq," *Washington Post*, August 15, 2006, sec. World, http://www.washingtonpost.com/wp-dyn/content/article/2006/08/14/AR2006081400477.html.

11 Quote from a British Defense Intelligence Staff report from 2006, quoted in Gordon and Trainor, *The Endgame*, 152.

12 Felter and Fishman, "Iranian Strategy in Iraq: Politics and 'Other Means,'" 70.

13 David Crist, *The Twilight War: The Secret History of America's Thirty-Year Conflict with Iran* (New York: Penguin, 2012), 466–67.

14 Michael Eisenstadt, "The Strategic Culture of the Islamic Republic of Iran: Religion, Expediency, and Soft Power in an Era of Disruptive Change" (Marine Corps University, expanded and revised edition, November 2015), 15, https://www.usmcu.edu/MES%20Documents/MESM_7_NOV_2015_lo.pdf.

avoid escalation to major conventional warfare."[15] John Negroponte, director of national intelligence, testified in an open hearing that "Tehran's intention to inflict pain on the United States and Iraq has been constrained by its caution to avoid giving Washington an excuse to attack it."[16]

There is some evidence that Iran incorporated lessons from past conflicts in its approach to covert intervention. As noted, Iran relied on smuggling routes that it had used against Saddam Hussein. Moreover, outside observers noted the reference point of the Soviet occupation of Afghanistan. A covert weapons supply approach by Iran was akin to the American weapons program in Afghanistan. It is plausible that such connections were noticed by Iran's key personnel. Prior to becoming Quds Force Chief, Qassem Suleimani personally helped run counter-narcotics operations in Iranian provinces bordering Afghanistan in the period after the US covert aid program against the Soviet Union ended.[17] Following his appointment in the late 1990s, Soleimani oversaw Tehran's "paramilitary and intelligence operations in Afghanistan."[18] Moreover, as Gordon and Trainor note regarding explosively formed penetrators (EFPs):

> Iran, in effect, was employing the same sort of strategy the United States had used to counter the Soviet invasion of Afghanistan. During that conflict, the Reagan administration had funneled Stinger antiaircraft missiles to the mujaheddin, which the fighters used with devastating effect to shoot down Soviet helicopters and constrain the Soviet military's mobility. By sending EFPs to the Shiite militias, the Iranians were helping their proxies contest the ability of the United States coalition to maneuver its armored vehicles around the country.[19]

What about detection and collusion? Iran's role was well known to American intelligence, as expected by the theory. According to intelligence

15 Gordon and Trainor, *The Endgame*, 321.
16 Quoted in Brian Ross, Richard Esposito, and Jill Rackmill, "Iraq Weapons—Made in Iran?," *ABCnews.com*, March 6, 2006, http://abcnews.go.com/Blotter/IraqCoverage/story?id=1692347&page=1.
17 Dexter Filkins, "The Shadow Commander," *New Yorker*, September 30, 2013, http://www.newyorker.com/magazine/2013/09/30/the-shadow-commander; Ali Alfoneh, "Brigadier General Qassem Suleimani: A Biography," American Enterprise Institute, *Middle Eastern Outlook* 1 (January 2011), https://www.aei.org/wp-content/uploads/2011/10/suleimani.pdf.
18 Jay Solomon, *The Iran Wars: Spy Games, Bank Battles, and the Secret Deals That Reshaped the Middle East* (New York: Random House Publishing, 2016), 38.
19 Gordon and Trainor, *The Endgame*, 153.

material cited by Gordon and Trainor, the earliest signs of a covert Iranian role through either the Quds Force or Iran's Ministry of Intelligence and Security reached American intelligence in 2004.[20] As its involvement shifted from training to weapons and then the more deadly EFP-type IEDs, evidence of Iran's role accumulated and was supplemented by intelligence shared by American partners.[21] Israel, for example, reportedly provided important corroboration through technical analysis of similar explosive devices that appeared in Lebanon.[22]

How did the United States respond? In the role of detector, the United States appears to have colluded for several years to help control the scope of the war in Iraq. Washington was concerned about a larger war, given that Iran had options to provide even more deadly weaponry should the covert contest escalate.[23] One high-level American strategic assessment listed the top threat to American interests in Iraq as "Iranian escalation significantly beyond their current level of covert action, sponsorship of insurgents, or intelligence and propaganda activity, which results in overt armed clashes between Coalition and Iranian forces."[24] American leaders generally feared that Iran's covert involvement could grow if confronted and could include more deadly assistance, including provision of missile capabilities that could jeopardize American airpower.[25]

Increasingly deadly attacks therefore put American leaders on the horns of a dilemma. In the first half of 2006, the Bush administration continued to worry that Iran's Quds Force could expand its role. As one former White

20 "Hints of Iranian operations in Iraq, both by the Quds Force and by MOIS, Iran's other intelligence organization, had been showing up since the early days of the war." See Gordon and Trainor, *The Endgame*, 315.

21 Covert Iranian intelligence personnel were also reportedly deployed within Iraq to oversee these programs. See Gordon and Trainor, *The Endgame*, 324–25.

22 According to Gordon and Trainor, "[t]he Israeli military had known about Iranian-supplied EFPs for some time and provided their findings to the Pentagon. Israeli troops operating in Hezbollah territory in southern Lebanon had first encountered one of the bombs in October 1998, according to a detailed technical assessment the Israelis shared with the Americans." Gordon and Trainor, *The Endgame*, 153–54.

23 Gordon and Trainor, *The Endgame*, 318.

24 See description of a high-level advisory team's ("Joint Strategic Assessment Team") report on "political or military shocks that could upend the surge strategy," where escalation with Iran is the first scenario listed. In Gordon and Trainor, *The Endgame*, 318–19.

25 "In Lebanon, Hezbollah had used a variety of other sophisticated weapons against Israeli armor, almost all of it supplied by Iran or Syria, alongside EFPs, and Abizaid feared that the same could become true of Iraq—that the Quds Force could put deadlier ordnance than the EFP in the hands of the Mahdi Army and its offshoots." Gordon and Trainor, *The Endgame*, 317.

House policymaker noted, "for many months American officials were torn between a desire to do something and a wish to avoid confrontation.... When a government is conflicted about what to do, the usual result is inaction."[26] Leaders in Washington were aware that "any assertion of an Iranian contribution to attacks on Americans in Iraq is both politically and diplomatically volatile."[27] As Crist recounts, a Pentagon memo from a senior general argued that "the Iranians were not making as much mischief as they could, so why stir things up by striking back, which might lead to a violent escalation. As long as Iran kept its support to a low level, some senior officers wanted to look the other way."[28] Going public with American intelligence had serious potential escalation implications. Bob Woodward's insider account of the period cites an influential strategy memo prepared by National Security Council official Phillip Zelikow, which links publicity of intelligence and hard-to-control escalation in terms very similar to the theory:

> There was strong evidence that starting in mid-2005, there has been a flow of advanced IED components coming into Iraq from Iran.... It was no longer just the lethality of the weapons that was important, but the significance that the weapons were coming from Iran. Some evidence indicated that the Iranian-backed terrorist group (Hezbollah) was training insurgents to build and use the shaped IEDs, at the urging of the Iranian Revolutionary Guard Corps. That kind of action was arguably an act of war by Iran against the United States. If we start putting out everything we know about these things, Zelikow felt, the administration might well *start a fire it couldn't put out.*[29]

One measure short of public accusation was attempted. The White House reportedly delivered a confidential note to Tehran through the Swiss government in July 2005 noting Iran's support for Shiite militia and the United States' awareness that this was leading to the deaths of American and British service members.[30] This appears to be a rare example of inter-adversary

26 The quotation is from Phillip Zellikow as cited in Gordon and Trainor, *The Endgame*, 319.

27 Michael R. Gordon, "Deadliest Bomb in Iraq Is Made by Iran, U.S. Says," *New York Times*, February 10, 2007, http://www.nytimes.com/2007/02/10/world/middleeast/10weapons.html.

28 Crist, *The Twilight War*, 523.

29 Woodward, *State of Denial*, 414–15. Emphasis added.

30 Michael R. Gordon and Scott Shane, "U.S. Long Worried That Iran Supplied Arms in Iraq," *New York Times*, March 27, 2007, http://www.nytimes.com/2007/03/27/world/middle east/27weapons.html.

private communication about covert dynamics in which the detector (the United States) indicates awareness of the intervener's covert role (Iran). The Bush administration's quiet approach, however, failed to change Iran's behavior, and the situation in Iraq continued to deteriorate.

By 2007, the American approach to Iran's covert role shifted. After a high-profile policy review of Iraq strategy, the White House chose to "surge" American forces and shift the tactics and size of the occupation footprint inside Iraq. As part of this pivot, the Bush administration also shifted to a strategy of public confrontation regarding Iran's covert role. As Gordon and Shane report, this reflected a conscious effort "to put new pressure on Tehran" through both action on the ground and "increasingly public complaints about Iran's role in arming Shiite militias."[31] President Bush's speech rolling out the surge strategy to the American public, for example, cited Iran by name; a US government public statement about Iran's military power described it as giving "strategic and operational guidance to militias and terrorist groups to target US Forces in Iraq."[32] The public relations campaign was accompanied by a strategy of confronting Iran's covert operations within Iraqi territory.[33] Together, these represent a simultaneous strategy shift, exposure, and direct action against a covert meddler.

Until further documentation is available, it is difficult to assess whether this shift from collusion to exposure is consistent with my theory. The escalation risks surrounding Iran and the United States had not meaningfully changed from 2005 to 2007. Accounts of the shift do not cite the role of third-party exposure, though news coverage of Iran's likely role was increasingly common over time. Moreover, available evidence points to exposure as part of an aggressive approach to send a message to Iran as the US doubled down via the surge. This suggests that an issue not addressed by my theory—the scope and ambition of the intervener's strategy—is relevant to exposure and collusion decisions. Exploring how other intervention features influence a detector's decision is thus a promising thread for future research.

Overall, key themes in this book appear in the covert confrontation of the United States by Iran. The initial American intervention to remove Saddam from power was a "first-mover" introduction of major power forces and localized, meaning that initial escalation risks were not severe. Iran's

---

31 Gordon and Shane, "U.S. Long Worried That Iran Supplied Arms in Iraq."

32 "Unclassified Report on the Military Power of Iran," April 2010, p. 3, https://fas.org/man/eprint/dod_iran_2010.pdf.

33 One especially influential raid in December led to the capture of members of Iranian intelligence and Quds Force personnel. See Crist, *The Twilight War*, 527.

leadership appears to have embraced covertness as a useful method for influencing developments in Iraq without creating a provocation and possible war with the United States. As the theory expects, Iran's major power rival detected its role early in the war. For two years (2004–2006), American leaders were publicly silent about this covert intervention and relied on private diplomacy to address it. According to accounts drawn from internal debates, this collusive response was a function of Washington's desire to avoid converting the Iraq war into a larger regional one. The 2007 exposure of Iran is less consistent with the theory and coincided with a strategic shift to the "surge" in late 2006. Overall, the case suggests that covert intervention remains a critical tool, detection via intelligence continues to give major powers a privileged view of backstage actions, and escalation dynamics help to make sense of covertness and collusion in a post–Cold War, post–9/11 setting.

Extensions

CYBERWAR

The idea of covertness and collusion as escalation-control tactics can be extended to other domains not addressed in the empirical chapters. Offensive military operations in cyberspace are one new domain in which issues of covertness and collusion are ripe for theorization. Indeed, historical comparisons between cyberthreats and cyberattacks, on the one hand, and the Cold War, on the other, are already common. One recent study of escalation dynamics in cyberwarfare found promise in "translating sources of Cold War instability to cyberspace."[34] Yet thus far, deriving lessons from nuclear deterrence is far more common than looking to lessons from covert conflict, at least in open-source publications.[35]

In the conceptual language of my theory, Internet-based attacks take place in a new kind of backstage, a segregated cyberspace where visibility is limited and where states and non-state actors can engage in coercive and other operations. Cyber weapons are not "overtly violent."[36] If not broadly exposed by states or non-state groups, a covert cyberattack can allow its

34 Martin C. Libicki, *Crisis and Escalation in Cyberspace*, MG-1215-AF (RAND Corporation, 2012), 123–32, http://www.rand.org/pubs/monographs/MG1215.html.

35 Mariarosaria Taddeo, "On the Risks of Relying on Analogies to Understand Cyber Conflicts," *Minds and Machines* 26, no. 4 (December 1, 2016): 317–21; Patrick Cirenza, "The Flawed Analogy Between Nuclear and Cyber Deterrence," *Bulletin of the Atomic Scientists*, February 22, 2016, https://thebulletin.org/flawed-analogy-between-nuclear-and-cyber-deterrence9179.

36 Lucas Kello, "The Meaning of the Cyber Revolution: Perils to Theory and Statecraft," *International Security* 38, no. 2 (October 1, 2013): 8.

sponsor to lower the risk that domestic hawkish actors will react and potentially constrain the target. Moreover, my theory suggests that the choice to conduct an action in cyberspace rather than alternative venues can be seen as an observable indicator of the attacker's resolve (it is doing more than inaction) and restraint (it is stopping short of more visible forms of kinetic attack). These insights are important because, as Jon Lindsay notes, IR theory is not traditionally well-equipped to understand the deniable dimension of cyber-coercion.[37] Moreover, an adversary observing its rival *limiting* its attacks to the cyber realm can infer that its rival continues to prefer keeping the rivalry "under the radar." This embodies both mechanisms developed in chapter 2.

The theory also implicates detection and reactions to cyberattacks. The book provides tools for thinking through a detector's options and considerations. Much has been written about the "attribution problem" in cyberspace, in which the true identity of the sponsor of a cyberattack is difficult to establish.[38] Yet major powers and others are investing significant resources in countering anonymity via cyber-forensics.[39] The theory suggests that successful forensic analysis should be followed by careful deliberation about how exposure and collusion might impact escalation. Remaining silent about culpability for an attack and exposing it are two very different options, as the American publicity of intelligence about Russian covert election meddling demonstrates. My theory and findings suggest that controlling risks of large-scale escalation can provide powerful incentives for detectors to stay silent. In contrast, lack of such escalation risk, or the exposure of a sponsor's identity by third-party non-state actors, should make exposure more attractive as a tool to diplomatically isolate and punish the sponsor. This is one way to interpret American exposure of Russian covert operations during the 2016 presidential election. Exposure was chosen only when the Obama administration had decided on a concrete set of proportional responses and after significant evidence of Russian culpability was already in the public sphere. The Obama administration also reportedly

---

37 Jon R. Lindsay, "Tipping the Scales: The Attribution Problem and the Feasibility of Deterrence Against Cyberattack," *Journal of Cybersecurity* 1, no. 1 (September 1, 2015): 53–67.

38 Martin C. Libicki, *Cyberdeterrence and Cyberwar* (Santa Monica, CA: RAND Corporation, 2009); Thomas Rid, "Cyber War Will Not Take Place," *Journal of Strategic Studies* 35, no. 1 (2012): 5–32; Jon R. Lindsay, "Stuxnet and the Limits of Cyber Warfare," *Security Studies* 22, no. 3 (July 1, 2013): 365–404.

39 As Lindsay notes, "the investigatory process can look to technical forensics as well as other intelligence sources and situational context, expanding the clues about means, motive, and opportunity that are available." Lindsay, "Tipping the Scales."

used covert cyber-retaliation in ways intended to be detected by Russia but not by wider audiences.[40]

In short, cyber-technology may function like the invention of flight or submarine warfare. As I describe in chapter 3, new technology can create opportunities for states to use force anonymously. These create new domains for covert activity. Like aerial bombing and subsurface naval attacks, cyber has created a domain within which states can influence a crisis or conflict without acknowledgment and with potentially limited exposure. This mode of covert activity likely has unique features, due in part to the regular presence of non-state actors (e.g., firms; hackers) on the cyber backstage. Yet cyberspace may also be a kind of new backstage in modern war that shows how technological change both enables and constrains states' capacity to act covertly.

CIVIL WAR AND TERRORISM

The theory can also be extended to make sense of some dynamics that arise in civil wars and terrorism. As noted in chapter 1, escalation control is but one example of a broader class of situations where collusive secrecy can emerge. I argue that mutual silence may often result any time individuals, firms, or governments can act secretly, observe one another doing so, and share fear of a mutually damaging outcome that is influenced by exposure dynamics. Political campaigns, for example, may include candidates that collusively hide compromising information due to the fear that the tit-for-tat exposure of opposition research might endanger both candidates.

The extension to civil conflict and terrorism is fairly straightforward and a promising direction for future research. Rebel and government groups may violently oppose one another but share a desire to avoid international criminal liability. This could lead them to jointly conduct a frontstage performance of civil war within the bounds of international law. Both sides might then stay silent about known atrocities of the other side, given that exposure would increase the chances of both sides incurring legal culpability.[41] The process of attributing and claiming terror attacks could have close

40 See description of deliberations and the response in Greg Miller, Ellen Nakashima, and Adam Entous, "Obama's Secret Struggle to Punish Russia for Putin's Election Assault," *Washington Post*, June 23, 2017, https://www.washingtonpost.com/graphics/2017/world/national-security /obama-putin-election-hacking/?tid=a_inl&utm_term=.e571dfl15cfa.

41 On denial and atrocities in post-conflict recovery, see Stanley Cohen, *States of Denial: Knowing about Atrocities and Suffering* (Cambridge, UK: Polity, 2001).

parallels. Both the targeted state and the perpetrating terror group might be drawn to a pseudo-collaborative process of restraint in attributing/claiming terror attacks. If both sides seek to avoid a major escalation of violence, and if both know that domestic constituents might intensify constraints when attacks are publicly confirmed (e.g., intra-regime pressure on leaders of the targeted state; intra-organizational pressure from within a terrorist organization), then collusion to hide and not acknowledge attacks could emerge.[42]

Other components of the theory could have implications beyond these domains. The distinct effects of official acknowledgment implicate other kinds of "open secrets" in international politics, as in the debate over acknowledging Israel's nuclear arsenal.[43] The basic intuition that non-acknowledgment makes inaction easier suggests a rationale for how leaders react to exposed secret trade negotiations. If states A and B negotiate controversial tariff reductions in private but have those concessions leaked, they may find non-acknowledgment a useful "fig leaf" to facilitate inaction. Future research could investigate how the acknowledgment by other bodies, such as multilateral organizations or influential major powers, influences postwar outcomes. For example, scholars could evaluate the impact of official UN investigations that gather information and formally acknowledge chemical weapons use in Syria.

Three Additional Questions

WHAT ABOUT THE INITIAL CHOICE TO INTERVENE?

My theory intentionally makes minimal assumptions about why major powers intervene in the first place. I make the wager that the value-added of a sustained focus on the *form* of intervention (covert vs. overt) and *reactions* to that choice (collusion vs. exposure) outweighs the benefits of specificity and analytical completeness. In practice, however, escalation and other dynamics are relevant to considerations about whether to use force in the first place. For example, the effectiveness of secrecy can influence whether an intervention is worth undertaking at all. Although it was a

42 Max Abrahms and Justin Conrad, "The Strategic Logic of Credit Claiming: A New Theory for Anonymous Terrorist Attacks," *Security Studies* 26, no. 2 (April 3, 2017): 279–304; Erin M. Kearns, Brendan Conlon, and Joseph K. Young, "Lying About Terrorism," *Studies in Conflict & Terrorism* 37, no. 5 (May 4, 2014): 422–39.

43 See discussion in both: Avner Cohen, *Israel and the Bomb* (New York: Columbia University Press, 1998); Avner Cohen, *The Worst-Kept Secret: Israel's Bargain with the Bomb* (New York: Columbia University Press, 2010).

peacetime operation, it is plausible that leaders' willingness to approve a covert operation to kill Osama bin Laden in Pakistan was influenced by the feasibility of effective secrecy. This suggests that, in practice, form and the initial decision to intervene are not independent. A related concern is se-lection effects. Although the book includes variation on the dependent variable (i.e., covert and overt cases), it analyzes only wars in which major powers have selected into caring about a local war and, for interveners, undertaking a foreign military intervention. Does this bias the inferences I make about the importance of escalation dynamics? More broadly, what im-plications, if any, does my theory have for the initial decision to intervene?

The theory and findings have two such implications. One is a by-product of my claims about escalation dynamics and the sequence of outside inter-ventions. I argue that escalation risks are severe for interventions that fol-low an initial intervention because the risk of a direct combat encounter rises dramatically. This suggests that there is a kind of first-mover advantage that is produced by the escalation-control problems I theorize. For exam-ple, an enabling condition for Soviet leaders in 1979 (chapter 7) or Ameri-can leaders in 1964 (chapter 6) to intervene overtly was the absence of other major powers from the local theater. Going in publicly allowed both to optimize the size and scope of intervention. In doing so, however, it pre-sented a new reality—a kind of a fait accompli—to other major powers.[44] The chapters describe how subsequent interventions were channeled to the covert realm to control escalation risks; yet doing so created sacrifices in scope, effectiveness, and public signaling. The theory therefore suggests that major powers will find additional incentives to intervene in the first place if escalation-related concerns are present and they would be the first major power to intervene. Put differently, escalation dynamics provide a good reason for early overt entry, or a kind of "rush to the entrance."

The book's findings also suggest that covertness creates new opportu-nities for intervention even for interveners that are not the first in. That is, escalation-control problems led to the refinement of covert forms of involvement; these, in turn, make it more feasible for major powers to in-tervene than a world in which the only choice was overt or no intervention. Removing the covert alternative leaves major powers with a stark choice. If forced to consider only these two options, many major powers might balk

44 A related point about red lines of conflict and fait accompli is developed more fully in Daniel Altman, "Advancing without Attacking: The Strategic Game around the Use of Force," *Security Studies* 27, no. 1 (2018): 58–88.

TABLE 8.3. Two Implications for Initial Intervention Decisions

Implication	Form of Intervention	Logic
First-mover advantage	Overt	Escalation dynamics make subsequent overt interventions dangerous. An initial overt intervener thus has scope and logistics advantages over any later covert interveners. If escalation-control goals are shared, moving first forces others to choose between no intervention and covert intervention.
More options, more interventions	Covert	Covert intervention adds a third option with escalation-control advantages. A choice of no intervention vs. overt intervention will lead major power to choose the former more often. Covert intervention allows influence in a local war and escalation control, expanding the acceptability of intervening in the first place.

at intervention, at least in part due to the threat of large-scale escalation. Techniques that limit public knowledge and avoid official acknowledgment allow a *via media* that balances the relevant tradeoffs. Interveners now can have moderate (but not strong) influence on the local conflict and retain moderate (but not perfect) escalation control. Thus, one implication of the theory is that the ready availability of covert intervention facilitates foreign meddling compared to a world where such options were not available. Table 8.3 summarizes these two implications for the initial decision to intervene.

Regarding selection bias, the points in table 8.3 suggest that the theory sheds light on the self-selection process. The book argues that escalation features lead to a self-selection process in which overt interventions appear only in conflicts that lack key escalation features. Otherwise, covertness is the dominant modality. This raises difficult questions for past studies that have excluded analysis of covert intervention. Conclusions based only on overt intervention will misleadingly underplay escalation factors precisely because the subset of interventions that reflect acute escalation concerns are not observed (i.e., covert). The intervener's concern for reputation or the role of individual leaders' beliefs may then loom as critical explanatory variables even though escalation considerations play a prior role in determining whether an intervention is overt or covert in the first place.

WHAT ABOUT MISTAKES AND EXPLOITATION?

Two problems regarding inferences have not been addressed in depth: mistakes and exploitation. The communication mechanism of the theory suggests a best-case scenario in which covert tools and collusive responses mutually support communication about limited war. Although my empirical findings suggest that this is common, readers may understandably wonder about the intrusion of a messier reality. China's early covert role in the Korean War in October and November 1950 (chapter 5) highlights these issues. American leaders detected but misunderstood China's reason for covertness. This mistake led the United States and its allies to fall victim to a large and effective surprise counterattack. This raises the question: Do major powers make mistakes in interpreting backstage behavior? And, if mistakes are possible, can covertness create new ways to exploit a rival?

Figure 8.1 sheds some light on the issue of mistakes. The American confusion in late 1950 resulted from a combination of factors. On the one hand, large-scale escalation was a sensible thing for China to fear and covertness could reasonably be expected to reduce domestic hawks' influence. On the other hand, American and Chinese leaders had very little prior experience

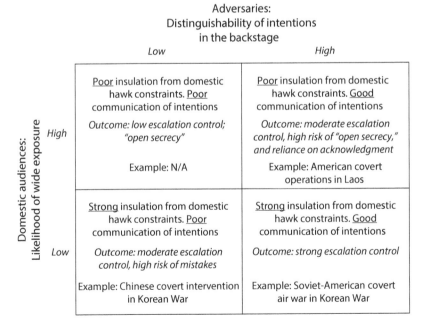

FIGURE 8.1. Conditions influencing escalation-control mechanisms.

in crises and none in limited war. The Chinese Communist Party's victory in the Chinese civil war was only a year or two old. Moreover, the two sides lacked good private communication channels to clarify their intentions akin to the Non-Intervention Committee during the Spanish Civil War. This is the lower left cell in figure 8.1.

Figure 8.1 shows that mistaken inferences and exploitation tend to arise in situations where distinguishability is low but domestic audiences can still be effectively excluded. When a detector has difficulty understanding a covert intervener's intentions despite witnessing backstage involvement, room for deception and misinterpretation is opened up. China in the first month of its entry into the Korean War therefore exploited the fact that the United States and China had no track record of covert rivalry and lacked a venue in which such activity could be clarified. This allowed China to "impersonate" a cautious, escalation-averse covert intervener and invited Washington's corresponding (but mistaken) inference. China's involvement appeared to American leaders as escalation-driven precisely because domestic audiences were, in that one-month window, effectively excluded from seeing backstage behavior. This suggests that a background understanding that limited war can motivate covert involvement can help an intervener seeking to surprise its rival.

WHAT ABOUT SOCIAL MEDIA AND LEAKS?

A final question is whether new technology has obviated secrecy's relevance. Leaks, smart phones, and social media have endangered states' ability to keep secrets and, presumably, to find value in acting covertly or colluding. Some analysts have speculated that such changes harbor an "end of secrecy" and a global version of "extreme glasnost."[45] For example, unauthorized leaks and citizen reporting via social media seem to be exposing covert behavior with some regularity. This was dramatized by the citizen bystander in Pakistan who broadcast a blow-by-blow account of helicopter noise and explosions during the raid that killed Osama bin Laden.[46] Can states really

---

[45] Ann M. Florini, "The End of Secrecy," in *Power and Conflict in the Age of Transparency*, ed. Bernard I. Finel and Kristin M. Lord (New York: Palgrave, 2002); Evgeny Morozov, "WikiLeaks and the Perils of Extreme Glasnost," *New Perspectives Quarterly* 28, no. 1 (January 1, 2011): 7–11.

[46] "Man Inadvertently Live Tweets Osama Bin Laden Raid," *Forbes*, May 2, 2011, http://www.forbes.com/sites/parmyolson/2011/05/02/man-inadvertently-live-tweets-osama-bin-laden-raid/.

hide any aspect of war? Put differently, what are the implications if the backstage has become more porous and visible?

Two points are worth making in this regard. First, one reason for caution is that states will adapt. Leaks and the organizational attempt to prevent them are a classic cat-and-mouse game.[47] What about social media? States are also adapting to public relations in an age of Twitter and Facebook. Moreover, adaptation and innovation are what led states to the development of different forms of covert intervention in the first place, as I develop in chapter 3. Secrecy and non-acknowledgment of external military involvement were a response to legal and political changes following World War I, which boosted the dangers of leaders' constraints and misunderstandings while increasing the destructiveness of war. If leaking or social media reduce states' confidence about secrecy effectiveness, they may develop new bureaucratic arrangements that build better reliability, work with other local partners rather than act directly, or cut out any partner that is likely to leak. If a given war is saturating coverage and discussion on social media, an outside power can limit their covert role to places like the air, sea, or cyber, where exposure risks are limited to state-based intelligence detection. If providing weaponry, covertly intervening states may limit the weaponry they send to "scrubbed" versions that cannot serve as evidence of involvement on Instagram or Twitter.

Second, the theoretical framework and empirical findings in this book suggest one way that states may adapt: shifting to open secrecy. The book is explicitly structured to address the practical reality of secrecy's exposure and develops theoretical tools for understanding how non-acknowledgment has political use even after wide exposure. As I described in chapter 2, general exposure reduces but does not eliminate how covertness and collusion can limit war. Like the Chinese in the Korean War and the Americans in Afghanistan, a widely visible covert intervention can still constitute a clear indicator of interest in limited war. This is one interpretation of Russia's "volunteer" intervention in Ukraine. Russian soldiers and equipment were exposed in Facebook posts and other social media.[48] Yet Putin still seemed

47 David E. Pozen, "The Leaky Leviathan: Why the Government Condemns and Condones Unlawful Disclosures of Information," *Harvard Law Review* 127, no. 2 (December 2013): 512–635.

48 Dmitry Volchek and Claire Bigg, "Ukrainian Bloggers Use Social Media to Track Russian Soldiers Fighting in East," *The Guardian*, June 3, 2015, sec. World news, https://www.the guardian.com/world/2015/jun/03/bloggers-social-media-russian-soldiers-fighting-in-ukraine; Paul Szoldra, "A Russian Soldier's Instagram Posts May Be the Clearest Indication of Moscow's

to find value in denying Russian involvement, however implausible. One explanation is that Russia believed this was a useful gesture indicating Moscow's limited aims to the United States and NATO, which would reduce the risk that Russian meddling would prompt a larger crisis or war. The broader implication is that greater risks of involuntary exposure may simply cause leaders to shift their judgment of covert intervention away from an assumption of effective secrecy to assessing its residual value even after discovery. This suggests that understanding the specific dynamics surrounding open secrecy and official (non-)acknowledgment is *more* rather than less important in a world of WikiLeaks and Twitter.

Implications for Policy

The theory and empirical findings have several implications for policy. A first set derives from dynamics present in intervention scenarios where covertness and collusion can arise. For example, the book suggests that policymakers need to attend to the multicausal nature of conflict escalation and the imperfect control they can exert. Policymakers and intelligence analysts should specifically incorporate the problems of domestic hawkish pressure and reliable communication about limited war as they assess other major powers and decide on actions. Another broad implication is the manipulability of domestic political constraints. Leaders that deploy covertness and respond with collusion can maintain the ability to act with restraint while saving face, both at home and for their adversaries. More broadly, the theory and empirics show the danger of public relations strategies that sharpen provocations and humiliate adversaries. Finally, policymakers should be attentive to the varied forms of covert intervention. Just as American leaders anticipated different kinds of covert assistance during the Vietnam War, analysts of the civil war in Syria or Russian involvement in Ukraine should be careful to attend to various options between "no intervention" and "overt intervention."

FOR INTERVENERS

Another set of policy implications are relevant to major powers considering how to intervene. One basic implication of the book is that such decisions must account for escalation-control problems that derive from domestic

---

Involvement in East Ukraine," *Business Insider*, July 31, 2014, http://www.businessinsider.com /russian-soldier-ukraine-2014-7.

politics and inter-adversary communication. Covert intervention should be seen as a useful way to inform one audience (i.e., an adversary likely to detect it) and keep other audiences in the dark (i.e., domestic hawkish elites). Identifying these audiences and effects is important in designing an optimal form and scope of intervention. Second, and related, intervening states should expect any covert intervention to be detected by major powers and select it only with this accounted for. The flipside of the difficulty in effectively concealing covert intervention is important: leaders should carefully assess the risks and benefits of wider exposure. Although collusion can keep a covert intervention on the backstage, exposure is also a possibility. Leaders should expect collusion only when other major powers share escalation concerns and when the likelihood of exposure by other, non-state sources is low. Third, leaders weighing intervention options should attend to issues of timing and location. As chapter 2 develops and the cases demonstrate, order and location of intervention matters. Overt intervention is best suited to an intervention that is the first by a major power (i.e., "first-mover advantage") and that is narrowly tailored to the existing locale of conflict. Finally, intervening leaders should understand the distinct implications of acknowledgment and the signaling value that may remain even after wide exposure. Even a covert intervention that becomes an "open secret" can still indicate deference to the limits of a war and an interest in maintaining those limits.

FOR DETECTORS

A third set of implications applies to detector states. A key theme in the book is that leaders that detect covert activity by other major powers can use secrecy and non-acknowledgment to retain control over the escalation process. Observers of covert intervention should form policy knowing that escalation risks may be decisively influenced by a decision to publicize. The cases therefore suggest that detectors should exercise care in how they use intelligence, especially when wider exposure by non-state actors has not occurred. More cautionary tales exist in the cases for detectors. One is the danger of misinterpretation. As I detail in chapter 5 on the Korean War, a major power like China can mimic an escalation-cautious covert intervener. American and British observers detected Chinese personnel covertly entering combat operations but interpreted the absence of publicity as an interest, like their own, in limiting the war. This enabled China to complete preparations for a large surprise attack and successfully execute it. For contemporary policymakers, this shows the importance of attending to the multiple potential logics for covertness and the risks of mistakes, especially when adversaries lack previous experience and opportunities for private diplomatic clarifications. Finally, detectors should also note the distinction between knowledge and acknowledgment effects. The recurring role of putative "volunteers" in the cases underscores that interventions can be visible but not officially confirmed through devices like volunteerism. The recurrence of "volunteer" as a cover for visible-but-unacknowledged military interventions is a possibility of which detectors must remain aware, especially given its recent reappearance in Russia's intervention in Eastern Ukraine and Iran's citation of "volunteers" in Syria.[49]

Implications for Scholarship

The book has implications for several research areas in IR. I cluster my discussion around three themes: the study of secrecy, the study of war, and topics and debates that transcend both, such as the nature of domestic politics and reputation.

STUDYING SECRECY

The theory and empirical findings contribute to growing scholarly interest in secrecy-related themes in IR. As noted in chapter 1, research in the past decade has addressed secrecy in bargaining, prewar crises, military operations, elite decision-making, and alliances.[50] Research has also focused on

49 Hossein Bastani, "Iran's Growing Role in Syria's War," *BBC News*, October 20, 2015, sec. Middle East, http://www.bbc.com/news/world-middle-east-34572756; Michael Kofman et al., "Lessons from Russia's Operations in Crimea and Eastern Ukraine," 2017, https://www.rand .org/pubs/research_reports/RR1498.html.

50 David Stasavage, "Open-Door or Closed-Door? Transparency in Domestic and International Bargaining," *International Organization* 58, no. 04 (2004): 667–703; Keren Yarhi-Milo, "Tying Hands Behind Closed Doors: The Logic and Practice of Secret Reassurance," *Security Studies* 22, no. 3 (2013): 405–35; Jonathan N. Brown, "Immovable Positions: Public Acknowledgment and Bargaining in Military Basing Negotiations," *Security Studies* 23, no. 2 (April 3, 2014): 258–92; Jonathan N. Brown, "The Sound of Silence: Power, Secrecy, and International Audiences in US Military Basing Negotiations," *Conflict Management and Peace Science* 31, no. 4 (September 1, 2014): 406–31; Corneliu Bjola and Stuart Murray, *Secret Diplomacy: Concepts, Contexts and Cases* (New York: Routledge, 2016); Shawn L. Ramirez, "Mediation in the Shadow of an Audience: How Third Parties Use Secrecy and Agenda-Setting to Broker Settlements," *Journal of Theoretical Politics*, September 25, 2017, 0951629817729227. On crisis bargaining, see Shuhei Kurizaki, "Efficient Secrecy: Public Versus Private Threats in Crisis Diplomacy," *American Political Science Review* 101, no. 03 (2007): 543–58; Jonathan N. Brown and Anthony S. Mar-

covert operations, deception and lying, and intelligence.[51] One of the book's contributions is developing a distinct escalation-focused understanding of what states do in the covert realm. I argue that covert activity during war is influenced by a widely shared desire to avoid large-scale escalation. Covertness and collusion can be means for controlling and thereby limiting war. Although these do not always dominate decision-making, my cases suggest that these factors often lead outside powers to select covert forms and give rise to otherwise puzzling collusion by others. Escalation considerations also help make sense of the reverse response, providing useful insights into when overt intervention and exposure are most attractive. This escalation-driven pattern differs most significantly from the typical view that secrecy is the product of competitive hoarding of information, or

cum, "Avoiding Audience Costs: Domestic Political Accountability and Concessions in Crisis Diplomacy," *Security Studies* 20 (April 2011): 141–70. On operational surprise in war, see Adam Meirowitz and Anne E. Sartori, "Strategic Uncertainty as a Cause of War," *Quarterly Journal of Political Science* 3, no. 4 (December 2008): 327–52; Branislav L. Slantchev, "Feigning Weakness," *International Organization* 64, no. 3 (2010): 357–88; David Lindsey, "Military Strategy, Private Information, and War," *International Studies Quarterly* 59, no. 4 (December 1, 2015): 629–4; Austin Carson, "Facing Off and Saving Face: Covert Intervention and Escalation Management in the Korean War," *International Organization* 70, no. 01 (2016): 103–31; Austin Carson and Keren Yarhi-Milo, "Covert Communication: The Intelligibility and Credibility of Signaling in Secret," *Security Studies* 26, no. 1 (January 2, 2017): 124–56. On elite decision-making, see Elizabeth N. Saunders, "War and the Inner Circle: Democratic Elites and the Politics of Using Force," *Security Studies* 24, no. 3 (July 3, 2015): 466–501. On alliances, see Jeffrey Ritter, "'Silent Partners' and Other Essays on Alliance Politics" (Dissertation, Harvard University, 2004); Muhammet Bas and Robert Schub, "Mutual Optimism as a Cause of Conflict: Secret Alliances and Conflict Onset," *International Studies Quarterly* 60, no. 3 (September 1, 2016): 552–64.

51 Alexander B. Downes and Mary Lauren Lilley, "Overt Peace, Covert War?: Covert Intervention and the Democratic Peace," *Security Studies* 19, no. 2 (2010): 266; Lindsey A. O'Rourke, *Covert Regime Change: America's Secret Cold War* (Ithaca, NY: Cornell University Press, 2018); Michael Poznansky, "Stasis or Decay? Reconciling Covert War and the Democratic Peace," *International Studies Quarterly*, March 1, 2015; Michael F. Joseph and Michael Poznansky, "Media Technology, Covert Action, and the Politics of Exposure," *Journal of Peace Research*, November 16, 2017, 0022343317731508. On deception, see John M. Schuessler, "The Deception Dividend: FDR's Undeclared War," *International Security* 34, no. 4 (2010): 133–65; John J. Mearsheimer, *Why Leaders Lie: The Truth about Lying in International Politics* (New York: Oxford University Press, 2011); Dan Reiter, "Democracy, Deception, and Entry into War," *Security Studies* 21, no. 4 (2012): 594–623; John M. Schuessler, *Deceit on the Road to War: Presidents, Politics, and American Democracy* (Ithaca, NY: Cornell University Press, 2015); Erik Gartzke and Jon R. Lindsay, "Weaving Tangled Webs: Offense, Defense, and Deception in Cyberspace," *Security Studies* 24, no. 2 (April 3, 2015): 316–48. On intelligence, see Joshua Rovner, *Fixing the Facts: National Security and the Politics of Intelligence* (Ithaca, NY: Cornell University Press, 2011); Robert Jervis, *Why Intelligence Fails: Lessons from the Iranian Revolution and the Iraq War* (Ithaca, NY: Cornell University Press, 2011); James Igoe Walsh, *The International Politics of Intelligence Sharing* (New

what I refer to as an operational security logic. Yet it also has implications for scholarship on the domestic origins of secrecy. Rather than treating domestic actors as a source of dovish constraint, the theoretical logic and empirical evidence are reminders that secrecy can be influenced by leaders' desire to control hawkish nationalism and rallying effects both in their own backyard and within that of their interlocutors.

Yet my claims about limited war and escalation are specific applications of a few broader departures from how secrecy dynamics are typically conceptualized in world politics, as I described in chapter 2. My theory embraces the practical reality that secrecy is subject to different kinds of exposure, that secrecy can have a stabilizing effect for social encounters, and that non-acknowledgment may have impacts distinct from knowledge manipulation. These are the foundation for the more distinctive claims in the theory. Most important, they help make sense of two puzzles: the emergence of mutual rather than exclusively selfish secrecy even among adversaries (collusion), and the utility of secrecy even after widespread exposure (open secrecy).

The book therefore invites future scholarship to attend more carefully to exposure dynamics. Doing so can reveal intriguing and non-obvious mechanisms and outcomes. In addition to the cooperative maintenance of secrecy, my findings support the basic idea that secrecy can communicate. Covert activity can simultaneously express resolve, restraint, and other foreign policy goals and interests, given that it tends to be observable to other major powers and their robust intelligence investments. Most existing work has understandably focused on secrecy as a modality that *avoids* communicating to certain audiences. This book joins with others in suggesting that minor and major powers may use covert tools to communicate a variety of messages to a variety of kinds of states.[52] The theory and findings also illustrate the value of dedicated research into the ways in which states tacitly and explicitly coordinate in hiding events. I find collusive secrecy in unlikely contexts, where adversaries compete but still display some degree of

---

York: Columbia University Press, 2013); Keren Yarhi-Milo, "In the Eye of the Beholder: How Leaders and Intelligence Communities Assess the Intentions of Adversaries," *International Security* 38, no. 1 (2013): 7–51; Keren Yarhi-Milo, *Knowing the Adversary: Leaders, Intelligence, and Assessment of Intentions in International Relations* (Princeton, NJ: Princeton University Press, 2014); Jonathan N. Brown and Alex Farrington, "Democracy and the Depth of Intelligence Sharing: Why Regime Type Hardly Matters," *Intelligence and National Security* 32, no. 1 (January 2, 2017): 68–84.

52 See also Carson and Yarhi-Milo, "Covert Communication."

cooperation in concealing explosive aspects of war, from interwar Spain to the US occupation of Iraq. Future research may address other cooperative forms of secrecy production and maintenance among adversaries, allies, and other groupings of states. Finally, the book shows the promise of exploring non-knowledge effects of secrecy in other empirical domains. Although I focus on the distinction between *knowledge about* and *acknowledgment of* state behavior, future research could assess the symbolic and other effects acting secretly may entail. For example, in an alliance, channeling cooperative state behavior to the backstage may be symbolic evidence of a continued commitment to joint action. Focusing exclusively on the audiences kept in the dark by such secret alliance activity would overlook its broader political effect.

STUDYING WAR

The book's insights into secrecy also shed a different light on key themes in scholarship on war. Two are especially important. First, the book provides a different view of the role of information in war. A wide range of research in IR has treated information in war as a strategic resource wielded against rival states to secure tactical or strategic advantage.[53] Deception and secrecy have been treated as factors that make mutual optimism more likely and war more common. The implication is that secrecy is a plague on peace that tends to lead to unnecessary war and feeds escalation.[54] More information is better for avoiding the most costly of wars.

Analyzing escalation dynamics in the covert sphere provides a different view. Secrecy's escalation-control function suggests that hiding information

53 E.g., James D. Fearon, "Rationalist Explanations for War," *International Organization* 49, no. 3 (Summer 1995): 379–414; Branislav L. Slantchev, "Feigning Weakness," *International Organization* 64, no. 3 (2010): 357–88.

54 For a catalog of problems created by secrecy, see Stephen Van Evera, *Causes of War: Power and the Roots of Conflict* (Ithaca, NY: Cornell University Press, 1999), 138–42; on misrepresentation and bargaining failures that lead to war, see Fearon, "Rationalist Explanations for War"; on statecraft during a crisis that reveals information and deters war, see Thomas Schelling, *The Strategy of Conflict* (Cambridge, MA: Harvard University Press, 1960); on costly signals to reveal information and avoid mutually destructive war, see James D. Fearon, "Signaling Foreign Policy Interests: Tying Hands versus Sinking Costs," *Journal of Conflict Resolution* 41, no. 1 (February 1997): 68–90; on information revealed through warfighting, see Robert Powell, "Bargaining and Learning While Fighting," *American Journal of Political Science* 48, no. 2 (April 1, 2004): 344–61; an overview of the "more information is better" view of the bargaining model of war in general is Dan Reiter, "Exploring the Bargaining Model of War," *Perspectives on Politics* 1, no. 01 (2003): 27–43.

can help *limit* war and that more public information can *fuel* war escalation.[55] To be clear, my theory also suggests that covertness and collusion help adversaries reach a better understanding; this is a "more information is better" story *among adversaries*. Yet my findings suggest that information about limit-crossing activity that is visible to publics can fuel domestic hawkish constraints and make action-reaction escalation cycles more acute. This suggests a distinction between information that is not just *common knowledge* among adversaries (i.e., observable covert activity) and information that is *public knowledge* (i.e., overt activity or widely exposed covert activity). This book suggests that the former helps to keep war limited, the latter fuels escalation, and thus curtailment of public knowledge can help control escalation dangers. This, in turn, produces an interesting and distinct implication for sources of transparency. The theory suggests that institutions like democracy and international organizations—often praised as sources of valuable information that help to avoid costly war—can have an important downside.[56] My theory suggests that such institutions could undermine the ability of major powers to manipulate information to control escalatory pressures and communicate their interest in limited war.

A second implication for scholars of war is about the study of escalation. The book highlights the problem of how wars escalate and how leaders assert control to limit them. The study of limited war and escalation largely fell out of fashion in IR after the end of the Cold War, when the specter of global nuclear conflict seemed to abate. Most broadly, this book joins a growing number of scholars interested in reviving the study of escalation dynamics and limited war to address topics like the rise of China.[57] The book also offers specific insights regarding limited war. It elevates the role

---

55 See also Bernard I. Finel and Kristin M. Lord, "The Surprising Logic of Transparency," *International Studies Quarterly* 43, no. 2 (June 1999): 315–39.

56 On the value of publicity in threats, see James D. Fearon, "Domestic Political Audiences and the Escalation of International Disputes," *American Political Science Review* 88, no. 3 (September 1994): 577–92; on the coercive boost from more transparent democratic institutions, see Kenneth A. Schultz, *Democracy and Coercive Diplomacy* (New York: Cambridge University Press, 2001); Dan Lindley, *Promoting Peace with Information: Transparency as a Tool of Security Regimes* (Princeton, NJ: Princeton University Press, 2007).

57 See, for example, Forrest E. Morgan et al., *Dangerous Thresholds: Managing Escalation in the 21st Century* (Santa Clara, CA: RAND Publishing, 2008); Avery Goldstein, "First Things First: The Pressing Danger of Crisis Instability in U.S.-China Relations," *International Security* 37, no. 4 (April 1, 2013): 49–89; Alex Weisiger, *Logics of War: Explanations for Limited and Unlimited Conflicts* (Ithaca, NY: Cornell University Press, 2013); Jeffrey Larsen and Kerry Kartchner, *On Limited Nuclear War in the 21st Century* (Stanford, CA: Stanford University Press, 2014); Carson, "Facing Off and Saving Face," 103–31; Caitlin Talmadge, "Would China Go Nuclear?

of "inadvertent" or hard-to-control escalation. This serves as an important reminder that escalation is a question not simply of deterrence success or failure but also of coping with spiral dynamics and domestic politics. The most unique contribution, however, directly results from the focus on the covert realm. Doing so provides new insight into the ways that leaders can manipulate visibility and acknowledgment to control escalation. As noted in chapter 2, older work on escalation dynamics and limited war typically focused on the binary choice to obey or transgress limits. This book shows that the choice is often among three options: obey, covertly violate, or overtly violate. This provides unique insight into the decisions that can prompt a crisis and the tools available to leaders should a crisis arise. The degree of escalation control following a militarized encounter in the South China Seas, for example, might depend on the quality of information available to outside audiences and the (lack of) official acknowledgment about key questions. This could then influence how China and the United States understand each other's intentions and the degree of hawkish constraint both face.[58]

BROADER DEBATES: DOMESTIC POLITICS

Beyond the study of secrecy and war, the book has implications for two broader debates in IR. One is whether and in what ways domestic politics shapes statecraft. A valuable finding of the empirical chapters is that the covert sphere often showcases authoritarian leaders using a surprising degree of cautious statecraft. Chapter 4 describes the way Hitler and his advisors carefully monitored British and French domestic politics and saw covertness as operationally limiting but critical to avoiding large-scale escalation prior to Germany's rearmament. Chapter 5 shows Stalin's sensitivity to the risks of large-scale escalation following North Korea's invasion and Washington's overt response. Covert activity—unobservable if we analyze only "overt" state behavior in war—is the place where caution about escalation pressure and desire for escalation control is most clearly displayed. This

Assessing the Risk of Chinese Nuclear Escalation in a Conventional War with the United States," *International Security* 41, no. 4 (April 1, 2017): 50–92.

58 On escalation and a U.S.-China clash, see among others Goldstein, "First Things First"; Jessica Chen Weiss, *Powerful Patriots: Nationalist Protest in China's Foreign Relations* (New York: Oxford University Press, 2014); Ja Ian Chong and Todd H. Hall, "The Lessons of 1914 for East Asia Today: Missing the Trees for the Forest," *International Security* 39, no. 1 (July 1, 2014): 7–43; Talmadge, "Would China Go Nuclear?"

narrative departs from some existing work. Jessica Weeks, for example, refers to Stalin-era Soviet behavior as an example of low-accountability personalist dictatorship that "increased the USSR's propensity to initiate international conflict, both by empowering a particularly ambitious leader and by insulating him from the costs of war."[59] This book's empirical findings suggest that appraising the risk orientation, ambition, and aggressiveness of authoritarian regimes requires assessing overt and covert activity.

Regarding democracies, a finding across the cases is that democratic leaders can limit knowledge of the covert interventions of other states. This is a distinct way in which intelligence manipulation can alter democratic accountability and constraints.[60] Chapter 7, for example, features American leaders in 1979 electing to keep private intelligence about deepening covert Soviet involvement in Afghanistan. In chapter 4, British leaders kept clear indications of Italian and German covert involvement secret. This pattern shows one way in which secrecy and deception in democracy are feasible, despite measures to ensure transparency.[61] It also provides motivation for theorizing the conditions under which liberal democracies operate with meaningful transparency and accountability as opposed to assuming it.[62] Collusion also has implications for debates about audience cost theory. Analysts of that theory's scope conditions have noted that "the theory assumes the public has sufficient information regarding crisis behavior, including, crucially, information that can be manipulated by leaders seeking to create audience costs. This is a very strong assumption and one that is empirically uncertain."[63] Moreover, Trachtenberg and others have shown that leaders often anticipate audience cost constraints and avoid

59 Jessica L. P. Weeks, *Dictators at War and Peace* (Ithaca, NY: Cornell University Press, 2014), 96.

60 Chaim Kaufmann, "Threat Inflation and the Failure of the Marketplace of Ideas: The Selling of the Iraq War," *International Security* 29, no. 1 (July 1, 2004): 5–48; Dan Reiter, "Democracy, Deception, and Entry into War," *Security Studies* 21, no. 4 (2012): 594–623; Schuessler, *Deceit on the Road to War*.

61 Reiter, "Democracy, Deception, and Entry into War"; Michael P. Colaresi, *Democracy Declassified: The Secrecy Dilemma in National Security* (New York: Oxford University Press, 2014).

62 E.g., Schultz, *Democracy and Coercive Diplomacy*; Dan Reiter and Allan C. Stam, *Democracies at War* (Princeton, NJ: Princeton University Press, 2010); Reiter, "Democracy, Deception, and Entry into War."

63 Erik Gartzke and Yonatan Lupu, "Still Looking for Audience Costs," *Security Studies* 21, no. 3 (2012): 396; for claims that place a heavy emphasis on domestic democratic transparency, see Schultz, *Democracy and Coercive Diplomacy*; Reiter, "Democracy, Deception, and Entry into War."

them through hedged public threats.[64] Democratic collusion combines these points. Collusion in maintaining the covertness of an intervention is an anticipatory action by vulnerable democratic leaders to avoid the constraint created by mobilized domestic constituents that care about honor, reputation, and so on. Moreover, this lesson applies as well to autocracies that face audience costs, where intelligence manipulation about covert behavior provides a way to loosen these constraints.

BROADER DEBATES: IMAGES AND INTENTIONS

The book also addresses a second broad debate about whether and how distrustful states under anarchy can communicate and make valid inferences about intentions. Scholars have long recognized that leaders are sensitive to the image they project to other states.[65] Moreover, a recurring axis of debate among realists is the degree to which intentions, which can be misrepresented and changed, can be inferred by adversaries.[66] Debates about signaling and, more recently, the ways adversaries make inferences respond to the same basic question of communication under anarchy.[67]

My theory and findings suggest that the covert sphere is one in which adversaries can send unique signals and gain unique insights. Covert activity specifically supports communication of a mix of resolve and restraint that I argue is ideally suited to sustaining limited war. Collusion decisions by major powers that detect covert behavior further reinforce this dynamic. This suggests that even if grand strategic intentions are "inscrutable," adversaries can act and observe in the backstage to make inferences about intentions *regarding limited war*.[68] The book also joins with other scholars in drawing on sociologist Erving Goffman for ideas about how

64 Marc Trachtenberg, "Audience Costs: An Historical Analysis," *Security Studies* 21, no. 1 (2012): 3–42; Jack Snyder and Erica D. Borghard, "The Cost of Empty Threats: A Penny, Not a Pound," *American Political Science Review* 105, no. 3 (August 2011): 437–56.

65 Robert Jervis, *The Logic of Images in International Relations* (New York: Columbia University Press, 1970).

66 See the defensive vs. offensive realism debate, e.g., Charles L. Glaser, "Realists as Optimists: Cooperation as Self-Help," *International Security* 19, no. 3 (1994): 50–90; John J. Mearsheimer, *The Tragedy of Great Power Politics* (New York: W. W. Norton, 2003).

67 Fearon, "Signaling Foreign Policy Interests," 68–90; on theorizing inferences, see Keren Yarhi-Milo, "In the Eye of the Beholder: How Leaders and Intelligence Communities Assess the Intentions of Adversaries," *International Security* 38, no. 1 (2013): 7–51; Yarhi-Milo, *Knowing the Adversary.*

68 Sebastian Rosato, "The Inscrutable Intentions of Great Powers," *International Security* 39, no. 3 (January 1, 2015): 48–88.

states manage their impressions and "perform" different kinds of roles.[69] I add consideration of the backstage as well as the frontstage and the basic insight that the availability of a backstage (covert/secret) allows governments to present coherent, strategically useful frontstage (overt/public) performances.

Conclusion

The scope of the book is limited in important ways. Parting the curtain on covert dynamics of war raises many questions for future research. Scholars might explore whether the other forms of "large-scale escalation" can motivate similar secrecy dynamics in non-conflict domains. It might also address pseudo-collaborative secrecy in substate violence, such as insurgencies and terrorism campaigns. The book also raises questions about broader themes. How else do adversaries cooperate to shut out or minimize the scrutiny of domestic actors and third-party leaders besides using secrecy? What kinds of tradeoffs, such as battlefield losses, influence the balance between escalation control and the drive to victory? While the book treats the limits that frame a given war as exogenous, future research might focus on how adversaries initially establish geographic or other salient thresholds and how those change over time. Much more work can be done to provide additional conceptualizations and typologies of secrecy's exposure and theorize alternative political, legal, and strategic consequences of exposure. Systematic data collection on leaks or other forms of exposure is another promising direction for future research. Beyond military intervention, effortful non-acknowledgment of historical genocide (e.g., Armenia) or nuclear weapons programs (e.g., Israel) are examples of other empirical domains where acknowledgment dynamics appear relevant.

The metaphor of war as a kind of theater performance with frontstages and backstages points to several additional strands of research. Future research could shed light on other "stage management" techniques besides secrecy and other "performances" besides limited war. Additional research into the kinds of collusion and cooperation that sustain performances is also promising. How do allies maintain secrets and backstage relationships over time? What institutional design features, like the Non-Intervention Committee in Spain, facilitate backstaging state activity? Moreover, I treat the "audience," or domestic hawkish constituents, as structural rather than

---

69 See scholars cited in chapters 1 and 2 on the theater analogy.

agential. Future research could better analyze how domestic hawkish sentiment varies in its expression and effectiveness, as well as whether the audience itself can refuse to acknowledge exposed secrets. Finally, I simplify the dynamics within the backstage to learning about limited-war interests. Future work might explore the microculture and norms that emerge on the backstage, including rules of communication, backstage-specific norms and relationships, and so on.

This book sought to develop a new approach to secrecy that could make sense of puzzling dynamics surrounding covert military intervention. I began by noting an ironic insight revealed by the end of the Cold War: American and Soviet leaders began their decades-long competition by colluding about a concealed air war over the Korean peninsula. Subsequent chapters documented a line connecting the escalation of World War I through the Spanish Civil War, the Cold War, and ultimately to the American occupation of Iraq. Across these conflicts, escalation control and secrecy are consistently linked. Nonetheless, the story is not all positive. This limited-war function requires that leaders dissemble and deceive. Each chapter features democratic leaders deceiving their own constituents about their own covert activities and those of other governments. Moreover, escalation dynamics and covertness can indirectly encourage troubling state behaviors. Major powers that are first movers can find advantage in going in quickly. More troubling, the option of covert intervention invites more great power involvement than otherwise might take place. Above all, the book argues for careful evaluation of the goals of secrecy, the dilemmas of exposure, and the promise and urgency of scholarly attention to what states do on the metaphorical backstage.

INDEX

Page numbers followed by *f* or *t* refer to figures or tables.

Abraham Lincoln Brigade, 134
Acheson, Dean, 152
acknowledgment: and atrocities, 297; and collusion, 60–61, 68; definition of, 39; and domestic hawks, 54–55; and escalation control, 71; in contrast with knowledge, 39; official and unofficial, 31; and open secrecy, 49; and sexual orientation, 39; and terror attacks 297
Afghanistan, 238–282; and Cold War, 238, 242; covert Soviet intervention in, 248–252; and cross-conflict learning, 245–248; and escalation risks, 243–245, 264–265, 282; interventions in, 240; and overt Soviet occupation, 239, 244, 257–260; and Soviet withdrawal, 274; and Stinger missile system, 272–275; US intervention in, 260–264
Afghan Army, 249
Agadir Crisis, 82
airpower, 90–91
Alliances: and escalation dynamics, 81, 180, 266; and Korean War, 148, 158, 196; and the Spanish Civil War, 117; and the War in Afghanistan, 262, 266. *See also* Sino-Soviet Mutual Defense Pact; US-Pakistan Agreement of Cooperation
al Qaeda, 239
American Volunteer Group, 96
Amin, Hafizullah, 258–259
Amstutz, Bruce, 247, 253–254, 254n47
anarchy, 3; communicating under, 5, 313; and escalation control, 12
Andong Province, 197
Andropov, Yuri, 258–260
anonymity, 87–93; and airpower, 90–91; and cyberattacks, 296; and submarines, 91–92; and technological change, 87

audience costs, 35, 51; and collusion, 312–313; and secrecy, 53
autocracy: theory's application to, 11, 66, 102n4, 313; China's intervention in Korean War, 172–179; and Germany's intervention in Spanish Civil War, 104, 108–114; and Soviet intervention in Korean War, 157–163; and Soviet intervention in Spanish Civil War, 104, 114–119. *See also* regime type
Austin, Warren, 155

backstage: access of major powers to, 49, 284–285; and communication and escalation control, 59–61; definition of, 41; for detector state, 66–68; and domestic hawks, 53–56; extensions to civil war, 297; extensions to cyberwar, 295–297; extensions to terrorism, 297; implications from social media, 302–303; for intervener, 63–66; key dynamics of, 43; in Korean War, 163, 166, 169, 175, 181, 183; and mistaken intentions, 301–302, 301f; and Non-Intervention Committee, 128–129; in Spanish Civil War, 106, 110, 113, 128, 140; and theater metaphor, 41–43; in Vietnam War, 194, 221, 230; in war in Afghanistan, 251, 255, 262, 264, 266, 276. *See also* frontstage; theater metaphor
Bagram Air Force Base, 249, 250, 253
Ball, George: on China and escalation risk in Vietnam, 196; on Russia and exposure risk in Vietnam, 232–233
Baloch separatists, 277
bargaining model of war, 43–44; 309n54; and domestic audience, 50–51; and secrecy, 53

Basic Principles Agreement, 245, 245n12

Bonaparte, Napoleon, 113–114

Bosnia, 288

Bosnian War, 65

Bradley, Omar, 154

Brezhnev, Leonid, 250, 258–259

British Broadcasting Corporation (BBC), 131

Brodie, Bernard: on escalation dangers after World War I, 78; on sanctuaries and the Korean War, 142

Brownell, Herbert, 171

Brzezinski, Zbigniew: and early Soviet presence in Afghanistan, 254; on exposure of covert Soviet role, 255, 255nn54 and 55; on Vietnam War analogy, 247–248

Bundy, McGeorge, 202; on press coverage of Laos covert operations, 202; and US overt entry into Vietnam, 234

Burma, 182

Bush, George W., 292, 294

Cambodia, 191; and independence, 192; and Operation Menu, 191; as peripheral area, 192

Carter, Jimmy, 244; and covert intervention in Afghanistan, 260; domestic hawks and Afghanistan, 244, 244n10; and SALT II treaty, 259; and use of Soviet weapons, 262

Casey, Stephen, 171, 171n95

Casey, William, 262–263

Central Intelligence Agency (CIA): assessment of covert Soviet activity in Korean War, 165, 167; and intervention in Afghanistan, 260–261, 263n87, 268–269; and collaboration with Pakistan, 239, 268; on Soviet reactions to Pakistan collaboration, 277; and Operation Paper, 182, 184; and US covert role in Laos, 193n9, 199–200

Chamberlain, Neville, 111; and British domestic constraints, 112; and intentions, 120; and escalation control, 127

Chennault, Claire, 97

Chile, 251

China: potential consequences of conflict escalation, 11, 46; and Cultural Revolution, 195, 214; and domestic politics changes, 194; intentions in Korean War, 173, 176n112; intentions and Vietnam War, 213; intervention in Korean War, 172; intervention in Vietnam, 188, 213; rise

of, 310; and rivalry with Soviet Union over North Vietnam support, 195; and volunteers in Korean War, 172, 176; and Afghanistan weapons program, 262, 266

Chinese Civil War, 174

Chinese Communist Party: conflict with Mao over Vietnam intervention, 197; and domestic politics, 149, 173; and internal division, 195; and volunteers, 178

Chinese Fourth Field Army, 174

Chinese Nationalists, 181; protection of, 184; and US covert aid, 145, 182. See also Operation Paper

Chinese People's Volunteers (CPV), 172, 174n106

Churchill, Winston, 111–112

Ciano, Galeazzo, 122; on Italian volunteers, 122; and overtness, 123n102

Civil Air Transport, 182

civil war: in Syria, Ukraine, and Yemen, 4; and Russian Civil War, 96; and Spanish Civil War, 99–141; and terrorism, 297; and theory's extensions to, 297–298. See also Spanish Civil War

Clark, Christopher, 83

Clausewitz, Carl von, 22; on escalation control, 11, 44

Cold War: and covert rules of the game and, 142, 245, 284, 282; and cyberwarfare, 295; and détente, 187, 239, 239n2, 244, 259; end of, 1, 182, 239; and limited war, 30, 142–143, 143n2, 245, 283; and limited-war scholarship, 19, 310; and pre–Cold War precursors, 94, 97; and Soviet intentions, 160; theory's extension beyond, 288–295; and US intentions, 194

collusion, 2, 7, 308; and civil wars, 297; and cyberwarfare, 295–296; definition of, 7, 32; and détente, 252, 255; and exposure, 7, 257, 294; of firms, 2; as a theoretical puzzle, 7–9; of rival candidates, 2; rationale and incentives for, 39–40, 55–56, 66–68; of United States and China, 180, 221; of United States and Iran, 292; of United States and Soviet Union, 155, 172, 212, 252, 255, 279. See also conspiracy of silence

Communist International (Comintern), 114

Condor Legion: and escalation control, 111; and intervention in Spanish Civil War, 24, 106, 131; restrictions on operations, 111; and secrecy measures, 107. See also Germany

conspiracy of silence, 2, 40, 62

Corum, James, 108

covert: along with overt intervention, 190; and audiences for, 5; definition of, 6; as enabler of US-Soviet conflict, 231; and limited war transgressions, 59 variation in, 191. *See also* secrecy

covert intervention: definition of, 6; and domestic dove logic, 13; examples of, 2; modern appeal of, 288; and operational security logic, 13; overlapping rationales for, 69; recent examples of, 6; and relation to secrecy and visibility, 31; techniques of, 31–32. *See also* secrecy

Creveld, Martin Van, 88

Crimean War, 81, 149

Cuban Missile Crisis, 2n4; and domestic constraints, 246; as escalation memory, 194, 246

cyber conflict, 20, 284; as backstage, 297; and detection, 296; and limited war, 295–296; and Russian election attack, 296

Davies, John, 150

Defense Intelligence Agency, 240n4

Delbos, Yvon, 113

Demilitarized Zone (DMZ), 207

democracy, 5, 8; as challenge to covertness, 310, 312; and escalation dynamics, 112, 151, 191; spread of, 85, 288; and World War I, 85–86. *See also* regime type

detector state, 28; behavior in Afghanistan, 241t; behavior in Korean War, 144t; behavior in Spanish Civil War, 101t; behavior in Vietnam, 190t; choices of, 36; definition of, 28; theory's predictions for, 72

détente, 239; end of Soviet-Afghanistan War, 239; Soviet desire in war in Afghanistan, 251–252, 281; strategic stability and, 244

Deutschland (battleship), 119, 131

Diem, Ngo Dinh, 192

domestic dove logic, 8, 10, 35; limitations of, 37; predictions of, 73

domestic hawks, 10; as audience, 13; definition of, 62; vs. domestic doves during the Vietnam War, 191, 191n5; and escalation factors, 52; post–World War II, 148; and US intervention in Korea, 170; and US intervention in Vietnam, 206; and World War I, 83

Douhet, Giulio, 90

drones, 23, 32; as covert innovation, 89

Eden, Anthony, 111; and British domestic constraints, 112; and defense of non-intervention diplomacy, 134

Edwards, Jill, 134

Eisenhower, Dwight, 185

escalation, 10, 310; conspicuous restraint and, 58; and cyberwarfare, 296; and détente, 245; inadvertent forms of, 46, 83; large-scale, costliness of, 45–46, 245, 282; large-scale, definition of, 29–30; and problem of communication, 56–61; and problem of domestic hawks, 49–56; scenarios in Afghanistan, 242–245, 264–266; scenarios in Korean War, 152; scenarios in Spanish Civil War, 104; scenarios in Vietnam War, 192–196, 204–207; severity of, 65; variation of within one war, 65; in World War I, 77–85

escalation control, 10; in Afghanistan, 244; communication and, 59–61; and Cold War détente, 251; and cyberwarfare, 296; definition of, 11, 30; domestic hawks and, 53–56; examples of, 47; in Korean War, 148; other intervention priorities and, 63–65; role of experience in, 47–48; role of learning in, 47–48; in Spanish Civil War, 109–111, 126, 133–135; in Vietnam War, 194

Egypt, 262

Ethiopia, 95

exposure, 7, 308; definition of, 33, 38; examples of avoiding, 135; forms of, 48, 48t; by media, 9, 69, 130, 210, 264, 302; policy implications regarding, 305–306; theory's logic for, 66–68, 72; and volunteers, 130

Fearon, James, 35

Finnemore, Martha, 76

First Indochina War, 194

first mover intervention, 66; advantages of, 299; covertness and, 249; examples of, 152, 214, 250; overtness and, 234

Foch, Ferdinand, 80

Formosa. *See* Taiwan

France: defeat in Vietnam, 192; domestic politics and Spanish Civil War, 112; and escalation control in the Spanish Civil War, 132; and Spanish Civil War, 104

Franco, Francisco: and German aid, 106; and ideology, 120; and Italian aid, 125; and Spanish coup, 99

frontstage: and collusion, 56; definition of, 41; for detector state, 66–68; and

frontstage (*continued*)
domestic politics, 51; and extensions to
civil war, 297; and extensions to terrorism,
297; for intervener, 63–66; in Korean
War, 155, 157, 169, 181; and theater metaphor, 41–44; in Vietnam War, 198; in war
in Afghanistan, 255–258, 266. *See also*
backstage; theater metaphor
Fussell, Paul, 80

Gaddis, John Lewis, 171–172
Gaiduk, Ilya, V., 225
Garthoff, Raymond, 251
Gates, Robert, 264, 271
Geneva Accords of 1962: and escalation,
199; and Laos neutrality, 193; and North
Vietnamese troops, 193n9; and Soviet-US
tacit agreement in Laos, 205, 211
Germany, 17t, 101t; and Condor Legion, 24,
106; and escalation control, 109; Foreign
Ministry and intelligence, 137; and
intervention in Spanish Civil War, 17t,
106–119; in World War I, 82–85. *See also*
Condor Legion; U-boats
Gleditsch, Kristian, 34
Goffman, Erving: and collusion, 62n121;
on impression management and stability, 40; in previous IR scholarship,
20–21n31, 313–314; and theater analogy/
performance 20, 24, 25n42, 41–42. *See
also* impression management
Gorbachev, Mikhail, 273–274
Gromyko, Andrei: authorization of overt
intervention in Afghanistan, 258–259;
and opposition to Soviet overt intervention, 252; on overtness of US operations in Laos, 211
Gulf of Tonkin Incident, 188, 209

Hall, Todd, 54, 83
Hart, Liddell, 45; on limited war, 94
Hawthorne, Nathaniel, 88
Herat uprising, 249
Hezbollah, 293
Hitler, Adolf, 4; and Condor Legion, 107;
and escalation control, 108, 132n149; and
goals in Spanish Civil War, 104, 108–109;
and intentions, 58. *See also* Germany
HMS Havock, 126
Ho Chi Minh: political consolidation, 192;
and US covert operations, 200
Ho Chi Minh Trail, 193; as target of covert
US bombing, 200

Hobbes, Thomas, 49
Hopf, Ted, 160
Howard, Michael, 81
Humphrey, Herbert, 196, 232
Hussein, Saddam: overthrow of, 288, 294;
weapons smuggling under, 289, 291. *See
also* Iraq

impression management, 40. *See also*
Goffman, Erving
Inchon landing, 147, 157, 197
India, 243; and escalation risk in war in
Afghanistan, 243, 264; and relationship
with Soviet Union, 243
International Brigades, 99, 114
international community, 37; and
punishment for intervention, 37
International Control Commission (ICC)
235
intervener state, 28; behavior in Afghanistan, 241t; behavior in Korean War, 144t;
behavior in Spanish Civil War, 101t;
behavior in Vietnam, 190t; choices of,
33–35; goals of, 63–66; signaling and,
60; interdependence among, 139;
theory's predictions for, 70–72
intervention: assumptions of the theory
regarding, 63–64; cases analyzed, 17t;
definition of, 27; examples of, 33–34;
existing explanations for, 66, 152, 214, 250, 299; forms
of, 63–64, 190, 241; location of,
65–67; as a selection issue, 298–299; timing of,
65–67. *See also* covert intervention; overt
intervention
Iran, 243; and covert intervention in Iraq,
290; as escalation risk, 243; rivalry with
Israel, 9, 288
Iranian Hostage Crisis, 255
Iraq, 17, 239; escalation scenarios in,
292–294; and Iranian covert weapons
program, 25, 98, 290; US occupation
of, 288–289. *See also* Saddam Hussein
Islamic Revolutionary Guard Corps (IRGC),
289
Israel: nuclear weapons program of, 10, 60,
298; provided intelligence to US in Iraq,
292; rivalry with Iran, 9, 288
Italy: and Black Shirts, 121; and Corps of
Volunteer Troops, CTV, 120; and ground
role in Spain, 121–124; and intervention
in Spanish Civil War, 17t, 119–128; and
naval role in Spain, 124–128

Jervis, Robert, 246

Jian, Chen: on Chinese volunteers in Korean War, 178; on Korea precedent in Vietnam War, 197

Johnson, Lyndon B, 22; and confirmation of Soviet presence in Vietnam, 228; and covert operations in Laos, 200, 201; overt intervention in Vietnam, 192, 234; and reassuring China regarding US bombing in Vietnam, 222; and Republican hawks in the Vietnam War, 195, 195n15; secrecy and Vietnam, 22, 24

Joint Chiefs of Staff (JCS); and prediction of Soviet intervention in Vietnam, 227; and Stinger missile program, 272n128

July Crisis, 84

Kahn, Herman, 29

Karmal, Babrak, 258

KGB: in Herat uprising, 249–250; and knowledge of covert operations in Laos, 208; and murder of Hafizullah Amin, 258

Kellogg-Briand Pact, 94

Kennan, George F., 81; on Soviet intervention options in Korean War, 169

Kennedy, John F., 192

Khamenei, Sayyid Ali Hosseini, 290

Khrushchev, Nikita, 195

Kinderlen-Waechter, Alfred von, 82

Kirilenko, Andrei, 259

Kirk, Ambassador Alan, G, 151, 159n30

Kissinger, Henry, 22

Korean People's Army (KPA), 146

Korean War, 142–186; China's intervention in, 172–179; and cross-conflict learning, 149–151; and escalation risk, 147–149; and Soviet collusion, 155–157; Soviet intervention in, 157–163; US intervention in, 151–155; US intervention in China during, 181–185; and volunteers, 175–179

Kosygin, Alexei: on aid refusal and concealment problems, 251–252; and opposition to Soviet overt intervention, 252; on Soviet prestige and Afghanistan, 251; on Vietnam War and conflict borders, 246

Kurizaki, Shuhei, 53

Laden, Osama Bin, 239

Laos, 192; as backstage for war in Vietnam, 198, as escalation risk, 196, and Ho Chi Minh Trail, 192–193, 200, 204; and independence, 192; as peripheral area,

192; as neutral periphery, 193; North Vietnam in, 193, 199, 204–206; US covert operations in, 188, 198–203

Larrabee, Stephen, 247

League of Nations, 94; and comparisons to Korean War, 155; and non-response to undeclared wars, 95n100

Levy, Jack, 82

Libya, 6; Italian bombing operations in, 90

Lieber, Kier, 83

limited war, 3, 12, 44; and adversary cooperation, 56n100; and alternative logics, 175; and Clausewitz, 44; and cross-conflict learning, 18, 47, 286, 291; and cyberwar, 295; definition of, 30; as a feature of modern warfare, 285, 288; and Morgenthau, 45; and nuclear weapons, 45; and salient thresholds, 12, 30; and specific meanings in Cold War, 30. *See also* escalation; escalation control

Logevall, Fredrik, 214

Lusitania, 92

MacArthur, Douglas, 146, 197; and counteroffensive in China, 172, 176; and escalation risk with Russia, 152; and forces in Korea, 172; and ground troops, 151; and intentional leaks, 154; and Korea counteroffensive, 157; and Soviet avoidance, 168, 168n85; on visibility of Chinese counteroffensive, 177n116

major powers, 13; as "actors," 13; definition of, 27; escalation potential, 70

Manchuria, 95, 182n140; Japanese invasion of, 95; Soviet covert operations, 157; and US covert operations, 182n140

McCarthy, Joseph, 171

McNaughton, John: on escalation risks in Laos, 204, 204n53; on US domestic politics and escalation pressure, 206

McNeil, William, 86

Mediterranean Sea, 121; and escalation dangers 104–105, 126, and Italian submarine campaign, 125; and Spanish Civil War, 104, 120

Mi, Li, 182, 182n141

Middle East, 244

MIG-15, 158, 164, 166, 167; and Chinese attribution, 168, 168n83

Militarized Interstate Dispute dataset, 34

Military Assistance Command, Vietnam-Studies and Observations Group, (MACVSOG), 200

Monteiro, Nuno, 27

Morgenthau, Hans, 45

Mueller, John, 78

Mussolini, Benito: and escalation control, 126, 132n149; and escalation in Spanish Civil War, 111; and intentions, 120; and rules of engagement, 126

National Intelligence Estimates, 166; and Chinese Fourth Field Army in Korean War, 175; and Chinese units in Vietnam War, 218; and Soviet cross-border operations, 277–279; on Soviet intentions in Vietnam, 227, 229–231; and Soviet pilots in Korean War, 164

National Security Agency (NSA), 165

National Security Council (NSC): and approval of covert intervention in China, 182; on early Soviet presence in Afghanistan, 254; and escalation in Afghanistan, 261, 265, 267; and escalation control in Korea, 152

National Security Decision Directive 166 (NSDD-166), 263, 273

nationalism, 50; as domestic constraint, 11, 51–52, 105; as escalation risk, 11, 26, 44, 45n63, 49–50, 308; and World War I, 81–83, 86

Nationalists (Spain), 99; escalation of, 102n5; territorial expansion, 103

Negroponte, John, 291

Newsom, David, 256

Nitze, Paul, 155; on American concealment of Soviet intervention, 171; and US domestic constraints, 156, 171

Nixon, Richard, 22; and Vietnam War, 22, 24, 188; and domestic politics during Vietnam War, 191

Non-Intervention Agreement, 124

Non-Intervention Committee: and backstaging, 128, 133; as early international institution, 103, 133; formation of, 100; and intelligence sharing, 136; and limited war, 106–107; and Spanish Civil War, 24; and volunteers, 124

North Atlantic Treaty Organization (NATO), 148

North Korea: and Korean War, 142, 151, 157; and military advances, 154; and request for military aid, 161, 172

NSC-68, 143

Nyon Agreement, 126–127

Obama, Barack: and covertness in Syrian, 288; and Iran, 296; response to Russian election interference (2016), 296–297

O'Brien, William, 4; on salient thresholds, 54, 65; on wars after 1945, 4

O'Neill, Barry, 54–55, 60–61, 173

open secrecy, 10, 39, 48; China in Korean War as, 173, 179–180; communicative effects of, 49, 60–61; definition of, 48; and social media, 303–304; as a theoretical puzzle, 9–10, 39, 60, 308; US intervention in Afghanistan and, 241, 262–263, 268; US intervention in Laos and, 188, 202, 212; and volunteers, 122; volunteers in Spanish Civil War and, 101, 122

Operation Brass Tacks (United States), 198

Operation Farmgate (United States), 192

Operation Menu (United States), 191

Operation Paper (United States), 182

Operation Prairie Fire (United States), 200

Operation Rolling Thunder (United States), 192

Operation Shining Brass (United States), 200

Operation X (Soviet Union), 114–115, 118

Operation Zet (Soviet Union), 96

operational security logic, 8–9, 10, 35; and the Korean War, 173; limitations of, 37; predictions of, 73; and the Vietnam War, 190, 234

overt intervention, 4; advantages of, 14–15, 35–36; definition of, 6; and Italian intervention, 123; and local area, 234; and overlapping interventions, 190; in the Spanish Civil War, 121; and US intervention, 154, 234

Pakistan, 6; and Afghanistan weapons program, 262, 266; and American drone strikes, 10, 241; and collaboration with Central Intelligence Agency, 239, 262; as escalation risk, 244, 264, 266; as peripheral area, 276; risk of conflict with Soviet Union, 266; Soviet military operations in, 276

Paris Peace Accords (1973), 187; termination of covert operations in Laos, 200

Pashtun separatists, 277

Pathet Lao, 193, 200, 203

Pentagon Papers, 201, 210; detection of Soviet intervention in Vietnam, 228; and opponents of overt intervention in

Vietnam, 234; and shift to overt inter-
vention in Vietnam, 235; as source, 191n6
People's Democratic Party of Afghanistan,
250
People's Liberation Army, 179; early
presence in Vietnam, 218
Phouma, Souvanna, 203
Popular Front, 99
Pravda: and coverage of Spanish Civil War,
116; and US aid to Afghan rebels, 271
Presidential Daily Briefs (PDB): Chinese
entry into Vietnam War, 220; early
reports of Soviet aid to North Vietnam,
228; reports of US-inflicted Soviet
casualties, 230
Privateers, 76n3
Pusan, 151
Putin, Vladimir, 304–305
Putnam, Robert, 51

Quds Force, 289–290. *See also* Islamic
Revolutionary Guard Corps (IRGC)

Radio Hanoi, 210
Radio Kabul, 258
Radio Peking, 210
Reagan, Ronald: and domestic hawks,
244n10; and Soviet weapon supply
network, 263; and Soviet withdrawal
from Afghanistan, 262, 274
Red Army: and escalation control, 118; and
Soviet withdrawal in Afghanistan, 275
regime type, 5; and domestic hawks, 62;
impact on crisis escalation, 11. *See also*
autocracy; democracy
reputation: and war in Afghanistan, 266, 271;
diplomacy and, 53n90; and domestic
politics, 312–313; implications of theory
for, 313–314; and intervener motives,
63–64, 300; and Korean War, 149; and
Vietnam War, 235
Ribbentrop, Joachim von, 109
Roosevelt, Franklin, 97
Rostow, Walt, 219
Rusk, Dean: directives for secrecy in Laos
operations, 203; on escalation risks with
Russians in Vietnam, 232; on mutual caution between US and Soviet Union, 233;
on overt attack in North Vietnam, 235
Russia: and covert operations, 9, 10; and
Russian Civil War, 96; US election
interference (2016) by, 296. *See also*
Soviet Union

Sadat, Anwar, 260
salient thresholds, 12, 59; in Afghanistan-
Stinger Missiles, 269, 270–275; definition
of, 30; and escalation control, 12; in
Korean War, 152; in Spanish Civil War,
110. *See also* escalation control; limited
war
SALT II Treaty, 259, 261
Saudi Arabia, 262
Saunders, Elizabeth, 34
Schelling, Thomas, 22; on escalation control, 12; on salient thresholds, 30; on
World War I and limited war, 82
secrecy: in anthropology, 39–40; and civil
wars, 297; as a collective act, 40; as
communication, 60; definition of, 5, 27;
and domestic hawk constraints, 53; existing logics of, 7n13, 8, 35–37, 306n50; and
exposure, 38–39, 47–49; logistics of,
14–15; and social media, 302–303; and
social stability, 39–40; in sociology, 39;
theoretical contributions, 283–284; vs.
covertness, 5–6, 16, 31
security dilemma, 82; and World War I, 82
Shevardnadze, Eduard, 274
Shultz, George, 274–275
signaling, 58, 313; and Afghanistan War,
267; and Korean War, 155, 172, 185; and
nuclear weapons, 185; and Vietnam War,
201, 210–217; and World War I, 82
Sino-Japanese War, 94
Sino-Soviet Mutual Defense Pact, 148
64th Fighter Aviation Corps, 158
Slantchev, Branislav, 173
Smoke, Richard: on escalation, 65; on
escalation control and preventive war,
101; on sanctuaries in war, 142n1
social media, 302–303; and open secrecy,
9–10; and other media technology, 69
Somalia, 6
South Korea: escalation risks in, 152;
invasion of, 146; and Korean War, 142
Soviet Air Defense, 208
Soviet Air Force Volunteers, 96
Soviet General Staff, 252
Soviet-Japanese Border Incident of 1937, 150
Soviet Union: and concealment in Korea,
159; and domestic politics changes, 194;
and escalation fears in Vietnam, 225;
as first mover in Afghanistan, 250; and
geostrategic goals in Korea, 160; and
GRU, 138, 208; and Herat uprising,
249; intelligence concealment, 139;

Soviet Union (*continued*)
and intervention in Afghanistan, 248, 257; and intervention in Korea, 157; and intervention in Pakistan, 276; and intervention in Spanish Civil War, 114; and intervention in Vietnam, 188, 222; NKVD, 115, 138; and Operation X, 114, 118; and post-Stalin factionalism, 244; risk of conflict with Pakistan, 266; and rivalry with China in North Vietnam, 195; and role minimization in Korea, 153; and volunteers in Vietnam, 223. *See also* Operation X; Russia

Spanish Air Force, 106

Spanish Army of Africa, 102; exposure of Italian involvement, 121, 132

Spanish Civil War, 99–141; British involvement in, 132–136; and Condor Legion, 106–108; detection and collusion, 128–132; and escalation risks, 103–105; French involvement in, 132–136; German intervention in, 106–114; Italian intervention in, 119–128; and Operation X, 114–116; Soviet intervention in, 114–119. *See also* Non-Intervention Committee

Spanish Foreign Legion, 133

Special National Intelligence Estimates (SNIE), 207, 231n166; on early Chinese presence in Vietnam, 218, 218n105; and prediction of Soviet intervention in Vietnam, 227; on Soviet escalation control in Vietnam, 229; on Soviet operations in Pakistan, 278

Stalin, Joseph: and collective security, 117; and concealment in Korea, 159, 162n56; and cooperation with China, 145n5, 147, 158, 172, 176; and covert operation in Mongolia, Manchuria, 96; death and domestic politics, 194–195; and domestic hawks, 51; and fear of escalation, 159; and Spanish Civil War, 104, 114; and strategic intentions, 116, 160

Stinger missile program, 241, 272–275, 280; as covert military aid, 272n127; development of, 272; and Gorbachev, 274–275; as overt military aid, 241, 272; and Soviet retaliation against Pakistan, 273; and State Department opposition, 275

Strachan, Hew, 78

stealth technology, 89

submarine technology, 91–92

Suleimani, Qassem, 291

Sullivan, William: on neutrality in Laos, 204; and role of diplomacy in Laos

military operations, 199; on Soviet constraints and Laos, 205

Sung, Kim Il, 146

Syria, 6; American aid operations in, 10; as example of modern covert war, 288

Syrian Civil War, 4, 10

Taiwan, 182; and Formosa, 184

Taraki, Nur Muhammad, 248, 251

Thailand, 182; and US collaboration in Laos, 211

theater metaphor, 5, 13, 41; and audience, 42; and backstage, 5, 13, 41, 183, 194, 266; and backstaging, 10, 14, 59, 62t, 113, 170, 198; and bargaining model of war, 43; and frontstage, 13, 41, 155; as narrative, 169; performance and, 5; war as, 41–42. *See also* backstage; frontstage

third-party exposure, 68, 130; in Afghanistan conflict, 254–255, 264; and censorship, 168–169; in Korean War, 167, 179; and Operation Paper, 184; in Spanish Civil War, 130; in Vietnam War, 202, 220, 230

38th parallel, 147

Thompson, Llewellyn, 231

Tocqueville, Alexis de, 50

Trachtenberg, Marc, 312

Truman Doctrine, 156n33

Truman, Harry: and anti-Soviet domestic hawks, 156; and domestic hawks, 51, 148, 170–171; and intelligence circulation, 166; and intelligence on Korea, 164; and Korean War, 146, 151; and response to invasion of South Korea, 146; and response to Soviet operations, 153; and Soviet collusion, 156; and UN endorsement, 155

Turner, Stanfield, 254

U-boats, 92

U-2 surveillance flights, 2n4

Ukraine, 6; civil war in, 4; Russian covert operations in, 9–10, 303

United Kingdom: and escalation control in Spanish Civil War, 132; exposure (lack of), 131; and media exposure, 131

United Nations (UN): and Chinese exposure in Korean War, 181; as frontstage, 155; and troop labels, 155

United Nations Command: in Korean War, technological superiority over Chinese forces, 174; US dominance of, 152

United Nations Security Council (UNSC): and police action against North Korea,

151; and response to invasion of South Korea, 146; Soviet intervention in Afghanistan, 254

United States: and covert aid operations, 10; and covert operations in Laos, 200; and covert rivalry with Iran, 292–295, as detector in Korea, 163; and drone program, 10, 241; intelligence analysis and Spanish Civil War precedent in Vietnam, 198; and intervention in China, 181; and intervention in Iraq, 288–289; and intervention in Korea, 151; and intervention in Laos, 188; and intervention in Russian Civil War, 96; and intervention in Vietnam, 192, 234, 235; and military concealment in Laos, 198; and public opinion, Vietnam, 195, 105n15; and weapons supply program in Afghanistan, 242

US-Pakistan Agreement of Cooperation (1959), 265

US Seventh Fleet, 225

USS Maine, 119

Ustinov, Dmitry, 258–259

Vandenberg, Hoyt, 169

Viet Cong, 234

Vietnam War, 187–237: and cross-conflict learning, 196–198; Chinese intervention in, 213–217; and escalation risk, 192–196; Soviet intervention in North Vietnam, 222–226; US intervention in, 233–235; US intervention in Laos and, 198–207

Vietnamization, 234n178

volunteers: and Chinese volunteers in Korean War, 162, 172, 174n106, 176, 177n117; for deniability in covert intervention, 6, 32, 32n17; and Iranian volunteers in Iraq, 288–295, 303; and Italian volunteers in Spanish Civil War, 122; and Russian volunteers in Ukraine, 32n17, 303–304; and Soviet and American volunteers in China before World War II, 96–97; and Soviet volunteers in Vietnam, 223. See also Chinese People's Volunteers

war: absence among major powers after 1945, 285; and the backstage, 41, 43; and communication, 56–58, 68–69; cooperation during, 21, 44; covert aspects of, 9; and cyber technology, 295–297; declared vs. undeclared, 93–97; destruc-tiveness of, 46; and domestic politics, 49–53, 69, 83–85, 311–313; escalation of, 19, 28–29, 310–311; information in, 18–19, 309–310; and limits, 30; local vs. major powers in, 28; military intervention and, 6, 27–30; and nationalism 44, 49–52, 83; and signaling intentions, 313–314; and technological change, 44, 86–93; as theater, 13–14, 41–44; and total war, 45; World War I and changes to, 75–93. See also bargaining model of war; escalation; escalation control

Weathersby, Kathryn, 160–162, 160n47, 162nn54 and 55

Weeks, Jessica, 312

Weizsacker, Ernst von, 138

Wheeler, Earle, 231

Whiting, Allen, 221

Wilson, Charles, 263

Wilson, Woodrow, 96

Woodward, Bob, 293

World War I: as critical juncture, 23, 76; and democratization, 85; destructiveness of, 77–80; and escalation cost, 85; and military technology, 86; and nationalism, 86; scale of, 79; and Spanish Civil War, 105

World War II, 16, 97; and volunteers, 32

Wright, Quincy, 45; on evolution of limited war, 95

Yalu River, 157, 158, 172, 175; and Korean War precedent, 197

yellow journalism, 81

Yemen, 6; civil war in, 4

Zedong, Mao, 145; collaboration with Joseph Stalin, 145n5, 147, 158, 172, 176; conflict with Communist Party over Vietnam intervention, 197; counter-offensive in Korea, 176; and domestic politics instability during Vietnam War, 195; fear of escalation in Vietnam War, 215; Korean War; intentions of, 173, 174, 174n106; intentions in Vietnam War, 214

Zelikow, Phillip, 293

Zia-ul-Haq, Muhammad: and "boiling pot" metaphor, 265, 265n93; and escalation in Afghanistan, 265; on Soviet intervention in Pakistan, 280; on Stinger missile program and escalation, 272–273

Zhai, Quiang: 213, 215

Zhang, Xiaoming, 162

A NOTE ON THE TYPE

This book has been composed in Adobe Text and Gotham. Adobe Text, designed by Robert Slimbach for Adobe, bridges the gap between fifteenth- and sixteenth-century calligraphic and eighteenth-century Modern styles. Gotham, inspired by New York street signs, was designed by Tobias Frere-Jones for Hoefler & Co.

Milton Keynes UK
Ingram Content Group UK Ltd.
UKHW011810241123
433186UK00003B/124